Vespa P/PX125, 150 & 200
Service and Repair Manual

by Pete Shoemark

*with Chapter 7 on the T5 and PX125/150/200 electric start models by Phil Mather
and Chapter 8 on the LML Star 2T model by Penny Cox*

Models covered

Vespa P125 X. 123cc. June 1978 to May 1982
Vespa PX125 E. 123cc. May 1982 to January 1993, February 1999 to 2014
Vespa PX125 T5. 123cc. March 1986 to October 1992
Vespa PX125 T5 Classic. 123cc. October 1992 to August 1999
Vespa P150 X. 150cc. November 1978 to January 1983
Vespa PX150 E. 150cc. January 1983 to 2014
Vespa P200 E. 198cc. June 1978 to May 1984
Vespa PX200 E. 198cc. March 1983 to 2003
LML Star 2T. 125cc. 1997 to 2014
LML Star 2T. 149cc. 1997 to 2014

(707-6AN10-168)

© Haynes Publishing 2014

A book in the Haynes Service and Repair Manual Series

ABCDE
FGHIJ
KLMNO
PQR
3

ISBN: 978 0 85733 984 3

British Library Cataloguing in Publication Data
A catalogue record for this book is available from the British Library.

Printed in the USA

Haynes Publishing
Sparkford, Yeovil, Somerset BA22 7JJ, England

Haynes North America, Inc
861 Lawrence Drive, Newbury Park, California 91320, USA

Haynes Publishing Nordiska AB
Box 1504, 751 45 UPPSALA, Sweden

Acknowledgements

Our thanks are due to Piaggio UK Ltd of Bromley who provided technical literature and a PX125E for the original edition of this manual. Special thanks must go to Mike Hayman who provided invaluable technical advice on the model range.

Thanks are also due to Fran Ridewood & Co of Wells for the PX125T5, Piaggio UK Ltd for the PX200E, South West Scooters of Yeovil for the disc-braked PX200E and Southampton Premier

Motorcycles Ltd for the LML Star 2T. We are also grateful to Tasso UK Ltd and E P Barrus Ltd for providing LML technical literature and advice.

Special thanks are due to Piaggio VE SpA, Italy, for permission to reproduce artwork from their publications.

NGK Spark Plugs (UK) Ltd provided information on plug maintenance and electrode conditions.

About this manual

The purpose of this manual is to present the owner with a concise and graphic guide which will enable him to tackle any operation from basic routine maintenance to a major overhaul. It has been assumed that any work would be undertaken without the luxury of a well-equipped workshop and a range of manufacturer's service tools.

To this end, the machine featured in the manual was stripped and rebuilt in our own workshop, by a team comprising a mechanic, a photographer and the author. The resulting photographic sequence depicts events as they took place, the hands shown being those of the author and the mechanic.

The use of specialised, and expensive, service tools was avoided unless their use was considered to be essential due to risk of breakage or injury. There is usually some way of improvising a method of removing a stubborn component, providing that a suitable degree of care is exercised.

The author learnt his motorcycle mechanics over a number of years, faced with the same difficulties and using similar facilities to those encountered by most owners. It is hoped that this practical experience can be passed on through the pages of this manual.

Where possible, a well-used example of the machine is chosen for the workshop project, as this highlights any areas which might be particularly prone to giving rise to problems. In this way, any such difficulties are encountered and resolved before the text is written, and the techniques used to deal with them can be incorporated in the relevant section. Armed with a working knowledge of the machine, the author undertakes a considerable amount of research in order that the maximum amount of data can be included in the manual.

A comprehensive section, preceding the main part of the manual, describes procedures for carrying out the routine maintenance of the machine at intervals of time and mileage. This section is included particularly for those owners who wish to ensure the efficient day-to-day running of their motorcycle, but who choose not to undertake overhaul or renovation work.

Each Chapter is divided into numbered sections. Within thyese sections are numbered paragraphs. Cross reference throughout the manual is quite straightforward and logical. When reference is made 'See Section 6.10' it means Section 6, paragraph 10 in the same Chapter. If another Chapter were intended, the reference would read, for example, 'See Chapter 2, Section 6.10'. All the photographs are captioned with a section/paragraph number to which they refer and are relevant to the Chapter text adjacent.

Figures (usually line illustrations) appear in a logical but numerical order, within a given Chapter. Fig. 1.1 therefore refers to the first figure in Chapter 1.

Left-hand and right-hand descriptions of the machine and their components refer to the left and right of a given machine when the rider is seated normally.

Motorcycle manufacturers continually make changes to specifications and recommendations, and these, when notified, are incorporated into our manuals at the earliest opportunity.

We take great pride in the accuracy of information given in this manual, but motorcycle manufacturers make alterations and design changes during the production run of a particular motorcycle of which they do not inform us. No liability can be accepted by the authors or publishers for loss, damage or injury caused by any errors in, or omissions from, the information given.

Contents

Right-hand view of the Vespa PX125 EFL

Engine and transmission unit

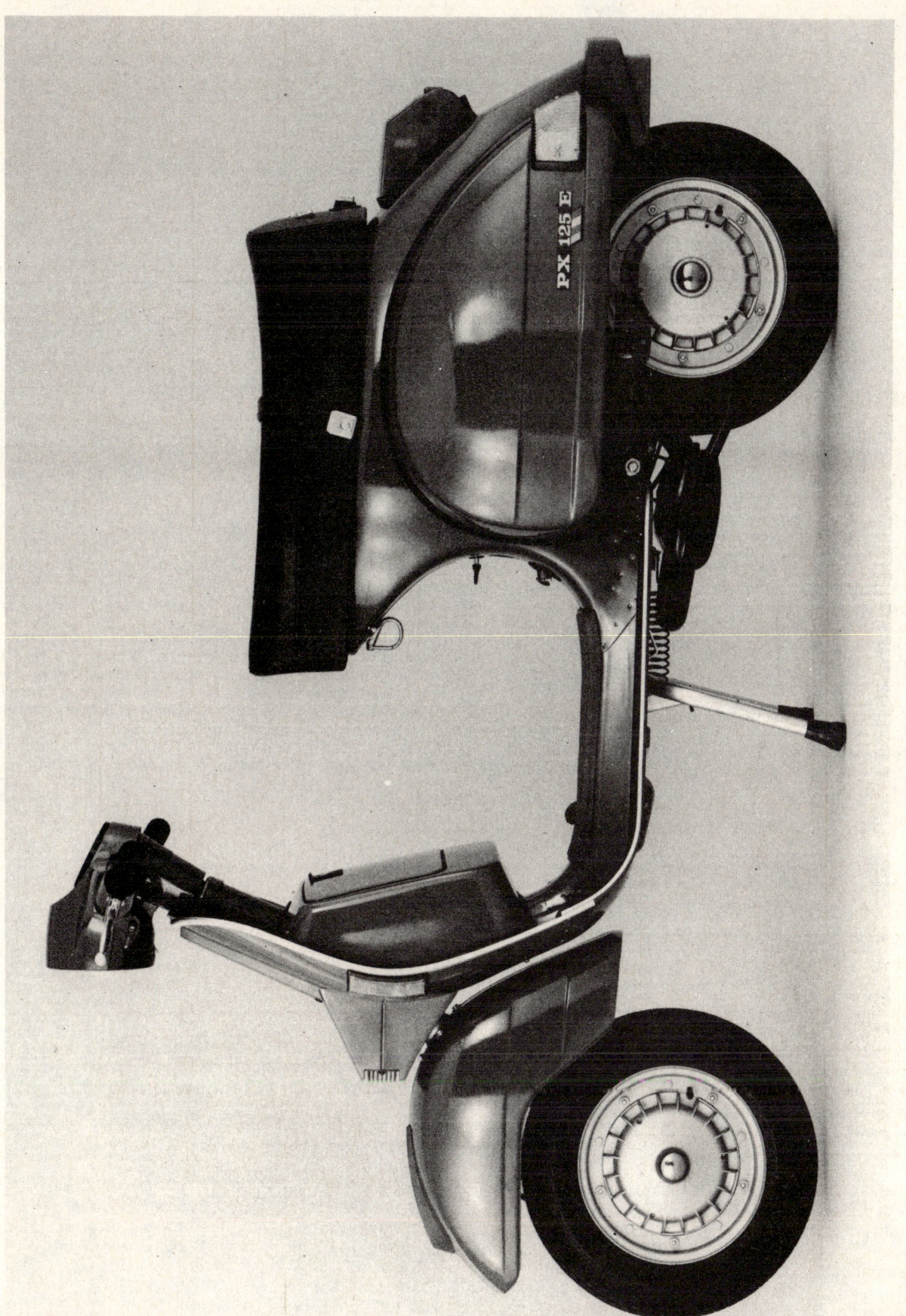

Left-hand view of the Vespa PX125 EFL

Introduction to the Vespa P and PX range

For information relating to later models see Chapter 7

The models featured in this manual are developed from the original Vespa scooters which first appeared in the late 1940s. Over the intervening years the range has evolved in many respects whilst still retaining the more significant characteristics of their ancestors. The PX series is descended from the earlier 180 cc and 200 cc Rally models which they replaced.

In June 1978 the P125 X and P200 E models were introduced in the UK, followed by the P150 X in November of the same year. In common with all previous Vespas, the new models were based on the welded steel monocoque frame incorporating an open footboard area and integral legshields. Again following earlier practice, the engine and transmission were built in unit, the complete assembly doubling as the 'swinging arm' member for the rear suspension.

At the front of the machine, the long steering column terminated in a single sided front fork to which was attached the trailing link suspension arrangement. This system allowed the front and rear wheels to be identical, and thus interchangeable, making it feasible to provide an optional spare wheel which could be carried beneath the left-hand side panel.

All models are equipped with a 12 volt electrical system. No battery is fitted, the entire system running from an ingenious ac (alternating current) voltage regulator.

During 1982 and 1983 the P125/150X and P200E were superseded by the PX models. The PX200E was largely unchanged from its predecessor although both the PX125 and 150 models were fitted with electronic ignition.

In 1989 Vespa celebrated its 40th anniversary and to commemorate this event a limited edition version of the PX125E was imported. Mechanically this machine was unchanged from the production model although it was fitted as standard with a spare wheel, wheel covers and handlebar mirrors. Also the T5 design spoiler and floor panel mat were fitted. These changes are mainly cosmetic and do not affect any of the procedures described in this manual. Mention of the wheel covers, mat and spoiler can be found in Chapter 7, Section 12.

Model dimensions and weights

For information relating to later models see Chapter 7

	P125 X	P150 X	P200 E
Overall length	1760 mm (69.3 in)	1760 mm (69.3 in)	1760 mm (69.3 in)
Overall width	695 mm (27.3 in)	695 mm (27.3 in)	695 mm (27.3 in)
Overall height	1110 mm (43.7 in)	1110 mm (43.7 in)	1110 mm (43.7 in)
Wheelbase	1235 mm (48.7 in)	1235 mm (48.7 in)	1235 mm (48.7 in)
Ground clearance	225 mm (8.9 in)	225 mm (8.9 in)	225 mm (8.9 in)
Dry weight	104 kg (229 lb)	104 kg (229 lb)	108 kg (238 lb)
Chassis No. prefix	VNX 1 T	VLX 1 T	VSX 1 T
Engine No. prefix	VNL 3 M	VLX 1 M	VSE 1 M

	PX125 E	PX150 E	PX200 E
Overall length	1760 mm (69.3 in)	1760 mm (69.3 in)	1760 mm (69.3 in)
Overall width	695 mm (27.3 in)	695 mm (27.3 in)	695 mm (27.3 in)
Overall height	1110 mm (43.7 in)	1110 mm (43.7 in)	1110 mm (43.7 in)
Wheelbase	1235 mm (48.7 in)	1235 mm (48.7 in)	1235 mm (48.7 in)
Ground clearance	225 mm (8.9 in)	225 mm (8.9 in)	225 mm (8.9 in)
Dry weight	104 kg (229 lb)	104 kg (229 lb)	108 kg (238 lb)
Chassis No. prefix	VNX 2 T	VLX 1 T	VSX 1 T
Engine No. prefix	VNX 1 M	VLX 1 M	VSE 1 M

Ordering spare parts

When ordering spare parts for any Vespa scooter it is advisable to deal direct with an official Vespa dealer who will be able to supply most items ex-stock. Where parts have to be ordered, an authorised dealer will be able to obtain them as quickly as possible. The engine and frame numbers must always be quoted in full. This avoids the risk of incorrect parts being supplied and is particularly important where detail modifications have been made in the middle of production runs. In some instances it will be necessary for the dealer to check compatibility of later parts designs with earlier models. The frame number is stamped into the right-hand side of the body, behind the side panel, and the engine number on a raised boss on the crankcase swinging arm extension.

It is recommended that genuine Vespa parts are used. Although pattern parts are often cheaper, remember that there is no guarantee that they are of the same specification as the original, and in some instances may be positively dangerous. Note also that the use of non-standard parts may invalidate the warranty in the event of a subsequent failure.

Some of the more expendable parts such as oils, greases, spark plugs, tyres and bulbs, can be obtained from auto accessory shops. These are often more conveniently located and may open during weekends. It is also possible to obtain parts on a mail order basis from specialists who advertise in the motorcycle magazines.

Engine number location

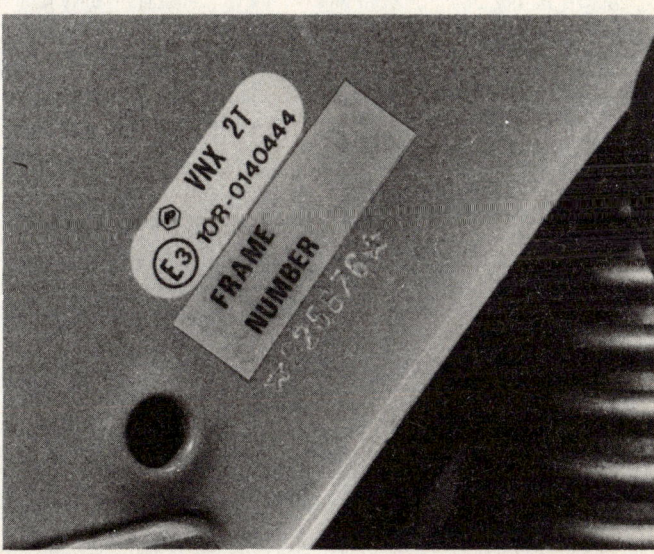

Frame number location

Safety first!

Professional motor mechanics are trained in safe working procedures. However enthusiastic you may be about getting on with the job in hand, do take the time to ensure that your safety is not put at risk. A moment's lack of attention can result in an accident, as can failure to observe certain elementary precautions.

There will always be new ways of having accidents, and the following points do not pretend to be a comprehensive list of all dangers; they are intended rather to make you aware of the risks and to encourage a safety-conscious approach to all work you carry out on your vehicle.

Essential DOs and DON'Ts

DON'T start the engine without first ascertaining that the transmission is in neutral.

DON'T suddenly remove the filler cap from a hot cooling system – cover it with a cloth and release the pressure gradually first, or you may get scalded by escaping coolant.

DON'T attempt to drain oil until you are sure it has cooled sufficiently to avoid scalding you.

DON'T grasp any part of the engine, exhaust or silencer without first ascertaining that it is sufficiently cool to avoid burning you.

DON'T allow brake fluid or antifreeze to contact the machine's paintwork or plastic components.

DON'T syphon toxic liquids such as fuel, brake fluid or antifreeze by mouth, or allow them to remain on your skin.

DON'T inhale dust – it may be injurious to health (see *Asbestos* heading).

DON'T allow any spilt oil or grease to remain on the floor – wipe it up straight away, before someone slips on it.

DON'T use ill-fitting spanners or other tools which may slip and cause injury.

DON'T attempt to lift a heavy component which may be beyond your capability – get assistance.

DON'T rush to finish a job, or take unverified short cuts.

DON'T allow children or animals in or around an unattended vehicle.

DON'T inflate a tyre to a pressure above the recommended maximum. Apart from overstressing the carcase and wheel rim, in extreme cases the tyre may blow off forcibly.

DO ensure that the machine is supported securely at all times. This is especially important when the machine is blocked up to aid wheel or fork removal.

DO take care when attempting to slacken a stubborn nut or bolt. It is generally better to pull on a spanner, rather than push, so that if slippage occurs you fall away from the machine rather than on to it.

DO wear eye protection when using power tools such as drill, sander, bench grinder etc.

DO use a barrier cream on your hands prior to undertaking dirty jobs – it will protect your skin from infection as well as making the dirt easier to remove afterwards; but make sure your hands aren't left slippery. Note that long-term contact with used engine oil can be a health hazard.

DO keep loose clothing (cuffs, tie etc) and long hair well out of the way of moving mechanical parts.

DO remove rings, wristwatch etc, before working on the vehicle – especially the electrical system.

DO keep your work area tidy – it is only too easy to fall over articles left lying around.

DO exercise caution when compressing springs for removal or installation. Ensure that the tension is applied and released in a controlled manner, using suitable tools which preclude the possibility of the spring escaping violently.

DO ensure that any lifting tackle used has a safe working load rating adequate for the job.

DO get someone to check periodically that all is well, when working alone on the vehicle.

DO carry out work in a logical sequence and check that everything is correctly assembled and tightened afterwards.

DO remember that your vehicle's safety affects that of yourself and others. If in doubt on any point, get specialist advice.

IF, in spite of following these precautions, you are unfortunate enough to injure yourself, seek medical attention as soon as possible.

Asbestos

Certain friction, insulating, sealing, and other products – such as brake linings, clutch linings, gaskets, etc – contain asbestos. *Extreme care must be taken to avoid inhalation of dust from such products since it is hazardous to health.* If in doubt, assume that they *do* contain asbestos.

Fire

Remember at all times that petrol (gasoline) is highly flammable. Never smoke, or have any kind of naked flame around, when working on the vehicle. But the risk does not end there – a spark caused by an electrical short-circuit, by two metal surfaces contacting each other, by careless use of tools, or even by static electricity built up in your body under certain conditions, can ignite petrol vapour, which in a confined space is highly explosive.

Always disconnect the battery earth (ground) terminal before working on any part of the fuel or electrical system, and never risk spilling fuel on to a hot engine or exhaust.

It is recommended that a fire extinguisher of a type suitable for fuel and electrical fires is kept handy in the garage or workplace at all times. Never try to extinguish a fuel or electrical fire with water.

Note: *Any reference to a 'torch' appearing in this manual should always be taken to mean a hand-held battery-operated electric lamp or flashlight. It does **not** mean a welding/gas torch or blowlamp.*

Fumes

Certain fumes are highly toxic and can quickly cause unconsciousness and even death if inhaled to any extent. Petrol (gasoline) vapour comes into this category, as do the vapours from certain solvents such as trichloroethylene. Any draining or pouring of such volatile fluids should be done in a well ventilated area.

When using cleaning fluids and solvents, read the instructions carefully. Never use materials from unmarked containers – they may give off poisonous vapours.

Never run the engine of a motor vehicle in an enclosed space such as a garage. Exhaust fumes contain carbon monoxide which is extremely poisonous; if you need to run the engine, always do so in the open air or at least have the rear of the vehicle outside the workplace.

The battery

Never cause a spark, or allow a naked light, near the vehicle's battery. It will normally be giving off a certain amount of hydrogen gas, which is highly explosive.

Always disconnect the battery earth (ground) terminal before working on the fuel or electrical systems.

If possible, loosen the filler plugs or cover when charging the battery from an external source. Do not charge at an excessive rate or the battery may burst.

Take care when topping up and when carrying the battery. The acid electrolyte, even when diluted, is very corrosive and should not be allowed to contact the eyes or skin.

If you ever need to prepare electrolyte yourself, always add the acid slowly to the water, and never the other way round. Protect against splashes by wearing rubber gloves and goggles.

Mains electricity and electrical equipment

When using an electric power tool, inspection light etc, always ensure that the appliance is correctly connected to its plug and that, where necessary, it is properly earthed (grounded). Do not use such appliances in damp conditions and, again, beware of creating a spark or applying excessive heat in the vicinity of fuel or fuel vapour. Also ensure that the appliances meet the relevant national safety standards.

Ignition HT voltage

A severe electric shock can result from touching certain parts of the ignition system, such as the HT leads, when the engine is running or being cranked, particularly if components are damp or the insulation is defective. Where an electronic ignition system is fitted, the HT voltage is much higher and could prove fatal.

Tools and working facilities

The first priority when undertaking maintenance or repair work of any sort on a motorcycle is to have a clean, dry, well-lit working area. Work carried out in peace and quiet in the well-ordered atmosphere of a good workshop will give more satisfaction and much better results than can usually be achieved in poor working conditions. A good workshop must have a clean flat workbench or a solidly constructed table of convenient working height. The workbench or table should be equipped with a vice which has a jaw opening of at least 4 in (100 mm). A set of jaw covers should be made from soft metal such as aluminium alloy or copper, or from wood. These covers will minimise the marking or damaging of soft or delicate components which may be clamped in the vice. Some clean, dry, storage space will be required for tools, lubricants and dismantled components. It will be necessary during a major overhaul to lay out engine/gearbox components for examination and to keep them where they will remain undisturbed for as long as is necessary. To this end it is recommended that a supply of metal or plastic containers of suitable size is collected. A supply of clean, lint-free, rags for cleaning purposes and some newspapers, other rags, or paper towels for mopping up spillages should also be kept. If working on a hard concrete floor note that both the floor and one's knees can be protected from oil spillages and wear by cutting open a large cardboard box and spreading it flat on the floor under the machine or workbench. This also helps to provide some warmth in winter and to prevent the loss of nuts, washers, and other tiny components which have a tendency to disappear when dropped on anything other than a perfectly clean, flat, surface.

Unfortunately, such working conditions are not always available to the home mechanic. When working in poor conditions it is essential to take extra time and care to ensure that the components being worked on are kept scrupulously clean and to ensure that no components or tools are lost or damaged.

A selection of good tools is a fundamental requirement for anyone contemplating the maintenance and repair of a motor vehicle. For the owner who does not possess any, their purchase will prove a considerable expense, offsetting some of the savings made by doing-it-yourself. However, provided that the tools purchased meet the relevant national safety standards and are of good quality, they will last for many years and prove an extremely worthwhile investment.

To help the average owner to decide which tools are needed to carry out the various tasks detailed in this manual, we have compiled three lists of tools under the following headings: *Maintenance and minor repair, Repair and overhaul,* and *Specialized*. The newcomer to practical mechanics should start off with the simpler jobs around the vehicle. Then, as his confidence and experience grow, he can undertake more difficult tasks, buying extra tools as and when they are needed. In this way, a *Maintenance and minor repair* tool kit can be built-up into a *Repair and overhaul* tool kit over a considerable period of time without any major cash outlays. The experienced home mechanic will have a tool kit good enough for most repair and overhaul procedures and will add tools from the specialized category when he feels the expense is justified by the amount of use these tools will be put to.

It is obviously not possible to cover the subject of tools fully here. For those who wish to learn more about tools and their use there is a book entitled *Motorcycle Workshop Practice Manual* (Bk no 1454) available from the publishers of this manual.

As a general rule, it is better to buy the more expensive, good quality tools. Given reasonable use, such tools will last for a very long time, whereas the cheaper, poor quality, item will wear out faster and need to be renewed more often, thus nullifying the original saving. There is also the risk of a poor quality tool breaking while in use, causing personal injury or expensive damage to the component being worked on.

For practically all tools, a tool factor is the best source since he will have a very comprehensive range compared with the average garage or accessory shop. Having said that, accessory shops often offer excellent quality tools at discount prices, so it pays to shop around. There are plenty of tools around at reasonable prices, but always aim to purchase items which meet the relevant national safety standards. If in doubt, seek the advice of the shop proprietor or manager before making a purchase.

The basis of any toolkit is a set of spanners. While open-ended spanners with their slim jaws, are useful for working on awkwardly-positioned nuts, ring spanners have advantages in that they grip the nut far more positively. There is less risk of the spanner slipping off the nut and damaging it, for this reason alone ring spanners are to be preferred. Ideally, the home mechanic should acquire a set of each, but if expense rules this out a set of combination spanners (open-ended at one end and with a ring of the same size at the other) will provide a good compromise. Another item which is so useful it should be considered an essential requirement for any home mechanic is a set of socket spanners. These are available in a variety of drive sizes. It is recommended that the ½-inch drive type is purchased to begin with as although bulkier and more expensive than the ⅜-inch type, the larger size is far more common and will accept a greater variety of torque wrenches, extension pieces and socket sizes. The socket set should comprise sockets of sizes between 8 and 24 mm, a reversible ratchet drive, an extension bar of about 10 inches in length, a spark plug socket with a rubber insert, and a universal joint. Other attachments can be added to the set at a later date.

Maintenance and minor repair tool kit

Set of spanners 8 – 24 mm
Set of sockets and attachments
Spark plug spanner with rubber insert – 10, 12, or 14 mm as appropriate
Adjustable spanner
C-spanner/pin spanner
Torque wrench (same size drive as sockets)
Set of screwdrivers (flat blade)
Set of screwdrivers (cross-head)
Set of Allen keys 4 – 10 mm
Impact screwdriver and bits
Ball pein hammer – 2 lb
Hacksaw (junior)
Self-locking pliers – Mole grips or vice grips
Pliers – combination
Pliers – needle nose
Wire brush (small)
Soft-bristled brush
Tyre pump
Tyre pressure gauge
Tyre tread depth gauge
Oil can
Fine emery cloth
Funnel (medium size)
Drip tray
Grease gun
Set of feeler gauges
Brake bleeding kit
Strobe timing light
Continuity tester (dry battery and bulb)
Soldering iron and solder
Wire stripper or craft knife
PVC insulating tape
Assortment of split pins, nuts, bolts, and washers

Repair and overhaul tool kit

The tools in this list are virtually essential for anyone undertaking major repairs to a motorcycle and are additional to the tools listed above. Concerning Torx driver bits, Torx screws are encountered on some of the more modern machines where their use is restricted to fastening certain components inside the engine/gearbox unit. It is therefore recommended that if Torx bits cannot be borrowed from a local dealer, they are purchased individually as the need arises. They are not in regular use in the motor trade and will therefore only be available in specialist tool shops.

Plastic or rubber soft-faced mallet
Torx driver bits
Pliers – electrician's side cutters
Circlip pliers – internal (straight or right-angled tips are available)
Circlip pliers – external
Cold chisel
Centre punch
Pin punch
Scriber
Scraper (made from soft metal such as aluminium or copper)
Soft metal drift

Steel rule/straight edge
Assortment of files
Electric drill and bits
Wire brush (large)
Soft wire brush (similar to those used for cleaning suede shoes)
Sheet of plate glass
Hacksaw (large)
Stud extractor set (E-Z out)

Specialized tools

This is not a list of the tools made by the machine's manufacturer to carry out a specific task on a limited range of models. Occasional references are made to such tools in the text of this manual and, in general, an alternative method of carrying out the task without the manufacturer's tool is given where possible. The tools mentioned in this list are those which are not used regularly and are expensive to buy in view of their infrequent use. Where this is the case it may be possible to hire or borrow the tools against a deposit from a local dealer or tool hire shop. An alternative is for a group of friends or a motorcycle club to join in the purchase.

Piston ring compressor
Universal bearing puller
Cylinder bore honing attachment (for electric drill)
Micrometer set
Vernier calipers
Dial gauge set
Cylinder compression gauge
Vacuum gauge set
Multimeter
Dwell meter/tachometer

Care and maintenance of tools

Whatever the quality of the tools purchased, they will last much longer if cared for. This means in practice ensuring that a tool is used for its intended purpose; for example screwdrivers should not be used as a substitute for a centre punch, or as chisels. Always remove dirt or grease and any metal particles but remember that a light film of oil will prevent rusting if the tools are infrequently used. The common tools can be kept together in a large box or tray but the more delicate, and more expensive, items should be stored separately where they cannot be damaged. When a tool is damaged or worn out, be sure to renew it immediately. It is false economy to continue to use a worn spanner or screwdriver which may slip and cause expensive damage to the component being worked on.

Fastening systems

Fasteners, basically, are nuts, bolts and screws used to hold two or more parts together. There are a few things to keep in mind when working with fasteners. Almost all of them use a locking device of some type; either a lock washer, lock nut, locking tab or thread adhesive. All threaded fasteners should be clean, straight, have undamaged threads and undamaged corners on the hexagon head where the spanner fits. Develop the habit of replacing all damaged nuts and bolts with new ones.

Rusted nuts and bolts should be treated with a rust penetrating fluid to ease removal and prevent breakage. After applying the rust penetrant, let it 'work' for a few minutes before trying to loosen the nut or bolt. Badly rusted fasteners may have to be chiseled off or removed with a special nut breaker, available at tool shops.

Flat washers and lock washers, when removed from an assembly should always be replaced exactly as removed. Replace any damaged washers with new ones. Always use a flat washer between a lock washer and any soft metal surface (such as aluminium), thin sheet metal or plastic. Special lock nuts can only be used once or twice before they lose their locking ability and must be renewed.

If a bolt or stud breaks off in an assembly, it can be drilled out and removed with a special tool called an E-Z out. Most dealer service departments and motorcycle repair shops can perform this task, as well as others (such as the repair of threaded holes that have been stripped out).

Conversion factors

Length (distance)

Inches (in)	x 25.4	= Millimetres (mm)	x 0.0394	= Inches (in)
Feet (ft)	x 0.305	= Metres (m)	x 3.281	= Feet (ft)
Miles	x 1.609	= Kilometres (km)	x 0.621	= Miles

Volume (capacity)

Cubic inches (cu in; in³)	x 16.387	= Cubic centimetres (cc; cm³)	x 0.061	= Cubic inches (cu in; in³)
Imperial pints (Imp pt)	x 0.568	= Litres (l)	x 1.76	= Imperial pints (Imp pt)
Imperial quarts (Imp qt)	x 1.137	= Litres (l)	x 0.88	= Imperial quarts (Imp qt)
Imperial quarts (Imp qt)	x 1.201	= US quarts (US qt)	x 0.833	= Imperial quarts (Imp qt)
US quarts (US qt)	x 0.946	= Litres (l)	x 1.057	= US quarts (US qt)
Imperial gallons (Imp gal)	x 4.546	= Litres (l)	x 0.22	= Imperial gallons (Imp gal)
Imperial gallons (Imp gal)	x 1.201	= US gallons (US gal)	x 0.833	= Imperial gallons (Imp gal)
US gallons (US gal)	x 3.785	= Litres (l)	x 0.264	= US gallons (US gal)

Mass (weight)

Ounces (oz)	x 28.35	= Grams (g)	x 0.035	= Ounces (oz)
Pounds (lb)	x 0.454	= Kilograms (kg)	x 2.205	= Pounds (lb)

Force

Ounces-force (ozf; oz)	x 0.278	= Newtons (N)	x 3.6	= Ounces-force (ozf; oz)
Pounds-force (lbf; lb)	x 4.448	= Newtons (N)	x 0.225	= Pounds-force (lbf; lb)
Newtons (N)	x 0.1	= Kilograms-force (kgf; kg)	x 9.81	= Newtons (N)

Pressure

Pounds-force per square inch (psi; lbf/in²; lb/in²)	x 0.070	= Kilograms-force per square centimetre (kgf/cm²; kg/cm²)	x 14.223	= Pounds-force per square inch (psi; lbf/in²; lb/in²)
Pounds-force per square inch (psi; lbf/in²; lb/in²)	x 0.068	= Atmospheres (atm)	x 14.696	= Pounds-force per square inch (psi; lbf/in²; lb/in²)
Pounds-force per square inch (psi; lbf/in²; lb/in²)	x 0.069	= Bars	x 14.5	= Pounds-force per square inch (psi; lbf/in²; lb/in²)
Pounds-force per square inch (psi; lbf/in²; lb/in²)	x 6.895	= Kilopascals (kPa)	x 0.145	= Pounds-force per square inch (psi; lbf/in²; lb/in²)
Kilopascals (kPa)	x 0.01	= Kilograms-force per square centimetre (kgf/cm²; kg/cm²)	x 98.1	= Kilopascals (kPa)
Millibar (mbar)	x 100	= Pascals (Pa)	x 0.01	= Millibar (mbar)
Millibar (mbar)	x 0.0145	= Pounds-force per square inch (psi; lbf/in²; lb/in²)	x 68.947	= Millibar (mbar)
Millibar (mbar)	x 0.75	= Millimetres of mercury (mmHg)	x 1.333	= Millibar (mbar)
Millibar (mbar)	x 0.401	= Inches of water (inH₂O)	x 2.491	= Millibar (mbar)
Millimetres of mercury (mmHg)	x 0.535	= Inches of water (inH₂O)	x 1.868	= Millimetres of mercury (mmHg)
Inches of water (inH₂O)	x 0.036	= Pounds-force per square inch (psi; lbf/in²; lb/in²)	x 27.68	= Inches of water (inH₂O)

Torque (moment of force)

Pounds-force inches (lbf in; lb in)	x 1.152	= Kilograms-force centimetre (kgf cm; kg cm)	x 0.868	= Pounds-force inches (lbf in; lb in)
Pounds-force inches (lbf in; lb in)	x 0.113	= Newton metres (Nm)	x 8.85	= Pounds-force inches (lbf in; lb in)
Pounds-force inches (lbf in; lb in)	x 0.083	= Pounds-force feet (lbf ft; lb ft)	x 12	= Pounds-force inches (lbf in; lb in)
Pounds-force feet (lbf ft; lb ft)	x 0.138	= Kilograms-force metres (kgf m; kg m)	x 7.233	= Pounds-force feet (lbf ft; lb ft)
Pounds-force feet (lbf ft; lb ft)	x 1.356	= Newton metres (Nm)	x 0.738	= Pounds-force feet (lbf ft; lb ft)
Newton metres (Nm)	x 0.102	= Kilograms-force metres (kgf m; kg m)	x 9.804	= Newton metres (Nm)

Power

Horsepower (hp)	x 745.7	= Watts (W)	x 0.0013	= Horsepower (hp)

Velocity (speed)

Miles per hour (miles/hr; mph)	x 1.609	= Kilometres per hour (km/hr; kph)	x 0.621	= Miles per hour (miles/hr; mph)

Fuel consumption*

Miles per gallon (mpg)	x 0.354	= Kilometres per litre (km/l)	x 2.825	= Miles per gallon (mpg)

Temperature

Degrees Fahrenheit = (°C x 1.8) + 32

Degrees Celsius (Degrees Centigrade; °C) = (°F - 32) x 0.56

It is common practice to convert from miles per gallon (mpg) to litres/100 kilometres (l/100km), where mpg x l/100 km = 282

Choosing and fitting accessories

A wide range of accessories is available for Vespa scooters, most of which can be supplied, and if necessary fitted, by any Vespa dealer. The list of equipment offered by the importers is extensive, and can be expected to fit without modification. It is also possible to purchase a number of similar 'universal' scooter accessories produced by various manufacturers and whilst these should pose no serious fitting problems, a certain amount of work may have to be undertaken.

Of the official Vespa range, additional luggage carrying equipment includes front and rear carriers, the latter being available with a top box if required. The level of weather protection can be further enhanced by fitting a windscreen or flyscreen. Also available are crashbars, rubber floor mats, grab rails, seats, backrests and chrome plated horn covers. Full details of these and other accessories can be obtained from Vespa dealers.

The fitting of accessories is generally straightforward, involving the removal of a few fasteners, positioning of the item to be fitted and the fitting of longer bolts to retain it. Whilst the job should be self-explanatory and well within the capabilities of most owners, a brief outline of the fitting procedure is given below, together with guidance on the selection of the best type, where appropriate.

Flyscreens and windscreens

The scooter rider is well protected from the elements from the waist down, and this protection can be extended by fitting a flyscreen or windscreen. The former is a very small screen which fits around the headlamp unit. Whilst it is less obtrusive than a full windscreen it will provide only limited protection, but it will divert most of the oncoming wind and rain from the torso. It must be noted, however, that it provides little hand protection, and some riders may find that any wind deflected from the body is directed at the rider's head, where it may cause buffeting.

The full windscreen provides a higher level of weather protection, but is more obtrusive. It is fitted in much the same way as the flyscreen, but is both wider and higher. It thus affords some measure of hand protection and should deflect wind and rain from all but the tallest rider's head.

The Vespa scooters covered by this manual are fitted with four threaded holes in the underside of the handlebar unit, and these provide mounting points for the windscreen or flyscreen brackets. The fitting procedure is similar for all screens, and consists of bolting the two mounting brackets to the handlebar. The screen blade should be positioned to leave a small gap between the plastic edging and the headlamp. This is because the screen will move slightly when the machine is ridden, and if it touches the handlebar it will tend to wear the paintwork away. With most designs it is possible to adjust the angle of the screen. This should be set to the position which gives best protection with minimum vibration of the screen blade, and can be determined by experiment.

Front carriers

Though all scooters are better equipped for the carrying of luggage than most motorcycles, many owners will require the additional capacity for bulky loads afforded by a luggage rack or carrier. The front-mounting types have two hooks which are fitted over the top of the legshields. Two rubber buffers hold the bottom of the rack clear of the bodywork, the assembly being held in position by two adjustable hooked rods. Fitting and removal of the rack takes only minutes, but note that the latter applies equally to potential thieves. Packages can be secured to the sprung luggage grid with bungy cords. On no account be tempted to carry heavy loads on a front carrier. Not only will this tend to distort the rack, but it may also damage the bodywork or impair the steering.

Rear carriers

The rear carrier fulfills the same role as the front unit described above, and most of the remarks can be applied to it. The rear fitment does have a number of advantages, notably the fact that it is bolted into position and is therefore more substantial and less prone to theft.

On some designs the top of the rack is retained by the seat latch post, whilst others may require bolt holes to be drilled in the body below the seat. The lower mountings normally make use of the number plate mounting holes, a brace bar running behind the plate.

It is possible to obtain a rear carrier complete with a lockable top box. This provides storage space for waterproof clothing and can be used to store the rider's helmet when the machine is parked. The box can double as a passenger backrest.

Crashbars

These are probably better described as side panel protectors, since this is their real function. In practice, it is unlikely that they will offer any real protection to the machine if it is dropped at any speed, but can save damage to the side panels if the machine falls over when stationary. They also fend off carelessly-opened car doors in car parks quite successfully.

The assembly is retained at the front by the stand mounting bolts and at the rear by a brace bar which utlises the number plate bolts. This arrangement also provides raised footrests for the passenger, which can avoid tangled feet on the rather cramped footboard area.

Backrests and grab rails

The purpose of a backrest will be obvious to anyone who has ridden on the back of a Vespa. With the exception of the rider there is little to hold onto, and in traffic there is a distinct tendency for the unwary passenger to make unplanned excursions from the rear of the machine.

A backrest will undeniably obviate this problem, but if finances permit, a rear carrier will provide a hand-hold and extra luggage capacity. Some rear carrier designs incorporate a backrest – the best of both worlds.

Grab rails also provide a means of retaining passengers, though without the comfort afforded by a backrest. Again, a rear carrier is a more useful accessory overall.

Other accessories

Of the remaining accessories, mirrors are an invaluable addition. These are available in various lengths and patterns, and aesthetics aside, the short-stemmed types are the best. The mirrors normally mount via brackets bolted to the underside of the handlebar unit in the same way as screens. If the machine is already fitted with a screen it may prove better to adapt the screen backrests to accept the mirrors than to fit still more bracketry. It should be noted that the standard motorcycle types of mirror cannot be fitted without a certain amount of fabrication work on the part of the owner, and that the stems will in any case be too short.

Also worth having is a floor mat. These simply lay over the existing rubber strips and make cleaning a good deal simpler. In addition, the paintwork is covered and will therefore be better preserved. Watch for corrosion due to water being held between the mat and the floorboard.

Of the remainder, a seat of a different design is perhaps worth considering if the old one is in need of renewal. Chrome plated horn covers are of no practical use, and while this may improve the machine in its owner's eyes may not make it easier to sell when the time comes.

A number of aftermarket exhaust systems are available, and this subject deserves a note of caution. Like every other motor vehicle manufacturer, Vespa have spent a good deal of time and effort obtaining a balance between performance, noise and economy, and it is therefore unlikely that any overall improvement can be made by an after-market manufacturer. It may be possible to improve one of these factors at the expense of another, but all too often accessory exhaust systems are generally less efficient. It should also be remembered that a change in the exhaust system is inevitably linked to changes in carburation, and if an alternative system is fitted some modification will probably be needed. As a general rule, stick to the manufacturer's original system, particularly during the warranty period, and do not expect a sympathetic reaction from the dealer or importer if a change of system results in engine damage.

Fault diagnosis

Contents

1 Introduction

This Section provides an easy reference-guide to the more common ailments that are likely to afflict your machine. Obviously, the opportunities are almost limitless for faults to occur as a result of obscure failures, and to try and cover all eventualities would require a book. Indeed, a number have been written on the subject.

Successful fault diagnosis is not a mysterious 'black art' but the application of a bit of knowledge combined with a systematic and logical approach to the problem. Approach any fault diagnosis by first accurately identifying the symptom and then checking through the list of possible causes, starting with the simplest or most obvious and progressing in stages to the most complex. Take nothing for granted, but above all apply liberal quantities of common sense.

The main symptom of a fault is given in the text as a major heading below which are listed, as Section headings, the various systems or areas which may contain the fault. Details of each possible cause for a fault and the remedial action to be taken are given, in brief, in the paragraphs below each Section heading. Further information should be sought in the relevant Chapter.

Engine does not start when turned over

2 No fuel flow to carburettor

● Fuel tank empty or level too low. Check that the tap is turned to 'On' or 'Reserve' position as required. If in doubt, prise off the fuel feed pipe at the carburettor end and check that fuel runs from the pipe when the tap is turned on.
● Tank filler cap vent obstructed. This can prevent fuel from flowing into the carburettor float bowl because air cannot enter the fuel tank to replace it. The problem is more likely to appear when the machine is being ridden. Check by listening close to the filler cap and releasing it. A hissing noise indicates that a blockage is present. Remove the cap and clear the vent hole with wire or by using an air line from the inside of the cap.
● Fuel tap or filter blocked. Blockage may be due to accumulation of rust or paint flakes from the tank's inner surface or of foreign matter from contaminated fuel. Remove the tap and clean it and the filter. Look also for water droplets in the fuel.
● Fuel line blocked. Blockage of the fuel line is more likely to result from a kink in the line rather than the accumulation of debris.

3 Fuel not reaching cylinder

● Float chamber not filling. Caused by float needle or floats sticking in up position. This may occur after the machine has been left standing for an extended length of time allowing the fuel to evaporate. When this occurs a gummy residue is often left which hardens to a varnish-like substance. This condition may be worsened by corrosion and crystalline deposits produced prior to the total evaporation of contaminated fuel. Sticking of the float needle may also be caused by wear. In any case removal of the float chamber will be necessary for inspection and cleaning.
● Blockage in starting circuit, slow running circuit or jets. Blockage of these items may be attributable to debris from the fuel tank by-passing the filter system or to gumming up as described in paragraph 1 Water droplets in the fuel will also block jets and passages. The carburettor should be dismantled for cleaning.
● Fuel level too low. The fuel level in the float chamber is controlled by float height. The fuel level may increase with wear or damage but will never reduce, thus a low fuel level is an inherent rather than a developing condition. Check the float height, renewing the float or needle if required.
● Oil blockage in fuel system or carburettor (petroil lubricated engines only). May arise when the machine has been parked for long periods and the residual petrol has evaporated. To rectify, dismantle and clean the carburettor and tap, flush the tank and fill with fresh petroil mixed in the correct proportions. This problem can be avoided by running the float bowl dry before the machine is stored for long periods. Do not attempt to use fuel which has become stale.

4 Engine flooding

● Float valve needle worn or stuck open. A piece of rust or other debris can prevent correct seating of the needle against the valve seat thereby permitting an uncontrolled flow of fuel. Similarly, a worn needle or needle seat will prevent valve closure. Dismantle the carburettor float bowl for cleaning and, if necessary, renewal of the worn components.
● Fuel level too high. The fuel level is controlled by the float height which may increase due to wear of the float needle, pivot pin or operating tang. A leaking float will cause an increase in fuel level, and thus should be renewed.
● Cold starting mechanism. Check the choke (starter mechanism) for correct operation. If the mechanism jams in the 'On' position subsequent starting of a hot engine will be difficult.
● Blocked air filter. A badly restricted air filter will cause flooding. Check the filter and clean or renew as required. A collapsed inlet hose will have a similar effect. Check that the air filter inlet has not become blocked by a rag or similar item.

5 No spark at plug

● Ignition switch not on.
● Engine stop switch off.
● Fuse blown. Check fuse for ignition circuit. See wiring diagram.
● Spark plug dirty, oiled or 'whiskered'. Because the induction mixture of a two-stroke engine is inclined to be of a rather oily nature it is comparatively easy to foul the plug electrodes, especially where there have been repeated attempts to start the engine. A machine used for short journeys will be more prone to fouling because the engine may never reach full operating temperature, and the deposits will not burn off. On rare occasions a change of plug grade may be required but the advice of a dealer should be sought before making such a change. 'Whiskering' is a comparatively rare occurrence on modern machines but may be encountered where pre-mixed petrol and oil (petroil) lubrication is employed. An electrode deposit in the form of a barely visible filament across the plug electrodes can short circuit the plug and prevent its sparking. On all two-stroke machines it is a sound precaution to carry a new spare spark plug for substitution in the event of fouling problems.
● Spark plug failure. Clean the spark plug thoroughly and reset the electrode gap. Refer to the spark plug section
in Chapter 3. If the spark plug shorts internally or has sustained visible damage to the electrodes, core or ceramic insulator it should be renewed. On rare occasions a plug that appears to spark vigorously will fail to do so when refitted to the engine and subjected to the compression pressure in the cylinder.
● Spark plug cap or high tension (HT) lead faulty. Check condition and security. Replace if deterioration is evident. Most spark plug caps have an internal resistor designed to inhibit electrical interference with radio and television sets. On rare occasions the resistor may break down, thus preventing sparking. If this is suspected, fit a new cap as a precaution.
● Spark plug cap loose. Check that the spark plug cap fits securely over the plug and, where fitted, the screwed terminal on the plug end is secure.
● Shorting due to moisture. Certain parts of the ignition system are susceptible to shorting when the machine is ridden or parked in wet weather. Check particularly the area from the spark plug cap back to the ignition coil. A water dispersant spray may be used to dry out waterlogged components. Recurrence of the problem can be prevented by using an ignition sealant spray after drying out and cleaning.
● Ignition or stop switch shorted. May be caused by water corrosion or wear. Water dispersant and contact cleaning sprays may be used. If this fails to overcome the problem dismantling and visual inspection of the switches will be required.
● Shorting or open circuit in wiring. Failure in any wire connecting any of the ignition components will cause ignition malfunction. Check also that all connections are clean, dry and tight.
● Ignition coil failure. Check the coil, referring to Chapter 3.
● Capacitor (condenser) failure. The capacitor may be checked most easily by substitution with a replacement item. Blackened contact

breaker points indicate capacitor malfunction but this may not always occur.

● Contact breaker points pitted, burned or closed up. Check the contact breaker points, referring to Chapter 3. Check also that the low tension leads at the contact breaker are secure and not shorting out.

6 Weak spark at plug

● Feeble sparking at the plug may be caused by any of the faults mentioned in the preceding Section other than those items in the first three paragraphs. Check first the contact breaker assembly and the spark plug, these being the most likely culprits.

7 Compression low

● Spark plug loose. This will be self-evident on inspection, and may be accompanied by a hissing noise when the engine is turned over. Remove the plug and check that the threads in the cylinder head are not damaged. Check also that the plug sealing washer is in good condition.

● Cylinder head joint leaking. This condition is often accompanied by a high pitched squeak from around the cylinder head and oil loss, and may be caused by insufficiently tightened cylinder head fasteners, or a warped cylinder head. Re-torqueing the fasteners to the correct specification may seal the leak in some instances but if damage has occurred this course of action will provide, at best, only a temporary cure.

● Low crankcase compression. This can be caused by worn main bearings and seals and will upset the incoming fuel/air mixture. A good seal in these areas is essential on any two-stroke engine.

● Worn disc valve. Disc valve wear is not common, but will cause similar symptoms to those described above. Overhaul will be necessary.

● Piston rings sticking or broken. Sticking of the piston rings may be caused by seizure due to lack of lubrication or overheating as a result of poor carburation or incorrect fuel type. Gumming of the rings may result from lack of use, or carbon deposits in the ring grooves. Broken rings result from over-revving, over-heating or general wear. In either case a top-end overhaul will be required.

Engine stalls after starting

8 General causes

● Improper cold start mechanism operation. Check that the operating controls function smoothly and, where applicable, are correctly adjusted. A cold engine may not require application of an enriched mixture to start initially but may baulk without choke once firing. Likewise a hot engine may start with an enriched mixture but will stop almost immediately if the choke is inadvertently in operation.

● Ignition malfunction. See Section 9. Weak spark at plug.

● Carburettor incorrectly adjusted. Maladjustment of the mixture strength or idle speed may cause the engine to stop immediately after starting. See Chapter 2.

● Fuel contamination. Check for filter blockage by debris or water which reduces, but does not completely stop, fuel flow, or blockage of the slow speed circuit in the carburettor by the same agents. If water is present it can often be seen as droplets in the bottom of the float bowl. Clean the filter and, where water is in evidence, drain and flush the fuel tank and float bowl.

● Intake air leak. Check for security of the carburettor mounting and hose connections, and for cracks or splits in the hoses. Check also that the carburettor top is secure.

● Air filter blocked or omitted. A blocked filter will cause an over-rich mixture; the omission of a filter will cause an excessively weak mixture. Both conditions will have a detrimental effect on carburation. Clean or renew the filter as necessary.

● Fuel filler cap air vent blocked. Usually caused by dirt or water. Clean the vent orifice.

● Choked exhaust system. Caused by excessive carbon build-up in the system, particularly around the silencer baffles. In many cases these can be detached for cleaning, though mopeds have one-piece systems which require a rather different approach. Refer to Chapter 2 for further information.

● Excessive carbon build-up in the engine. This can result from failure to decarbonise the engine at the specified interval or through excessive oil consumption. On pump-fed engines check pump adjustment. On pre-mix (petroil) systems check that oil is mixed in the recommended ratio.

Poor running at idle and low speed

9 Weak spark at plug or erratic firing

● Spark plug fouled, faulty or incorrectly adjusted. See Section 4 or refer to Chapter 3.

● Spark plug cap or high tension lead shorting. Check the condition of both these items ensuring that they are in good condition and dry and that the cap is fitted correctly.

● Spark plug type incorrect. Fit plug of correct type and heat range as given in Specifications. In certain conditions a plug of hotter or colder type may be required for normal running.

● Contact breaker points pitted, burned or closed-up. Check the contact breaker assembly, referring to Chapter 3.

● Ignition timing incorrect. Check the ignition timing statically and dynamically, ensuring that the advance is functioning correctly.

● Faulty ignition coil. Partial failure of the coil internal insulation will diminish the performance of the coil. No repair is possible, a new component must be fitted.

● Faulty capacitor (condenser). A failure of the capacitor will cause blackening of the contact breaker point faces and will allow excessive sparking at the points. A faulty capacitor may best be checked by substitution of a serviceable replacement item.

● Defective flywheel generator ignition source. Refer to Chapter 3 for further details on test procedures.

10 Fuel/air mixture incorrect

● Intake air leak. Check carburettor mountings and air cleaner hoses for security and signs of splitting. Ensure that carburettor top is tight.

● Mixture strength incorrect. Adjust slow running mixture strength using pilot adjustment screw.

● Pilot jet or slow running circuit blocked. The carburettor should be removed and dismantled for thorough cleaning. Blow through all jets and air passages with compressed air to clear obstructions.

● Air cleaner clogged or omitted. Clean or fit air cleaner element as necessary. Check also that the element and air filter cover are correctly seated.

● Cold start mechanism in operation. Check that the choke has not been left on inadvertently and the operation is correct. Where applicable check the operating cable free play.

● Fuel level too high or too low. Check the float height, renewing float or needle if required. See Section 3 or 4.

● Fuel tank air vent obstructed. Obstructions usually caused by dirt or water. Clean vent orifice.

11 Compression low

● See Section 7.

Acceleration poor

12 General causes

● All items as for previous Section.

● Choked air filter. Failure to keep the air filter element clean will allow the build-up of dirt with proportional loss of performance. In extreme cases of neglect acceleration will suffer.

● Choked exhaust system. This can result from failure to remove accumulations of carbon from the silencer baffles at the prescribed intervals. The increased back pressure will make the machine noticeably sluggish. Refer to Chapter 2 for further information on decarbonisation.

● Excessive carbon build-up in the engine. This can result from failure to decarbonise the engine at the specified interval or through excessive oil consumption. On pump-fed engines check pump adjustment. On pre-mix (petroil) systems check that oil is mixed in the recommended ratio.

● Ignition timing incorrect. Check the contact breaker gap and set within the prescribed range ensuring that the ignition timing is correct. If the contact breaker assembly is worn it may prove impossible to get the gap and timing settings to coincide, necessitating renewal.

● Ignition timing incorrect. Check the ignition timing as described in Chapter 3. Where no provision for adjustment exists, test the electronic ignition components and renew as required.

● Carburation fault. See Section 10.

● Mechanical resistance. Check that the brakes are not binding. On small machines in particular note that the increased rolling resistance caused by under-inflated tyres may impede acceleration.

Poor running or lack of power at high speeds

13 Weak spark at plug or erratic firing

● All items as for Section 9.

● HT lead insulation failure. Insulation failure of the HT lead and spark plug cap due to old age or damage can cause shorting when the engine is driven hard. This condition may be less noticeable, or not noticeable at all at lower engine speeds.

14 Fuel/air mixture incorrect

● All items as for Section 10, with the exception of items relative exclusively to low speed running.

● Main jet blocked. Debris from contaminated fuel, or from the fuel tank, and water in the fuel can block the main jet. Clean the fuel filter, the float bowl area, and if water is present, flush and refill the fuel tank.

● Main jet is the wrong size. The standard carburettor jetting is for sea level atmospheric pressure. For high altitudes, usually above 5000 ft, a smaller main jet will be required.

● Jet needle and needle jet worn. These can be renewed individually but should be renewed as a pair. Renewal of both items requires partial dismantling of the carburettor.

● Air bleed holes blocked. Dismantle carburettor and use compressed air to blow out all air passages.

● Reduced fuel flow. A reduction in the maximum fuel flow from the fuel tank to the carburettor will cause fuel starvation, proportionate to the engine speed. Check for blockages through debris or a kinked fuel line.

15 Compression low

● See Section 7.

Knocking or pinking

16 General causes

● Carbon build-up in combustion chamber. After a high mileage has been covered a large accumulation of carbon may occur. This may glow red hot and cause premature ignition of the fuel/air mixture, in advance of normal firing by the spark plug. Cylinder head removal will be required to allow inspection and cleaning.

● Fuel incorrect. A low grade fuel, or one of poor quality may result in compression induced detonation of the fuel resulting in knocking and pinking noises. Old fuel can cause similar problems. A too highly leaded fuel will reduce detonation but will accelerate deposit formation in the combustion chamber and may lead to early pre-ignition as described in item 1.

● Spark plug heat range incorrect. Uncontrolled pre-ignition can result from the use of a spark plug the heat range of which is too hot.

● Weak mixture. Overheating of the engine due to a weak mixture can result in pre-ignition occurring where it would not occur when engine temperature was within normal limits. Maladjustment, blocked jets or passages and air leaks can cause this condition.

Overheating

17 Firing incorrect

● Spark plug fouled, defective or maladjusted. See Section 5.

● Spark plug type incorrect. Refer to the Specifications and ensure that the correct plug type is fitted.

● Incorrect ignition timing. Timing that is far too much advanced or far too much retarded will cause overheating. Check the ignition timing is correct.

18 Fuel/air mixture incorrect

● Slow speed mixture strength incorrect. Adjust pilot air screw.

● Main jet wrong size. The carburettor is jetted for sea level atmospheric conditions. For high altitudes, usually above 5000 ft, a smaller main jet will be required.

● Air filter badly fitted or omitted. Check that the filter element is in place and that it and the air filter box cover are sealing correctly. Any leaks will cause a weak mixture.

● Induction air leaks. Check the security of the carburettor mountings and hose connections, and for cracks and splits in the hoses. Check also that the carburettor top is secure and that the vacuum gauge adaptor plug (where fitted) is tight.

● Fuel level too low. See Section 3.

● Fuel tank filler cap air vent obstructed. Clear blockage.

19 Lubrication inadequate

● Petrol/oil mixture incorrect. The proportion of oil mixed with the petrol in the tank is critical if the engine is to perform correctly. Too little oil will leave the reciprocating parts and bearings poorly lubricated and overheating will occur. In extreme case the engine will seize. Conversely, too much oil will effectively displace a similar amount of petrol. Though this does not often cause overheating in practice it is possible that the resultant weak mixture may cause overheating. It will inevitably cause a loss of power and excessive exhaust smoke.

● Oil pump settings incorrect. The oil pump settings are of great importance since the quantities of oil being injected are very small. Any variation in oil delivery will have a significant effect on the engine. Refer to Chapter 3 for further information.

● Oil tank empty or low. This will have disastrous consequences if left unnoticed. Check and replenish tank regularly.

● Transmission oil low or worn out. Check the level regularly and investigate any loss of oil. If the oil level drops with no sign of external leakage it is likely that the crankshaft main bearing oil seals are worn, allowing transmission oil to be drawn into the crankcase during induction.

20 Miscellaneous causes

● Engine fins clogged. A build-up of mud in the cylinder head and cylinder barrel cooling fins will decrease the cooling capabilities of the fins. Clean the fins as required.

Clutch operating problems

21 Clutch slip

● No clutch lever play. Adjust clutch lever end play according to the procedure in Chapter 1.

● Friction plates worn or warped. Overhaul clutch assembly, replacing plates out of specification.

● Steel plates worn or warped. Overhaul clutch assembly, replacing plates out of specification.

● Clutch spring broken or worn. Old or heat-damaged (from slipping clutch) springs should be replaced with new ones.
● Clutch release not adjusted properly. See the adjustments section of Chapter 1.
● Clutch inner cable snagging. Caused by a frayed cable or kinked outer cable. Replace the cable with a new one. Repair of a frayed cable is not advised.
● Clutch release mechanism defective. Worn or damaged parts in the clutch release mechanism could include the shaft, cam, actuating arm or pivot. Replace parts as necessary.
● Clutch hub and outer drum worn. Severe indentation by the clutch plate tangs of the channels in the hub and drum will cause snagging of the plates preventing correct engagement. If this damage occurs, renewal of the worn components is required.
● Lubricant incorrect. Use of a transmission lubricant other than that specified may allow the plates to slip.

22 Clutch drag

● Clutch lever play excessive. Adjust lever at bars or at cable end if necessary.
● Clutch plates warped or damaged. This will cause a drag on the clutch, causing the machine to creep. Overhaul clutch assembly.
● Clutch spring tension uneven. Usually caused by a sagged or broken spring. Check and replace springs.
● Transmission oil deteriorated. Badly contaminated transmission oil and a heavy deposit of oil sludge on the plates will cause plate sticking. The oil recommended for this machine is of the detergent type, therefore it is unlikely that this problem will arise unless regular oil changes are neglected.
● Transmission oil viscosity too high. Drag in the plates will result from the use of an oil with too high a viscosity. In very cold weather clutch drag may occur until the engine has reached operating temperature.
● Clutch hub and outer drum worn. Indentation by the clutch plate tangs of the channels in the hub and drum will prevent easy plate disengagement. If the damage is light the affected areas may be dressed with a fine file. More pronounced damage will necessitate renewal of the components.
● Clutch housing seized to shaft. Lack of lubrication, severe wear or damage can cause the housing to seize to the shaft. Overhaul of the clutch, and perhaps the transmission, may be necessary to repair damage.
● Clutch release mechanism defective. Worn or damaged release mechanism parts can stick and fail to provide leverage. Overhaul clutch cover components.
● Loose clutch hub nut. Causes drum and hub misalignment, putting a drag on the engine. Engagement adjustment continually varies. Overhaul clutch assembly.

Gear selection problems

23 Gearchange imprecise

● Gearchange cables maladjusted. Check that cables are set to give minimal free play, so that gear positions align correctly with index mark.
● Gearchange cables corroded or damaged. Inspect cables and lubricate or renew as required.

24 Gear selection difficult or impossible

● Clutch not disengaging fully. See Section 22.
● Gearchange cable(s) damaged or broken. Check and renew as required. See Chapter 4 for details.
● Gear selector cruciform worn or broken. This component is made of a softer material than that of the gearbox pinions to prevent damage to the latter. Dismantle the engine unit as described in Chapter 1 and renew the cruciform.

25 Jumping out of gear

● Detent mechanism worn or damaged. Remove selector box cover and check operation of the detent mechanism. Renew pawl or spring as necessary.
● Gear selector cruciform worn or broken. Dismantle engine unit and renew as required.
● Worn gear pinions or bearings. Strip engine unit and renew as required.

26 Overselection

● Gearchange cables badly adjusted.
● Detent mechanism worn or damaged. Remove selector box cover and check operation of the detent mechanism. Renew pawl or spring as necessary.
● Gear selector cruciform worn or broken. Dismantle engine unit and renew as required.
● Worn gear pinions or bearings. Strip engine unit and renew as required.

Abnormal engine noise

27 Knocking or pinking

● See Section 16.

28 Piston slap or rattling from cylinder

● Cylinder bore/piston clearance excessive. Resulting from wear, or partial seizure. This condition can often be heard as a high, rapid tapping noise when the engine is under little or no load, particularly when power is just beginning to be applied. Reboring to the next correct oversize should be carried out and a new oversize piston fitted.
● Connecting rod bent. This can be caused by over-revving, trying to start a very badly flooded engine (resulting in a hydraulic lock in the cylinder) or by earlier mechanical failure. Attempts at straightening a bent connecting rod are not recommended. Careful inspection of the crankshaft should be made before renewing the damaged connecting rod.
● Gudgeon pin, piston boss bore or small-end bearing wear or seizure. Excess clearance or partial seizure between normal moving parts of these items can cause continuous or intermittent tapping noises. Rapid wear or seizure is caused by lubrication starvation.
● Piston rings worn, broken or sticking. Renew the rings after careful inspection of the piston and bore.

29 Other noises

● Big-end bearing wear. A pronounced knock from within the crankcase which worsens rapidly is indicative of big-end bearing failure as a result of extreme normal wear or lubrication failure. Remedial action in the form of a bottom end overhaul should be taken; continuing to run the engine will lead to further damage including the possibility of connecting rod breakage.
● Main bearing failure. Extreme normal wear or failure of the main bearings is characteristically accompanied by a rumble from the crankcase and vibration felt through the frame and footrests. Renew the worn bearings and carry out a very careful examination of the crankshaft.
● Crankshaft excessively out of true. A bent crank may result from over-revving or damage from an upper cylinder component or gearbox failure. Straightening of the crankshaft is not possible in normal circumstances; a replacement item should be fitted.
● Engine mounting loose. Tighten all the engine mounting nuts and bolts.
● Cylinder head joint leaking. The noise most often associated with a leaking head joint is a high pitched squeaking, although any other noise consistent with gas being forced out under pressure from a small orifice can also be emitted. Joint leakage is often accompanied by oil

seepage from around the mating joint or from the cylinder head holding down bolts and nuts. Leakage results from insufficient or uneven tightening of the cylinder head fasteners, or from random mechanical failure. Retightening to the correct torque figure will, at best, only provide a temporary cure. The joint faces should be reground at the earliest opportunity.

● Exhaust system leakage. Popping or crackling in the exhaust system, particularly when it occurs with the engine on the overrun, indicates a poor joint either at the cylinder port or at the exhaust pipe/silencer connection. Failure of the gasket or looseness of the clamp should be looked for.

Abnormal transmission noise

30 Clutch noise

● Clutch outer drum/friction plate tang clearance excessive.
● Clutch outer drum/spacer clearance excessive.
● Clutch outer drum/thrust washer clearance excessive.
● Primary drive gear teeth worn or damaged.
● Clutch shock absorber assembly worn or damaged.

31 Transmission noise

● Bearing or bushes worn or damaged. Renew the affected components.
● Gear pinions worn or chipped. Renew the gear pinions.
● Metal chips jammed in gear teeth.This can occur when pieces of metal from any failed component are picked up by a meshing pinion. The condition will lead to rapid bearing wear or early gear failure.
● Gearbox oil level too low. Top up immediately to prevent damage to gearbox and engine.
● Gearchange mechanism worn or damaged. Wear or failure of certain items in the selection and change components can induce mis-selection of gears (see Section 24) where incipient engagement of more than one gear set is promoted. Remedial action, by the overhaul of the gearbox, should be taken without delay.

Exhaust smokes excessively

32 White/blue smoke (caused by oil burning)

● Petrol/oil ratio incorrect. Ensure that oil is mixed with the petrol in the correct ratio. The manufacturer's recommendation must be adhered to if excessive smoking or under-lubrication is to be avoided.
● Oil pump settings incorrect. Check and reset the oil pump as described in Chapter 2.
● Crankshaft main bearing oil seals worn. Wear in the main bearing oil seals, often in conjunction with wear in the bearings themselves, can allow transmission oil to find its way into the crankcase and thence to the combustion chamber. This condition is often indicated by a mysterious drop in the transmission oil level with no sign of external leakage.
● Accumulated oil deposits in exhaust system. If the machine is used for short journeys only it is possible for the oil residue in the exhaust gases to condense in the relatively cool silencer. If the machine is then taken for a longer run in hot weather, the accumulated oil will burn off producing ominous smoke from the exhaust.

33 Black smoke (caused by over-rich mixture)

● Air filter element clogged. Clean or renew the element.
● Main jet loose or too large. Remove the float chamber to check for tightness of the jet. If the machine is used at high altitudes rejetting will be required to compensate for the lower atmospheric pressure.
● Cold start mechanism jammed on. Check that the mechanism works smoothly and correctly and that, where fitted, the operating cable is lubricated and not snagged.

● Fuel level too high. The fuel level is controlled by the float height which can increase as a result of wear or damage. Remove the float bowl and check the float height. Check also that floats have not punctured; a punctured float will lose buoyancy and allow an increased fuel level.
● Float valve needle stuck open. Caused by dirt or a worn valve. Clean the float chamber or renew the needle and, if necessary, the valve seat.

Poor handling or roadholding

34 Directional instability

● Steering head bearing adjustment too tight. This will cause rolling or weaving at low speeds. Re-adjust the bearings.
● Steering head bearing worn or damaged. Correct adjustment of the bearing will prove impossible to achieve if wear or damage has occurred. Inconsistent handling will occur including rolling or weaving at low speed and poor directional control at indeterminate higher speeds. The steering head bearing should be dismantled for inspection and renewed if required. Lubrication should also be carried out.
● Bearing races pitted or dented. Impact damage caused, perhaps, by an accident or riding over a pot-hole can cause indentation of the bearing, usually in one position. This should be noted as notchiness when the handlebars are turned. Renew and lubricate the bearings.
● Steering column bent. This will occur only if the machine is subjected to a high impact such as hitting a curb or a pot-hole. The steering column should be renewed; do not attempt to straighten the column.
● Front or rear tyre pressures too low.
● Front or rear tyre worn. General instability, high speed wobbles and skipping over white lines indicates that tyre renewal may be required. Tyre induced problems, in some machine/tyre combinations, can occur even when the tyre in question is by no means fully worn.
● Engine pivot bushes worn. Difficulties in holding line, particularly when cornering or when changing power settings indicates wear in the bushes. The engine unit should be removed from the machine and the bushes renewed.
● Tyres unsuitable for machine. Not all available tyres will suit the characteristics of the frame and suspension, indeed, some tyres or tyre combinations may cause a transformation in the handling characteristics. If handling problems occur immediately after changing to a new tyre type or make, revert to the original tyres to see whether an improvement can be noted. In some instances a change to what are, in fact, suitable tyres may give rise to handling deficiences. In this case a thorough check should be made of all frame and suspension items which affect stability.

35 Steering bias to left or right

● Wheels out of alignment. This can be caused by impact damage to the frame, swinging arm, wheel spindles or front forks. Although occasionally a result of material failure or corrosion it is usually as a result of a crash.

36 Handlebar vibrates or oscillates

● Tyres worn or out of balance. Either condition, particularly in the front tyre, will promote shaking of the fork assembly and thus the handlebars. A sudden onset of shaking can result if a balance weight is displaced during use.
● Tyres badly positioned on the wheel rims. A moulded line on each wall of a tyre is provided to allow visual verification that the tyre is correctly positioned on the rim. A check can be made by rotating the tyre; any misalignment will be immediately obvious.
● Wheel rims warped or damaged. Inspect the wheels for runout as described in Chapter 5.
● Swinging arm bearings worn. Renew the bearings.
● Wheel bearings worn. Renew the bearings.

● Steering head bearings incorrectly adjusted. Vibration is more likely to result from bearings which are too loose rather than too tight. Re-adjust the bearings.

37 Poor front suspension performance

● Damping components worn or corroded. Advanced normal wear of the suspension unit internals is unlikely to occur until a very high mileage has been covered. Continual use of the machine with damaged oil seals which allows the ingress of water, or neglect, will lead to rapid corrosion and wear. Dismantle the unit for inspection and overhaul.

38 Front fork judder when braking (see also Section 46)

● Wear between the front suspension linkage components. Renewal of the affected components is required.
● Slack steering head bearings. Re-adjust the bearings.
● Warped brake drum. If irregular braking action occurs fork judder can be induced in what are normally serviceable forks. Renew the damaged brake components.

39 Poor rear suspension performance

● Rear suspension unit damper worn out or leaking. The damping performance of most rear suspension units falls off with age. This is a gradual process, and thus may not be immediately obvious. Indications of poor damping include hopping of the rear end when cornering or braking, and a general loss of positive stability.
● Weak rear spring. If the suspension unit spring fatigues it will promote excessive pitching of the machine and reduce the ground clearance when cornering. Although replacement springs are available separately from the rear suspension damper unit it is probable that if spring fatigue has occurred the damper units will also require renewal.
● Swinging arm flexing or bearings worn. See Sections 34 and 36.
● Bent suspension unit damper rod. This is likely to occur only if the machine is dropped or if seizure of the piston occurs. If either happens the suspension unit should be renewed.

Abnormal frame and suspension noise

40 Front end noise

● Spring weak or broken. Makes a clicking or scraping sound. Fork oil will have a lot of metal particles in it.
● Steering head bearings loose or damaged. Clicks when braking. Check, adjust or replace.
● Fork clamps loose. Make sure all fork clamp pinch bolts are tight.
● Steering column bent. Good possibility if machine has been dropped. Repair or replace column.

41 Rear suspension noise

● Fluid level too low. Leakage of a suspension unit, usually evident by oil on the outer surfaces, can cause a spurting noise. The suspension unit should be renewed.
● Defective rear suspension unit with internal damage. Renew the suspension units as a pair.

Brake problems

42 Brakes are spongy or ineffective

● Brake cable deterioration. Damage to the outer cable by stretching or being trapped will give a spongy feel to the brake lever. The cable should be renewed. A cable which has become corroded due to old age or neglect of lubrication will partially seize making operation

very heavy. Lubrication at this stage may overcome the problem but the fitting of a new cable is recommended.
● Worn brake linings. Determine lining wear using the external brake wear indicator on the brake backplate, or by removing the wheel and withdrawing the brake backplate. Renew the shoe/lining units as a pair if the linings are worn below the recommended limit.
● Worn brake camshaft. Wear between the camshaft and the bearing surface will reduce brake feel and reduce operating efficiency. Renewal of one or both items will be required to rectify the fault.
● Worn brake cam and shoe ends. Renew the worn components.
● Linings contaminated with dust or grease. Any accumulations of dust should be cleaned from the brake assembly and drum using a petrol dampened cloth. Do not blow or brush off the dust because it is asbestos based and thus harmful if inhaled. Light contamination from grease can be removed from the surface of the brake linings using a solvent; attempts at removing heavier contamination are less likely to be successful because some of the lubricant will have been absorbed by the lining material which will severely reduce the braking performance.

43 Brake drag

● Incorrect adjustment. Re-adjust the brake operating mechanism.
● Drum warped or oval. This can result from overheating or impact. The condition is difficult to correct, although if slight ovality only occurs, skimming the surface of the brake drum can provide a cure. This is work for a specialist engineer. Renewal of the complete wheel hub is normally the only satisfactory solution.
● Weak brake shoe return springs. This will prevent the brake lining/shoe units from pulling away from the drum surface once the brake is released. The springs should be renewed.
● Brake camshaft, lever pivot or cable poorly lubricated. Failure to attend to regular lubrication of these areas will increase operating resistance which, when compounded, may cause tardy operation and poor release movement.

44 Brake lever or pedal pulsates in operation

● Drums warped or oval. This can result from overheating or impact. This condition is difficult to correct, although if slight ovality only occurs skimming the surface of the drum can provide a cure. This is work for a specialist engineer. Renewal of the hub is normally the only satisfactory solution.

45 Drum brake noise

● Drum warped or oval. This can cause intermittent rubbing of the brake linings against the drum. See the preceding Section.
● Brake linings glazed. This condition, usually accompanied by heavy lining dust contamination, often induces brake squeal. The surface of the linings may be roughened using glass-paper or a fine file.

46 Brake induced fork judder

● Worn front suspension linkage, or worn or badly adjusted steering head bearings. These conditions, combined with uneven or pulsating braking as described in Section 44 will induce more or less judder when the brakes are applied, dependent on the degree of wear and poor brake operation. Attention should be given to both areas of malfunction. See the relevant Sections.

Electrical problems

47 Total electrical failure

● Break in horn circuit wiring. However unlikely this may seem, it can result in the entire electrical system being isolated. Refer to Chapter 6 for details on this and other possible causes.

48 Circuit failure

● Cable failure. Refer to the machine's wiring diagram and check the circuit for continuity. Open circuits are a result of loose or corroded connections, either at terminals or in-line connectors, or because of broken wires. Occasionally, the core of a wire will break without there being any apparent damage to the outer plastic cover.

● Switch failure. All switches may be checked for continuity in each switch position, after referring to the switch position boxes incorporated in the wiring diagram for the machine. Switch failure may be a result of mechanical breakage, corrosion or water.

49 Bulbs blowing repeatedly

● Vibration failure. This is often an inherent fault related to the natural vibration characteristics of the engine and frame and is, thus, difficult to resolve. Modifications of the lamp mounting, to change the damping characteristics, may help.

● Intermittent earth. Repeated failure of one bulb, particularly where the bulb is fed directly from the generator, indicates that a poor earth exists somewhere in the circuit. Check that a good contact is available at each earthing point in the circuit.

● Faulty ac voltage regulator. Test by substitution. See Chapter 6 for details.

Vespa P/PX 125, 150, 200 and T5 component locations - right-hand side

1	Engine idle speed adjuster	4	Speedometer cable	7	Rear brake cable adjuster
2	Engine oil tank	5	Front brake cable adjuster	8	Gearbox drain plug
3	Headlamp adjuster	6	Rear brake stop lamp switch	9	Gear change selector box

Vespa P/PX 125, 150, 200 and T5 component locations - left-hand side

1	Horn	4	Fuel gauge sender unit	7	Stand pivot and spring
2	Clutch switch	5	Seat lock	8	Front hub
3	Steering stem	6	Rear hub		

Routine maintenance

For information relating to later models see Chapter 7

Periodic routine maintenance is a continuous process which should commence immediately the machine is used. The object is to maintain all adjustments and to diagnose and rectify minor defects before they develop into more extensive, and often more expensive, problems.

It follows that if the machine is maintained properly, it will both run and perform with optimum efficiency, and be less prone to unexpected breakdowns. Regular inspection of the machine will show up any parts which are wearing, and with a little experience, it is possible to obtain the maximum life from any one component, renewing it when it becomes so worn that it is liable to fail.

Regular cleaning can be considered as important as mechanical maintenance. This will ensure that all the cycle parts are inspected regularly and are kept free from accumulations of road dirt and grime.

Cleaning is especially important during the winter months, despite its appearance of being a thankless task which very soon seems pointless. On the contrary, it is during these months that the paintwork, chromium plating, and the alloy casings suffer the ravages of abrasive grit, rain and road salt. A couple of hours spent weekly on cleaning the machine will maintain its appearance and value, and highlight small points, like chipped paint, before they become a serious problem.

The various maintenance tasks are described under their respective mileage and calendar headings, and are accompanied by diagrams and photographs where pertinent.

It should be noted that the intervals between each maintenance task serve only as a guide. As the machine gets older, or if it is used under particularly arduous conditions, it is advisable to reduce the period between each check.

For ease of reference, most service operations are described in detail under the relevant heading. However, if further general information is required, this can be found under the pertinent Section heading and Chapter in the main text.

Although no special tools are required for routine maintenance, a good selection of general workshop tools is essential. Included in the tools must be a range of metric ring or combination spanners, a selection of crosshead screwdrivers, and two pairs of circlip pliers, one external opening and the other internal opening. Additionally, owing to the extreme tightness of most casing screws, an impact screwdriver, together with a choice of large or small cross-head screw bits, is absolutely indispensable. This is particularly so if the engine has not been dismantled since leaving the factory.

Daily

The checklist shown below should be carried out prior to riding the machine each day. The procedure should take only a few moments, and will significantly reduce the risk of unexpected failure in use.

(a) Check brake operation
(b) Check clutch and throttle operation
(c) Check oil tank level, where fitted
(d) Check fuel tank level
(e) Check tyre pressures and condition of tread and sidewalls
(f) Check the electrical system

Weekly, or every 100 miles (160 km)

1 Topping up the engine oil tank (where fitted)

Unlock and open the dualseat to gain access to the oil filler cap. Top up with a good quality two-stroke engine oil to within about one inch of the filler neck. It is important that the tank level is maintained at all times. If it is suspected that the level has fallen too low, or if the system has been disconnected at any point, fill the **FUEL** tank with a 50:1 (2%) fuel/oil mixture to ensure adequate lubrication while the system primes itself.

Later models are equipped with an oil level sight glass set in the centre body panel. Oil must be visible in the sight glass at all times.

2 Checking the tyre condition and pressures

The importance of maintaining the correct tyre pressures cannot be stressed too highly, the safety of the rider and other road users being at risk if regular checks are ignored or postponed. To this end it is a good idea to keep an accurate pocket pressure gauge with the machine's toolkit and to have access to a simple footpump at home. It should be noted that not every filling station gauge is accurate, and that tyre pressure checks should only be made when the tyres are cold to ensure consistent readings. The tyre pressures shown below are for original equipment tyres, and non-standard fitments may require modified settings. A reputable tyre supplier will be able to advise on this point when the tyres are fitted.

Tyre pressures (cold)

Front	17.6 psi
Rear (solo)	25.8 psi
Rear (with passenger)	36.7 psi

When checking the tyre pressures, examine the tyre treads and sidewalls for signs of damage or excessive wear. If cracks or splitting are noted, renew the tyre or have it examined by a specialist. Remove any small stones which may have become embedded in the treads, ensuring that no damage to the fabric carcass has occurred. Check the tread depth around the tyre's circumference. The minimum depth in the UK is 1 mm; this should be considered an absolute lower limit, 2 mm being a safer allowance.

3 General maintenance and inspection

It is recommended that one month be considered the maximum interval for cleaning the machine, but that if possible, cleaning should be carried out on a weekly basis, especially during the winter months. This will make the cleaning job much easier and will usually bring to the owner's attention faults such as loose fasteners which might otherwise be missed. Although a less pleasant task in winter, remember that cleaning is even more important, if only to remove potentially corrosive road salt. If appearance is not of paramount importance, spray the cleaned machine's cycle parts (avoiding the brakes, seat and tyres!) with a silicone-based maintenance spray, such as WD 40. This will inhibit corrosion and electrical problems, and cleaning will be made easier on the next occasion.

Monthly, or every 500 miles (800 km)

1   Checking, cleaning and re-gapping the spark plug

Remove the spark plug cap and unscrew the plug using a plug spanner to avoid damage. The appearance of the plug can be used to assess the general condition of the engine.

Examine the condition of the plug electrodes. If they are worn or badly contaminated the plug should be renewed. Plugs are relatively inexpensive, and attempting to reuse an old and worn plug is a false economy.

A sound plug can be cleaned using a brass wire brush of the type sold for this purpose in motor accessory shops, or by abrasive cleaning. Many garages offer this service, and inexpensive home units are available. If the abrasive method is chosen, make sure that any residual particles are removed from the plug before it is refitted.

Check the electrode gap using feeler gauges. The recommended gap is 0.6 mm (0.024 in). If adjustment is required, bend the outer, earth, electrode to give the specified gap. On no account try to bend the centre electrode; the porcelain insulator will invariably be broken.

The correct replacement plug is as shown below. Do not fit a plug of a different value or engine damage may result. The plug threads should be greased lightly prior to installation. Tighten the plug firmly by hand, then tighten it by a further quarter turn with the plug spanner. This will ensure that the plug seals correctly without risk of damage to the plug threads in the cylinder head. Remember to keep a new plug of the correct type and gap setting in the toolkit.

Recommended spark plug types

Model:	P125 X	P150 X	P200 E
Marelli	CW 6N AT	CW 6N AT	CW 6N AT
Bosch	W 225 T1	W 225 T1	W 225 T2
Champion	L 86	–	N4
AC	43 F	43 F	43 XL
NGK	B7HS	B7HS	B7HS
Model:	PX125 E	PX150 E	PX200 E
Marelli	CW 6N	CW 6N	CW 6L
Bosch	W 5A	W 5A	W 5C
Champion	L 86	L 86	N4
AC	43 F	43 F	43 XL
NGK	B6HS	B6HS	B6ES

2   Throttle cable adjustment

The throttle cable should be adjusted to give 2 – 3 mm (0.08 – 0.12 in) free play measured at the twist grip flange. To effect adjustment, slacken the adjuster locknut and turn the adjuster in or out as required, then secure the locknut. The adjuster is located at the lower end of the cable, where it enters the air filter casing. After adjustment, start the engine and check that the idle speed does not alter when the handlebars are turned from lock to lock. If necessary, readjust or re-route the cable to prevent this.

3   Checking engine idle speed and mixture adjustment

This Section need only be carried out if there have been problems with erratic idling or stalling. If the engine idles reliably, do not disturb it. Start the engine and allow it to idle. If when the handlebar is turned from lock to lock the idle speed varies, check the adjustment of the throttle cable as described above, and also the routing of the throttle cable.

Locate and identify the throttle stop screw and the pilot mixture screw. The former protrudes through the top of the air filter casing, whilst the latter can be reached by passing a screwdriver through the access hole at the back of the casing after the rubber blanking plug has been removed.

Start the engine and allow it to reach normal operating temperature, preferably by taking it on a short run. Set the throttle stop screw to obtain the slowest reliable idle speed. Moving to the pilot mixture screw, turn it inwards by a quarter turn at a time, noting the number of quarter turns and the effect this has on the idle speed. Turn the screw to its original position, then repeat the process, this time turning it outwards. The screw should now be set to the position which gives the fastest reliable idle speed. If necessary, reduce the idle speed using the throttle stop screw.

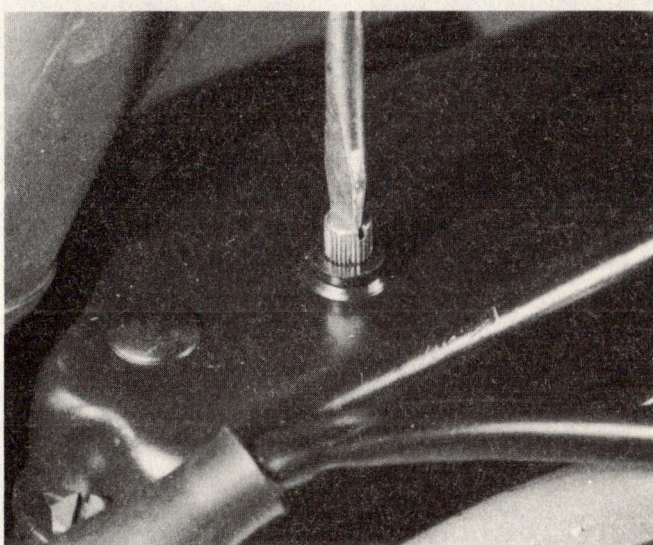
Throttle stop screw protrudes through air filter cover

Pilot mixture screw can be reached via hole in air filter casing (arrowed)

4   Clutch cable adjustment

Check the operation of the clutch, and check that there is about 2 mm (0.08 in) free play measured between the lever stock and the blade. If adjustment is required, this is carried out at the lower end of the cable. Where there is insufficient range in the cable adjuster, reposition the solderless nipple on the inner cable, then carry out fine adjustment using the threaded adjuster.

5   Brake adjustment

Brake adjustment is to some extent a matter of personal preference, but as a general rule the cable should be adjusted so that the brake starts to operate as soon as the lever or pedal is operated, but without causing drag when at rest. Each brake cable incorporates a threaded adjuster and locknut at its lower end. Two different types of front brake adjuster have been fitted to these machines. Adjustment will either be by means of a knurled nut at the cable lower end, or by an adjuster nut and locknut which abut against the hub casting. Both types are shown overleaf, the latter being similar to the rear brake arrangement. Where there is insufficient range in the rear brake cable adjuster (or front brake, as applicable) reposition the cable inner in the anchor plate at the end of the operating arm, then carry out fine adjustment using the threaded adjuster.

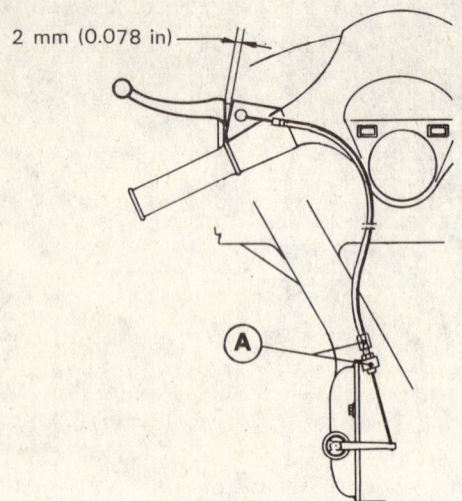

2 mm (0.078 in)

Clutch cable adjustment

A   Adjusting screw and locknut

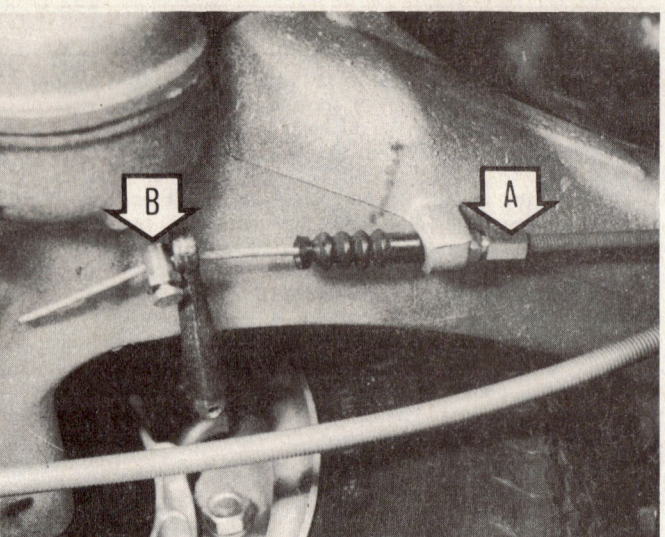

A: Clutch cable adjuster. B: Solderless nipple

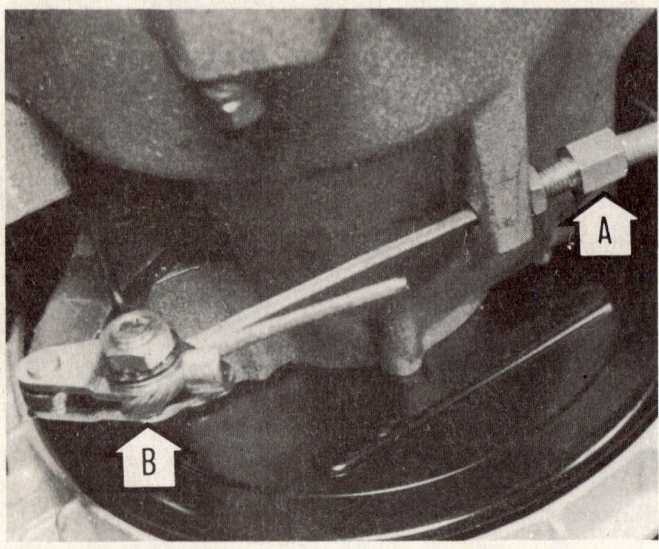

A: Rear brake cable adjuster. B: Cable anchor plate

Front brake adjuster is incorporated in cable inner (alternative type, as rear brake – see text)

6   Gearchange cable adjustment

Select neutral gear, then check that the neutral mark on the handlebar control aligns with the index mark. Check also that there is minimal free play in the cables. If this becomes excessive, gearchanging will become imprecise and awkward. Adjustment is effected at the lower end of the cables where they enter the selector box.

If the gear position marks do not align properly this can be corrected by slackening one adjuster and tightening the other. Once positioned correctly, tighten both cables to remove free play, but take care not to place them under tension, which can result in breakage of one of the cables.

3 Monthly, or every 2500 miles (4000 km)

Carry out the operations listed under the previous headings, then complete the following.

1   Decarbonising the engine

This operation should be carried out at the above intervals unless experience has indicated otherwise. Where the machine is used for a lot of short journeys without reaching full operating temperature, the build-up of carbon in the engine is likely to be rapid. If on the other hand it is used for longer trips, or is used only occasionally, the interval can be extended.

Decarbonisation can be carried out with the engine installed, and should take less than an hour to accomplish. Start by removing the right-hand side panel. Remove the spark plug cap, then release the single bolt and screw which secure the cylinder cowl. Remove the exhaust port clamp bolt and silencer mounting bolt and remove the exhaust system. Remove the extended nut from the cylinder head stud, then slacken evenly and progressively the four cylinder head nuts and lift the head away. For further details on the above, refer to Section 6 of Chapter 1.

Examine and clean off the cylinder head as described in Section 17 of Chapter 1. To remove accumulated carbon from the piston, turn the engine over until the piston is at the top of the bore, then wipe a ring of grease around the edge of the piston to trap any residual carbon particles. Carefully scrape off the carbon, taking care not to score the piston crown or the bore surface. Wipe out the carbon, then lower the piston slightly in the bore. Carefully wipe away the residual carbon which will have been trapped in the grease.

Before the cylinder head is refitted, check that all traces of carbon have been removed and that the mating faces are clean and dry. Place the cylinder head over the holding studs (spark plug thread uppermost) then fit the washers and cylinder head nuts. These should be tightened evenly and in a diagonal sequence to 1.3 – 1.8 kgf m (9.4 – 13.0 lbf ft) on the 125 and 150 models, or to 1.7 – 2.2 kgf m (12.3 – 15.9 lbf ft) in the case of the 200 models.

Remove any carbon build-up from the exhaust port, taking care not to score the piston wall. The condition of the port will give some indication of the state of the exhaust system. If badly choked, the system will require thorough cleaning with caustic soda, but if the carbon accumulation is light, cleaning the tailpipe will normally suffice. For details refer to Section 11 of Chapter 2. Before refitting the cylinder cowl, remove any debris which may have become lodged in the cooling fins of the cylinder barrel, to prevent overheating.

2   Topping up the gearbox oil

With the machine on its stand on a level surface, remove the filler/level plug which is located below and to the rear of the selector box. The transmission oil level should be just level with the threads of the filler hole. If topping up is required, add SAE 30 motor oil or SAE 80 gear oil using a syringe or small funnel. Allow any surplus to run out of the casing, then fit the plug and wipe down the engine casing.

3   Cleaning the air filter element

Remove the right-hand side panel and the air filter cover. Release the element retaining screws and lift it out of the casing. The element should be washed thoroughly in petrol until all accumulated dirt has been removed. Blow the element dry with compressed air, or leave it in a well ventilated place until the petrol has evaporated.

Before refitting the element it should be examined closely for damage. If in any doubt as to its condition, renew it. It should be noted that unfiltered air entering the engine can cause very serious damage, for the reasons outlined in Section 9 of Chapter 2. When fitting the element, check that it and the cover seal correctly.

4   General lubrication

Remove the gear selector box cover and check the operation of the selector ratchet mechanism. Apply grease to the mechanism, then refit the cover. Lubricate with engine oil or WD 40 the stand pivots, and check the condition of the stand return spring. Grease the front brake lever and the rear brake pedal pivots, and check that both brakes operate smoothly and easily. If any stiffness is noted, strip and overhaul the brake (see Chapter 5) and grease the brake cams and the speedometer drive gears.

6 Monthly, or every 5000 miles (8000 km)

Carry out the operations listed under the previous headings, then complete the following.

1   Changing the gearbox oil

With the engine at normal operating temperature, remove the gearbox drain and filler/level plugs and allow the oil to drain fully. Clean the drain plug threads and refit it, using a new sealing washer if required. Refill with SAE 30 motor oil or SAE 80 gear oil until the oil is just level with the filler/level plug threads, then refit the plug.

2   Checking the contact breaker gap (P125 X and P150 X only)

Referring to Section 5 of Chapter 3 for details, check the contact breaker gap and adjust as required. The condition of the contact faces should be examined, and they should be cleaned or renewed where necessary. The felt wick which lubricates the contact breaker cam should be greased lightly.

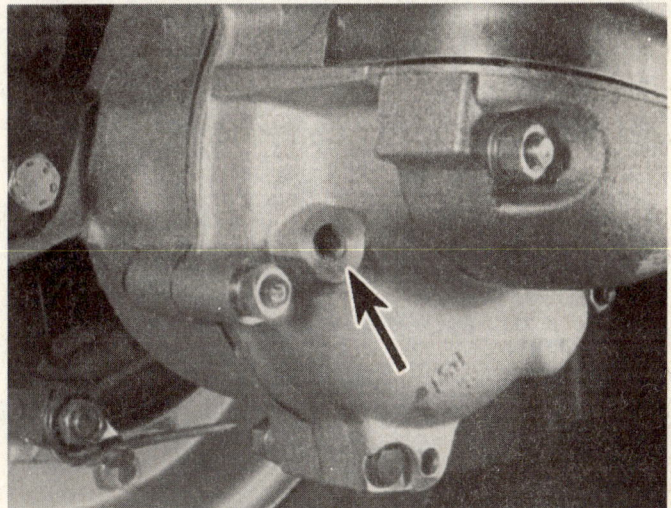

Gearbox oil should be level with filler hole threads

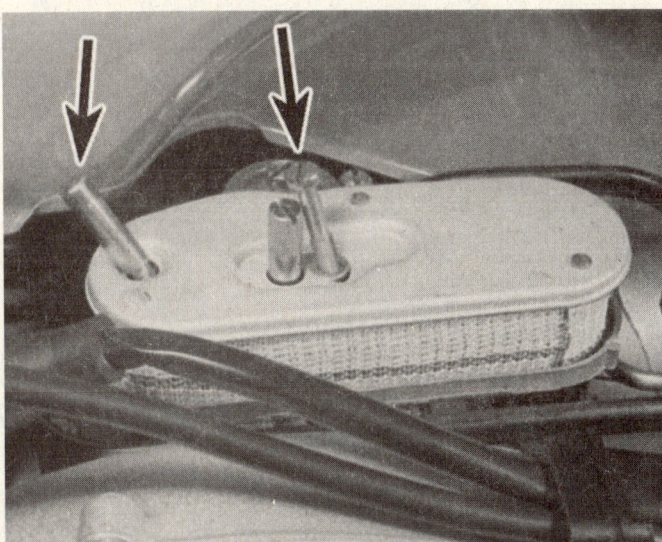

Filter is retained by two screws (arrowed)

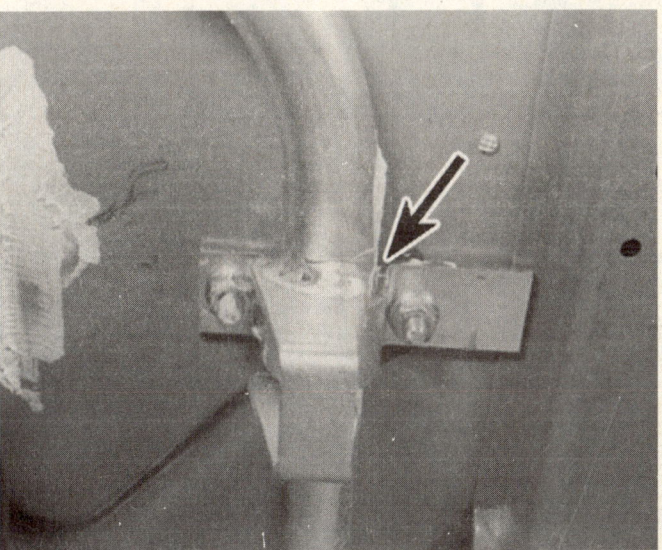

Lubricate stand pivots (arrowed) and check return spring

Gearbox drain plug is located at lowest point of casing

3   Lubricating the control cables

The operation of the various control cables will be improved and their lives greatly extended by regular lubrication. This is accomplished by freeing the upper end of the cable as described in Section 8 of Chapter 4, and then forcing oil through it until it emerges at the lower end. Proprietary cable oilers are available from most motorcycle dealers which allow this operation to be carried out quickly and easily. Alternatively, if time is no object, tape a plastic bag around the top of the outer cable, fill the bag with engine oil and allow it to drain through overnight.

Vespa produce an ingenious cable oiler of their own design which allows the cable to be lubricated with an aerosol maintenance spray such as WD 40. The tool clamps over the end of the cable, and where there is sufficient clearance, it can be lubricated without being disconnected. The tool can be ordered from Vespa dealers as Part Number 19.1.20018.

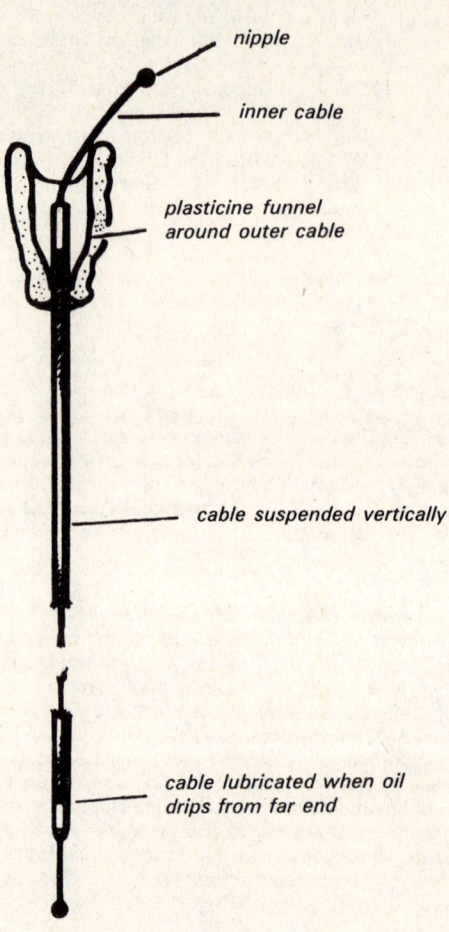

Oiling a control cable

Chapter 1 Engine and transmission

For information relating to later models see Chapter 7

Contents

Specifications

P125 X, PX125 E models

Engine

Type	Single cylinder fan-cooled two-stroke
Bore	52.5 mm (2.066 in)
Stroke	57.0 mm (2.240 in)
Displacement	123.4 cc (7.52 cu in)
Compression ratio	8.2:1 (8.5:1, PX125 E)

Cylinder head

Type	Cast aluminium alloy

Cylinder barrel

Type	Cast iron
Standard bore size	52.5 mm (2.067 in)
1st oversize	52.7 mm (2.075 in)
2nd oversize	52.9 mm (2.083 in)
3rd oversize	53.1 mm (2.091 in)

Piston

Standard diameter.......................................	52.330 mm (2.0602 in)
Ring end gap..	0.20 - 0.35 mm (0.008 - 0.014 in)
Service limit	2.0 mm (0.08 in)

Crankshaft assembly
Maximum runout:
At mainshaft ends .... 0.03 mm (0.0012 in)
At flywheel faces .... 0.02 mm (0.0079 in)

Clutch
Type .... Wet, multiplate
No. of friction plates 3
No. of plain plates 2

Gearbox
Type .... 4-speed, constant mesh
Overall ratios:
1st .... 14.47:1 (16.43:1, PX125 E)
2nd .... 10.28:1 (10.98:1, PX125 E)
3rd .... 7.31:1 (7.60:1, PX125 E)
Top .... 5.36:1 (5.83:1, PX125 E)

Torque wrench settings

Component	kgf m	lbf ft
Alternator stator screws	0.3 – 0.4	2.17 – 2.89
Kickstart lever nut	2.3 – 2.6	16.64 – 18.81
Pickup mounting screw:		
P125 X	Not applicable	Not applicable
PX125 E	0.2 – 0.25	1.45 – 1.81
Clutch centre nut	4.0 – 4.5	28.93 – 32.55
Input shaft nut	3.0 – 3.5	21.70 – 25.32
Alternator rotor nut	6.0 – 6.5	43.40 – 47.01
Carburettor sleeve nuts	1.6 – 2.0	11.57 – 14.47
Clutch cover bolts	0.6 – 0.8	4.34 – 5.79
Cylinder head nuts	1.3 – 1.8	9.40 – 13.02

P150 X, PX150 E models
Engine
Type .... Single cylinder fan-cooled two-stroke
Bore .... 57.8 mm (2.276 in)
Stroke .... 57.0 mm (2.240 in)
Displacement .... 149.56 cc (9.19 cu in)
Compression ratio .... 8.2:1 (8.0:1, PX150 E)

Cylinder head
Type .... Cast aluminium alloy

Cylinder barrel
Type .... Cast iron
Standard bore size .... 57.8 mm (2.276 in)
1st oversize .... 58.0 mm (2.283 in)
2nd oversize .... 58.2 mm (2.291 in)
3rd oversize .... 58.4 mm (2.299 in)

Piston
Standard diameter .... 57.585 mm (2.2671 in)
Ring end gap .... 0.20 - 0.40 mm (0.008 - 0.016 in)
Service limit .... 2.0 mm (0.08 in)

Crankshaft assembly
Maximum runout:
At maximum ends .... 0.03 mm (0.0012 in)
At flywheel faces .... 0.02 mm (0.0079 in)

Clutch
Type .... Wet, multiplate
No. of friction plates 3
No. of plain plates 2

Gearbox
Type .... 4-speed, constant mesh
Overall ratios:
1st .... 14.47:1, (15.38:1, PX150 E)
2nd .... 10.28:1, (10.46:1, PX150 E)
3rd .... 7.31:1, (7.24:1, PX150 E)
Top .... 5.36:1, (5.39:1, PX150 E)

Torque wrench settings

Component	kgf m	lbf ft
Alternator stator screws	0.3 – 0.4	2.17 – 2.89
Kickstart lever nut	2.3 – 2.6	16.64 – 18.81
Pickup mounting screws:		
P125 X	Not applicable	Not applicable
PX125 E	0.2 – 0.25	1.45 – 1.81
Clutch centre nut	4.0 – 4.5	28.93 – 32.55
Input shaft nut	3.0 – 3.5	21.70 – 25.32
Alternator rotor nut	6.0 – 6.5	43.40 – 47.01
Carburettor sleeve nuts	1.6 – 2.0	11.57 – 14.47
Clutch cover bolts	0.6 – 0.8	4.34 – 5.79
Cylinder head nuts	1.3 – 1.8	9.40 – 13.02

P200 E, PX200 E models

Engine

Type	Single cylinder fan-cooled two-stroke
Bore	66.5 mm (2.618 in)
Stroke	57.0 mm (2.240 in)
Displacement	197.97 cc (12.080 cu in)
Compression ratio	9.8:1 (8.8:1, PX200 E)

Cylinder

Type	Cast aluminium alloy

Cylinder barrel

Type	Cast iron
Standard bore size	66.5 mm (2.618 in)
1st oversize	66.7 mm (2.626 in)
2nd oversize	66.9 mm (2.634 in)
3rd oversize	67.1 mm (2.642 in)

Piston

Standard diameter	66.292 mm (2.6099 in)
Ring end gap	0.25 - 0.40 mm (0.008 - 0.016 in)
Service limit	2.0 mm (0.08 in)

Crankshaft assembly

Maximum runout:	
At mainshaft ends	0.03 mm (0.0012 in)
At flywheel faces	0.02 mm (0.0079 in)

Clutch

Type	Wet, multiplate
No. of friction plates	3
No. of plain plates	2

Gearbox

Type	4-speed, constant mesh
Overall ratios:	
1st	14.47:1, (13.42:1, PX200 E)
2nd	10.28:1, (9.13:1, PX200 E)
3rd	7.31:1 (6.32:1, PX200 E)
Top	5.36:1 (4.71:1, PX200 E)

Torque wrench settings

Component	kgf m	lbf ft
Alternator stator screws	0.3 – 0.4	2.17 – 2.89
Kickstart lever nut	2.3 – 2.6	16.64 – 18.81
Pickup mounting screws	0.2 – 0.25	1.45 – 1.81
Clutch centre nut	4.0 – 4.5	28.93 – 32.55
Input shaft nut	3.0 – 3.5	21.70 – 25.32
Alternator rotor nut	6.0 – 6.5	43.40 – 47.01
Carburettor sleeve nuts	1.6 – 2.0	11.57 – 14.47
Clutch cover bolts	0.6 – 0.8	4.34 – 5.79
Cylinder head nuts	1.7 – 2.2	12.30 – 15.91
Exhaust pipe stub	7.5 – 8.0	54.25 – 57.86

1 General description

The engine is a single-cylinder fan-cooled two-stroke built in unit with the gearbox, clutch and transmission components. An extension of the engine/transmission casing runs forward, forming the engine mounting and pivot point, thus using the entire assembly as the rear suspension member.

Mixture from the enclosed carburettor is drawn down into the crankcase via a rotary valve arrangement formed by the left-hand flywheel. This controls induction timing precisely, and has the effect of increasing the torque produced by the engine. The cylinder barrel is of cast iron, whilst the cylinder head and piston are light alloy. The piston is carried on a caged needle roller bearing in the small-end eye of the connecting rod.

The crankshaft is a pressed-up assembly comprising the connecting rod and roller big-end bearing, supported on a crankpin between the two flywheels. The assembly is supported by a caged ball bearing on its left-hand end and by a needle-roller bearing at the right-hand end.

A cover at the left-hand end of the crankcase houses the crankshaft-mounted clutch and also the drive to the oil metering device, where fitted. At the opposite end of the crankshaft is the flywheel generator assembly, the rotor doubling as the engine cooling fan. This forces air through the ducting which encloses the cylinder barrel and head to provide engine cooling.

Below and to the rear of the clutch lies the gearbox input shaft, power being transmitted to it from the clutch by a pair of helical gears. The gearbox is of the constant-mesh type, selection of a particular ratio being made by an unusual cruciform selector incorporated in the hollow output shaft. The cruciform is able to slide within the shaft, its position being controlled by the selector box at the right-hand end of the casing. This in turn is controlled by a pair of cables running from the handlebar gear change control.

The left-hand end of the output shaft projects through the bearing and oil seal and carries the combined wheel hub and brake drum. The rear brake shoes are mounted on the outside of the engine/transmission casing.

2 Operations with the engine unit in the frame

1 A number of carefully thought out details on the engine unit have made it possible to remove almost every internal component without removing the left-hand engine casing from the body section. Although many owners will prefer to work with the unit on the workbench, it should be noted that it is not unknown for the engine pivot bolt to seize in its bonded rubber inserts, making removal of the bolt almost impossible without extensive workshop facilities. Details for each operation are broadly similar to those given in the remainder of this Chapter, where many tasks assume that the unit is on the workbench. If the work has to be carried out with the engine in position, the following preliminary work should be carried out.

    a) Remove the side panels and detach the fan and cylinder cowlings.
    b) Release the gear selector box, lodging it clear of the engine unit
    c) Disconnect the clutch and rear brake cables
    d) Disconnect the wiring harness at the junction box near the coil
    e) Disconnect the fuel pipe, and also the oil pipe where fitted
    f) Remove the exhaust system
    g) Slacken and remove the rear suspension unit lower mounting bolt

2 Once these components have been carried out the rear of the body should be lifted, allowing the engine unit to pivot downwards. Support the body using axle stands or wooden blocks. For further details on specific operations, refer to the appropriate Section in this Chapter.
3 A number of components or assemblies can be worked on with the engine in position and without having to lower the rear of the unit, these being as follows.

    1) Cylinder head, barrel and piston
    2) Flywheel generator assembly
    3) Gear selector box

3 Operations requiring engine unit removal

1 As has been mentioned above, it is possible to work on almost any area of the unit without removing it from the body section. Whilst this may be necessary in the circumstances discussed, it is normally far preferable to remove the unit so that work can proceed in the relative comfort of the workbench. This approach ensures that access is unobstructed and is less likely to result in dirt entering the engine.

Removal of the engine unit should take about 20-30 minutes and is easily carried out unaided.

4 Removing the engine/transmission unit

1 Place the machine on its centre stand, leaving adequate working space on both sides and to the rear. Remove both side panels and place them somewhere safe to avoid damage. Place a drain tray below the gearbox drain plug, remove the plug and allow the transmission oil to drain fully. Note that the oil will drain much more quickly if the engine is warm.
2 While the oil is draining, release the single screw which secures the wiring junction box to the rear of the fan cowling. Disconnect the wiring and lodge it clear of the engine. On some later models the junction box has been replaced by a multi-pin connector block which should be unplugged to free the wiring. Pull off the spark plug cap and remove the single bolt which retains the cylinder cowling. Remove the single screw which passes through the cylinder and fan cowling, then manoeuvre the cylinder cowl clear of the cylinder.
3 When the transmission oil has finished draining, refit and tighten the drain plug. Remove the two nuts which retain the gear selector box to the crankcase, using a box spanner or a thin-walled socket. To free the selector box, operate the handlebar control, turning it well beyond the 4th gear position. As the control is moved, the box will move outwards until the mechanism can be disengaged, and the box and cables moved clear of the engine. It will be found helpful if the engine is turned as the gearchange control is operated.
4 Moving to the underside of the unit, disconnect the rear brake cable by unscrewing the nut which clamps the cable inner. Unscrew the cable adjuster and lodge the cable clear of the engine. The clutch cable should also be disconnected by releasing the small solderless nipple which is fitted to the end of the inner cable.
5 Remove the top of the carburettor/air cleaner case and release the air cleaner element to gain access to the fuel pipe. Check that the fuel tap is turned off, then slide the wire clip away from the stub. This can be done by squeezing the ends of the clip together with pliers and sliding it along the pipe. On machines fitted with a separate oil tank, the oil pipe should be disconnected at the metering device stub and the end of the pipe plugged to prevent the oil from escaping. Pull both pipes clear of the carburettor case.
6 Locate the choke cable and unhook the looped end of the inner wire from the operating arm. Disconnect the throttle cable from the carburettor or metering device lever, as appropriate, and pull both cables clear of the carburettor case.
7 The engine/transmission unit is now ready for removal and it is helpful, though not essential, to have some assistance at this stage. Start by removing the nut and bolt which secures the lower end of the rear suspension unit to the crankcase. The body will probably tip forward slightly until the front wheel rests on the ground. Slacken the engine pivot bolt nut until it lies flush with the end of the bolt, then tap the end of the bolt to start it moving in its bushes.
8 If the engine unit has not been removed for some years it is possible that the bolt may have become rusted into the metal sleeves through which it passes. Often it can be freed by liberal application of WD40 or a similar releasing fluid, and if possible this should be allowed several hours to penetrate.
9 If this fails to free the bolt, removal is likely to present a serious problem. This is because the sleeves will tend to tear out of the rubber bushes to which they are bonded, but will not pass through the holes in the body section. The only solution is to have the pivot bolt cut or drilled out to allow the unit to be removed. It is then possible to drive out the damaged bolt and bushes, but it should be noted that fitting new bushes may require the special tools available to Vespa dealers.
10 An alternative to the above is to carry out the engine overhaul work without removing the unit from the body section by raising the body and allowing the engine to pivot downwards (see Section 2 of this Chapter).
11 If the pivot bolt moves relatively easily, remove the nut completely and use a long bar to tap it out of its bore. Take care not to damage the threads during removal. Support the unit as the drift is removed, then manoeuvre the unit clear of the body. Note that it will be necessary to tilt the engine slightly so that the cylinder barrel does not foul the adjacent bodywork. Once clear of the body, place the unit on the work bench to await further dismantling.

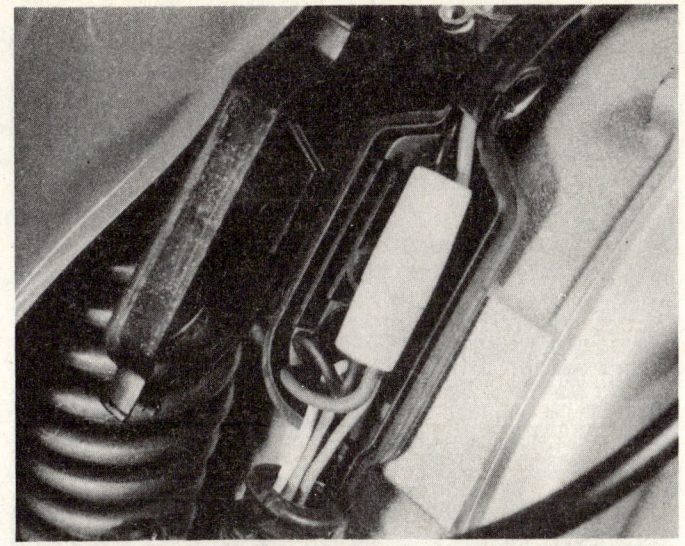

4.2 Release junction box from crankcase and disconnect wiring

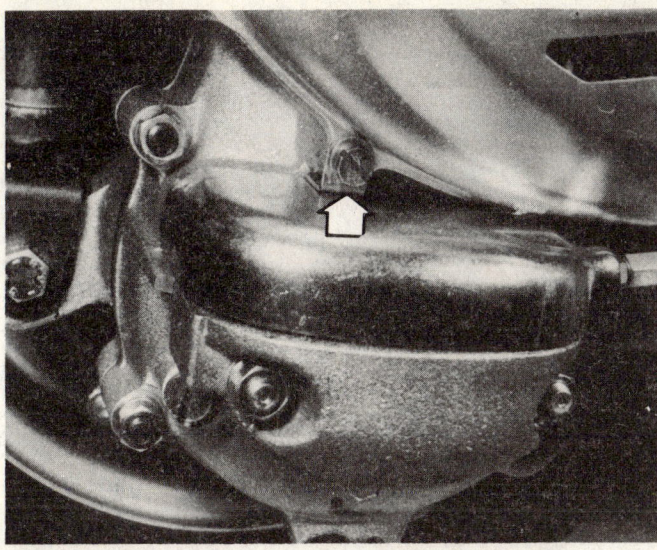

4.3a Remove single screw (arrowed) and lift away cover

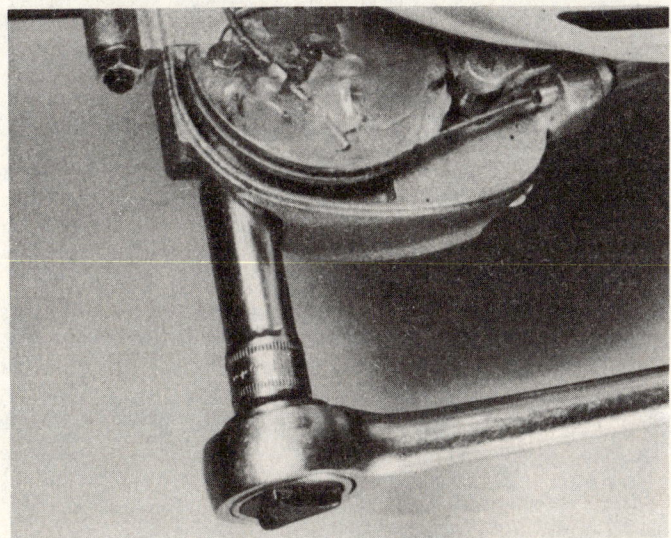

4.3b Use box spanner or thin-walled socket to remove selector box mounting nuts

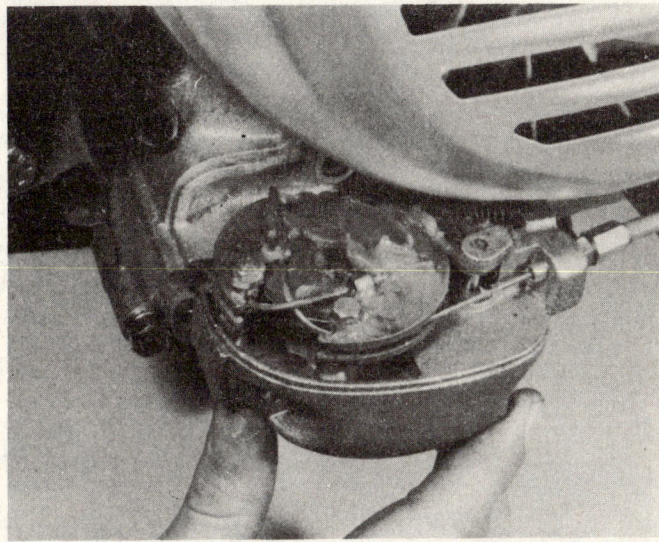

4.3c Turn gearchange control to push box clear of crankcase

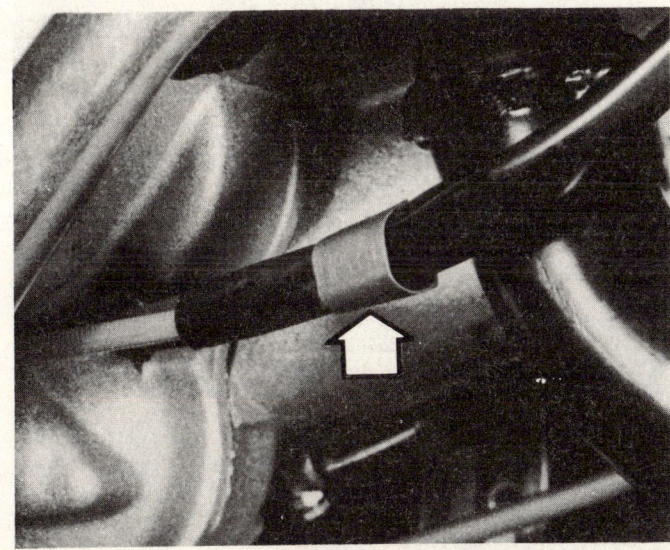

4.3d Free cables from guide clip (arrowed)

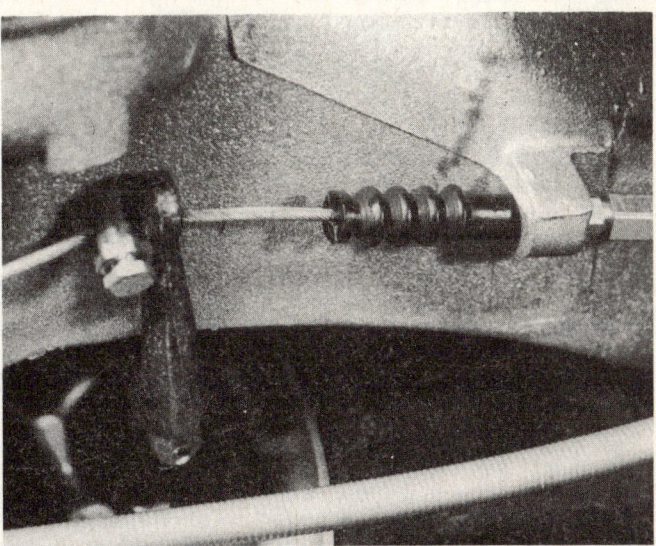

4.4 Release the solderless nipple to free clutch cable

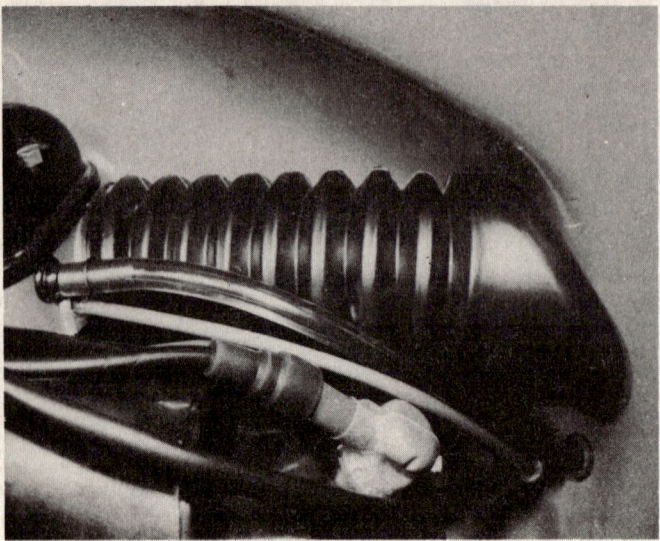

4.5a Pull off the air filter intake hose

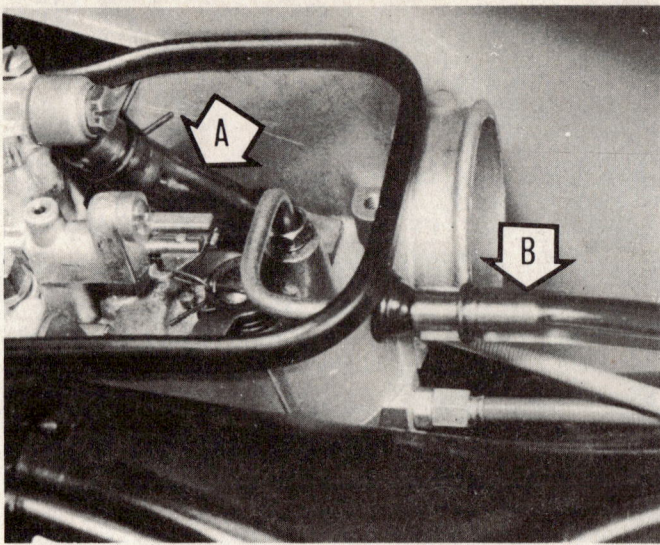

4.5b Disconnect the fuel pipe (A) and oil pipe (B)

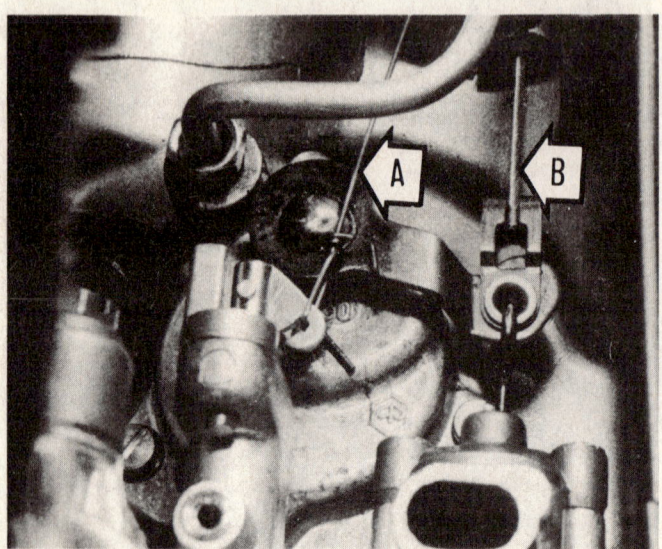

4.6 Unhook the choke cable (A) and throttle cable (B)

4.7 Release the engine mounting bolts (arrowed) and lift the unit clear of the body

5   Dismantling the engine/transmission unit: general

1   Before any dismantling work is undertaken, the external surfaces of the unit should be thoroughly cleaned and degreased. This will prevent the contamination of the engine internals, and will also make working a lot easier and cleaner. A high flash point solvent, such as paraffin (kerosene) can be used, or better still, a proprietary engine degreaser such as Gunk. Use old paintbrushes and toothbrushes to work the solvent into the various recesses of the engine castings. Take care to exclude solvent or water from the electrical components and inlet and exhaust ports. The use of petrol (gasoline) as a cleaning medium should be avoided, because the vapour is explosive and can be toxic if used in a confined space.

2   When clean and dry, arrange the unit on the workbench, leaving a suitable clear area for working. Gather a selection of small containers and plastic bags so that parts can be grouped together in an easily identifiable manner. Some paper and a pen should be on hand to permit notes to be made and labels attached where necessary. A supply of clean rag is also required.

3   Before commencing work, read through the appropriate section so that some idea of the necessary procedure can be gained. When removing the various engine components it should be noted that great force is seldom required, unless specified. In many cases, a component's reluctance to be removed is indicative of an incorrect approach or removal method. If in any doubt, re-check with the text.

6   Dismantling the engine/transmission unit: removing the cylinder head, barrel and piston

1   If the cylinder head, barrel and piston are to be removed with the engine unit installed in the body section, it should be noted that the head can be removed for decarbonisation or examination with little preparatory work. Removal of the barrel is likely to be impaired by the bodywork, and it may prove necessary to lower the engine as described in Section 2. In most instances it is preferable to remove the unit from the frame to gain better access and to lessen the chance of dirt entering the crankcase.

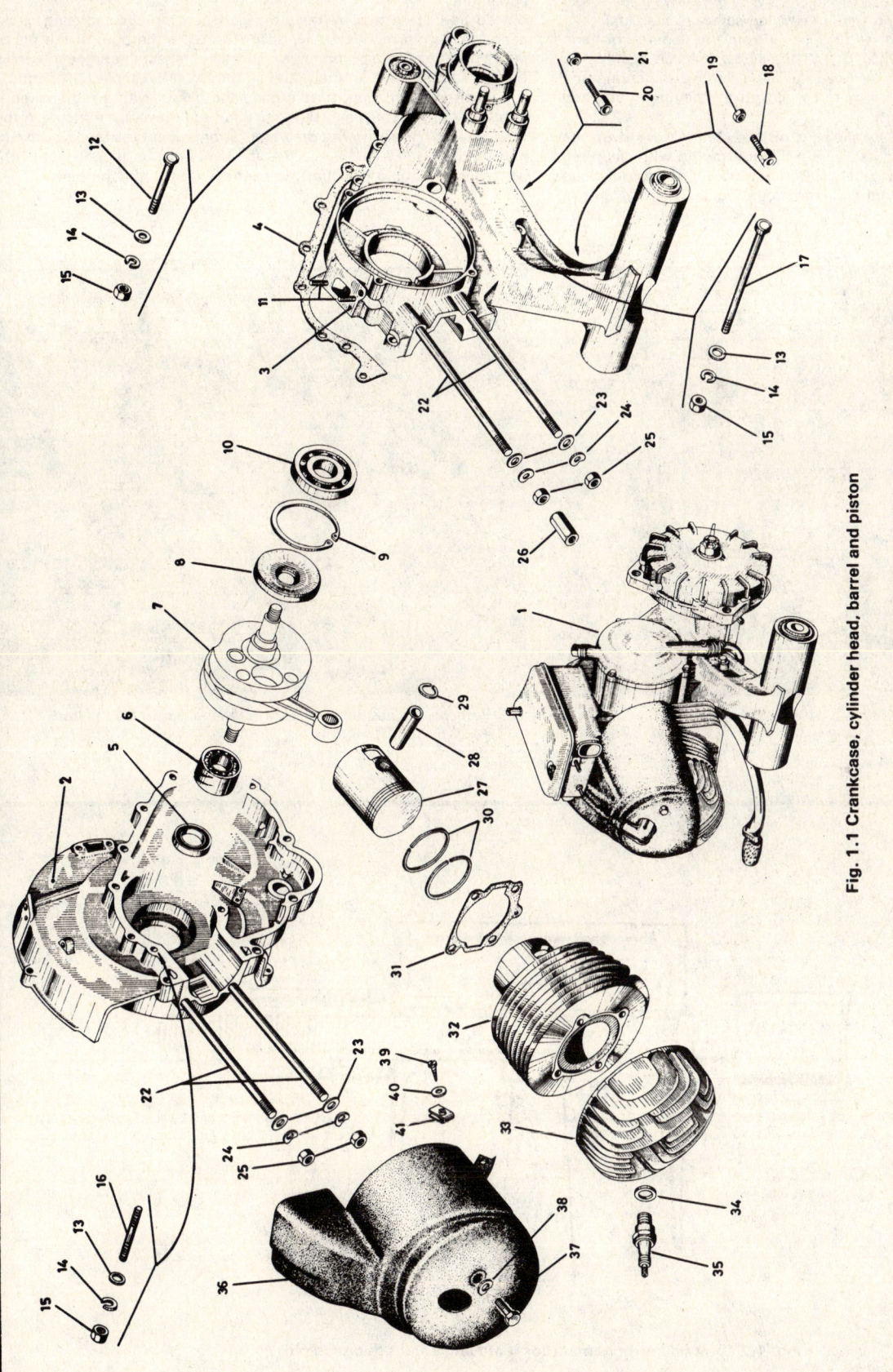

Fig. 1.1 Crankcase, cylinder head, barrel and piston

1 Engine/transmission unit
2 Right-hand crankcase
3 Left-hand crankcase
4 Gasket
5 Oil seal
6 Right-hand main bearing
7 Crankshaft
8 Oil seal
9 Circlip
10 Left-hand main bearing
11 Stud
12 Bolt
13 Washer
14 Spring washer
15 Nut
16 Stud
17 Bolt
18 Clutch cable adjuster screw
19 Locknut
20 Rear brake cable adjuster screw
21 Locknut
22 Stud
23 Washer
24 Spring washer
25 Nut
26 Hexagonal stud extension
27 Piston
28 Gudgeon pin
29 Circlip
30 Piston rings
31 Cylinder base gasket
32 Cylinder barrel
33 Cylinder head
34 Sealing washer
35 Spark plug
36 Cylinder cowl
37 Bolt
38 Spring washer
39 Screw
40 Washer
41 Clip

2   Start by removing the right-hand side panel. Pull off the spark plug HT cap, then remove the plastic cylinder cowl by unscrewing the single bolt near the spark plug and the fan cowling screw at the side.

3   Remove the hexagonal stud extension from the upper right-hand cylinder head stud and place it with the cowl. Slacken evenly and progressively the four cylinder head nuts and remove the spring and plain washers. The head can now be slid up the holding studs and removed.

4   The barrel is removed by sliding it off the studs. Move it up the studs by about an inch and pack the crankcase mouth with clean rag to prevent the ingress of any debris. Continue to pull the barrel clear, supporting the piston as it emerges from the bore. Carefully remove the aluminium cylinder base gasket; this can be re-used if in good condition.

5   To free the piston, remove the gudgeon pin circlips using circlip pliers. If the pin moves easily, push it through the bore of the piston until the latter can be lifted away. Displace the small-end needle roller bearing and place it on the gudgeon pin for safe keeping. If the pin is a tight fit in the piston, try warming the piston with a rag soaked in very hot water. This will expand the alloy and may ease removal. If this fails, use a home-made drawbolt arrangement as shown in the accompanying line drawing. The pin should not be tapped out of the piston as there is a risk that the connecting rod may be bent.

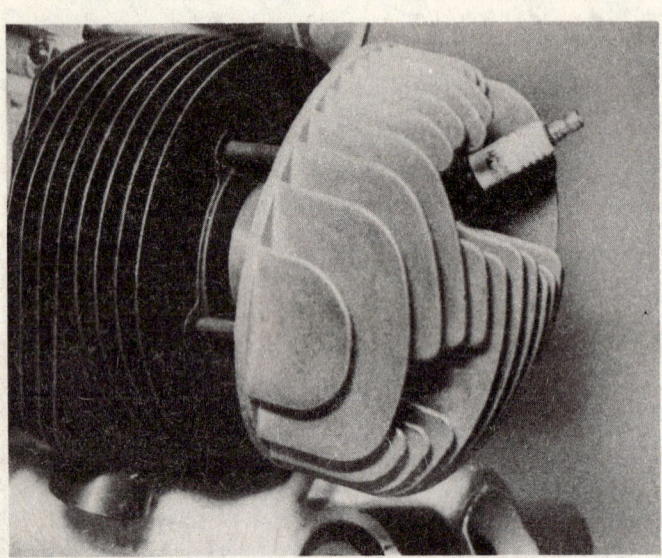

6.3 Lift away the cylinder head, followed by barrel

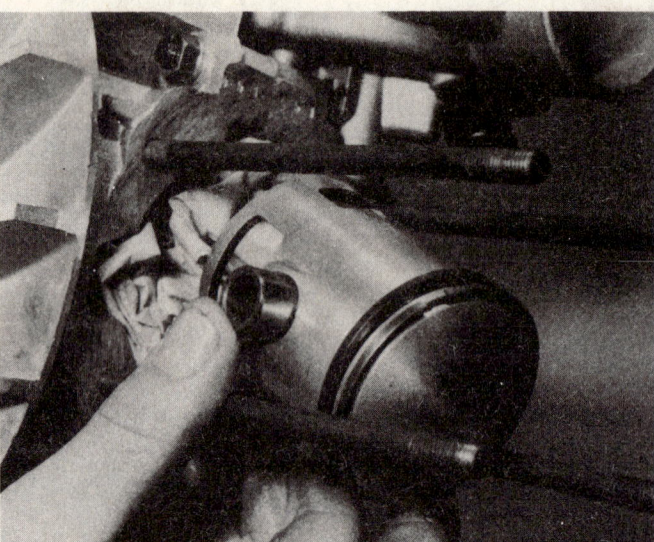

6.5 Remove circlips and displace gudgeon pin to free piston

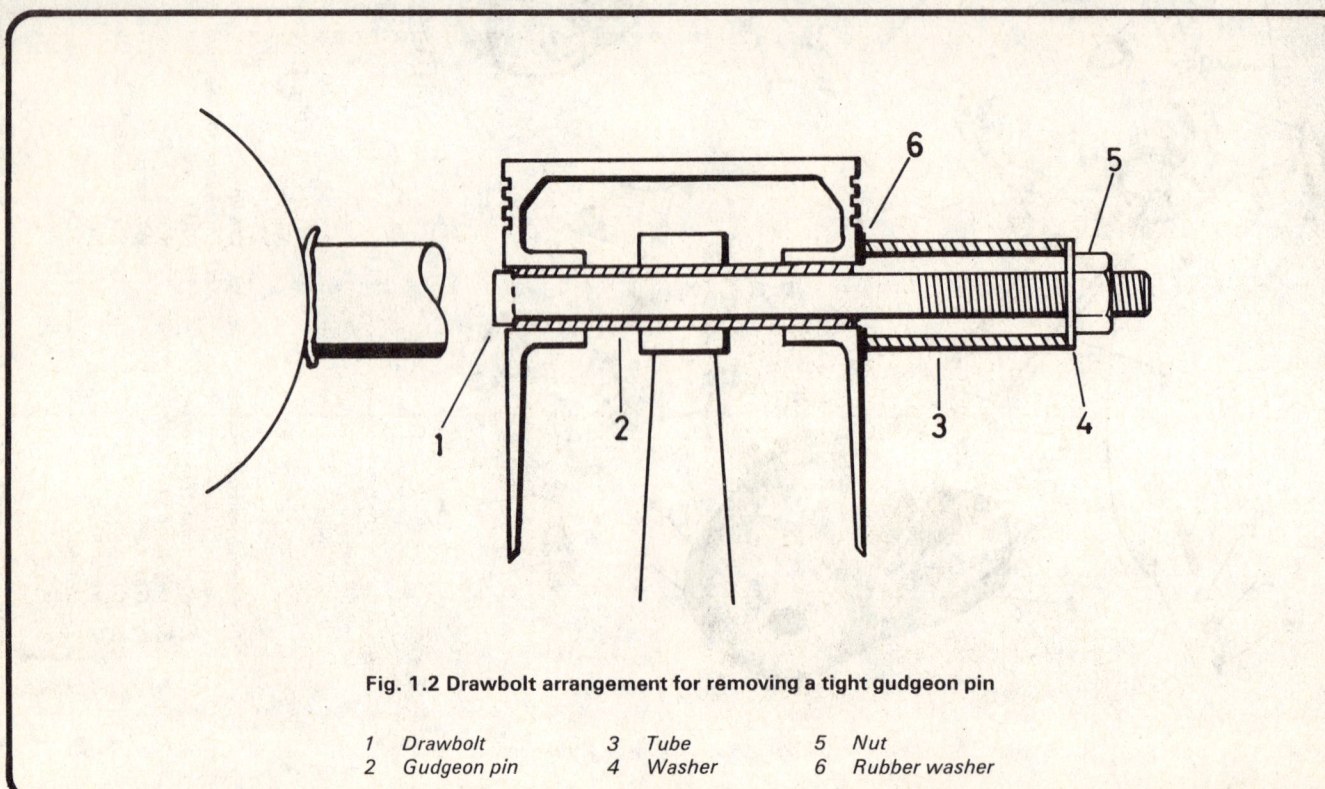

Fig. 1.2 Drawbolt arrangement for removing a tight gudgeon pin

1	Drawbolt	3	Tube	5	Nut
2	Gudgeon pin	4	Washer	6	Rubber washer

7   Dismantling the engine/transmission unit: removing the fly-wheel generator assembly

1   Before attempting to remove the generator rotor note that an extractor, Part Number T.0048564 will be required to draw it off the crankshaft taper. The use of a legged puller is **not** recommended due to the risk of damage and limited access at the rotor edge. On contact breaker ignition models there is a small slot in the face of the rotor which can be used as a method of holding it while the retaining nut is slackened. A holding tool, Part Number T.0031760 should be hooked over the kickstart shaft and the other end engaged in the slot. A resourceful owner can make up a version of this tool, which is essentially a double ended hook, from a length of $\frac{3}{8}$ in steel bar or similar.

2   On the models fitted with electronic ignition, the holding tool cannot be used, there being no slot in the rotor. In the absence of an official alternative, it is recommended that the method described below is used. Note that the cooling fins on the rotor are brittle and **must not be used to lock it.**

3   The generator assembly can be removed with the engine unit in or out of the body. Start by removing the screws which secure the fan cowling in position and lift it away. Lock the crankshaft using the tool mentioned above or a home-made version and remove the retaining nut. In the case of electronic ignition models, or where the holding tool is not available an alternative holding method will be required.

4   The easiest method to try is to select TOP gear (using the gear change if the engine is in the body, or by pushing the selector rod fully inwards if removed). Apply the rear brake fully and attempt to slacken the nut. If an impact driver is available, this may prove more effective than a socket and lever bar. This method will work unless the nut is abnormally tight, in which case proceed as follows.

5   If the engine is being stripped and the cylinder head, barrel and piston have been removed, the crankshaft can be locked by passing a round metal bar through the connecting rod small-end eye and resting its ends on wooden blocks placed against the crankcase mouth. This method is shown in the accompanying photograph.

6   Fit the extractor to the thread in the rotor and tighten the central bolt to draw the rotor off its taper. If it proves reluctant to move, tap the end of the central bolt lightly but sharply to jar it free. Remember that the crankshaft is a pressed-up assembly and can be distorted if hit hard, so take care.

7   With the rotor removed, the stator can be freed where necessary. In the case of contact breaker models, the stator edge and crankcase should be marked by scribing a line across them as a rough guide to alignment during reassembly. The electronic ignition models, fitted with the 'star' type generators, have the timing marks cast in and thus the stator need not be marked. It is good practice, however, to check these prior to removal. In the case of the P200 E there is a simple raised line on each part. The later PX models have two stator marks; '1T' in the case of the 125 and 150, and 'A' in the case of the 200.

8   Slacken the stator retaining screws and lift it clear of the crankcase. Free the wiring junction box from the top of the casing and feed the wires through to permit the stator to be lifted clear.

8   Dismantling the engine/transmission unit: removing the carburettor, air filter case and oil metering device

1   This operation can be carried out with the engine unit in or out of the body section. Start by removing the two screws which retain the air filter cover, noting that the throttle stop screw, which protrudes through a grommet in the cover, need not be disturbed. Lift the cover away.

2   Remove the two screws which retain the air filter element and lift it away from the top of the carburettor. Slacken and remove the two sleeve bolts which retain the carburettor. Lift the carburettor slightly, and disconnect the throttle rod from the lever on the oil metering device. If the fuel pipe is still connected, check that the fuel tap is off, slide the clip clear of the stub and then disconnect the pipe. The carburettor can now be lifted clear of the air filter casing.

3   If it is still attached at this stage, disconnect the oil pipe at the protruding stub from the metering device. Note that the end of the pipe should be plugged to prevent the oil in the tank from draining. Unhook the throttle cable from the metering device lever, unscrew the cable adjuster, and pull it clear of the casing.

4   Unless it requires attention, the oil metering device can be left attached to the air filter case and removed with it. Carefully remove the carburettor gasket from the mounting studs to reveal the air filter case screw. Remove the screw and lift away the case. The drive spindle for the metering device may remain in the crankcase or may lift out with the air filter casing.

5   If required, the metering device can be dismantled with the air filter case in position. Release the screws which secure the oil metering device cover and lift it away. Lift out the driven gear, washer and spring and place them with the cover. If the drive spindle is to be removed, it too can be lifted out of the case.

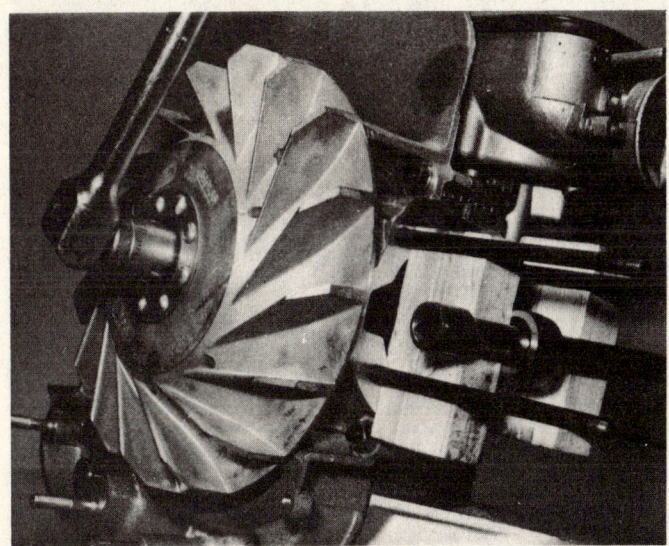

7.5 Method of locking crankshaft whilst rotor nut is removed

7.6 Use threaded extractor to draw rotor off crankshaft

9   Dismantling the engine/transmission unit: removing the clutch

1   The clutch assembly is mounted on the left-hand end of the crankshaft, and thus is somewhat inaccessible with the engine in position. It is possible to gain access to it by lowering the engine unit as described in Section 2, though normally it is recommended that work on the clutch is carried out with the engine unit on the workbench. It should also be noted that a special peg spanner is normally required to free the clutch centre nut, and this can be ordered through Vespa dealers as Part Number T.0030627. In an emergency, and given the facilities, it is possible to make a suitable tool as described later in this Section.

2   Slacken and remove the three screws which retain the clutch outer cover and lift it away. Note that the short pushrod at the centre of the cover may drop free and must be retained. Using a small screwdriver, unhook the spring retainer which locates the clutch thrust plate and lift it away to reveal the clutch centre nut. Straighten the locking tab which secures the nut using an electrical screwdriver.

3   It will be necessary to hold the clutch assembly while the retaining nut is slackened. In the absence of the holding tool, Part Number T.0031729, a strap wrench can be used to good effect. Slacken the slotted nut using the peg spanner mentioned above, then lift away the clutch as an assembly. If the peg spanner is not available, an improvised version can be made as described below.

4   A home-made version of the peg spanner was made up using a damaged 12 mm $\frac{3}{8}$ drive socket, chosen because it was sufficiently hard to remove the nut. A piece of thick-walled steel tubing can be used but this will require hardening before use. Apply a thin coat of paint to the face of the socket, then press it onto the nut, leaving paint on the outer face of the raised tangs. Wipe the socket clean, then press it onto the nut to mark the face of the socket in segments.

5   Using a hacksaw, mark the areas to be filed away (the painted segments). Carefully remove the marked areas, taking care to keep the faces square. This can be done using files, but the job is much easier if an angle grinder is available. Check the fit on the nut frequently; it is important that a good fit is obtained or the nut may be damaged, making removal next to impossible. If tubing was used, it should be hardened after it has been shaped by heating the working end to a dull cherry red colour, then quenching it in water.

6   We found that the nut can be removed more easily if the modified socket is fitted to an impact driver. This has an additional advantage in that there is less tendency for the clutch to turn during slackening. An assistant was able to hold the clutch outer drum by hand after wrapping some rag around it.

9.4 Heavily modified 12 mm socket used to remove clutch nut

Fig. 1.3 Crankshaft assembly, clutch, oil metering device and engine mounting bushes

1 Crankshaft	14 Spring washer	28 Spring	42 Right-hand buffer	55 Oil metering device
2 Rotor nut	15 Bolt	29 Backplate	43 Washer	driven gear
3 Shakeproof washer	16 O-ring	30 Bush	44 Left-hand buffer	56 Washer
4 Woodruff key	17 Oil breather	31 Rivets	45 Spacer	57 Gasket
5 Metal sleeve	18 Thrust plate	32 Location washer	46 Connecting rod	58 Driven gear assembly
6 Rubber bush	19 Retaining clip	33 Clutch centre	47 Thrust washer	59 Washer
7 Oil metering device	20 Short pushrod	34 Primary gear assembly	48 Plate	60 Drive spindle
drive gear	21 Lever	35 Friction plate	49 Tab washer	61 O-ring
8 Small-end bearing	22 Clutch outer cover	36 Plain plate	50 Nut	62 Spring
9 Woodruff key	23 Sealing washer	37 Friction plate (outer)	51 Circlip	63 Oil pipe
10 Locking washer	24 Return spring	38 Circlip	52 Washer	64 Spring washer
11 Clutch centre nut	25 Clutch operating arm	39 Clutch assembly	53 Stud	65 Screw
12 Circlip	26 Clutch drum	40 Spacer	54 Oil metering device	
13 Washer	27 Cup	41 Sleeve	cover	

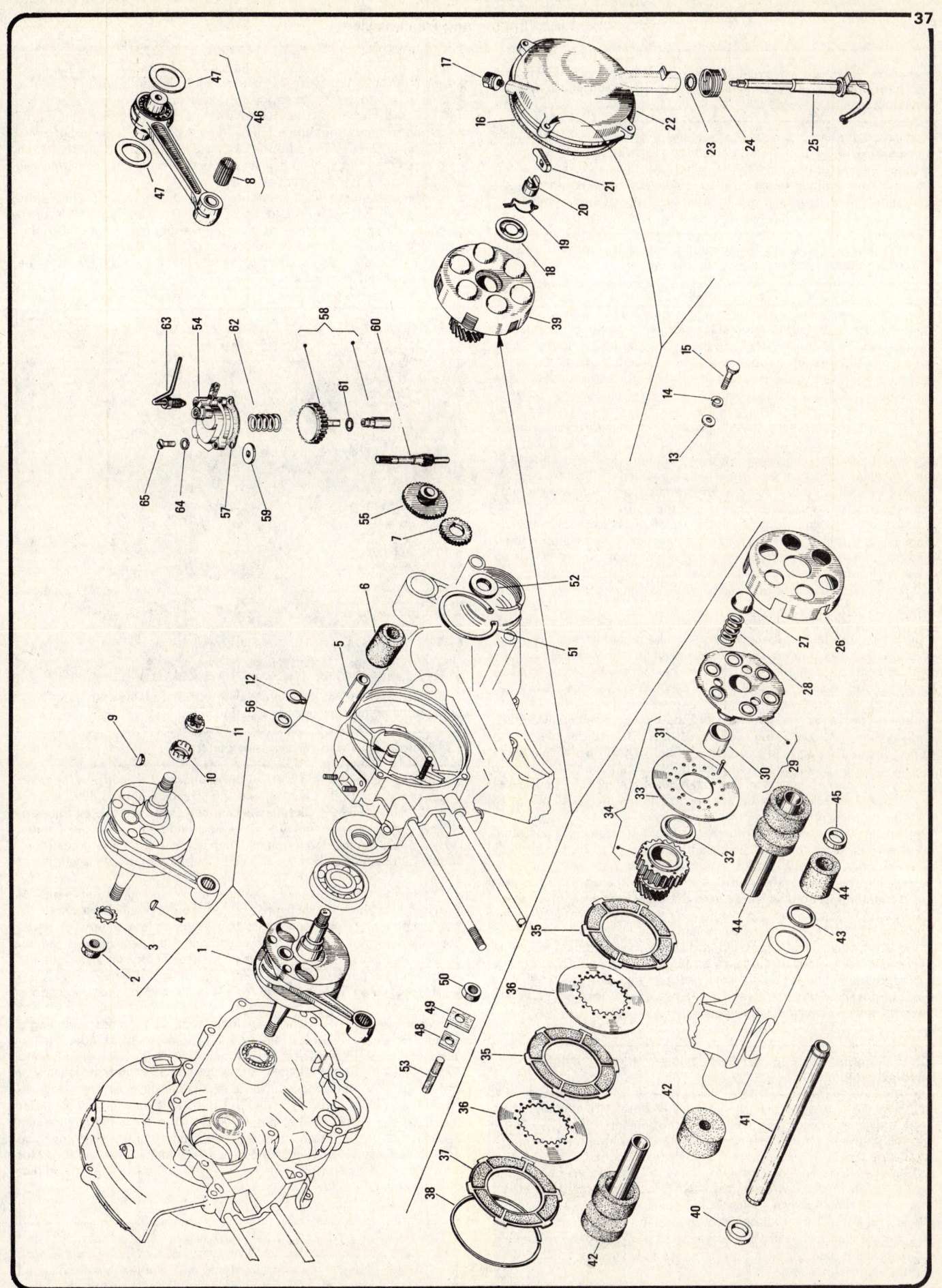

10 Dismantling the engine/transmission unit: removing the oil metering device drive gears

1   The oil metering device is driven by a pair of gears from the crankshaft. These are mounted behind the clutch and can be attended to after it has been removed. The crankshaft gear shares the clutch Woodruff key and can be slid off the crankshaft end. The driven gear is retained by a circlip and has a thrust washer fitted on either face.

11 Dismantling the engine/transmission unit: separating the crankcase halves and removing the crankshaft

1   The crankcase halves can be separated once the cylinder head and barrel, the gear selector box and the flywheel generator have been removed. If it is wished to remove the crankshaft assembly it will also be necessary to detach the clutch assembly and oil metering device drive gears from its left-hand end. it should be noted that some of the crankcase nuts are deeply recessed and cannot be removed using conventional sockets or spanners; an 11 mm box spanner or deep socket will be required.

2   The crankcase halves are secured by seven short studs and a single long stud, each of these passing right through the casing and terminating in a shaped head to prevent rotation. It is impossible to fit the long stud in other than the correct position, and obvious from which side each stud fits, so no notes need be made. Remove the nuts and washers, then displace and remove the studs.

3   With the fasteners removed it should be possible to lift away the crankcase right-hand half, leaving the crankshaft assembly and transmission components in place in the left-hand half. As the left-hand crankcase comes away, it is likely that the kickstart idler gear spring will drop free. This should be placed with the crankcase half for safe keeping.

4   If the casing proves reluctant to move, it is permissible to tap around the joint face with a soft-faced mallet or similar to start it, but on no account lever between the two casings; this will damage the jointing face, causing leakage. Once the casing has begun to move, it can be rocked to and fro until it pulls clear of the crankshaft.

5   When removing the crankshaft from the left-hand crankcase half it must be borne in mind that the crankshaft is a pressed up assembly, and can be distorted if the ends are struck. The official method of removal is to use a special tool, Part Number T.0038886 consisting of a thick steel plate which bolts to the three clutch cover threads, with an extractor bolt at its centre. The ingenious and well equipped owner may be able to fabricate a suitable version of this tool, but failing this another method must be found.

6   It is possible to tap the crankshaft out of the casing, provided that great care is taken to avoid damaging it. If in any doubt it is strongly recommended that the aid of a Vespa dealer is enlisted. Start by positioning the crankshaft at BDC (bottom dead centre), that is, with the crankpin at its furthest point from the crankcase mouth. Make up a hardwood wedge, and tap it between the flywheels opposite the crankpin. DO NOT force the flywheels apart.

7   With the flywheels supported in this way distortion is unlikely to occur, and the crankshaft can now be tapped very carefully out of the left-hand bearing, using a soft metal drift to avoid damage. Great care must be taken at this stage, and it is advisable to have assistance to support the crankshaft as it emerges.

12 Dismantling the engine/transmission unit: removing the transmission components

1   With the crankcase halves separated as described start by lifting away the kickstart idler gear from the end of the input shaft, placing it with its spring in the right-hand crankcase half for safe keeping.

2   If it is still in place, remove the rear wheel and hub. The two can be removed together to save time. Prise off the plated cap at the centre of the hub, then straighten and remove the split pin which secures the rear hub nut. Slacken and remove the nut, and pull the wheel and hub off the end of the output shaft. Though not essential, it is a good idea to remove the brake shoes and backplate to prevent contamination (see Chapter 5). Alternatively, cover the shoes with a plastic bag or some rag.

3   Temporarily refit the rear hub nut flush with the end of the output

shaft to protect the threads. Using a soft-faced mallet, drive the shaft through the bearing, removing it together with the gears.

4   As an alternative to the above, the gears can be removed with the shaft in position as follows. Remove the large circlip from the right-hand end of the output shaft, followed by the thrust washer. Lift away each gear in turn, taking care that they are kept in order and that each gear faces the right way. This last point is especially important and will avoid a lot of potential confusion.

5   To free the input shaft, straighten the tab washer and remove the retaining nut at its left-hand end. The shaft can now be tapped through, noting that there is an uncaged needle roller race at its right-hand end and some provision must be made to store the rollers safely. Once the shaft has been displaced, the gear cluster can be manoeuvred out of the casing.

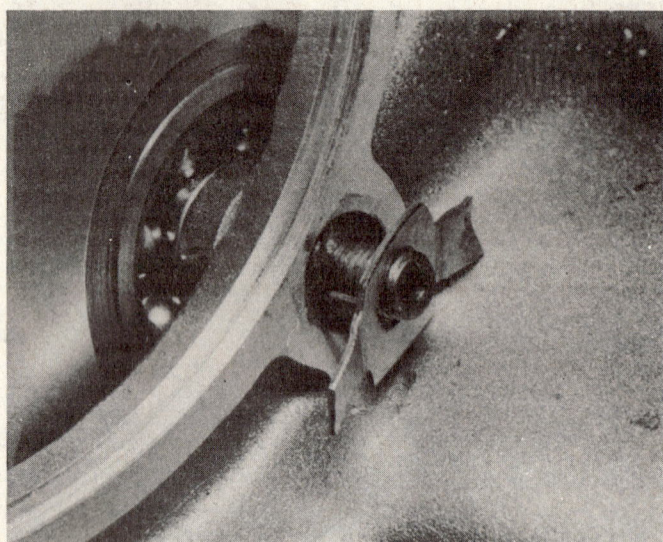

12.5 Left-hand end of input shaft with nut and plain washer removed, showing tab washer location

13 Examination and renovation: general

1   Before examining the parts of the dismantled engine unit for wear, it is essential that they should be cleaned thoroughly. Use a petrol/paraffin mix or a high flash-point solvent to remove all traces of old oil and sludge which may have accumulated within the engine. Where petrol is included in the cleaning agent, normal fire precautions should be taken and cleaning should be carried out in a well-ventilated place.

2   Examine the crankcase castings for cracks or other signs of damage. If a crack is discovered, it will require a specialist repair.

3   Examine carefully each part to determine the extent of wear, checking with the tolerance figures listed in the Specifications section of this Chapter or in the main text. If there is any doubt about the condition of a particular component, play safe and renew.

4   Use a clean lint free rag for cleaning and drying the various components.

5   Various instruments for measuring wear are required, including a vernier gauge or external micrometer and a set of standard feeler gauges. Also an internal and an external micrometer will be required to check wear limits. Additionally, although not absolutely necessary, a dial gauge and mounting bracket is invaluable for accurate measurement of end float, and play between components of very low diameter bores, where a micrometer cannot reach. After some experience has been gained, the state of wear of many components can be determined visually or by feel and thus a decision on their suitability for continued service can be made without resorting to direct measurement.

14 Crankshaft assembly: examination and renovation

1   The crankshaft is a pressed-up unit comprising two steel flywheels, connected by a crankpin, the latter forming the inner

bearing surface of the needle roller big-end bearing. The crankshaft turns on two mainshafts, supported on the left-hand end by a caged ball bearing and on the right by a needle roller bearing. The assembly is pressed together to fine tolerances, and it is important to avoid dropping or knocking the crankshaft, or mis-alignment may result.

2   In normal service, the assembly will give many thousands of miles of use, requiring no attention. The most likely cause of problems is worn or damaged main or big-end bearings, usually due to a failed lubrication supply. In the case of a failed main bearing, excessive rumbling or vibration will be noted when the engine is running. In extreme cases the increased movement of the crankshaft will cause the associated oil seal to fail, leading to loss of primary compression and poor running. If main bearing failure is suspected, refer to Section 15 for further information.

3   A worn big-end bearing will produce a pronounced knocking noise, most audible when the engine is under load, and increasing as the engine speed rises. This should not be confused with small-end bearing wear which produces a lighter, metallic rattle. The condition of the big-end bearing is best assessed after the cylinder head, barrel and piston have been removed. Grasp the end of the connecting rod and attempt to push it up and down. If any free play can be felt, it is safe to assume that the bearing must be renewed, but take care not to mistake the small amount of normal side-to-side play for bearing wear.

4   If the bearing requires renewal, the crankshaft should be removed from the crankcase and taken to a Vespa dealer for overhaul. The work demands the use of a press and a number of special tools, and the rebuilt crankshaft must be aligned with considerable accuracy if the machine is to run correctly.

5   The matter of alignment is particularly important on Vespa engines which employ rotary valve induction. This relies upon a precise fit between the machined edge of the flywheel and the corresponding crankcase surface. If badly aligned, the flywheel may drag on the crankcase, causing erratic running or even mechanical damage. For further information on the rotary valve arrangement, see Chapter 2.

6   For those owners having access to V-blocks and a dial gauge, the accuracy of alignment can be checked. There should be less than 0.03 mm (0.0012 in) eccentricity at the mainshaft ends, and less than 0.02 mm (0.0008 in) at the flywheel face.

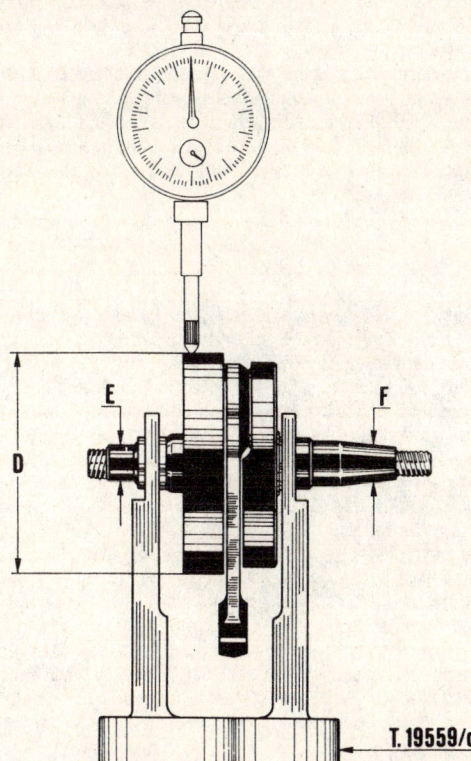

Fig. 1.4 Checking crankshaft runout

D Less than 0.02 mm (0.0008 in) runout
E and F Less than 0.03 mm (0.0012 in) runout

15 Main bearings: examination and renovation

1   The main bearings may be checked after the crankshaft has been removed as described above. In the case of the right-hand bearing, the condition of the inner race and the rollers are easily checked by visual examination; they should show a perfect and polished appearance with no visible pitting or marking. If the crankshaft is fitted into the right-hand crankcase half, there should be no discernible free play in the bearing.

2   Check the left-hand bearing, after washing out any residual oil, by turning the inner race. The bearing should run smoothly, any tight spots or irregularities being indicative of wear or damage and the need for renewal.

3   Renewal of the bearings requires a certain degree of skill if damage is to be avoided, and many owners may prefer to have the job carried out by a Vespa dealer. Note also that a bearing extractor is required to draw the inner race of the right-hand main bearing off the crankshaft; **it should not be levered off.**

Right-hand (roller) main bearing

4   Fit the Vespa extractor, Part Number T.0014499 with adaptor 23 to the inner race, then tighten the centre bolt to draw it off the crankshaft end. Alternatively, a suitable commercial extractor may be used. The race will be a tight fit over the shaft, and attempts to lever it off will result in crankshaft misalignment.

5   Lever out and discard the oil seal, using a screwdriver or a similar tool. Vespa produce another tool to draw out the inner bearing and this can be ordered as Part Number T.0021467, with adaptors 2 and 18. In the absence of this tool, first heat the casing by immersing it in boiling water. This will expand the alloy, releasing its grip on the bearing. Now try banging the casing, joint face downwards, on a clean wooden bench. With luck the bearing may be jarred free and drop out of its recess. Failing this, use a large socket as a drift and carefully drive out the old bearing.

6   When refitting the inner race, support the crankshaft securely on blocks placed under the left-hand flywheel. Find a piece of steel plate (or a suitable open-ended spanner) and fit this between the flywheels. This wedge must be a good fit between the flywheels and should be positioned directly opposite the crankpin. Do not force it into position. Note that if the crankshaft is not supported in this way it will be distorted as the race is fitted.

7   Heat the inner race in oil to 100°C, then place it over the crankshaft end. Using a tubular drift made from a piece of 26 mm I.D. tubing, tap the race down the shaft. Note that the race **must not** be driven right down to the shoulder. Its final position should be such that the outer face is 16 mm (0.63 in) above the shoulder, and it is worth making up a simple thickness gauge before the race is fitted to ensure that this position is achieved.

8   To fit the outer race, again heat the casing in boiling water, drying it off before the bearing is inserted. Using a large round drift, tap the bearing home squarely until its inner edge lies flush with the casing. Grease the sealing face of the new oil seal, then turn the casing over and tap it squarely into its recess, leaving the outer face flush with the casing.

Left-hand (ball) main bearing

9   Prise out the old oil seal using a screwdriver, then remove the large circlip which locates the bearing. Note that on machines without the oil metering device, a second circlip is fitted outboard of the bearing. The remaining models have two washers fitted in place of the circlip. The extractor, Part Number T.0021467 together with adaptors 1 and 2 can be used to extract the bearing.

10   In the absence of this tool, first heat the casing by immersing it in boiling water. This will expand the alloy, releasing its grip on the bearing. Now try banging the casing, joint face downwards, on a clean wooden bench. With luck the bearing may be jarred free and drop out of its recess. Failing this, use a large socket as a drift and carefully drive out the old bearing.

11   The new bearing can be tapped into position, having first heated the casing in boiling water and dried it off. Refit the locating circlip, then carefully tap home the new oil seal, the seal face of which should be greased prior to installation.

15.2a Check left-hand main bearing by turning inner race

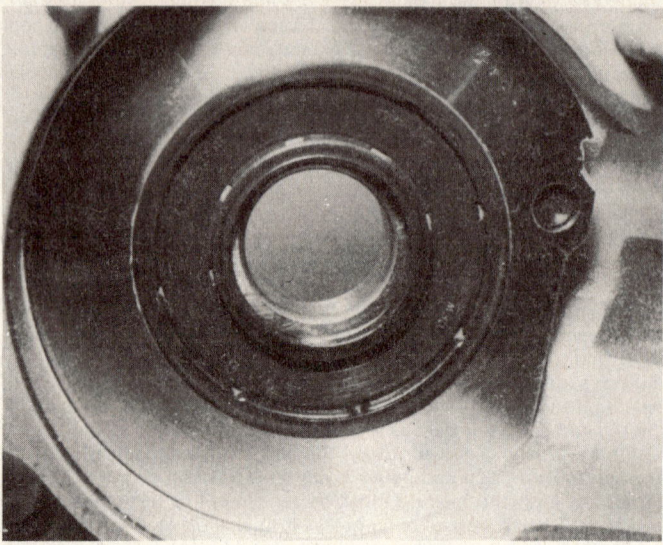

15.2b Left-hand main bearing seal is fitted inboard of bearing

16 Transmission bearings: examination and renovation

1   The input shaft gear cluster is supported by internal bearings, and these are described in Section 22 of this Chapter. The output shaft is carried by a caged ball bearing at its left-hand end and by a needle roller bearing on the right.

2   The left-hand (ball) bearing can be removed after the rear hub oil seal has been prised out and the circlip removed. Do not discard the oil seal at this stage. The bearing can be removed by driving it out to the left, using a socket as a drift. This is made easier if the casing is heated by immersing it in boiling water to expand the alloy and relax its grip on the bearing.

3   When fitting the new bearing, take care to ensure that it enters the bore squarely and fully, tapping it home using a socket against the outer race. Refit the circlip.

4   Before the new seal is fitted, check carefully the size marked on the side and compare this with the old seal. Two different seals may be fitted, depending on the size of hub boss. The seal may be either 27 mm or 30 mm, and it is important to ensure that the correct one is fitted. Note that it is possible to fit either seal to either hub, but that oil leakage will occur unless the correct one is chosen.

5   Note also that the seal bears upon the hub boss, and it is essential that this is unmarked. If any scoring or burrs are present the seal will be destroyed very quickly. Very light damage can be polished out, using fine abrasive paper, but deep scores or pits will necessitate renewal of the hub.

6   The right-hand (needle roller) bearing can be dealt with in much the same way as the right-hand main bearing. The Vespa extractor, Part Number T.0021467, with adaptors 9 and 16, can be used to remove it, or it can be driven out after the casing has been heated with boiling water. The new bearing should be fitted flush with the inner face of the casting.

16.2a Prise out the old seal, but retain it as pattern

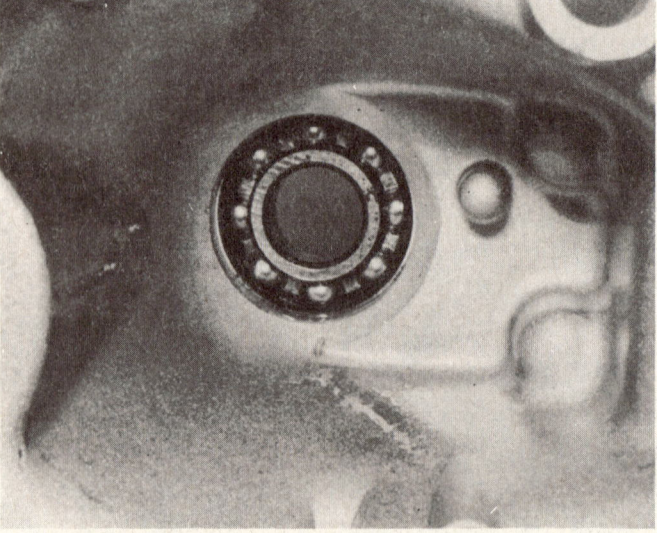

16.2b Bearing can be driven out from inside of casing

17 Cylinder head: examination and renovation

1 Remove all accumulated carbon from the cylinder head using a blunt scraper. Remember that aluminium alloy is a relatively soft material and will be scored easily if care is not taken. In particular, be very careful not to mark the joint face. Though not essential, the cylinder head surface can be finished using metal polish, the resulting shiny surface being more resistant to subsequent carbon build-up.

2 Check the condition of the spark plug thread, which is easily damaged if the plug has been over-tightened. A damaged thread can be reclaimed by fitting a Helicoil thread insert. Most dealers or small engineering firms can offer this service, providing a cheap and effective alternative to fitting a new head.

3 The head to barrel joint is made by ground faces on each part, no gasket being used. Of the two, the head is more likely to allow leakage due to the softer material used. Leakage is often evident in the form of an obvious score or burning across the surface.

4 It is permissible to repair minor scoring or distortion by lapping the head on a flat surface. Tape a sheet of fine abrasive paper to a sheet of glass. The head can then be lapped in a rotary motion until the damaged area has been removed. To show up any low spots, first cover the mating surface with a spirit-based felt marker.

5 Do not attempt to remove a significant amount of material in this fashion; if the distortion or damage is more serious, take the head to a Vespa dealer for expert advice. The dealer may be able to have the head surface ground, but this will inevitably raise the compression ratio, possibly to an unacceptable level. In serious cases the cylinder head will have to be renewed.

18 Cylinder barrel: examination and renovation

1 Examine the bore surface for wear or damage. If deep scoring is evident it will be necessary to have the barrel rebored to suit the next oversize of piston. This job is best entrusted to a Vespa dealer who will be able to supply the appropriate piston and get the barrel bored to suit, usually within a few days. Very light scoring can be removed by honing, provided that this does not enlarge the bore beyond the specified tolerance. Again, this is outside the scope of most owners, and should be entrusted to a Vespa dealer or a specialist engineering company.

2 A used but undamaged bore will have a wear ridge near the top, denoting the upper limit of piston ring travel. The extent of bore wear can be measured using a bore micrometer, taking several readings above the wear ridge and several just below it. Subtract the original bore size from the largest reading to establish the amount of wear that has taken place.

3 The following table gives the bore and piston dimensions for the various models and oversizes and should be used in conjunction with the accompanying line drawing. Note that the bore diameter reading (dimension E) should be made 25 mm below the top of the bore surface on 125 and 150 models, and 30 mm in the case of the 200 models (dimension A). Note also that in the case of newly rebored cylinders, the bore diameter (E) must exceed the piston diameter (C) by the following amounts on assembly:

P125 X, PX125 E   0.180 mm (0.007 in)
P150 X, PX150 E   0.225 mm (0.009 in)
P200 E, PX200 E   0.215 mm (0.008 in)

Cylinder bore dimensions, mm (in)

	125 cc	150 cc	200 cc	Tolerance
(E) Standard bore	52.5 (2.067)	57.8 (2.276)	66.5 (2.618)	-0.005, +0.025 (-0.0002, +0.001)
(E) 1st oversize	52.7 (2.075)	58.0 (2.283)	66.7 (2.626)	-0.000, +0.020 (-0.000, +0.0008)
(E) 2nd oversize	52.9 (2.083)	58.2 (2.291)	66.9 (2.634)	-0.000, +0.020 (-0.000, +0.0008)
(E) 3rd oversize	53.1 (2.091)	58.4 (2.299)	67.1 (2.642)	-0.000, +0.020 (-0.000, +0.0008)

Piston dimensions, mm (in)

	P125 X	P150 X	P200 E	Tolerance
(C) Standard piston	52.330 (2.0602)	57.585 (2.2671)	66.292 (2.6099)	±0.015 (±0.0006)
(C) 1st oversize	52.530 (2.0681)	57.785 (2.2750)	66.495 (2.6179)	±0.010 (±0.0004)
(C) 2nd oversize	52.730 (2.0760)	57.985 (2.2830)	66.695 (2.6258)	±0.010 (±0.0004)
(C) 3rd oversize	52.930 (2.0839)	58.185 (2.2907)	66.895 (2.6337)	±0.010 (±0.0004)

	PX125 E	PX150 E	PX200 E	Tolerance
(C) Standard piston	52.305 (2.0593)	57.585 (2.2671)	66.292 (2.6099)	±0.015 (±0.0006)
(C) 1st oversize	52.505 (2.0671)	57.785 (2.2750)	66.495 (2.6179)	±0.010 (±0.0004)
(C) 2nd ovrsize	52.705 (2.0750)	57.985 (2.2830)	66.695 (2.6258)	±0.010 (±0.0004)
(C) 3rd oversize	52.905 (2.0829)	58.185 (2.2907)	66.895 (2.6337)	±0.010 (±0.0004)

4 If it is intended to fit a new piston and rings into the original bore, it must be remembered that the unworn rings may strike the ridge, fracturing them. A specialist engineering shop may be able to remove the ridge, and will be able to advise on this point. Note also that the piston and bore are matched during assembly, and both components will be marked by a letter. If a new piston is fitted in an existing bore, it is important that the letters match, so quote this when ordering the new component.

5 It will also be necessary to roughen slightly the bore surface to assist the new rings in bedding in to the bore surface. This is best done by honing, or with a 'glaze buster', but can be approximated at home by careful use of fine abrasive paper. Move the paper in rotary motion around the bore surface until the shiny surface is just removed. Take care not to remove a significant amount of metal, and be very careful that all traces of abrasive dust are removed from the bore and ports afterwards.

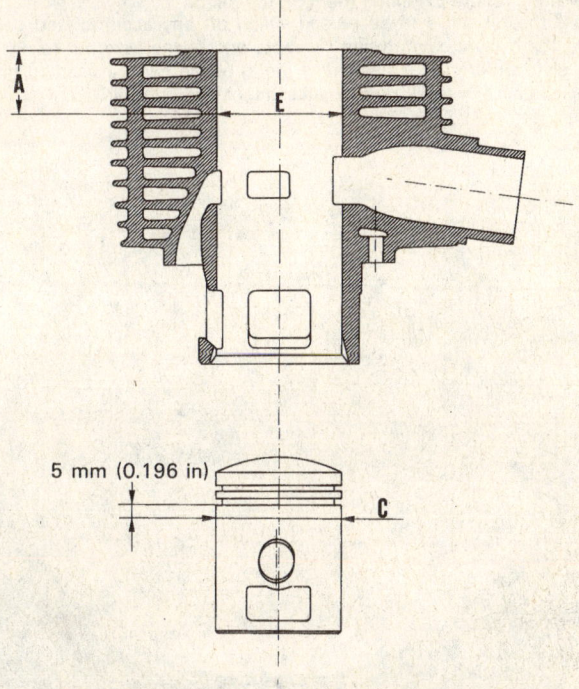

5 mm (0.196 in)

Fig. 1.5 Cylinder barrel and piston measurement points (see text)

19 Piston and rings: examination and renovation

1   If examination of the bore surface has indicated the need for reboring, this Section can be ignored, since a new piston will be required to suit the oversized bore.

2   Check the piston surface for scoring or other damage. If the scoring is light, the piston can normally be reused, but any deep scoring or smearing of the surface is indicative of serious wear or of seizure in the past, and will require the piston to be renewed. Where damage of this type is noted, it is uncommon for the bore surface to have escaped damage.

3   The above checks are adequate for most purposes, but if it is felt necessary, the piston dimensions can be checked as described above. Note that this will require the use of a micrometer and that all measurements are taken at right angles to the gudgeon pin bore.

4   The piston rings should be free to move in their grooves, though they are prevented from rotating in use by small pegs; these stop the ring ends from becoming caught in the ports. If the rings are trapped in the grooves this may be due to burring of the piston material due to seizure or by gumming caused by accumulated oil residue.

5   The rings should be removed to allow the grooves to be cleaned out properly, and if care is taken this can be accomplished by spreading the ring ends slightly with the thumbs and lifting the ring clear. A safer method in view of the brittle nature of the rings is to use three thin steel strips such as old feeler gauges as shown in the accompanying line drawing. This method is a useful way of freeing gummed rings. It will be noted that the top ring is of the L-section Dykes type, and thus is unlikely to be confused with the second ring.

6   Carefully clean out the ring grooves before refitting the piston rings. No exact figures are available to indicate the allowable ring to groove clearance, but as a rough guide the maximum clearance on similar engines is about 0.05 mm (0.002 in). If greatly in excess of this, renew the piston as an assembly.

7   Piston ring wear should be checked by carefully installing each ring in an unworn portion of the bore about 13 mm (1/2 in) up from the bottom. Use the piston to position the ring square to the bore. Use feeler gauges to measure the gap between the ends of the ring and compare the result to the specifications at the beginning of this Chapter. If either ring shows an end gap in excess of the wear limit, renewal will be required. It is good practice to fit new piston rings whenever the engine is overhauled. Always check the end gap of the new rings before installing them on the piston.

8   If the piston is to be reused, clean off any accumulated carbon from the crown, using a blunt scraper and taking care not to dig into the piston material. If desired, a metal polish can be used to give a bright finish. This will reduce subsequent carbon build up.

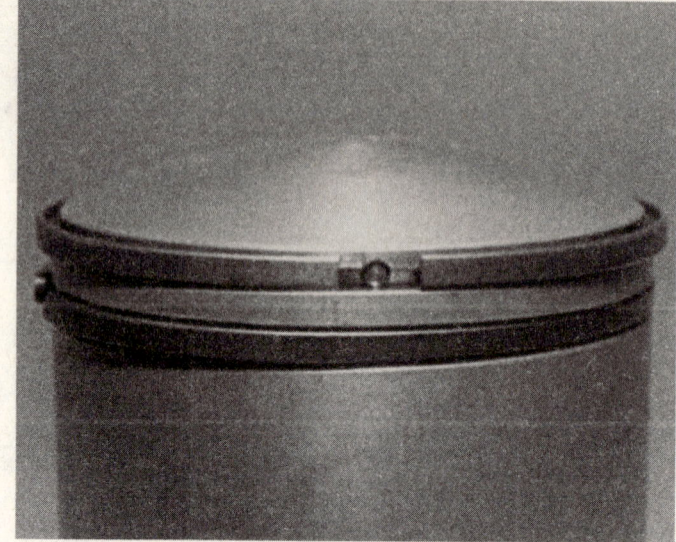

19.4 Check that ring location pegs are secure in ring grooves

19.5 Note L-section Dykes top ring

19.7 Clean carbon from piston crown. Arrow mark denotes exhaust port side of piston

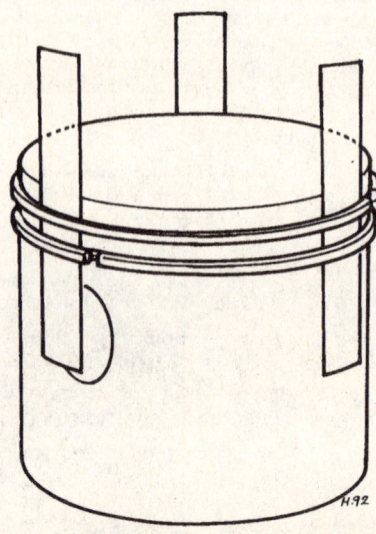

Fig. 1.6 Freeing gummed piston rings

20 Small-end bearing: examination and renovation

1   Small-end bearing wear is characterised by a metallic rattle when the engine is run. When checking for wear do not confuse play in the small-end bearing with excessive clearance between the gudgeon pin and piston.

2   The bearing is of the caged needle roller type in which the connecting rod small-end eye forms the outer race and the gudgeon pin the inner race. It follows that these and the bearing itself must be in good condition; if wear is suspected, examine them closely.

3   If marking or indenting of the gudgeon pin is noted, it should be renewed. The same applies to the connecting rod small-end eye, remembering that to renew the connecting rod it will be necessary to have the crankshaft overhauled or, where possible, to have the small-end eye honed to accept a larger category bearing. It is recommended that the advice of a Vespa dealer is sought on this point. The bearing itself should show no signs of wear or marking of the rollers.

4   If the various surfaces are unmarked, but play can be detected when assembled, it may be possible to fit a new cage of a larger category. Note that the service limit for bearing clearance is 0.02 mm (0.0008 in). Each connecting rod and bearing is marked with a category number. On 200 cc models, these must normally be matched as follows.

    Use a 1st category connecting rod with a 4th category bearing
    Use a 2nd category connecting rod with a 3rd category bearing
    Use a 3rd category connecting rod with a 2nd category bearing
    Use a 4th category connecting rod with a 1st category bearing

If the engine proves noisy with this combination, fit a bearing of the next lowest category.

5   In the case of the 125 and 150 cc models, use a bearing of the same category as the connecting rod. If this proves noisy in use, fit a bearing of the next highest category.

21 Clutch assembly: dismantling, examination and renovation

1   The clutch assembly can be dismantled for examination after it has been removed as described in Section 9 of this Chapter. It can be dismantled by removing the large circlip which retains the plates inside the clutch drum. This will require that the assembly is compressed against the pressure of the clutch springs. If it is available, use the compression tool Part Number T.0020322.

2   As an alternative, clamp the clutch between soft vice jaws, using a piece of tubing or similar as a spacer. The spacer should be placed against the outer face of the clutch drum, so that the springs are compressed as the vice is tightened (see photograph).

3   Compress the clutch until pressure is taken off the clutch plates. Prise out one end of the circlip, then work it out of its groove. Release the compression tool or vice and lift out the clutch springs and plates. It should be noted that on some models one dished plate may be fitted. Note that this **must** be refitted facing in the same direction, so make sure that it is not turned round while the clutch is apart. If fitted incorrectly, the clutch may tend to grab in use.

4   In the absence of specific wear limits, the condition of the clutch plates should be checked visually, where necessary by comparison with new parts. If in any doubt, take the clutch components to a Vespa dealer who will be able to advise on this point. Normally, if the clutch has been slipping in use, this will be evident in the form of an obviously worn or glazed surface on the friction material.

5   The plain plates will not normally require renewal unless they have been seriously overheated by clutch slip and have warped as a result. Such damage is usually characterised by discolouration.

6   The springs will weaken in time and may eventually become permanently compressed. allowing clutch slip to occur. The springs can be compared with new ones, and should be renewed if obviously weakened. Note that this is a relatively uncommon cause of slippage, and that the clutch friction plates should always be checked first.

7   Examine the slots in the clutch drum and the splines on the centre for indenting and wear. This is not likely to be a problem unless a very high mileage has been covered, but if present may cause erratic clutch operation. Light indenting of the drum slots can be relieved by carefully filing the edges smooth, but if more serious wear is found, the drum should be renewed.

8   The clutch centre is integral with the primary gear, this being attached to the left-hand plain plate by rivets. If spline or gear tooth wear is found, the centre should be renewed, either as a complete assembly with the plain plate, or by drilling out the rivets and riveting the plate to a new clutch centre. This last job is best entrusted to a Vespa dealer. Finally, check for wear between the clutch centre and the backplate brush. If there is obvious wear, renew the bush.

9   To reassemble the clutch, place the drum on the workbench and fit the spring cups and springs into their holes. Offer up the clutch backplate, making sure that the springs locate in the recesses in the backplate. Lubricate and fit the thrust washer and backplate bush, then place the clutch centre assembly over the bush.

10   Build up the friction and plain plates alternately, noting that the last friction plate has friction material on one side only. Compress the assembly in the same way as was using during dismantling, and secure with the circlip. Check that the circlip seats fully in its groove.

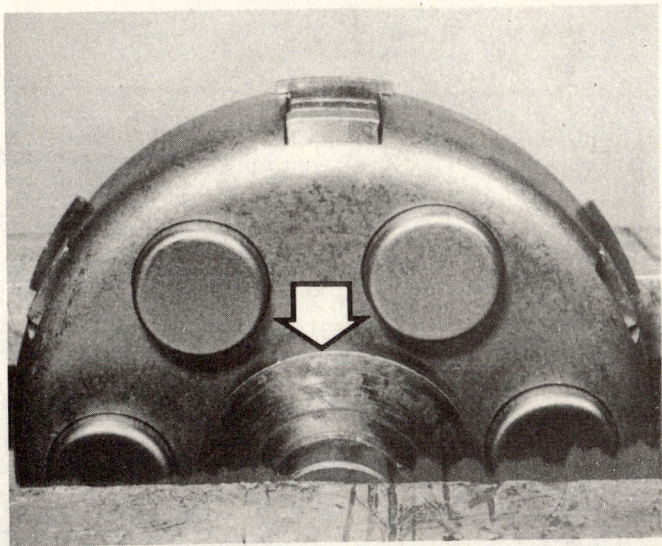

21.2a Compress clutch between soft vice jaws, using home-made spacer (arrowed) on spring side

21.2b With clutch compressed, peel out the circlip (arrowed)

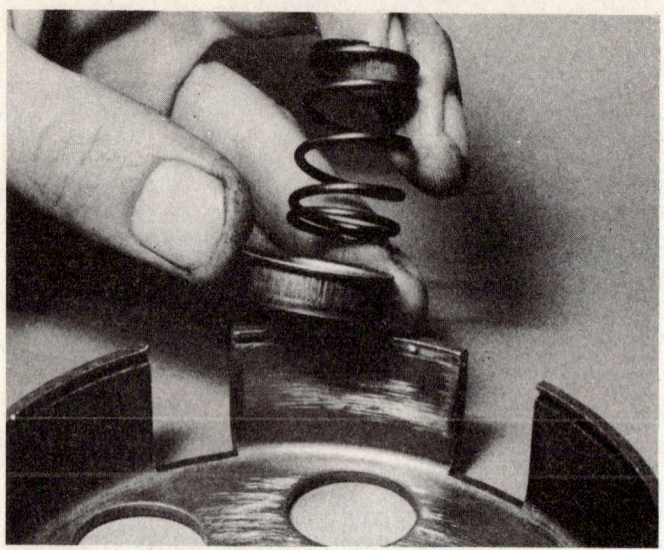

21.9a Fit cups and springs into clutch drum...

21.9b ... offer up the backplate, making sure that springs engage in recesses

21.9c Fit the thrust washer and backplate bush ...

21.9d ... then fit the clutch centre

21.10a Fit plain plates and ...

21.10b ... friction plates alternately

21.10c Final friction plate has friction material on inner face only

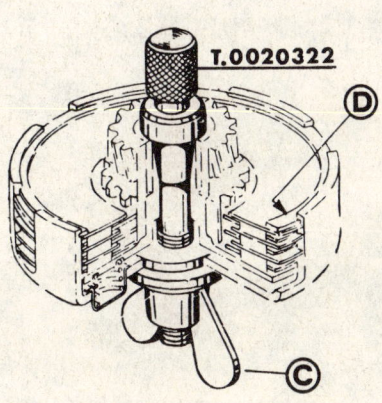

T.0020322

Fig. 1.7 Clutch compression tool in use

C   Wingnut   D   Circlip

22 Transmission components: examination and renovation

Input shaft
1   The input shaft cluster comprises the four integral transmission gears, together with the helically-cut primary driven gear. The latter incorporates a spring shock absorber unit to damp out transmission snatch. The whole assembly is carried on a steel shaft and is supported by a journal ball bearing at the left-hand end and an uncaged needle-roller bearing at the right-hand end.
2   To remove the shaft and bearings, release the circlip which retains the left-hand bearing in the primary driven gear. Push the shaft through to the right to expose the needle rollers, which should be removed for safe keeping. Support the primary driven gear, left-hand side downwards, on wooden blocks. Using a soft metal drift to avoid damage to the shaft end, tap the shaft through the cluster to displace the bearing.
3   Wash out the left-hand bearing in clean petrol to remove any residual oil, then check for wear by spinning it. The needle rollers of the right-hand bearing should be smooth and undamaged as should the surfaces of the shaft and gear cluster on which they bear. If pitting or scoring is discovered, renew the affected parts.
4   If the gear teeth show any signs of pitting or chipping, it will be necessary to renew the cluster. This can be purchased as an assembly,

complete with the primary driven gear and shock absorber assembly, or the latter components can be built onto a new bare cluster. This latter job, or the renewal of the shock absorber components, requires the riveted shock absorber unit to be dismantled, and is best entrusted to a Vespa dealer.

Output shaft
5   The output shaft gears are retained on the shaft by a large circlip. Once this has been removed the thrust washer and the gears may be slid off. Note that the gears should be placed carefully in order to ensure that none are reversed during reassembly.
6   The shaft is hollow through part of its length and this section houses the gear selector cruciform or 'spider'. To release the spider from the shaft, unscrew the selector rod, noting that it has a **left-hand** thread. Flats are provided on the rod for this purpose. Once the rod has been removed, turn the spider in the shaft, noting that one pair of legs is curved to permit this. The spider can now be withdrawn through the slots in the shaft.
7   The part most likely to be worn is the spider itself, this being made of a relatively soft material to protect the more expensive parts (like the shaft and gears) from selection damage. Check the gear teeth for chipping or damage, renewing parts as required.
8   When ordering replacement transmission parts, it is worth taking the damaged component as a pattern. The gear train has been modified on occasions to improve interchangeability between the various models, and the above precaution will assist the storeman in identifying the correct replacement part for a particular machine.
9   When rebuilding the cluster, remember that the spider must be fitted first, its legs being slightly offset away from the selector rod. Make certain that the gears are fitted exactly as they were; it is possible to reverse one or more of the gears, and this can cause some degree of confusion. The accompanying photographs illustrate the reassembly sequence.
10   Once the circlip has been fitted, the end-float on the shaft must be checked. A special forked thickness gauge, Part Number T.0060824, is available for this purpose. It is designed to ensure that the gear remains square on the shaft to avoid a false reading, but it is possible to make do by using two feeler gauges as shown in the accompanying photograph.
11   The correct initial clearance is 0.15 – 0.40 mm (0.006 – 0.016 in), whilst the service limit is 0.50 mm (0.020 in). If an excessive clearance is noted, remove the circlip and substitute a thicker thrust washer. These are available in the following sizes.

Output shaft thrust washers

Standard thickness	2.05 mm (0.081 in)
1st oversize	2.20 mm (0.087 in)
2nd oversize	2.35 mm (0.093 in)
3rd oversize	2.50 mm (0.098 in)
4th oversize	2.65 mm (0.104 in)

All sizes +0.00, −0.06 mm (+0.000, −0.002 in)

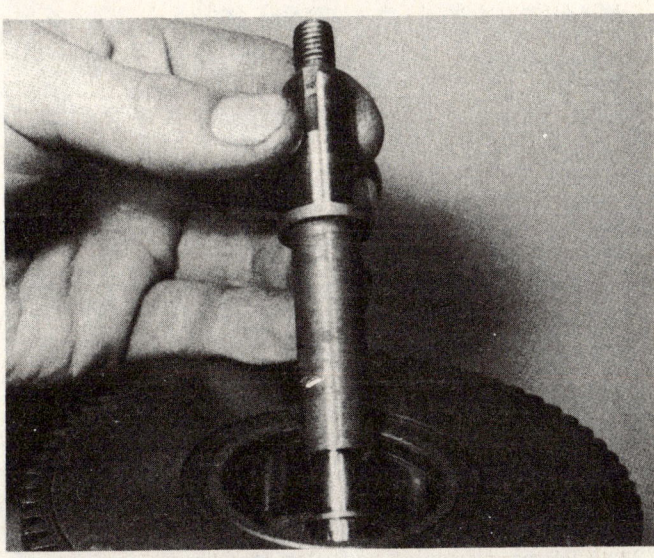

22.4a To reassemble input shaft assembly, fit shaft as shown ...

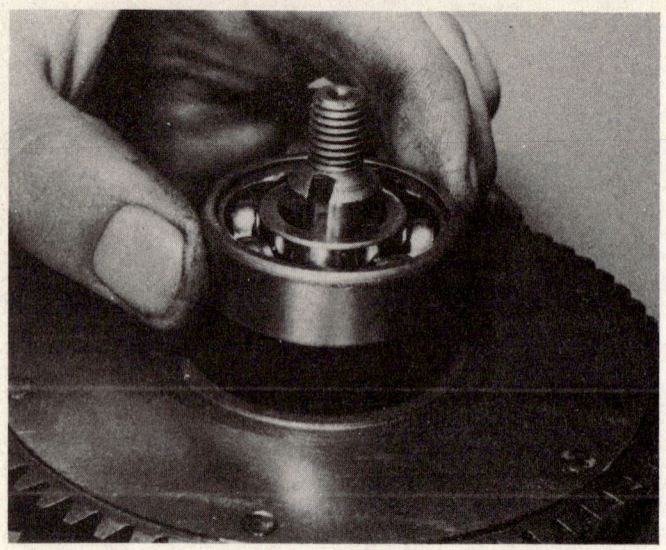

22.4b ... then offer up the left-hand bearing

22.4c Drive bearing home using a large socket ...

22.4d ... and secure with circlip

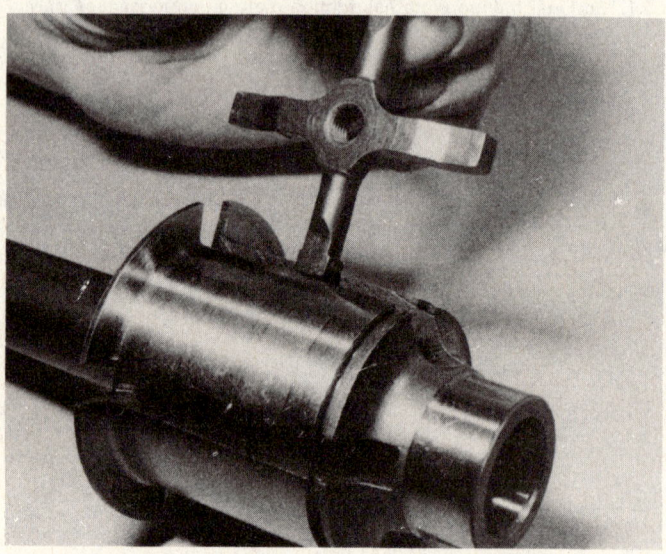

22.9a Slide spider into shaft and turn through 90 degrees – note radius on legs to permit this

22.9b Tighten selector rod, noting **left-hand** thread

22.9c Fit 4th gear over shaft as shown ...

22.9d ... followed by the 3rd gear ...

22.9e ... 2nd gear and ...

22.9f ... 1st gear. Note direction of each gear

22.9g Fit thrust washer as shown and secure with circlip

22.10 Check end float using **two** feeler gauges as shown

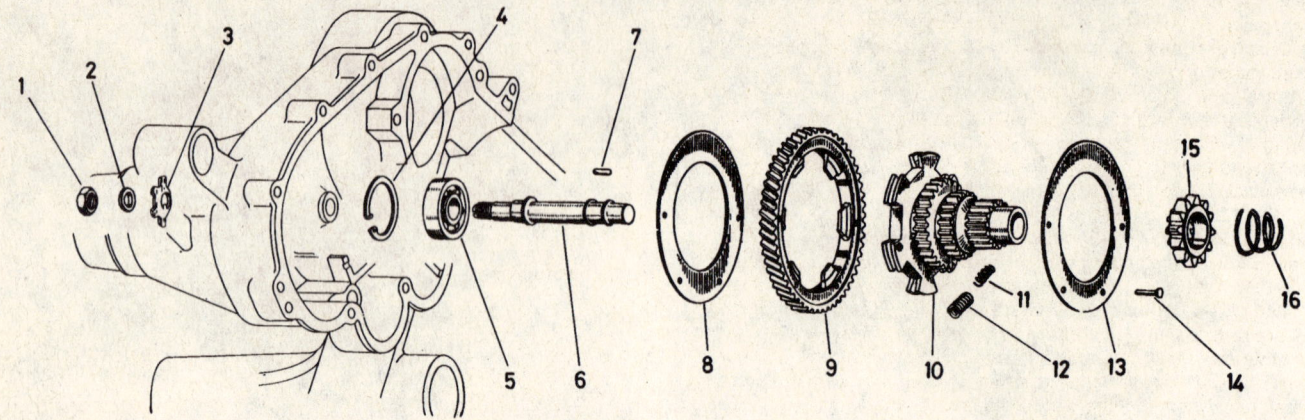

Fig. 1.8 Input shaft assembly

1	Nut	5	Bearing	9	Primary driven gear	13	Outer plate
2	Washer	6	Input shaft	10	Gear cluster	14	Rivets
3	Tab washer	7	Needle roller	11	Spring (inner)	15	Kickstart idler gear
4	Circlip	8	Inner plate	12	Spring (outer)	16	Spring

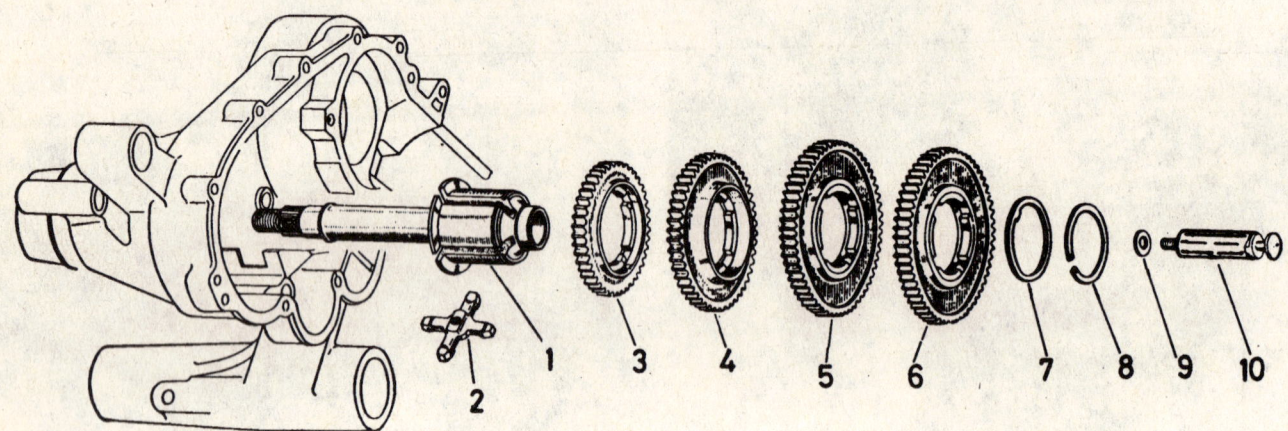

Fig. 1.9 Output shaft assembly

1	Output shaft	4	3rd gear	7	Thrust washer	9	Washer
2	Cruciform (spider)	5	2nd gear	8	Circlip	10	Selector rod
3	4th gear	6	1st gear				

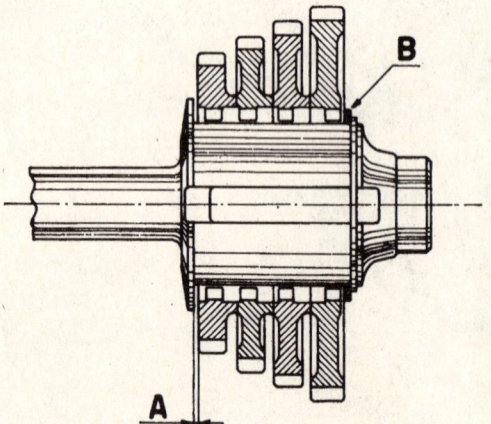

Fig. 1.10 Measuring output shaft end float

A　Endfloat measurement point　　　　B　Thrust washer

23 Kickstart mechanism: examination and renovation

1　The kickstart mechanism is a robust assembly which will require little attention in normal use. The most probable cause of problems is a broken return spring, a self-evident condition, or slippage caused by worn ratchet teeth.

2　If the return spring is broken or shows signs of cracking, it must be renewed. Disengage the spring by grasping it with pliers and unhooking the end from its anchor point. The new spring is refitted by reversing this operation. If the ratchet teeth show signs of wear, renew the starter gear to prevent further slippage. It is a sound precaution to renew the light spring which loads the starter gear at the same time.

24 Engine reassembly: general

1　Before reassembly of the engine/gear unit is commenced, the various component parts should be cleaned thoroughly and placed on a sheet of clean paper, close to the working area.

2　Make sure all traces of old gaskets have been removed and that the mating surfaces are clean and undamaged. Great care should be taken when removing old gasket compound not to damage the mating surface. Most gasket compounds can be softened using a suitable solvent such as methylated spirits, acetone or cellulose thinner. The type of solvent required will depend on the type of compound used. Gasket compound of the non-hardening type can be removed using a soft brass-wire brush of the type used for cleaning suede shoes. A considerable amount of scrubbing can take place without fear of harming the mating surfaces. Some difficulty may be encountered when attempting to remove gaskets of the self-vulcanising type, the use of which is becoming widespread, particularly as cylinder head and base gaskets. The gasket should be pared from the mating surface using a scalpel or a small chisel with a finely honed edge. Do not, however, resort to scraping with a sharp instrument unless necessary.

3 Gather together all the necessary tools and have available an oil can filled with clean engine oil. Make sure that all new gaskets and oil seals are to hand, also all replacement parts required. Nothing is more frustrating than having to stop in the middle of a reassembly sequence because a vital gasket or replacement has been overlooked. As a general rule each moving engine component should be lubricated thoroughly as it is fitted into position.

4 Make sure that the reassembly area is clean and that there is adequate working space. Refer to the torque and clearance setting wherever they are given. Many of the smaller bolts are easily sheared or overtightened. Always use the correct size screwdriver bit for the cross-head screws and never an ordinary screwdriver or punch. If the existing screws show evidence of maltreatment in the past, it is advisable to renew them as a complete set.

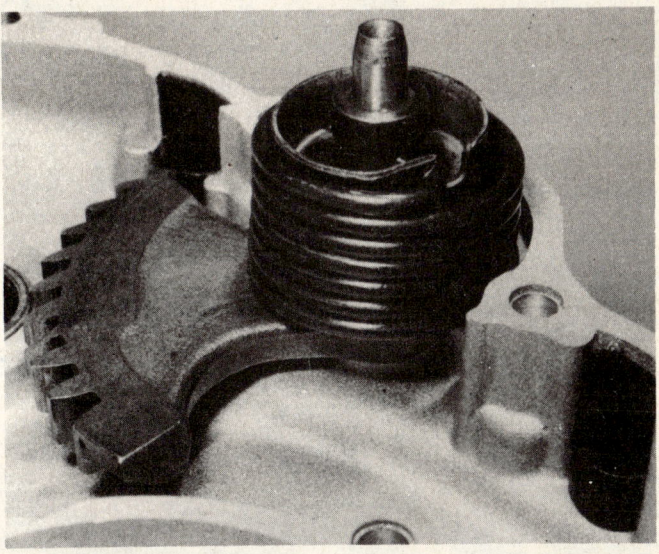

23.1 Check kickstart mechanism for wear. Renew rubber stops if worn or damaged

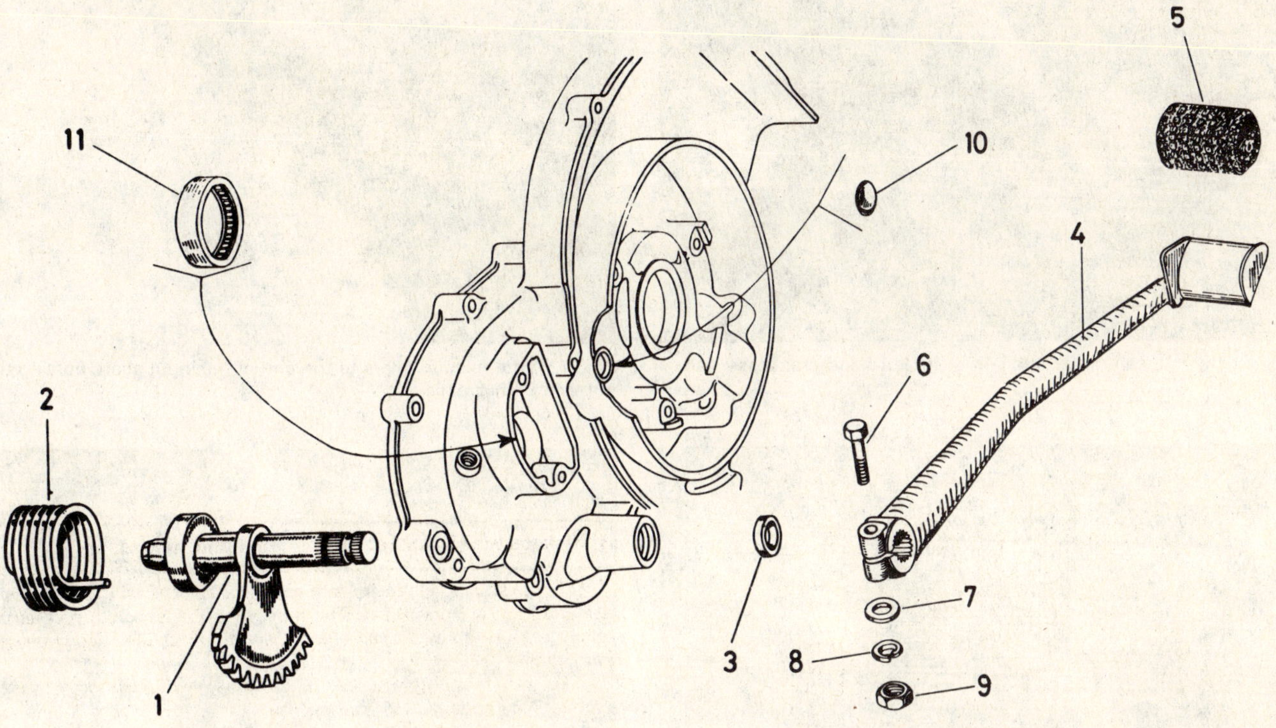

Fig. 1.11 Kickstart mechanism

1	Kickstart quadrant	5	Pedal rubber	9	Nut
2	Return spring	6	Bolt	10	Cap
3	Oil seal	7	Plain washer	11	Bearing
4	Kickstart pedal	8	Spring washer		

25 Engine reassembly: refitting the crankcase components

1   Support the crankcase left-hand half on wooden blocks, leaving sufficient space below it for the crankshaft end to protrude after fitting. Lubricate the lip of the main bearing oil seal. Offer up the crankshaft and push it fully home in the bearing. It is likely that it will be necessary to tap the crankshaft into place, and care must be taken to avoid distorting the assembly. A wedge should be fitted opposite the crankpin as described in the removal sequence. Place a length of tubing over the right-hand mainshaft end and use this to drive the crankshaft home.

2   If not yet in place, fit the needle rollers to the right-hand end of the input shaft, sticking them in place with grease. Offer up the input shaft, securing it with the tab washer and nut. Tighten the nut to 3.0 – 3.5 kgf m (21.7 – 25.3 lbf ft(then bend up the locking tab to secure it.

3   Install the output shaft assembly, tapping it fully home. At this stage, check that all four gear ratios select normally, operating the selector rod manually to obtain each one. If there are selection problems, check that the output shaft gears have been fitted correctly, resolving the problem before moving on.

4   Place the kickstart gear over the end of the input shaft, noting that the ratchet teeth must face the gear cluster. Fit the kickstart gear spring to the inside of the crankcase right-hand half, holding it in place with a dab of grease. Lubricate all shaft ends with clean engine oil. Before fitting the new crankcase gasket to the right-hand cover, check that the kickstart rubber stops are securely in place and that they do not protrude beyond the gasket face. Fit the new gasket, holding it in place with a film of grease or RTV jointing compound.

5   Offer up the crankcase right-hand half, lowering it into position over the shaft ends. Using the palm of the hand or a soft-faced mallet, gently tap the joint closed. Note that it will be necessary to temporarily refit the kickstart lever so that the quadrant can be moved slightly as the casing halves meet. This small amount of movement will allow the joint to close fully.

6   Fit the crankcase studs, washers and nuts, noting that the cable guide is fitted to the right-hand end of the longer stud. Tighten the nuts evenly and progressively, to prevent warpage. Check that the crankshaft assembly turns smoothly, with no sign of fouling on the crankcase. If necessary, separate the crankcase halves and check the crankshaft alignment before progressing further.

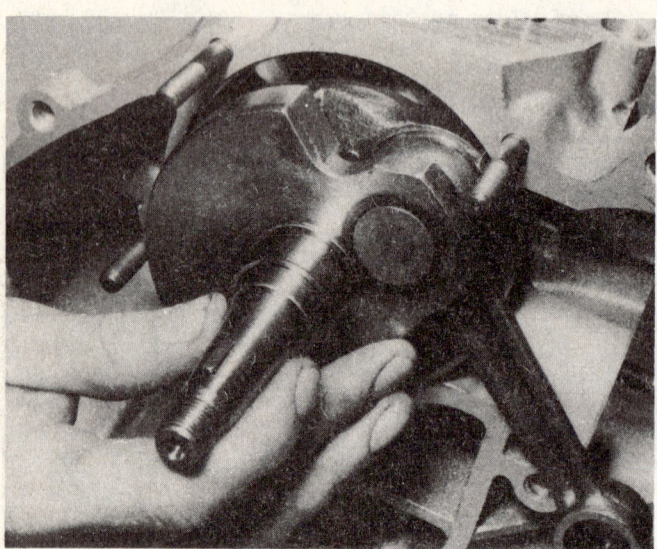

25.1 Fit the crankshaft assembly into the left-hand crankcase half

25.2a Fit the needle rollers to the end of the input shaft, holding them in place with grease

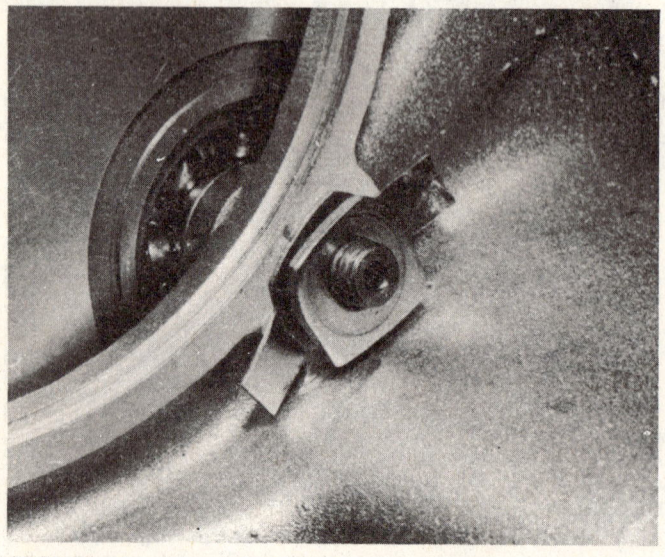

25.2b Fit tab washer and plain washer as shown ...

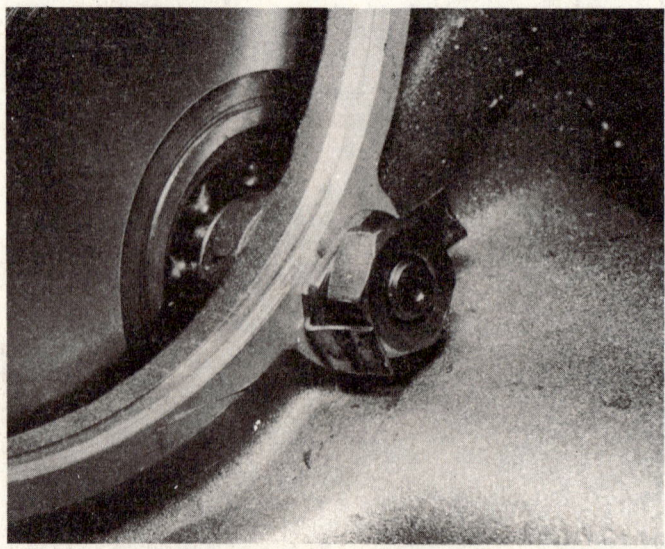

25.2c ... then tighten nut and bend up the locking tab

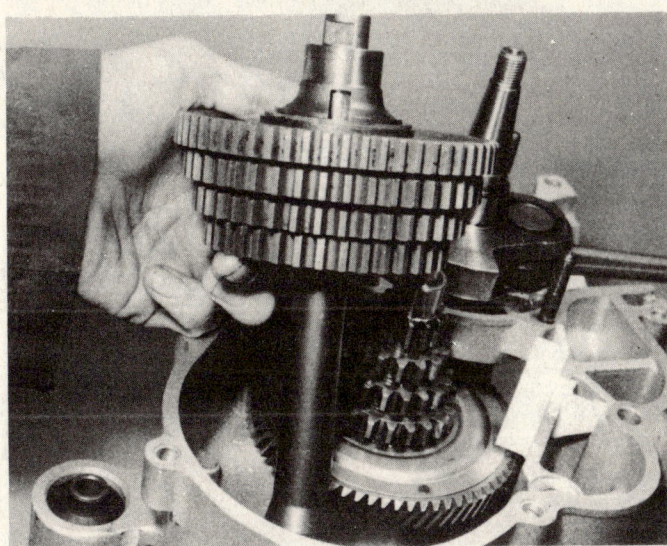

25.3 Fit the output shaft assembly as shown, then check gearbox operation

25.4a Fit kickstart gear over input shaft, ratchet teeth innermost

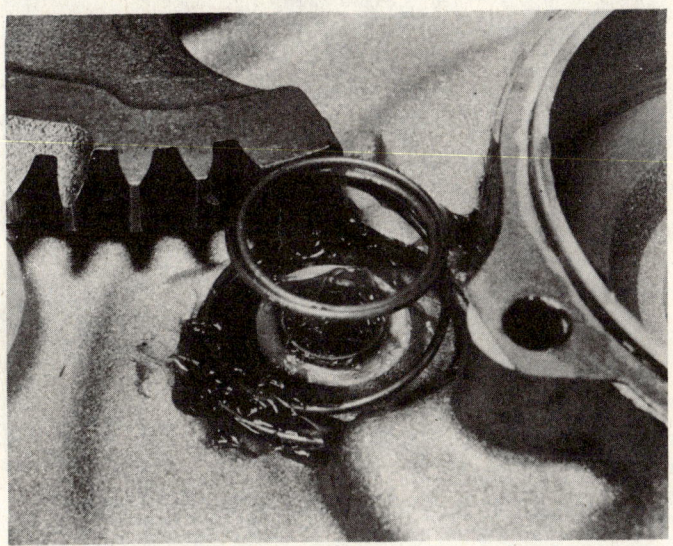

25.4b Hold kickstart spring in place with a dab of grease

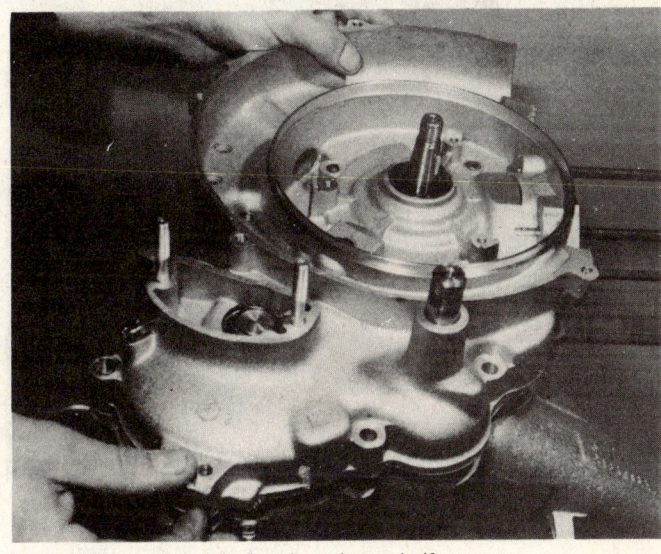

25.5a Offer up the right-hand crankcase half ...

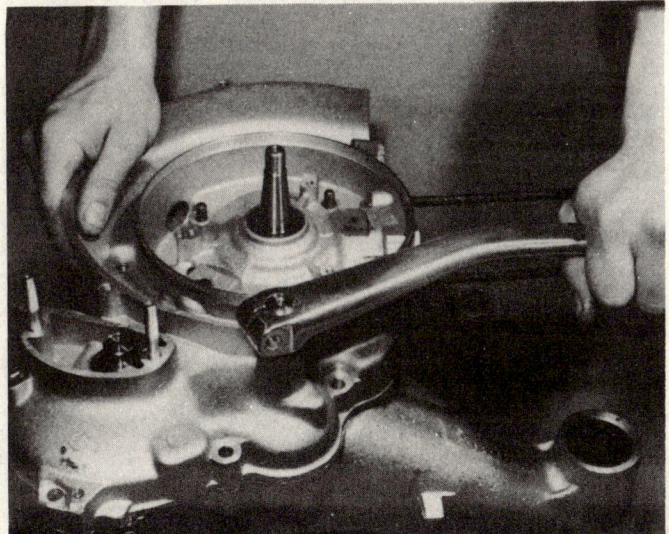

25.5b ... moving kickstart quadrant as shown to allow joint to seat fully

26 Engine reassembly: refitting the oil metering device drive and the clutch assembly

1   Fit the plain washer, driven gear and second plain washer to the stub inside the clutch housing, securing them with a new circlip. Place the metering device shaft in its bore, ensuring that the scroll meshes correctly. Fit the Woodruff key to its slot in the crankshaft end, then fit the metering device drive gear.

2   Offer up the assembled clutch, sliding it fully home on the crankshaft. Place the locking washer over the shaft end, then fit and tighten the slotted nut to 4.0 – 4.5 kgf m (28.9 – 32.5 lbf ft). Note that it will be necessary to lock the clutch while the nut is tightened, using the method employed during removal.

3   Refit the clutch release plate to the clutch drum, ensuring that the retaining clip engages correctly. Check that the short pushrod is in position inside the clutch cover, and that the O-ring is intact, then offer up the cover. Fit and tighten the cover bolts, tightening them to 1.6 – 2.0 kgf m (11.6 – 14.5 lbf ft).

26.1a Fit the plain washer to the stub inside the clutch housing ...

26.1b ... followed by the driven gear ...

26.1c ... a second washer and the circlip which retains them

26.1d Slide the metering device shaft into place

26.1e Fit the Woodruff key and the drive gear to the crankshaft

26.2a Offer up the assembled clutch ...

26.2b ... then fit the locking washer and retaining nut

26.2c Tighten the nut and secure it by bending over one of the locking tabs

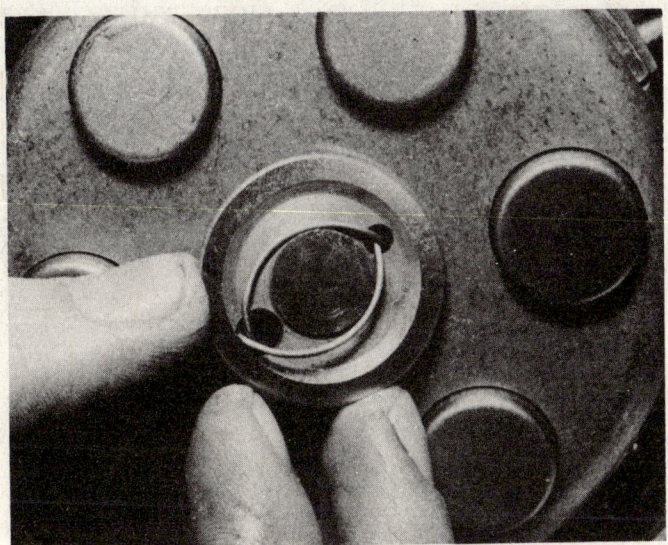

26.3a Fit the release plate to the clutch centre

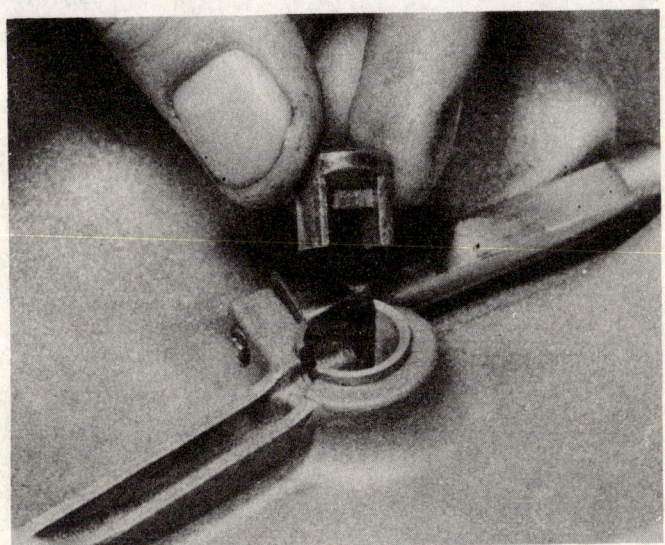

26.3b Check that the pushrod is in position and greased

26.3c Offer up the cover, using a new O-ring as required

27 Engine reassembly: refitting the oil metering device, carburettor and air filter casing

1   Place a new gasket on the crankcase mating face then offer up the lower section of the air cleaner casing, securing it with the single cheese-headed screw. Install the oil metering device gear, spring and washer. Fit the oil metering device cover, using a new gasket, and manoeuvre the oil pipe through the casing grommet. Secure the cover, tightening the screws evenly.

2   Offer up the carburettor, using a new gasket, and secure it with the two sleeve bolts. Where an oil metering device is fitted, connect the throttle valve wire to the oil metering device lever. If the engine unit is in the body section, the control cables, oil and fuel pipes, air filter element and cover can be refitted, otherwise leave these operations until the unit has been installed.

28 Engine reassembly: refitting the flywheel generator

1   Note that when the generator stator has been removed it is essential that the ignition timing is checked and reset during re-assembly. The procedure varies according to the model and ignition system fitted, and details will be found in Chapter 3 of this manual. It is stressed that inaccurate ignition timing will lead to poor running and may cause engine damage. This Section covers the refitting of the stator and rotor and describes the initial positioning of the rotor. The ignition timing must be checked properly once the engine unit is installed.

2   Offer up the stator assembly, feeding the leads up through the tunnel in the casing. Place the stator in position and fit the retaining screws finger tight. On machines with contact breaker ignition, align the reference marks made during removal, then tighten the screws. On P200 E models, line up the raised timing marks. In the case of the PX models, align the stator '1T' mark (PX125 E and PX150 E) or the 'A' mark (PX200 E) with the fixed mark on the crankcase.

3   Clean the crankshaft taper, fit the Wodruff key in its slot, then offer up the rotor, shakeproof washer and retaining nut. Lock the crankshaft to prevent it turning, then fit and tighten the nut. The final torque figure is 6.0 – 6.5 kgf m (43.4 – 47.0 lbf ft), but it is suggested that the nut is not tightened fully until the timing has been checked.

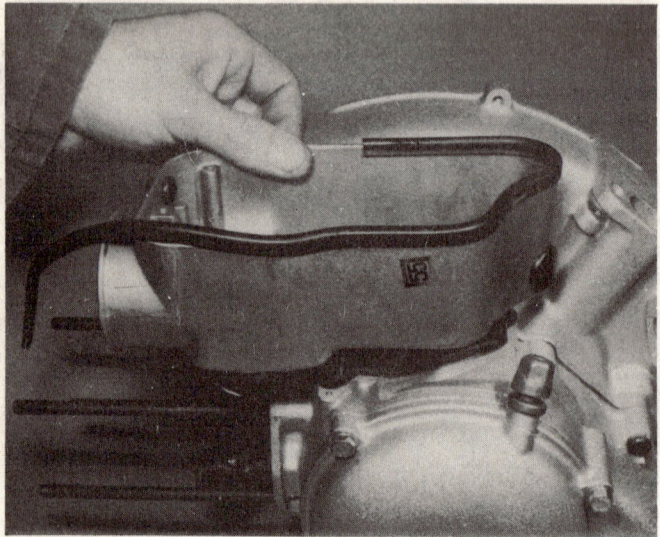

27.1a Fit the lower section of the air filter casing, using a new gasket

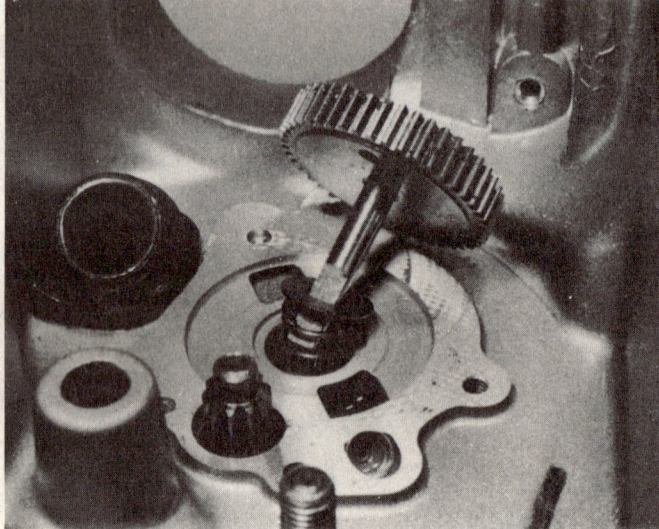

27.1b Install the spring, washer and gear as shown and fit a new gasket to the cover

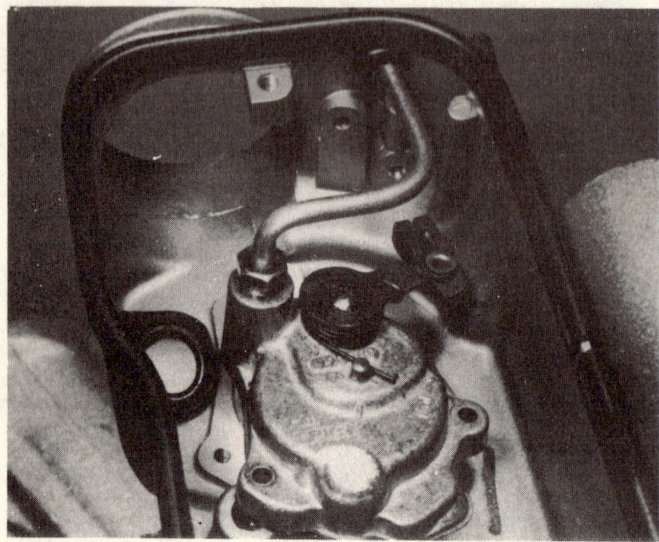

27.1c Offer up the cover, manoeuvring the pipe through the casing grommet

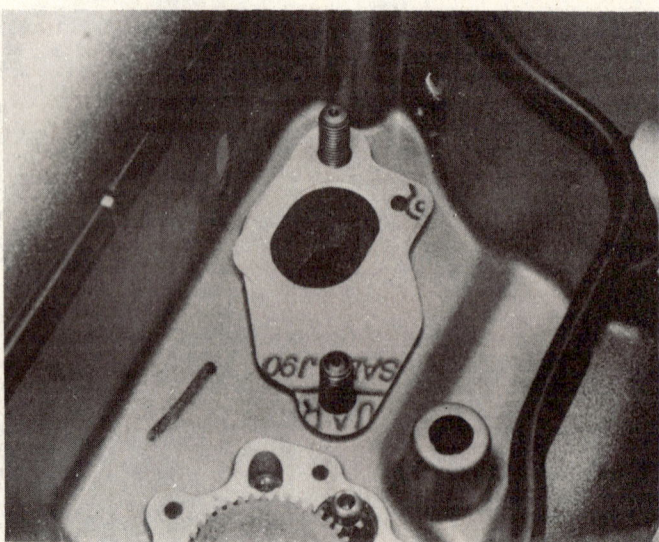

27.2a Fit a new gasket and install the carburettor ...

27.2b ... hooking throttle wire (arrowed) over metering device lever

28.2a Offer up the alternator stator, feeding the wiring through the tunnel in the crankcase

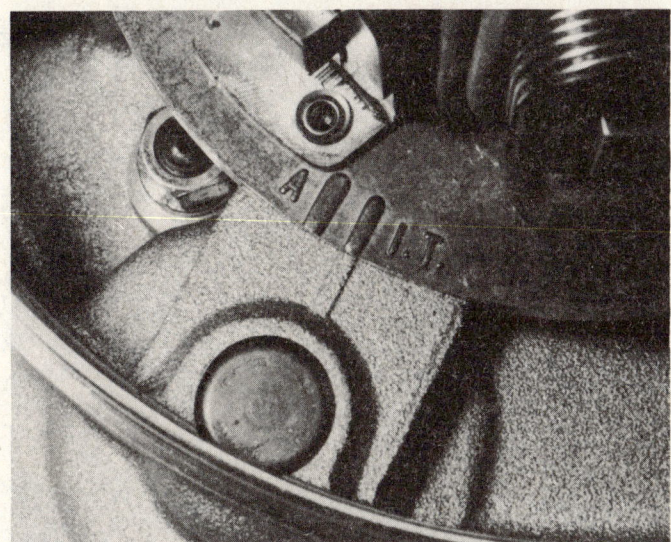

28.2b Align the timing mark (PX125/150 E shown) ...

28.2c ... then tighten stator screws

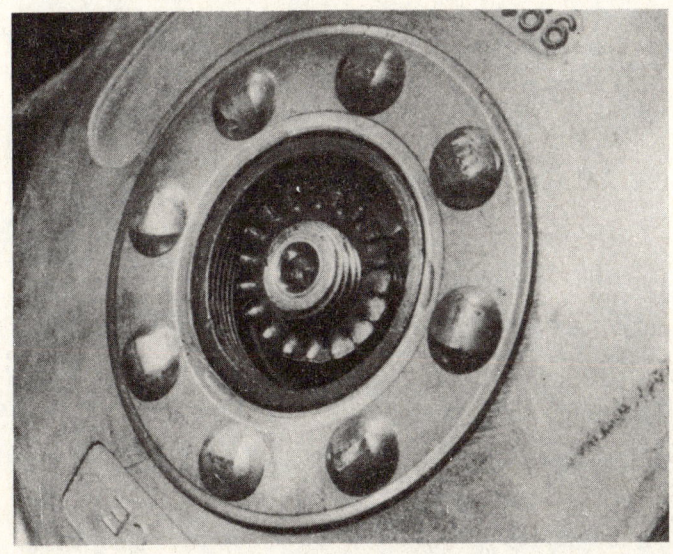

28.3a Fit rotor and shakeproof washer

28.3b Secure the nut and fit plastic cap

29 Engine reassembly: refitting the piston, cylinder barrel and cylinder head

1   Pack some clean rag into the crankcase mouth to prevent dirt or dropped circlips from entering the crankcase. Fit the needle roller bearing into the connecting rod small-end eye and lubricate it with engine oil. Offer up the piston and slide the gudgeon pin into place to retain it. If necessary, warm the piston in very hot water to ease fitting, but remember to dry it off thoroughly. Retain the gudgeon pin using **new** circlips.

2   Examine carefully the aluminium cylinder base gasket. If it is in good condition it can be re-used, but normally it is good practice to renew it as a precaution. Slide the gasket into position over the holding studs.

3   Check that the cylinder bore is clean, then lubricate it and the piston with engine oil. Arrange the piston rings so that the ends are located against the small pegs. Offer up the barrel, noting that the exhaust port faces downwards, then guide the piston into the bore by hand.

4   The barrel has a tapered lead-in at the bottom of the bore, and this will help to guide the rings home. The rings should be compressed slightly as the barrel is slid into place, and a careful check should be kept to ensure that the rings remain correctly positioned in relation to their location pegs. Once the rings have entered the bore, remove the rag from the crankcase mouth and slide the barrel down against the base gasket.

5   Clean the mating surfaces of the barrel and cylinder head, then fit the head over the studs, noting that the spark plug should face upwards. Fit the plain washers, shakeproof washers and the head nuts. The nuts should be tightened progressively, in a diagonal sequence, to prevent warpage, turning each nut by a quarter turn at a time. The final torque figure is 1.3 - 1.8 kgf m (9.4 -13.0 lbf ft) for the 125 and 150 models, and 1.7 - 2.2 kgf m (12.3 - 15.9 lbf ft) for the 200 models.

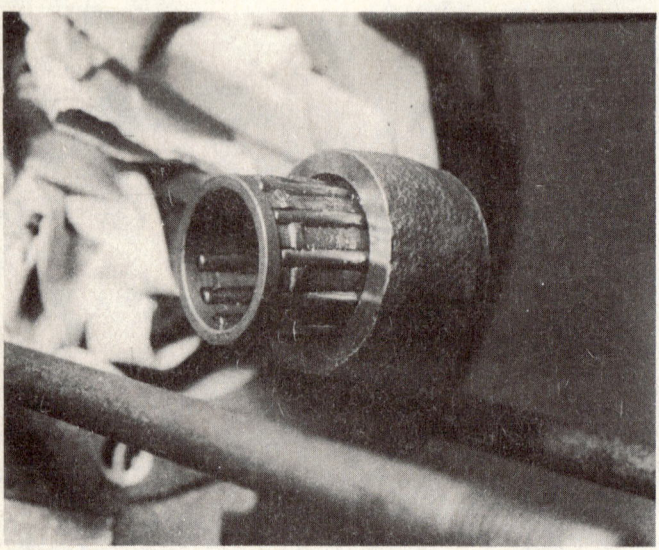

29.1a Pack crankcase mouth with rag, then fit small-end bearing

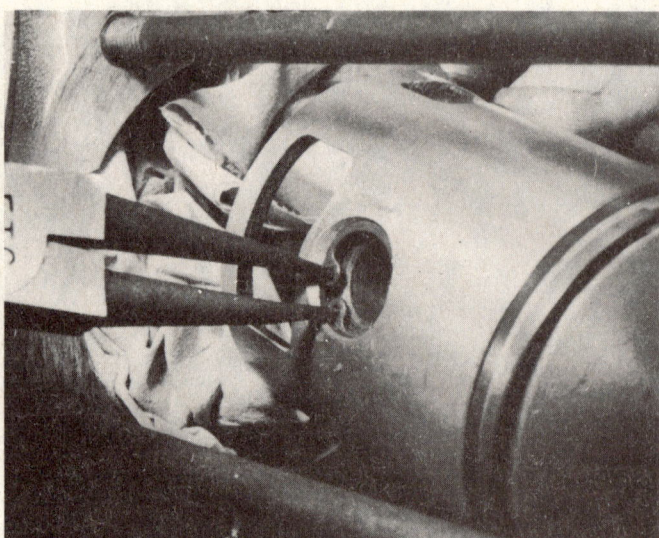

29.1b Fit piston with arrow facing downwards, and secure with new circlips

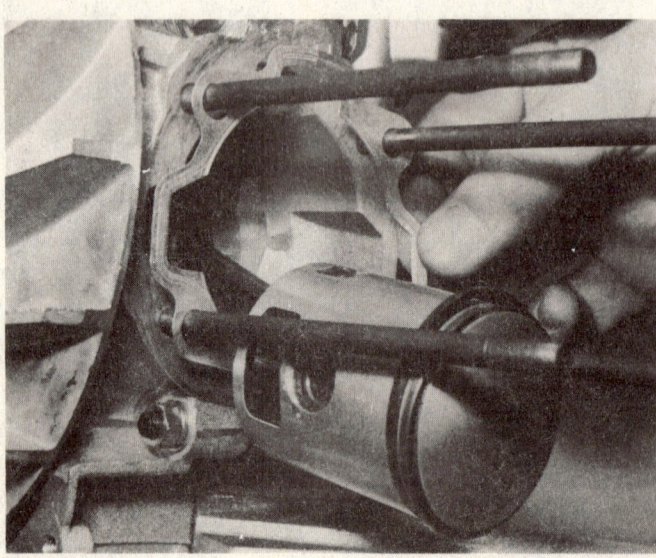

29.2 Remove rag from crankcase and fit base gasket

29.3 Feed piston into bore, then slide it home against the crankcase

29.5 Tighten head nuts in sequence shown to prevent warpage

30 Fitting the engine/transmission unit into the frame

1   If it was removed in the course of the overhaul, the rear brake assembly and the rear wheel can be refitted at this stage. See Chapter 5 for further details. Offer up the exhaust system, securing it with the clamp bolt at the exhaust port and the single fixing bolt which secures the silencer to the swinging arm cross member.

2   The engine/transmission unit can be fitted single-handed, but it is considerably easier if an assistant is available to help guide it into place. Check that all cables and electrical leads are well clear of the engine as it is moved into position, and tie the rear suspension unit to the rear of the machine with wire to allow the wheel to be slid into place.

3   It will be necessary to tip the unit slightly so that the rear wheel can be manoeuvred under the rear of the body. Once this is partly in position, lift the front of the unit into place, taking care not to damage the paintwork near the cylinder recess.

4   Release the wire holding the rear suspension unit, then fit it over the lower mounting. Slip the bolt into position to hold it. Lift the front cross member into position between the lower edges of the body, using a screwdriver to align it with the pivot bolt holes. Push the greased pivot bolt through from the right-hand side, rocking the unit as necessary to allow the threaded end to emerge. Fit the pivot bolt plain

Fig. 1.12 Gear selector box

1 Cover	11 Gear selector box
2 Pin	12 Nut
3 Block	13 Spring washer
4 Ratchet block	14 Plain washer
5 Tapered pin	15 Gasket
6 Special screw	16 Oil filler/level plug
7 Ratchet plate	17 Sealing washer
8 Spring	18 Drain plug
9 Adjuster	19 Sealing washer
10 Locknut	20 Stud

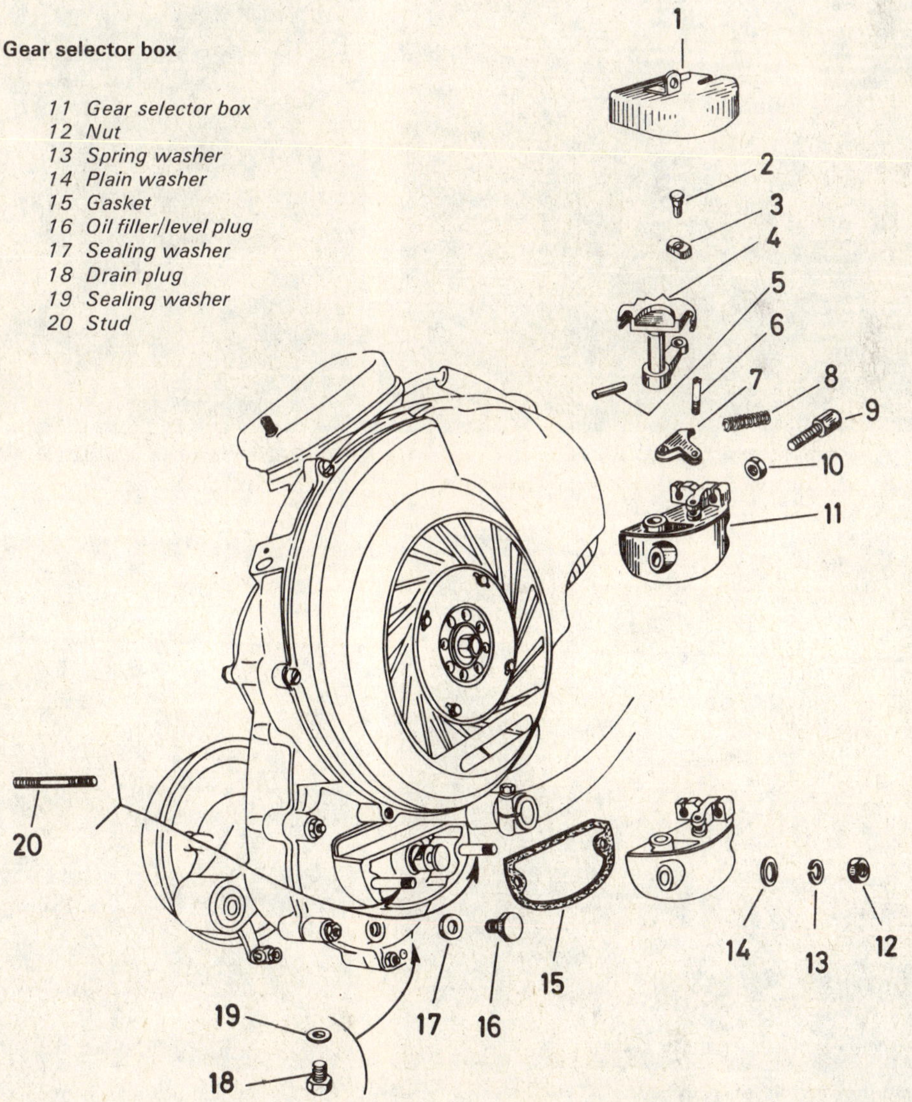

washer, shakeproof washer and retaining nut, tightening it to 6.1 - 7.5 kgf m (44.1 - 54.3 lbf ft). Fit the rear suspension unit lower mounting washers and nut, noting that the correct torque setting is 1.3 - 2.3 kgf m (9.4 - 16.6 lbf ft).

5   Reconnect the rear brake and clutch cables. In the case of the rear brake cable, screw the adjuster fully home, then position the cable inner in its clamp to give about 2-3 mm free play. Check that the wheel will turn freely, but that the brake commences operation soon after the pedal begins to move. When fitting the clutch cable, thread the inner through the lever end, then position the solderless nipple to give about 1-2 mm free play at the end of the handlebar lever. Refit the kickstart lever, tightening the pinch bolt securely. The prescribed torque figure is 2.3 - 2.6 kgf m (16.6 - 18.8 lbf ft).

6   Turn the handlebar gear selector control well beyond the 4th gear position and check that the selector rod is pulled fully outwards. Fit a new gasket over the selector box holding stub. Engage the pivoting block at the end of the selector box bellcrank in the grooved end of the selector rod. Turn the handlebar selector control back towards the 1st gear position to draw the box over the holding studs, then fit and tighten the washers and retaining nuts. Route the gearchange cables through the guide.

7   Reconnect the generator output and ignition coil leads at the crankcase-mounted junction box, then refit it to the crankcase. Pass the fuel pipe into the air filter casing and reconnect it to its stub. Where applicable, reconnect the oil feed pipe to the external stub. Refit the air filter element, followed by the casing lid.

8   Check that the transmission oil drain plug is secure, then remove the small filler plug and top up with SAE 30 motor oil or SAE 80 gear oil until it just emerges from the filler hole. It is a good idea to allow the machine to stand for a few minutes until any surplus oil has drained off. Topping up is made easier using a syringe or small funnel.

9   On machines fitted with a metered engine oil supply, note that the initial filling of fuel should be a 2% (50:1) mixture of petrol and self-mixing two-stroke oil. This is because the oil system will take some time to prime itself. The additional oil will obviate any risk of seizure while this takes place, but may cause some exhaust smoke for a while.

10   The engine should now be started and test run as described below, and the ignition timing checked. This procedure is described in Chapter 2. Check the engine idle speed once it has warmed up, and set it to the lowest reliable idle using the throttle stop screw which protrudes through the air filter lid.

11   After the timing has been checked, refit the fan and cylinder cowling. Recheck the transmission oil level and the various cable adjustments, then road-test the machine.

30.1 Refit exhaust system, tightening clamp securely

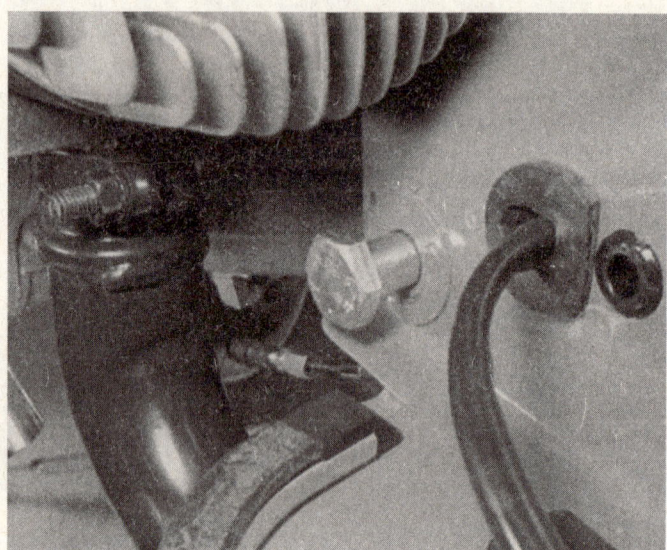
30.4 Grease pivot bolt and slide it into place

30.6 Refit selector box and fit retaining nuts

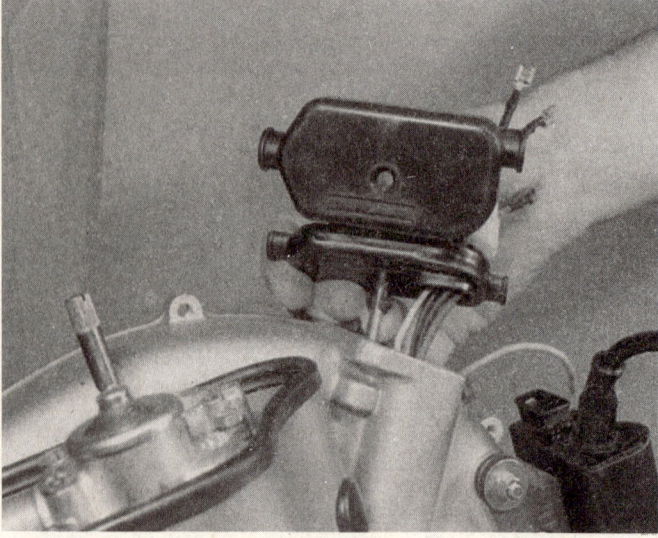
30.7a Fit junction box and reconnect wiring

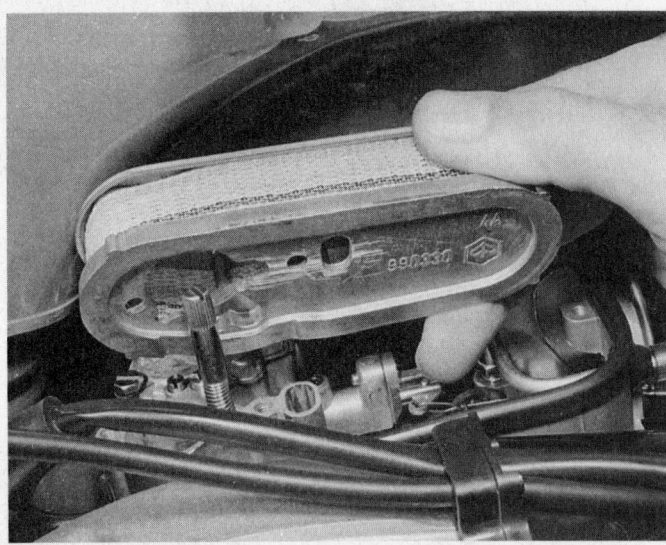

30.7b Fit fuel and oil pipes, then install air filter and cover

31 Starting and running the rebuilt engine

1   Attempt to start the engine using the usual procedure adopted for a cold engine. Do not be disillusioned if there is no sign of life initially. A certain amount of perseverance may prove necessary to coax the engine into activity even if new parts have not been fitted. Should the engine persist in not starting, check that the spark plug has not become fouled by the oil used during re-assembly. Failing this, go through the fault finding charts and work out what the problem is methodically.

2   When the engine does start, keep it running as slowly as possible to allow the oil to circulate. Open the choke as soon as the engine will run without it. During the initial running, a certain amount of smoke may be in evidence due to the oil used in the reassembly sequence being burnt away. The resulting smoke should gradually subside.

3   Check the engine for blowing gaskets and oil leaks. Before using the machine on the road, check that all the gears select properly, and that the controls function correctly.

32 Taking the rebuilt machine on the road

1   Any rebuilt machine will need time to settle down, even if parts have been replaced in their original order. For this reason it is highly advisable to treat the machine gently for the first few miles to ensure oil has circulated throughout the lubrication system and that new parts fitted have begun to bed down.

2   Even greater care is necessary if the engine has been rebored or if a new crankshaft has been fitted. In the case of a rebore, the engine will have to be run in again, as if the machine were new. This means greater use of the gearbox and a restraining hand on the throttle until at least 500 miles have been covered. There is no point in keeping to any set speed limit; the main requirement is to keep a light loading on the engine and to gradually work up performance until the 500 mile mark is reached. These recommendations can be lessened to an extent when only a new crankshaft is fitted. Experience is the best guide since it is easy to tell when an engine is running freely.

3   Remember that a good seal between the piston and the cylinder barrel is essential for the correct functioning of the engine. A rebored two-stroke engine will require more careful running-in, over a long period, than its four-stroke counterpart. There is a far greater risk of engine seizure during the first hundred miles if the engine is permitted to work hard.

4   If at any time a lubrication failure is suspected, stop the engine immediately and investigate the cause. If an engine is run without oil, even for a short period, irreparable engine damage is inevitable.

5   Do not tamper with the exhaust system or run the engine without the baffle fitted to the silencer. Unwarranted changes in the exhaust system will have a marked effect on engine performance, invariably for the worse. The same advice applies to dispensing with the air cleaner or the air cleaner element.

6   When the initial run has been completed allow the engine unit to cool and then check all the fittings and fasteners for security. Re-adjust any controls which may have settled down during initial use.

Chapter 2 Fuel system and lubrication

For information relating to later models see Chapter 7

Contents

Specifications

Fuel tank capacity
Overall .... 8 litres (1.76 Imp gallons)
Reserve (not applicable to models with fuel gauge) .... 2 litres (0.46 Imp gallons)

Fuel grade .... Leaded (unleaded suitable for 1980-on models)

Carburettor

	P125 X	PX125 E
Make	Dell'Orto	Dell'Orto
Type	SI 20/20 D	SI 20/20 D
Venturi size	20 mm (0.79 in)	20 mm (0.79 in)
Main jet:		
Without automatic mixer	98/100	100/100
With automatic mixer	98/100	99/100
Slow running jet:		
Without idle air hole	48/100	45/100
With idle air hole	160/100	140/100
Air jet	160/100	160/100
Throttle valve	6823.01	6823.08
Mixer tube	BE 3	BE 5
Atomiser	280/100	280/100
Starter jet	60/100	60/100

Carburettor	P150 X	PX150 E
Make	Dell'Orto	Dell'Orto
Type	SI 20/20 D	SI 20/20 D
Venturi size	20 mm (0.79 in)	20 mm (0.79 in)
Main jet:		
Without mixer device	102/100	102/100
With mixer device	116/100	100/100
Slow running jet:		
Without idle air hole	48/100	48/100
With idle air hole	160/100	160/100
Air jet	160/100	160/100
Throttle valve	6823.01	6823.01
Mixer tube	BE 3	BE 3
Atomiser	280/100	280/100
Starter jet	60/100	60/100

Carburettor	P200 E	PX200 E
Make	Dell'Orto	Dell'Orto
Type	SI 24/24 E	SI 24/24 E
Venturi size	24 mm (0.95 in)	24 mm (0.95 in)
Main jet:		
Without mixer device	118/100	118/100
With mixer device	116/100	116/100
Slow running jet:		
Without idle air hole	55/100	55/100
With idle air hole	160/100	160/100
Air jet	160/100	160/100
Throttle valve	8492.4	8492.04
Mixer tube	BE 3	BE 3
Atomiser	300/100	300/100
Starter jet	60/100	60/100

Air filter

Type .... Pleated fabric and gauze

Engine lubrication

Type .... Pre-mixed petrol and oil (petroil) or optional gravity-fed metered oil supply by 'LS' device

Pre-mix petrol/oil ratio .... 50 : 1 (2%)

Oil grade (all models) .... Good quality two-stroke oil

Gearbox lubrication

Oil grade .... SAE 30 motor oil or SAE 80 gear oil

Capacity .... To level hole

Torque wrench settings

Carburettor sleeve nuts .... 1.6 - 2.0 kgf m (11.57 - 14.47 lbf ft)

1 General description

The fuel system comprises a fuel tank contained within the main body section from which fuel is fed by gravity to the float chamber of the carburettor via a three position tap. The 'Off', 'On' the 'Reserve' (where applicable) positions of the tap are controlled from a remote tap lever which projects from the body below the dual seat. A separate cable-operated choke knob controls the cold start circuit, providing the enriched mixture required for this purpose.

The carburettor is a downdraught slide-type instrument housed in a cast alloy casing mounted on the top of the crankcase. The casing also houses the oil metering device, where fitted, and the air filter element, air being drawn from inside the body via a large intake hose. This arrangement ensures that air entering the engine is free of airborne dust which might otherwise cause engine wear, and also serves to silence induction noise.

Like all two-stroke engines, the Vespa unit employs a system of ports in the cylinder barrel which control induction timing. As a supplement to this, one of the engine flywheels is carefully machined to function as a disc valve. This allows much closer control of the incoming mixture than would otherwise be possible, and has been used to good effect in extracting the maximum useful power from the engine over a wide range of engine speeds.

After combustion has taken place, the exhaust gases are expelled through a compact one-piece exhaust system mounted below the engine/transmission unit. The system serves to reduce exhaust noise and provides the necessary degree of back pressure required to balance the induction system.

The crankcase components are lubricated either by a small amount of oil mixed with the fuel which is deposited inside the engine during combustion, or by an optional oil metering system. This latter arrangement allows a suitable amount of oil to flow by gravity from a separate oil tank through a throttle-controlled metering system to the engine. This ensures that the exact amount of oil is available at all engine speeds, and obviates the need for pre-mixing fuel and oil. Note that it is almost impossible to say which models have been equipped with this system, it having been an option for some years. Those machines so equipped can be recognised by the oil tank filler cap below the seat and by the oil level sight glass near the fuel tap lever.

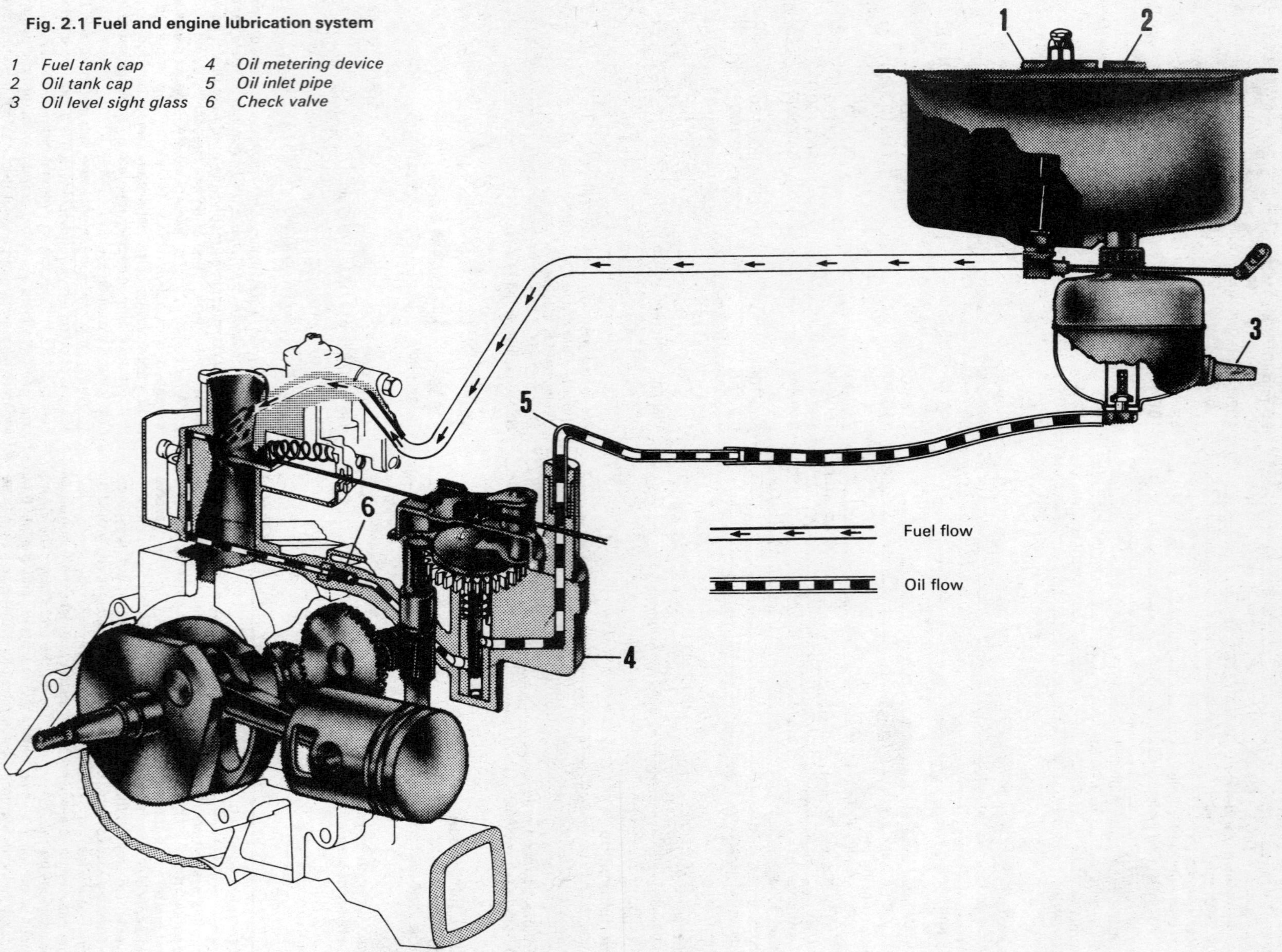

Fig. 2.1 Fuel and engine lubrication system

1 Fuel tank cap
2 Oil tank cap
3 Oil level sight glass
4 Oil metering device
5 Oil inlet pipe
6 Check valve

Fuel flow

Oil flow

2 Fuel tank: removal and refitting

1   Check that the fuel tap is turned to the 'Off' position, and remove the right-hand side panel. Remove the air filter cover and element to gain access to the fuel pipe. Squeeze together the 'ears' of the pipe retaining clip and slide this clear of the stub, then work the pipe off the stub using a screwdriver. Pull the pipe out through the grommet in the side of the air filter casing and push it through into the body section. On machines fitted with the oil metering system, disconnect the oil feed pipe at the stub, plugging the pipe with a bolt or similar to retain the oil. Push the pipe through into the body.

2   Remove the bolts which secure the dual seat to the body and lift it away, together with the helmet hook bracket, where fitted. On PX models it will be necessary to turn the side panel catches outwards to clear the seat bracket. Where the machine is equipped with a fuel gauge, pull out the fuel gauge wiring grommet to reveal the wiring connector, then separate the wiring at the connector.

3   Unscrew the remaining tank fixing bolts, then remove the grommet from around the tap lever shaft, and the oil tank sight glass, if applicable. The tank can now be lifted out of the body section, together with the oil tank, where fitted. If the tank is stuck to the gasket it may first be necessary to carefully work it free using a screwdriver. Take care not to damage the paint finish. As the tank comes free, guide the tap lever through the hole in the body.

4   If it is necessary to separate the fuel and oil tanks, a special wrench, Part Number T.0062850 will be required. Failing this, a socket can be used, but note that sufficient extension bars to reach from the oil filler cap to the base of the tank will be required. Once the oil pipe union bolt is released, the large knurled plastic ring at the neck of the oil tank can be released and the tanks separated. The oil tank is fitted by reversing the above procedure. Note that the oil pipe should be positioned so that it faces forward before the union nut is secured.

5   Reassembly is a straightforward reversal of the removal sequence. Before the tank is lowered into place, check that the fuel and oil pipes are pushed through their respective grommets. As the tank is positioned, guide the tap lever through the hole in the body.

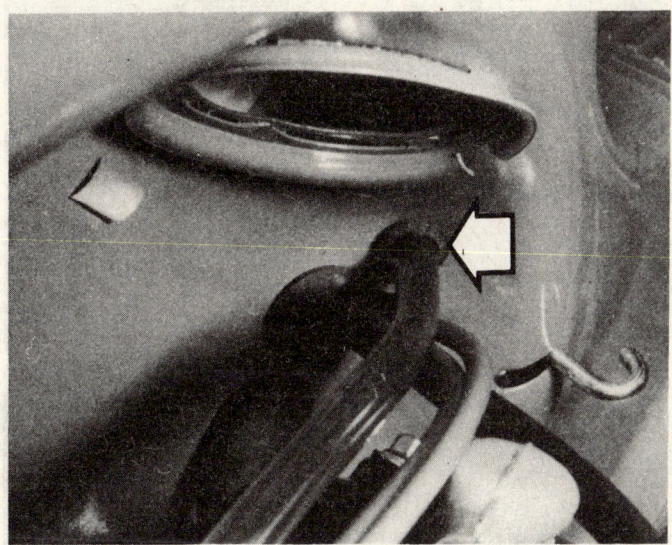

2.1 Disconnect the fuel pipe and push through grommet (arrowed) into body

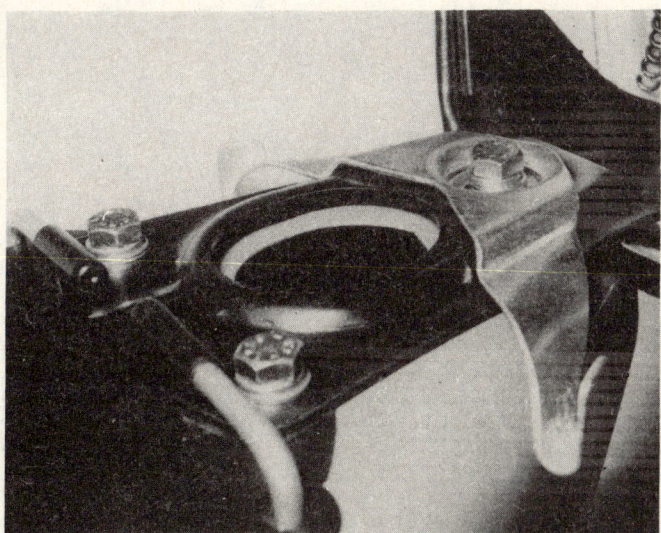

2.2a Remove the three seat hinge bolts and remove seat

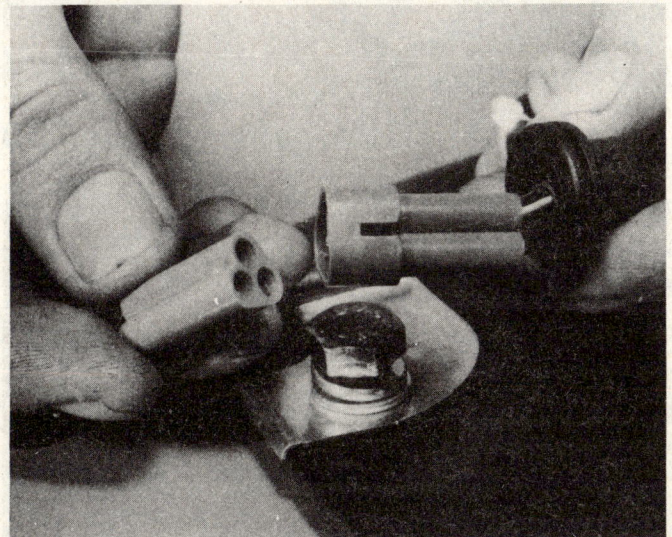

2.2b Disconnect fuel gauge wiring (where fitted)

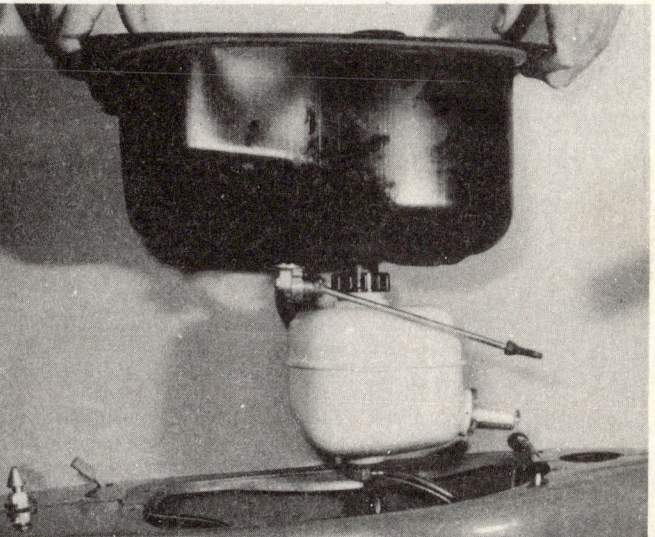

2.3 Fuel tank can now be removed, together with oil tank (where fitted)

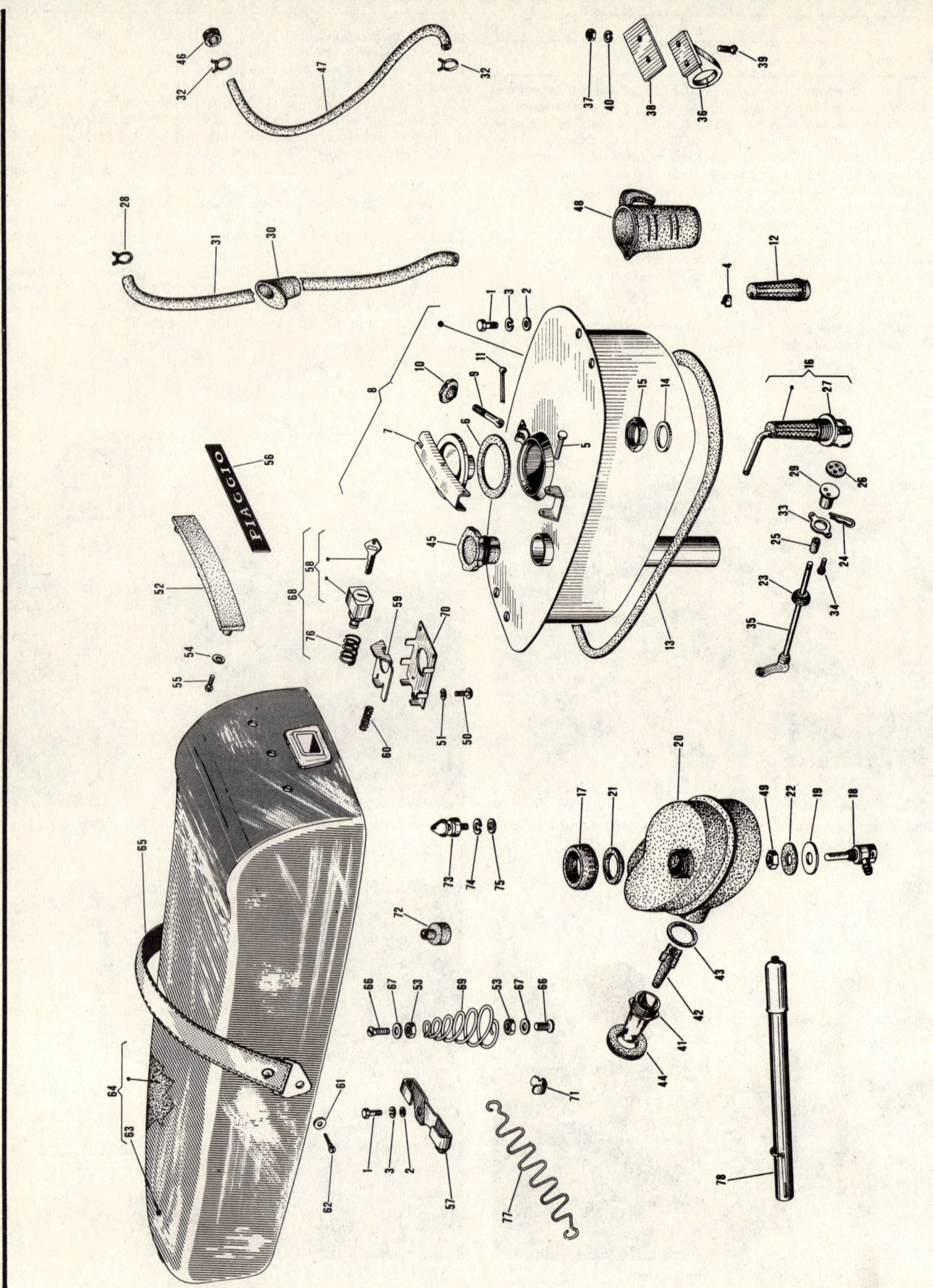

Fig. 2.2 Fuel tank, oil tank and dualseat

1	Bolt	27	Tap body	53	Nut
2	Plain washer	28	Clip	54	Washer
3	Spring washer	29	Tap rotor	55	Screw
4	Clip	30	Grommet	56	Badge
5	Pivot pin	31	Fuel pipe	57	Helmet hook
6	Sealing ring	32	Clip	58	Seat lock barrel
7	Fuel filler cap	33	Plate	59	Latch plate
8	Fuel tank assembly	34	Screw	60	Spring
9	Threaded pin	35	Tap lever	61	Washer
10	Knurled nut	36	Luggage hook	62	Screw
11	Split pin	37	Nut	63	Seat cover
12	Fuel filter	38	Plate	64	Seat assembly
13	Fuel tank gasket	39	Screw	65	Strap
14	Sealing washer	40	Spring washer	66	Screw
15	Nut	41	Oil sight glass	67	Washer
16	Fuel tap assembly	42	Insert	68	Seat lock assembly
17	Knurled ring	43	Sealing washer	69	Seat spring
18	Union	44	Grommet	70	Lock base
19	Washer	45	Oil filler cap	71	Clip
20	Oil tank	46	Grommet	72	Buffer
21	Sealing washer	47	Oil pipe	73	Latch pillar
22	Sealing washer	48	Measuring jug	74	Spring washer
23	Grommet	49	Nut	75	Plain washer
24	R-pin	50	Screw	76	Lock barrel spring
25	Sleeve	51	Washer	77	Seat spring
26	Tap seal	52	Backing piece	78	Tyre pump

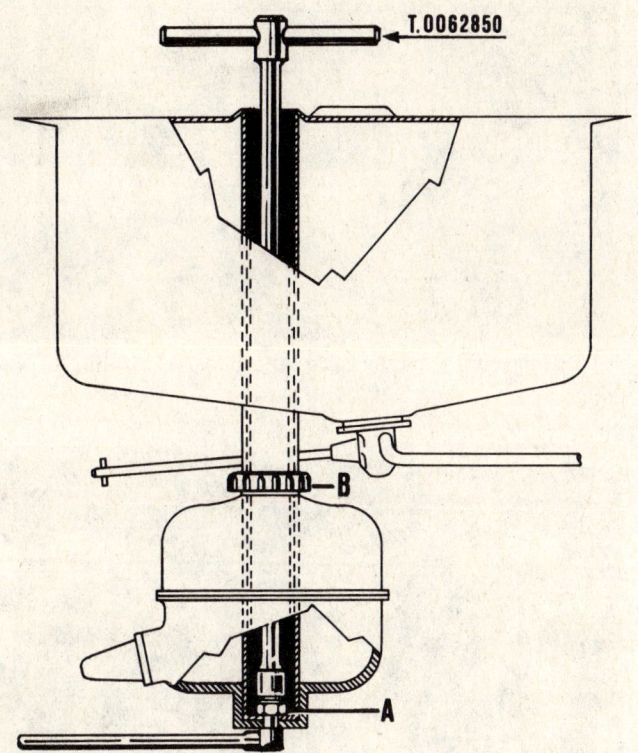

Fig. 2.3 Oil and fuel tank separation

A   Oil tank union nut   B   Knurled ring

---

3 Fuel tap: removal and refitting

1   The fuel tap is mounted on the underside of the fuel tank and is secured by a large diameter nut fitted on the inside of the tank. Before attempting removal, a special wrench, Part Number T 0032973, will be essential to release the nut. This can be purchased through (or perhaps borrowed from) a Vespa dealer, and is not too expensive. Most fuel tap faults can be attended to with the tap attached to the tank, as described below.

2   Remove the fuel tank as described in Section 2, then drain the tank contents into a metal can. The tap lever can be removed, if necessary, by pulling out the R-pin which retains it. Remove the two screws which retain the tap cover plate and pull out the tap rotor. If the tap has been leaking, the most likely cause of problems is the seal. If this is scored or damaged it should be prised out and renewed. The tap can now be assembled by reversing the dismantling sequence. Do not overtighten the two cover plate screws, and check that the tap turns smoothly before refitting the tank.

3   If tap removal is unavoidable, use the special wrench inserted through the tank filler hole to release the retaining nut and lift the body clear of the tank base. When refitting the tap body, use a new sealing washer to avoid any risk of subsequent leakage.

3.2a Remove cover plate screws and lift away tap lever ...

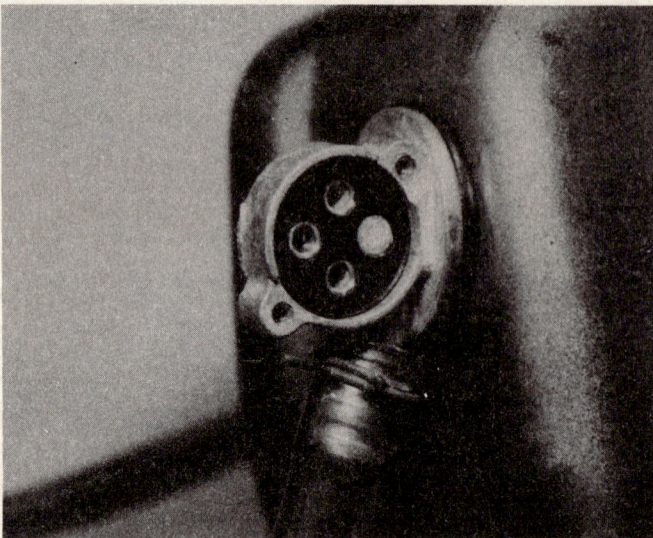

3.2b ... to gain access to tap seal

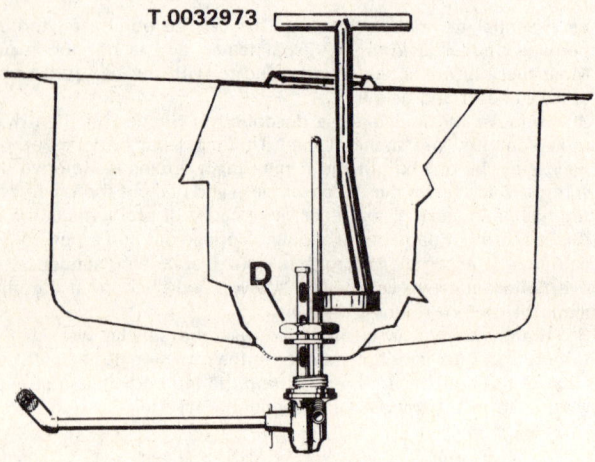

T.0032973

Fig. 2.4 Fuel tap removal using special tool

D   Tap securing nut

4   Fuel feed pipe: renewal

1   The fuel pipe is made from translucent plastic and is of the push-on type, secured with wire retaining clips. The condition of the pipe should be checked periodically, and it should be renewed if it becomes brittle or shows signs of splitting. Note that because part of the pipe is inside the body there is a risk of leakage not being obvious at the tap end.

2   To renew the pipe it will first be necessary to remove the fuel tank as described in Section 2. Use only the correct fuel pipe as a replacement; it is possible to buy pipe of the correct size that is not resistant to fuel. This will rapidly become brittle as the plasticiser is leached out by the fuel, and so should be avoided. On no account should natural rubber tubing be used, even as a temporary measure. This material will dissolve in fuel leaving a sticky deposit throughout the fuel system and carburettor.

5   Carburettor: removal and refitting

1   Remove the right-hand side panel, then remove the lid of the air filter casing and the filter element to reveal the carburettor. Unhook the throttle cable. This is attached to the oil metering unit lever, where fitted, or direct to the throttle slide operating rod on models with pre-mix lubrication. Disconnect the choke cable from the end of the plunger unit. Check that the fuel tap lever is turned to the 'Off' position.

2   Slacken and remove the two sleeve nuts which retain the carburettor to its mounting studs. Lift the instrument slightly to gain access to the fuel pipe clip. Grasp the ends of the clip and squeeze them together to allow it to be slid down the pipe. Using a screwdriver, work the pipe off its stub. On models with a metered oil supply, disengage the throttle slide operating rod from the lever. The carburettor can now be lifted clear of the casing.

3   The carburettor is installed by reversing the removal sequence, using a new gasket on the mounting flange. The two sleeve bolts should be tightened evenly and not excessively, to avoid warping the carburettor mounting flange. Once the carburettor and air filter cover have been installed and the cover refitted, check the pilot mixture and idle speed adjustments as described later in this Chapter.

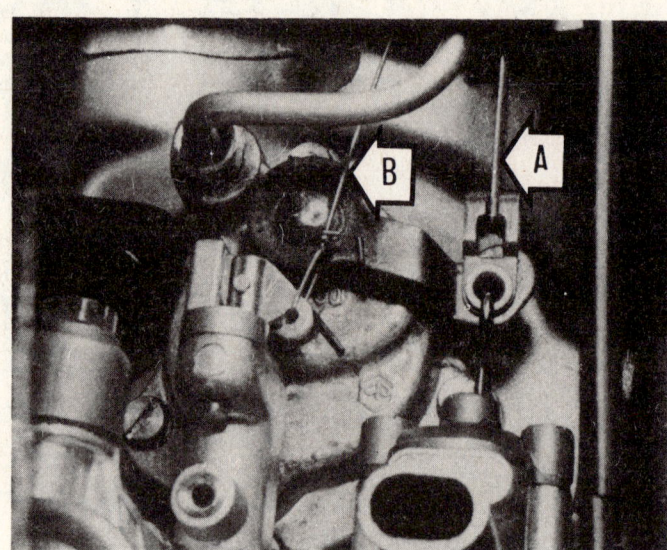

5.1 Disconnect the throttle cable (A) and choke cable (B)

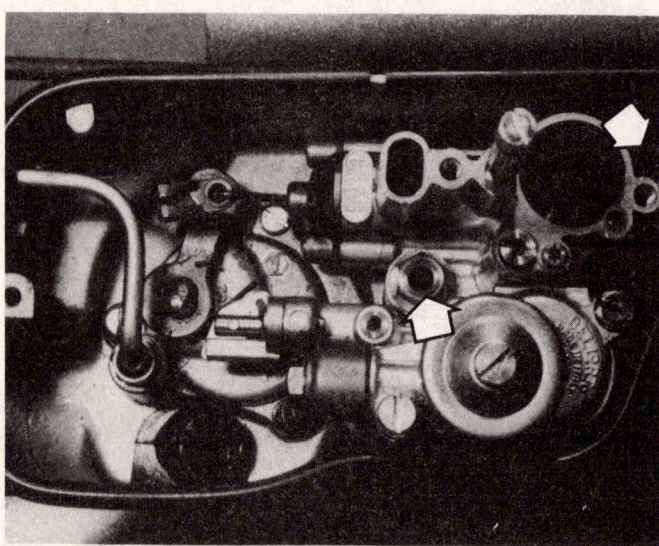

5.2 Carburettor is retained by two sleeve nuts (arrowed)

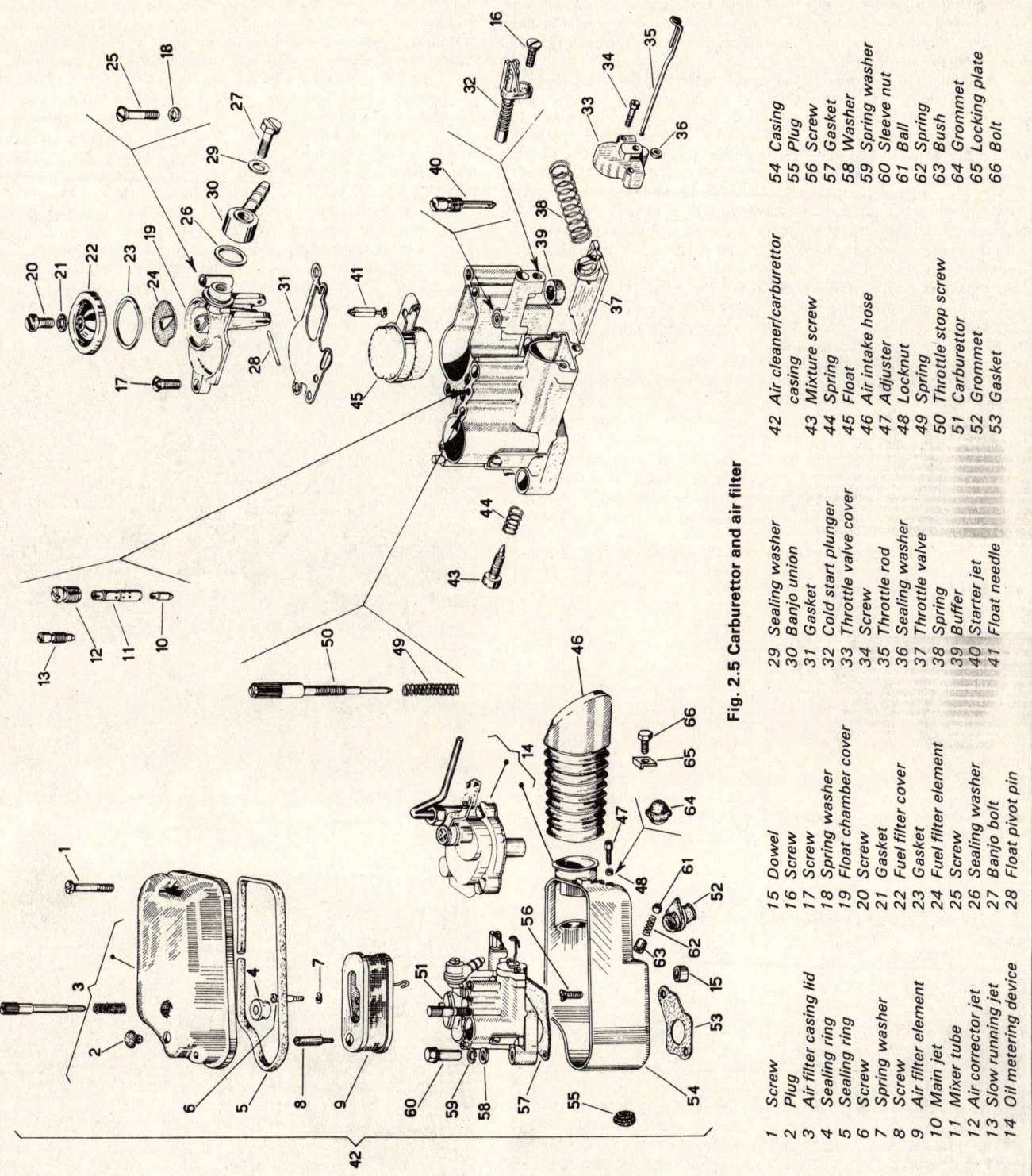

Fig. 2.5 Carburettor and air filter

1 Screw
2 Plug
3 Air filter casing lid
4 Sealing ring
5 Sealing ring
6 Screw
7 Spring washer
8 Screw
9 Air filter element
10 Main jet
11 Mixer tube
12 Air corrector jet
13 Slow running jet
14 Oil metering device

15 Dowel
16 Screw
17 Screw
18 Spring washer
19 Float chamber cover
20 Screw
21 Gasket
22 Fuel filter cover
23 Gasket
24 Fuel filter element
25 Screw
26 Sealing washer
27 Banjo bolt
28 Float pivot pin

29 Sealing washer
30 Banjo union
31 Gasket
32 Cold start plunger
33 Throttle valve cover
34 Screw
35 Throttle rod
36 Sealing washer
37 Throttle valve
38 Spring
39 Buffer
40 Starter jet
41 Float needle

42 Air cleaner/carburettor casing
43 Mixture screw
44 Spring
45 Float
46 Air intake hose
47 Adjuster
48 Locknut
49 Spring
50 Throttle stop screw
51 Carburettor
52 Grommet
53 Gasket

54 Casing
55 Plug
56 Screw
57 Gasket
58 Washer
59 Spring washer
60 Sleeve nut
61 Ball
62 Spring
63 Bush
64 Grommet
65 Locking plate
66 Bolt

6   Carburettor: dismantling, examination and reassembly

1   The fuel pipe connects via a union retained to the carburettor body by a banjo bolt. This need not be disturbed unless specific attention is required due to leakage. When refitting the union, use new sealing washers and position the fuel pipe stub so that it faces downwards and is angled slightly away from the carburettor body. Beware of over-tightening the banjo bolt.

2   A circular cover above the fuel inlet houses the fuel filter element. This should be removed and the filter cleaned, particularly where there is evidence of dirt or water contamination of the fuel tank. Note that if such contaminants are found anywhere in the carburettor, the tank should be removed and flushed out to prevent subsequent problems (see Section 2 of this Chapter).

3   To gain access to the float assembly, remove the two screws which retain the float chamber cover and lift it away. Try to avoid damage to the gasket, which can be re-used if it is intact. The float is held on the underside of the cover by a pivot pin, and this should be displaced to free it. A small screwdriver or a similar tool can be used to push the pin out. The float needle fits into a slot on the float arm.

4   The throttle valve assembly is located behind a cover on the side of the carburettor and can be withdrawn after the two retaining screws have been released. The cold start (choke) plunger is fitted in the adjacent bore and is removed in a similar fashion.

5   If it is wished to remove the long throttle stop screw or the smaller mixture screw it is advisable to first make a note of their settings so that these can be duplicated during reassembly. Screw each one inwards, noting the number of turns and part turns until the screw seats lightly. Make a written note of the settings, then remove the screws. When refitting them, screw them both home until they seat, then back each one off by the required number of turns.

6   Two jets are screwed into the carburettor body near the throttle stop screw. The smaller of the two is the slow running jet. The larger one is, in fact, three successive jets which are pushed together. Starting at the top, these are the air corrector jet, the mixer tube and the main jet. The final jet is located in a bore next to the float bowl. This is the starter jet.

7   When the carburettor has been dismantled, the component parts should be washed carefully in clean petrol. Check each jet carefully for obstructions, blowing them through with compressed air. If a com-pressed air supply is not available, the tyre pump supplied with the machine or a foot pump will usually suffice. If there is a stubborn blockage, do not resort to attempting to clear it with a piece of wire; this will almost invariably enlarge or score the carefully calibrated jet drilling. As a last resort a fine nylon bristle may be used.

8   Check the float for signs of leakage, indicated by the presence of fuel inside it. If the float has developed a leak it should be renewed; there is no satisfactory method of repairing a plastic float without upsetting the float height setting. The float needle will wear after many

years use and may eventually fail to seat correctly or may stick in the seating. If it has a pronounced wear ridge on its seating face, it should be renewed.

9   Check the fit of the throttle valve in its bore. It should be a sliding fit without significant up-and-down play. After extended use, the valve may wear leading to excessive play and attendant air leakage problems. This is characterised by an audible rattle from the carburettor when the engine is running, and it will probably be impossible to obtain an even tickover or normal fuel consumption and performance. If the new valve fails to cure the problem, check for wear in the body. This can only be corrected by renewing the body casting.

10 The cold start plunger assembly is unlikely to require attention during the normal life of the machine. When the choke knob is pulled out, the cable-operated plunger opens, allowing fuel to be drawn through the starter jet. If the cold start device operates erratically, check that the plunger is unworn. If renewal is necessary, note that the plunger assembly incorporates the return spring and cover; the component parts are not available separately.

11 When reassembling the carburettor in the reverse of the dismantling sequence, refer to the accompanying photographs for details. Note that the carburettor castings are rather brittle, and care should be taken to avoid damage to these or the jets. When the assembled instrument has been refitted, check the idle speed and mixture settings as described later in this Chapter.

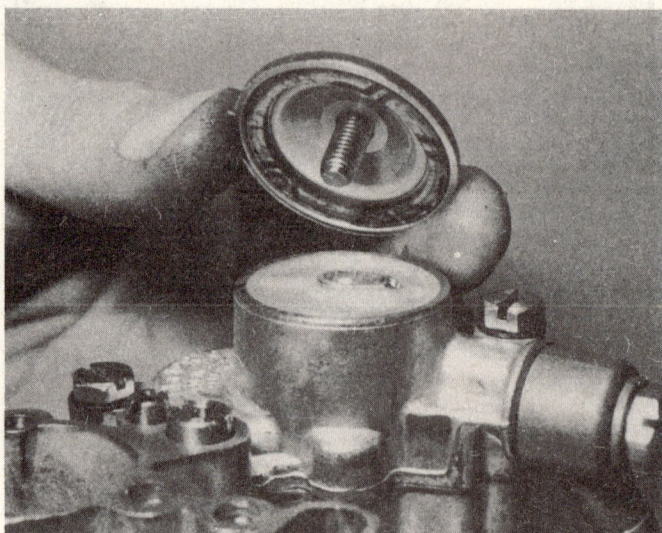

6.2a Circular cover should be removed ...

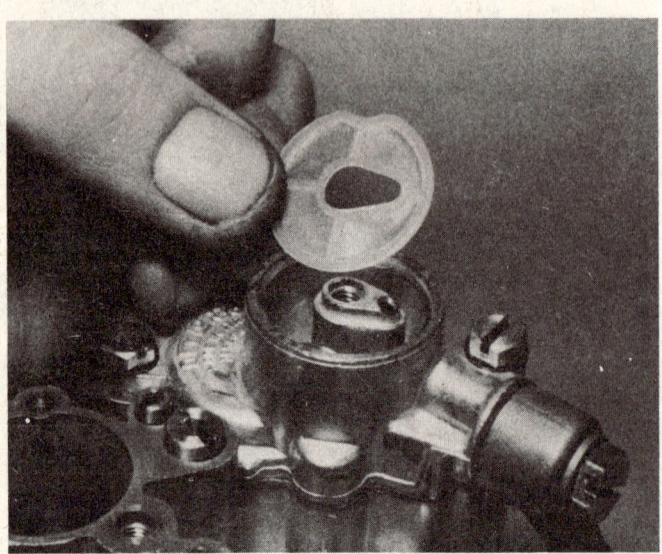

6.2b ... to gain access to fuel filter for cleaning

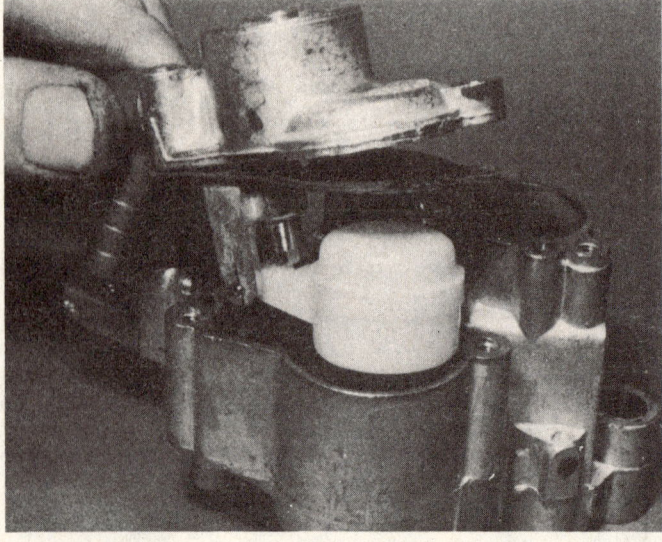

6.3a Remove cover to reveal float assembly

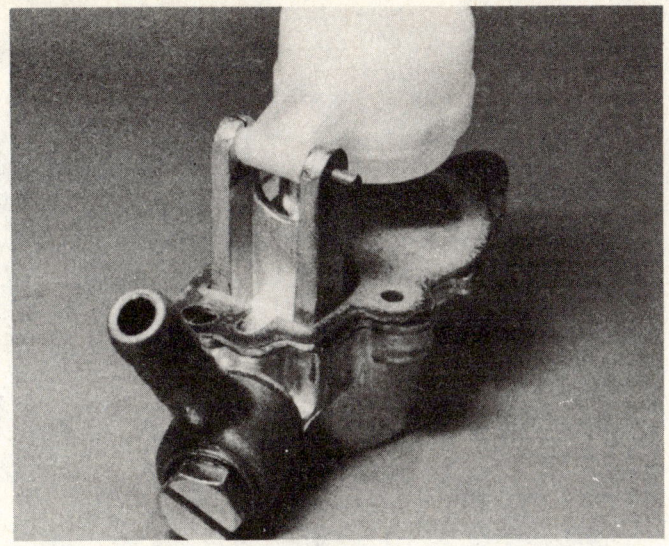

6.3b Displace the float pivot pin ...

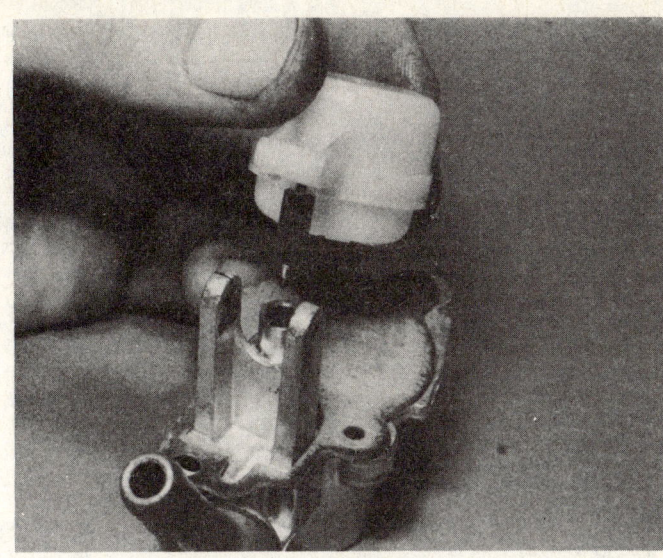

6.3c ... and lift away the float and needle

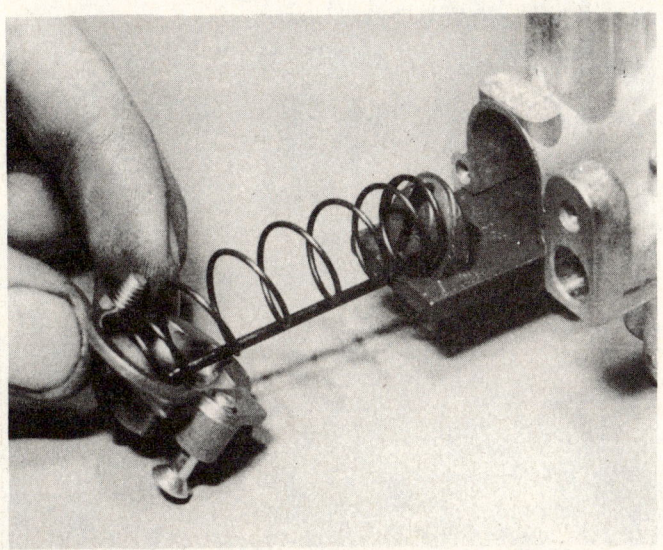

6.4a Throttle valve assembly can be withdrawn after the two retaining screws have been released

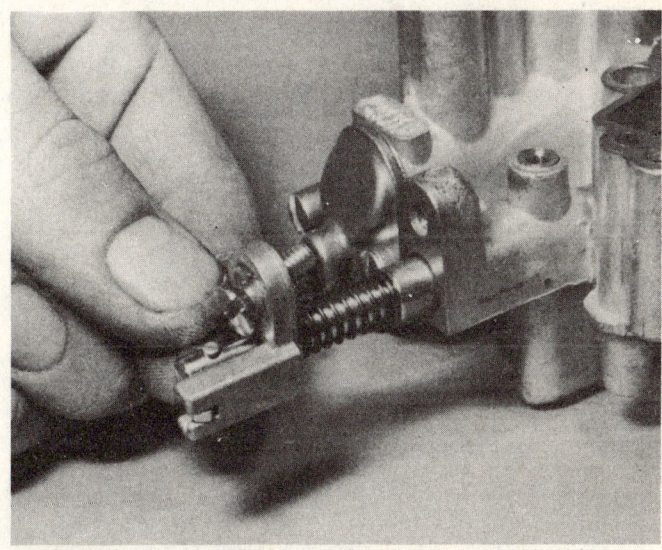

6.4b Cold-start plunger assembly is located in adjacent bore

6.5a Note positions of throttle stop screw ...

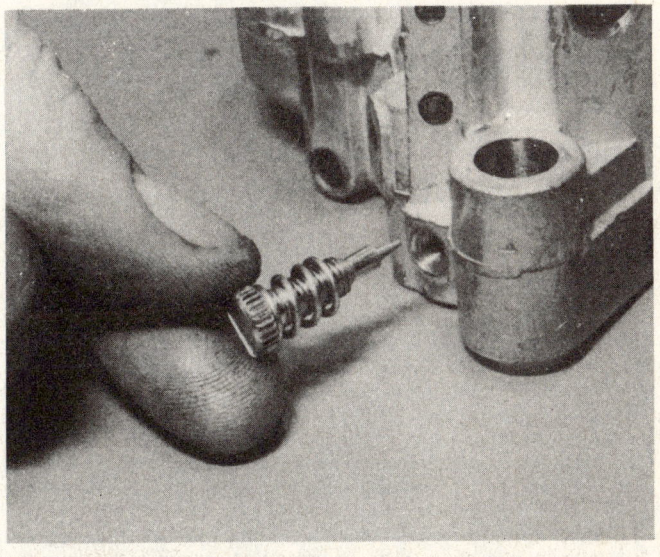

6.5b ... and smaller pilot mixture screw before removal

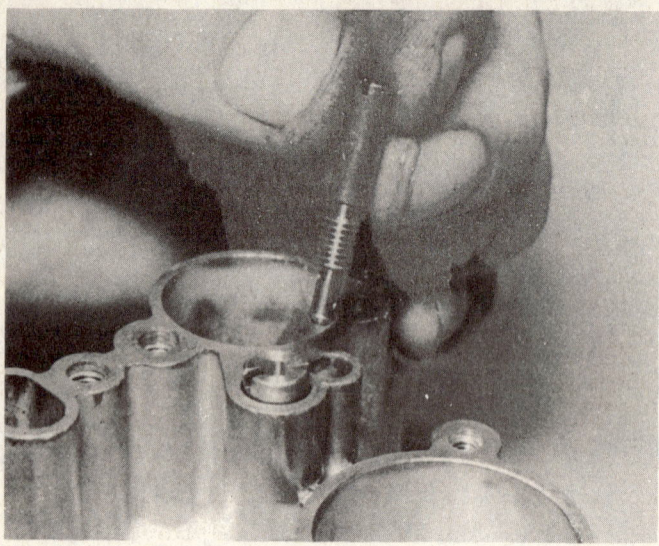

6.6a Slow running jet location

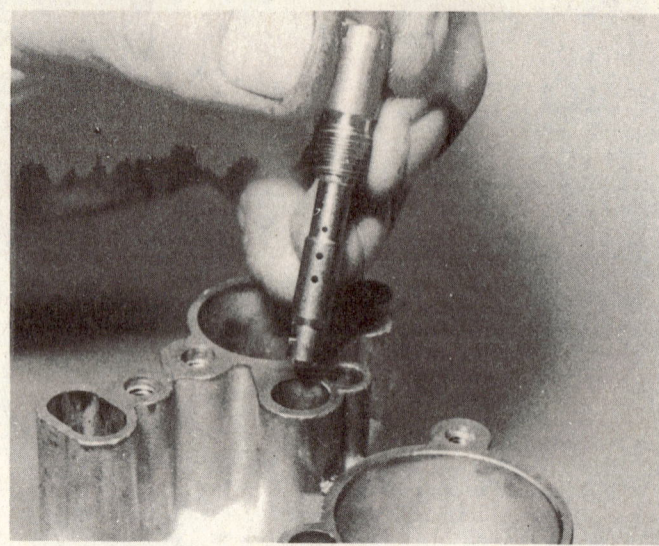

6.6b Main jet assembly location

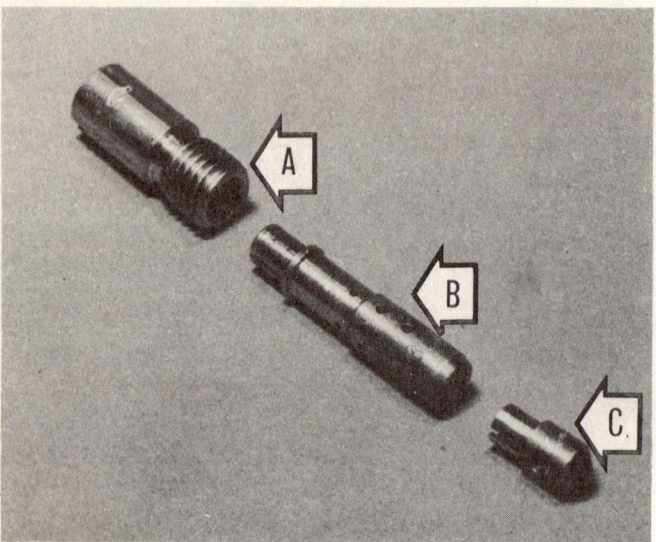

6.6c A: Air corrector jet B: Mixer tube C: Main jet

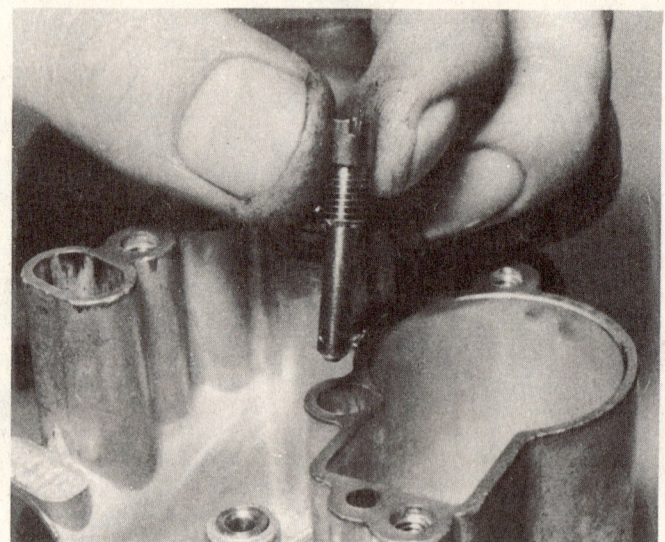

6.6d Starter jet location

7 Carburettor: checking the settings

1   The various jet sizes, throttle valve cutaway and needle position are predetermined by the manufacturer and should not require modification. Check with the specifications list at the beginning of this Chapter if there is any doubt about the sizes fitted. If a change appears necessary, it can often be attributed to a developing engine fault unconnected with the carburettor. Although carburettors do wear in service, this process occurs slowly over an extended length of time and hence wear of the carburettor is unlikely to cause sudden or extreme malfunction. If a fault does occur, check first other main systems, in which a fault may give similar symptoms, before proceeding with carburettor examination or modification.

2   Where non-standard items, such as exhaust systems or air filters, have been fitted to a machine, some alterations to carburation may be required. Arriving at the correct settings often requires trial and error, a method which demands skill borne of previous experience. In many cases the manufacturer of the non-standard equipment will be able to advise on correct carburation changes.

3   As a rough guide, up to $\frac{1}{8}$ throttle is controlled by the pilot jet, $\frac{1}{8}$ to $\frac{1}{2}$ by the throttle valve cutaway, and higher speeds by a combination of the throttle valve position and the main jet. These are very approximate divisions, and in practice there is no clear cut division, there being a degree of overlap between each one.

4   It is worth noting that what appears to be a carburation problem may be due to an induction fault attributable to the disc valve arrangement (see Section 9). If alterations to the carburation must be made, always err on the side of a slightly rich mixture. A weak mixture will cause the engine to overheat, which, on a two-stroke engine in particular, may cause engine seizure. Reference to the ignition Chapter will show how, after some experience has been gained, the condition of the spark plug electrodes can be interpreted as a reliable guide to mixture strength.

8 Carburettor: adjustment

1   Before any dismantling or adjustment is undertaken, eliminate all other possible causes of running problems, checking in particular the spark plug, contact breaker gap and condition (where appropriate), ignition timing, air filter and the exhaust system. Checking and

cleaning these items as necessary will often resolve a mysterious flat spot or misfire.

2   The first stage in adjustment is to ensure that the jet sizes are correct and that the fault is not due to obstruction of a jet or carburettor drilling. This will require the removal and dismantling of the carburettor as described in Sections 5 and 6.

3   Once the carburettor has been checked and refitted and the air filter element and cover installed, the engine should be run until it reaches normal operating temperature. If practicable, take the machine for a short run to ensure this. Stop the engine and remove the right-hand side panel. Prise out the small blanking grommet at the rear of the air filter casing to gain access to the pilot mixture screw.

4   Start the engine, then set the throttle stop screw to obtain the slowest reliable idle speed. Turn the pilot mixture screw inwards by $\frac{1}{4}$ turn at a time and note the effect on the idle speed, counting the number of $\frac{1}{4}$ turns for reference. When the engine begins to falter, return the screw to its original position and repeat the above process, this time turning it outwards. Using this method it should be possible to find the position at which the engine settles idles fastest and most reliably. The screw can then be set at this point.

5   Reduce the idle speed once more and repeat the above sequence to find the optimum setting. Once set, open and close the throttle a few times to check that the engine settles down to a consistent idle, making any necessary fine adjustments to the throttle stop screw to ensure this.

6   After any adjustment or dismantling work has been completed, check that the throttle cable is set to give about 1-2 mm free play. No specified clearance is given, but the object is to set the adjuster to give the minimum clearance necessary to ensure consistent operation. In particular, check that the idle speed remains constant when the handlebar is turned from lock to lock. If the idle speed rises, slacken the adjuster slightly to eliminate this.

9   Disc valve induction systems: description and fault diagnosis

1   As has been mentioned, the Vespa engines covered in this manual employ a disc valve induction system as a method of controlling precisely the timing of the incoming mixture. Unlike similar arrangements, no additional disc valve components are fitted, the left-hand engine flywheel being carefully machined to fulfill this additional function.

2   It will be appreciated that to operate effectively the flywheel must run extremely close to the crankcase and inlet port to form an effective seal when the port is covered, and this can be seen if the carburettor and air filter casing is removed and the engine turned using the kickstart lever. The arrangement is robust and reliable, but only if the incoming air is absolutely clean.

3   If unfiltered air is drawn into the engine, any dust particles will be deposited on the edge of the flywheel and held there by the oil film. If these are larger than the normal clearance between the flywheel and the casing, they are likely to become trapped between the two. The particle will then become embedded in the soft alloy casing, damaging it and possibly scoring the edge of the flywheel.

4   As the resultant air leakage increases, the efficiency of the disc valve falls off, and the engine will begin to run erratically. The usual symptoms are poor starting and erratic idling. The surface of the flywheel can be checked visually by removing the air filter, opening the throttle and viewing the flywheel as it is rotated slowly. The surface should be absolutely smooth with no visible scoring. If damage is visible check it further as follows.

5   Remove the carburettor and turn the crankshaft until the area of worst scoring is visible in the port. Fill the port with two-stroke oil, and time how long it takes to drain into the crankcase. On a good engine this should take 1 minute or more, but if it drains in less than 15 seconds it is safe to assume that remedial action is required.

6   Repairing damage of this type necessitates the removal of the crankshaft for examination, and reference should be made to Chapter 1 for details. It is advisable to seek the advice of a Vespa dealer when assessing the extent of damage. In extreme cases it may be necessary to renew the crankshaft and the crankcases to resolve the problem.

7   In consideration of the above, it need hardly be stressed that it is vital that the air filter element is kept clean and that the engine is **never** run with the element missing. The standard induction system is very well designed to avoid damage of this type, and given regular maintenance this should never occur.

10   Air filter: examination and renovation

1   The air filter element is housed in a casing below the right-hand side panel, together with the carburettor and the oil metering device, where fitted. Maintenance is confined to cleaning and re-oiling the element at the specified intervals, and this should be combined with a careful examination of the element.

2   Remove the two screws which retain the air filter cover and lift it away. Release the two screws which hold the element to the carburettor and lift it clear. Wash the element in clean petrol until all traces of dirt have been removed. Allow the element to dry completely, or blow it dry with compressed air.

3   Check the entire surface of the element for damage, and renew it if any holes or splits are discovered. Make sure that the element seats properly and that the cover seal is in place and complete. It is essential that all air reaching the engine should pass through the filter, for reasons described in Section 9.

11   Exhaust system: maintenance

1   The exhaust system is a one-piece welded steel arrangement, bolted to the underside of the engine transmission unit. It is finished with a black heat-dispersing coating. The system is essentially a sealed unit and cannot be dismantled for cleaning. No removable baffle is fitted.

2   As with all two-stroke engines, there will be a build-up of carbon over a period of time, largely due to the deposits which result from excess engine oil being burnt off. Given the unusually low oil percentage in the fuel, this will take some time to occur.

3   As an interim measure, the exhaust tailpipe can be kept clear using a length of stiff wire (a length cut from a wire coathanger is ideal for this). This job, which can be done with the system in place and takes only a few moments, will keep the worst of the carbon at bay.

4   If the problem is more serious, it will be necessary to renew the system or to adopt a more drastic approach to cleaning. In either case the system should be lifted away after the exhaust port clamp bolt and the main silencer mounting bolt have been released. Before making any further attempt at cleaning, check the system for rusting. If this has got to the stage where the metal has become thin or small holes are appearing, renew it.

5   If the system is sound but obviously choked with carbon, try the following method. Obtain from a chemist some caustic soda. This should be mixed with water in the ratio of 3 lbs caustic soda to 1 gallon of water. Add the soda to the water slowly, stirring it to dissolve the powder or crystals. **On no account** should water be added to the caustic soda powder; it will react violently and can be extremely dangerous due to its corrosive properties. Wear protective clothing, gloves and eye protection when handling caustic soda.

6   Use a cork or make a wooden bung to plug the end of the exhaust tailpipe and place the silencer well out of the way of passers by and out of doors. Pour the solution into the exhaust pipe until the system is full. **Do not** plug the open end of the system. Leave the silencer overnight to allow the caustic soda to dissolve. After the process is complete, pour out the caustic soda, remove the bung and flush the system with fresh water to remove any residue.

7   Bear in mind that it is very important to take great care when using caustic soda as it is a **very dangerous chemical**. Always wear protective clothing, which must include eye protection. If the solution does come into contact with the eyes or skin it must be washed clean **immediately** with clean, fresh running water. In the case of an eye becoming contaminated, seek expert medical advice **immediately**. Also, the solution must not be allowed to come into contact with aluminium alloy – especially at the above recommended strength – caustic soda reacts violently with aluminium and will cause severe damage to the component.

8   When cleaning the exhaust system, do not forget to remove any carbon deposits from the exhaust port itself. Use a blunt edged scraping tool of suitable shape and size, and take great care not to damage the piston or to scratch the surface of the port. If the port is severely blocked, the cylinder barrel should be removed for a major decarbonising operation.

9   Do not attempt to modify the exhaust system in any way. The exhaust system is designed to give the maximum power possible yet

meet legal requirements and produce the minimum noise level. Quite apart from the legal aspects of attempting to modify the exhaust of one of the restricted machines described in this Manual, it is very unlikely that an unskilled person could improve the performance of any of the machines by working on the exhaust. If an aftermarket accessory system is being considered, check very carefully that it will maintain or increase performance when compared with the standard system. Very few 'performance' exhaust systems live up to the claims made by manufacturers, and even fewer offer any performance increase at all over the standard component.

10 The final point to be borne in mind when considering the exhaust system is the finish. The matt-black painted finish employed is cheaper to renovate but less durable than a conventional chrome-plated system. It is inevitable that the original finish will deteriorate to the point where the system must be removed from the machine and repainted, therefore some thought must be given to the type of paint to be used. Reference to the advertisements in the national motorcycle press, or to a local Vespa dealer will help in selecting the most effective finish. The best are those which require the paint to be baked on, although some aerosol sprays are almost as effective. Whichever finish is decided upon, ensure that the surface is properly prepared according to the paint manufacturer's instructions and that the paint itself is correctly applied.

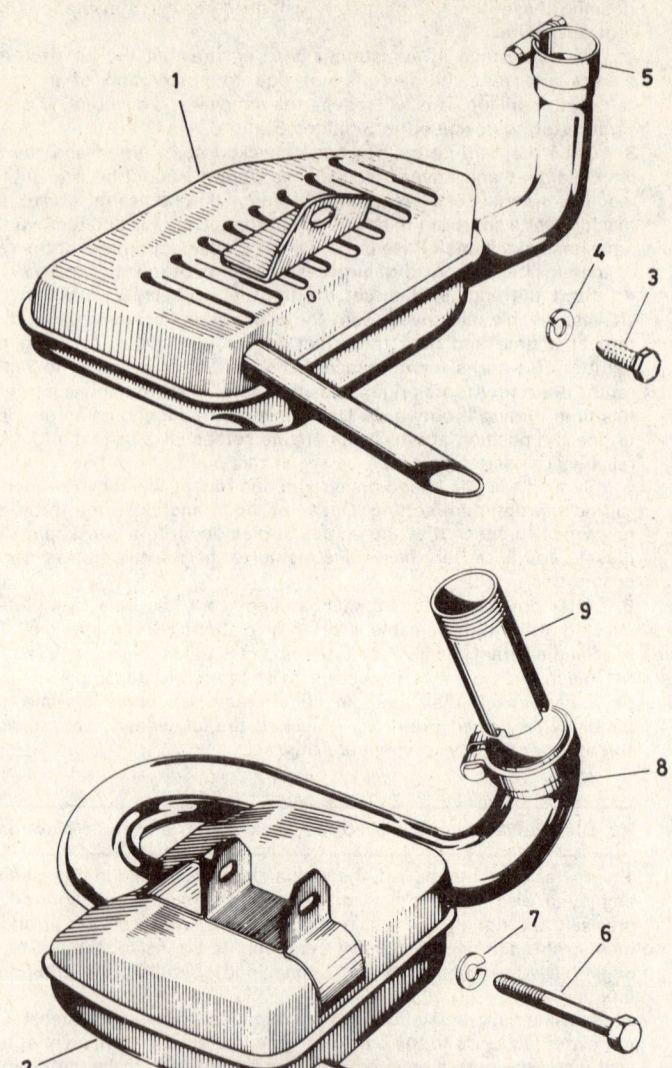

12 Engine lubrication: general description

1   Vespa scooters have traditionally used petroil engine lubrication, where a measured amount of self-mixing two-stroke oil is added to the fuel each time the tank is filled. At one time many garages had two-stroke pumps delivering the correct fuel at a number of mixture ratios, or kept an oil pump on the forecourt to add the required amount of oil after the petrol had been dispensed.

2   These are now uncommon, and it is inadvisable to expect the average filling station to stock two-stroke oil. On machines using pre-mixed oil and petrol, a supply of oil should always be carried in the toolbox. If the measure supplied with the machine has been lost, note that the mixing ratio is 2% or 50 : 1. This means that the following quantities of oil must be added to the petrol when refuelling.

    0.16 Imp pint oil to 1 gallon petrol
    3.20 Imp fl oz oil to 1 Imp gallon petrol
    90.1 cc oil to 1 Imp gallon petrol
    20 cc oil to 1 litre petrol

3   On many later models an oil metering system was fitted. On these machines, identified by the oil filler cap beneath the seat and the oil sight glass below the fuel tap, oil is delivered automatically in the correct quantity, the owner having only to ensure that the oil tank is kept filled.

4   Oil from the tank is fed to the inlet tract by gravity, passing through a crankshaft driven metering device on the way. The metering device is interconnected with the throttle, thus allowing the delivery rate to be increased as the throttle is opened. The system is fully automatic and requires no maintenance. Note that if the system is disturbed in the course of an engine overhaul it is important that the first tankful of fuel is a 50 : 1 mixture of petrol and oil. This is because it will take a little time for the system to prime and begin operating, there being no provision for bleeding the oil circuit.

Fig. 2.6 Exhaust system

1 Exhaust system – 125 and 150 models	5 Clamp 6 Bolt
2 Exhaust system – 200 models	7 Spring washer 8 Clamp
3 Bolt	9 Threaded insert
4 Spring washer	

Chapter 3 Ignition system

For information relating to later models see Chapter 7

Contents

Specifications

Ignition system

Type:

P125 X and P150 X .... Coil and contact breaker

All other models .... Electronic

Ignition advance:

P125 X and P150 X .... 21° ± 1° BTDC

PX125 E and PX150 E .... 18° ± 1° BTDC

P200 E and PX200 E .... 23° ± 1° BTDC

Contact breaker (P125 X and P150 X)

Gap .... 0.3 - 0.5 mm (0.012 - 0.020 in)

Electronic ignition

Source coil resistances .... 500 ± 20 ohms

Pickup winding resistances .... 110 ± 5 ohms

Spark plug

Recommended fitments:

Model	P125 X	P150 X	P200 E
Marelli	CW 6N AT	CW 6N AT	CW 6N AT
Bosch	W225 T1	W 225 T1	W 225 T2
Champion	L 86	N/A	N 4
AC	43 F	43 F	43 XL

Model	PX125 E	PX150 E	PX200 E
Marelli	CW 6N	CW 6N	CW 6L
Bosch	W 5A	W 5A	W 5C
Champion	L 86	L 86	N 4
AC	43 F	43 F	43 XL
NGK	B6HS	B6HS	B6ES
Electrode gap (all models)	0.6 mm (0.24 in)	0.6 mm (0.24 in)	0.6 mm (0.24 in)

Torque wrench settings

Component	kgf m	lbf ft
Alternator stator screws	0.3 - 0.4	2.17 - 2.89
Alternator rotor nut	6.0 - 6.5	43.4 - 47.0
Pickup mounting screws	0.2 - 0.25	1.45 - 1.81

1 General description

The P125 X and P150 X models are equipped with conventional coil and contact breaker ignition systems, whilst the P200 E and all of the later PX models feature electronic ignition. Though in general the electronic system is preferable to the earlier type, each has advantages and disadvantages. The two basic arrangements are described below.

Conventional ignition

Power from an ignition source coil built into the flywheel generator is fed via the contact breaker points to the primary windings of the ignition HT (high tension) coil. A cam incorporated in the flywheel rotor controls the opening of the contact breaker points. As the contacts separate, the electromagnetic field in the preliminary windings collapses. This in turn induces a high tension pulse in the HT coil secondary windings. This is applied to the spark plug electrodes, producing the ignition spark at the required time.

The above arrangement has been the usual method of providing ignition on most internal combustion engines during several decades, and is thus well proven. The main disadvantage is the need for regular maintenance of the contact breaker points to compensate for wear and erosion. On the other hand, the system is a simple electro-mechanical arrangement, easily and inexpensively repaired if it does fail, and requiring no specialised equipment or knowledge.

Electronic ignition

The electronic system fitted to the later models eliminates the main cause of problems in the conventional points system; namely the contact breaker itself. An alternating current (ac) is supplied from the ignition source coil in the stator to the ignition unit. Inside the unit it is rectified, or converted to direct current (dc) by a diode, and the resulting charge stored by a capacitor.

Also built into the stator is a small pickup coil, the purpose of which is to supply a small trigger pulse as a magnet if the rotor passes it. In this sense it replaces the mechanical contact breaker with an electronic unit having no moving parts to wear out. The trigger pulse is applied to a device known as a thyristor or silicon controlled rectifier (scr). This functions as an electronic switch, allowing the charge stored in the capacitor to discharge through the HT coil primary windings. As in the conventional system this induces the required HT pulse which is fed to the spark plug.

The electronic system offers a number of advantages over its predecessor, notably freedom from the need for maintenance or adjustment, accuracy at all engine speeds and long-term reliability. Against this it must be kept in mind that in the event of failure, repair is likely to be more expensive and diagnosis more difficult.

2   Spark plug: checking and resetting the gap – all models

1   The standard plug recommendations are shown in the Specifications at the beginning of this Chapter, and should be adhered to for all normal purposes. Only in exceptional circumstances would a change from the prescribed grade be advisable, and the advice of a Vespa dealer should be sought if persistent plug fouling or electrode erosion is experienced. In the majority of cases the fault will be attributable to some other cause, such as incorrect carburation, incorrect engine lubrication or a partially blocked or leaking exhaust system. Bear in mind that an unwarranted change of plug grade could cause engine damage.

2   Carry a new, spare plug on the machine at all times, ensuring that it is of the correct type and that the electrode gap has been set accurately. Plug failure is not as common on modern two-strokes as it was on earlier and cruder designs, but it is worth noting that few filling stations will stock the correct grade of plug in the event of such an occurrence. Plug failure is by far the most common cause of ignition problems, and it is good practice to fit a new plug to eliminate this possibility before carrying out a full test of the system.

3   Spark plugs are relatively inexpensive, and in general it is preferable to renew a suspect plug as a precaution, even if it appears unworn. If, however, the existing plug is to be cleaned and re-gapped, start by scraping off the accumulated carbon from the electrodes and the porcelain insulator, using a small screwdriver and a wire brush. The opposing faces of the electrodes can be burnished using fine abrasive paper.

4   As an alternative to the above method, some garages offer an abrasive cleaning service, and there are home units which do a similar job. If the plug is in sound condition, these methods are quite acceptable, but make sure that all traces of abrasive grit are removed from the plug before it is refitted.

5   The recommended electrode gap is 0.6 mm (0.024 in) and this should be checked using feeler gauges. If adjustment is necessary, alter the gap by bending the outer (earth) electrode only, preferably using an electrode setting tool. On no account bend or lever against the centre electrode. This will almost invariably crack the porcelain

insulator, pieces of which can cause extensive damage if they drop into the engine when it is running.

6   Before refitting the plug, coat its threads sparingly with molybdenum or graphite grease to aid future removal. Use only a plug spanner to fit the plug. Tighten the plug by hand only at first, then secure it with a quarter turn to seat it firmly on the sealing ring. Note that it is easy to overtighten plugs and that damage to the cylinder head threads may result.

7   If the plug threads in the cylinder head have become stripped or damaged, they can be repaired by having a Helicoil insert fitted. The head should be removed (see Chapter 1) and taken to a motorcycle dealer or engineering works offering this service. This repair method is quick and inexpensive and avoids the expense of a new cylinder head.

3   Checking the spark plug cap and HT lead: all models

1   Problems of erratic running or spasmodic cutting out can often be traced to damage or earthing of the plug cap or HT lead. Although both are well protected by the side panel, condensation formed while the machine is parked in damp conditions, or damage to the HT lead caused by chafing against the engine unit or the side panel, can produce some mystifying problems.

2   In many instances it will be possible to see tiny sparks around the plug cap or HT lead at night; a sure sign that arcing is occurring. The cap and lead should be examined closely for damage and any dirt or moisture cleaned off. If the lead has become dirty it is quite possible for HT leakage to occur by 'tracking' to earth on the engine or body. This can usually be stopped by cleaning the lead and spraying it with WD 40 or similar.

3   It is also possible for the plug cap to break down internally and if this is suspected, try fitting a new cap. Physical damage to the HT lead is normally obvious by a wear mark or groove in the insulation. As a temporary measure, clean the lead thoroughly, then bind the damaged area with PVC insulating tape. Remember to re-route the lead to avoid a recurrent problem.

4   Renewing the lead poses something of a dilemma because it is integral with the ignition coil. If the damaged area is several inches away from the coil body, the lead can be cut and a new section fitted, using a threaded connector. An Auto-electrical specialist should be able to supply a suitable connector or offer advice on how best to deal with the problem. As a last resort, renew the coil and lead as an assembly.

4   Checking the ignition system: P125 X and P150 X (contact breaker) models only

1   In the event of a partial or complete failure of the ignition system it is important to ensure that the spark plug is working normally, preferably by fitting a new plug. For further information see Section 2 of this Chapter. If this does not resolve the problem, check the HT lead and plug cap as described in Section 3.

2   The next area to be checked is the contact breaker. Although wear normally develops gradually, it is possible that the fixed contact securing screw may have become loose, allowing the gap to close up. Check and adjust or renew the contact breaker assembly as required, referring to Section 5 for details.

3   Where the plug seems to spark normally, but the engine refuses to run correctly, it is possible that the ignition timing may have slipped, though it must be stressed that this is not common. The ignition timing sequence is described in Section 6 of this Chapter.

4   If the above checks fail to locate the fault, attention should be turned to the system wiring and connections. Refer to Section 7 of this Chapter, in conjunction with the wiring diagram at the end of the book.

5   In most cases the fault will have been located at this stage, but where this is not the case it can be assumed that the HT coil, ignition source coil or the condenser is at fault. These are best checked by substituting a new component, there being no specific test details available for these parts. Note also that if any of the stator coils is to be renewed it is essential to have access to the appropriate fixture to ensure accurate alignment. It follows that it will be necessary to entrust this operation to a Vespa dealer who will be equipped with the necessary parts and tooling to carry out the work.

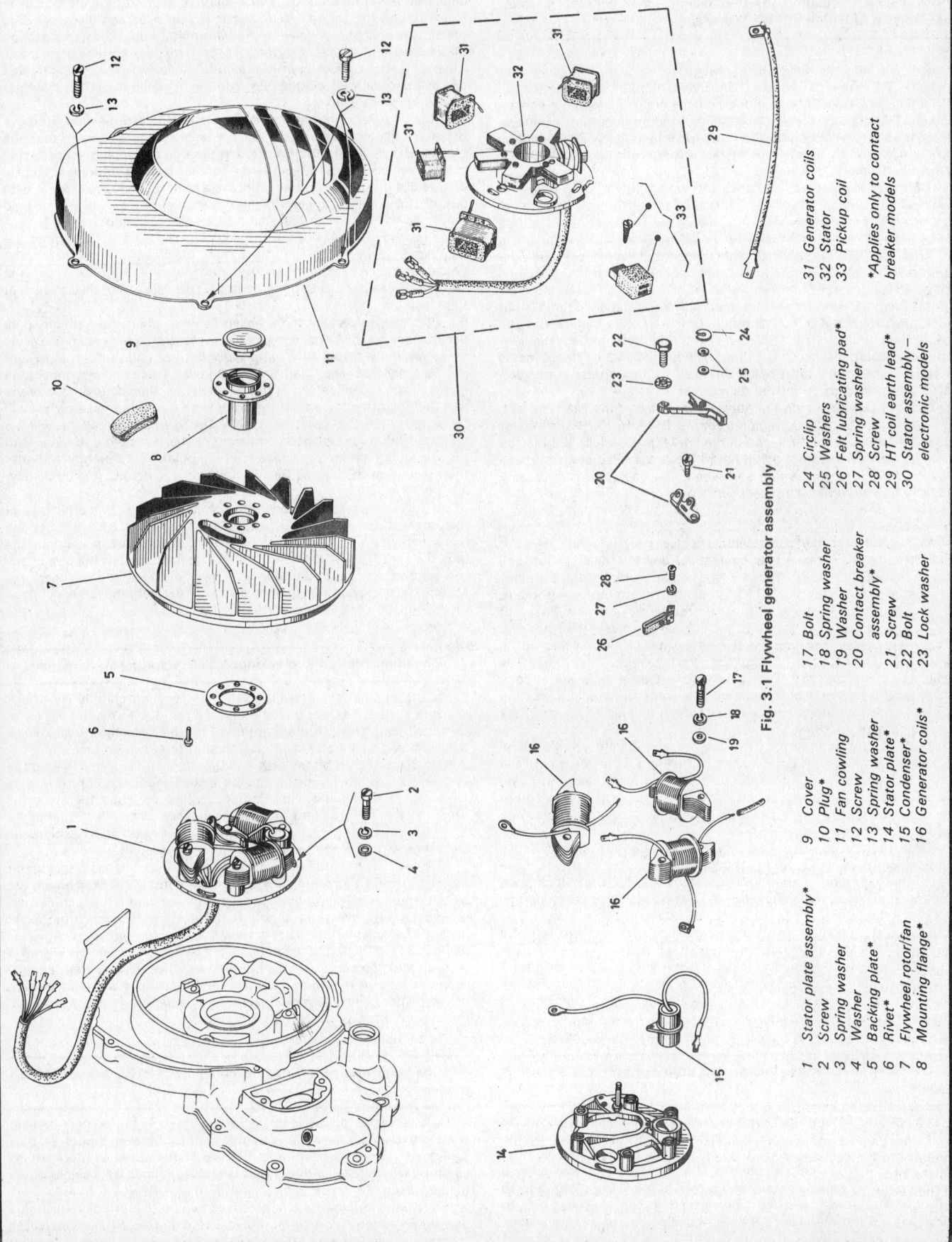

Fig. 3.1 Flywheel generator assembly

1 Stator plate assembly*
2 Screw
3 Spring washer
4 Washer
5 Backing plate*
6 Rivet*
7 Flywheel rotor/fan
8 Mounting flange*

9 Cover
10 Plug*
11 Fan cowling
12 Screw
13 Spring washer
14 Stator plate*
15 Condenser*
16 Generator coils*

17 Bolt
18 Spring washer
19 Washer
20 Contact breaker
   assembly*
21 Screw
22 Bolt
23 Lock washer

24 Circlip
25 Washers
26 Felt lubricating pad*
27 Spring washer
28 Screw
29 HT coil earth lead*
30 Stator assembly –
   electronic models

31 Generator coils
32 Stator
33 Pickup coil

*Applies only to contact
breaker models

5 Checking, adjusting and renewing the contact breaker assembly: P125 X and P150 X models

Adjustment

1   Remove the right-hand side panel and detach the fan cowling after releasing its retaining screws. The flywheel rotor incorporates an inspection slot through which the contact breaker assembly can be viewed. The contact breaker is mounted on the generator stator, in about the 2 o'clock position. Turn the rotor by hand while observing the contact breaker points. Set the rotor in the position at which the points are fully open.

2   Examine the contact surfaces for wear, pitting or burning. If significantly damaged it will be impossible to set the gap accurately, and the contact breaker assembly should be renewed as described below. Any oil or grease deposits should be removed by drawing a piece of stiff card moistened with methylated spirits between the contact faces. More stubborn deposits can be removed by judicious use of a fine contact file or emery board.

3   Measure the contact breaker gap using feeler gauges. If this is not within the prescribed 0.3 – 0.5 mm (0.012 – 0.020 in) limits, the gap should be reset as follows. Slacken slightly the fixed contact securing screw (located near the outer edge of the fixed contact). The object is to set the screw so that it holds the fixed contact lightly in position whilst allowing it to be moved as required.

4   Using a screwdriver in the notch at the edge of the fixed contact, open or close the gap as required until a 0.4 mm (0.016 in) feeler gauge is a light sliding fit between the contacts. Carefully tighten the screw to hold this setting, trying not to move the fixed contact in the process. Re-check the setting and repeat the operation if necessary until the gap is within the prescribed limits.

Renewal

5   If inspection of the contact breaker assembly has indicated the need for renewal, obtain a new contact set and a rotor extractor tool, Part Number T. 0048564, from a Vespa dealer. Note that the extractor is essential to this operation which should not be attempted without it.

6   Remove the right-hand side panel and the fan cowling. Prise out the plastic cap from the centre of the flywheel to reveal the rotor nut. It will be necessary to prevent the rotor from turning as the nut is removed, and a special holding tool, Part Number T. 0031760 is available for this purpose. This is little more than a stout metal hook which locates in the inspection hole in the rotor, the free end locating over the kickstart shaft. Most owners should be able to approximate this, using scrap materials.

7   Slacken and remove the retaining nut and lift out the plain and shakeproof washers. Fit the extractor, screwing it fully home with the centre bolt unscrewed. The centre bolt can now be tightened to draw the rotor off the crankshaft taper. If it proves stubborn, tap the end of the extractor bolt to jar it free. Lift away the rotor and retrieve the Woodruff key if this drops free.

8   Before removing the old contact breaker assembly, note carefully the position of the leads and insulating washers. It is vital that these are refitted correctly or the ignition system will not work. It is good practice to make a sketch showing the relative position of each part as it is removed.

9   Fit the new contact breaker assembly by reversing the removal sequence, having first degreased the contact faces. When fitting the fixed contact securing screw, leave it very slightly loose to permit adjustment. Refit the rotor, tightening the retaining nut to 6.0 – 6.5 kgf m (43.4 – 47.0 lbf ft). Set the contact breaker gap as described in paragraphs 1 – 4 above.

6 Checking and setting the ignition timing: P125 X and P150 X models

1   To set the ignition timing, a piston stop and a degree disc will be required. These can be ordered as Vespa parts through a dealer, the stop being Part Number T. 0030259 and the degree disc Part Number T.0023465. In the likely event that the tools are not available, a proprietary degree disc can be used provided it can be adapted to fit the rotor. Note also that it will be necessary to cut an access hole to match that of the rotor, once the disc position has been established. The piston stop is easily fabricated from a discarded spark plug as follows.

2   Clamp the plug in a vice and carefully hacksaw around the spun-over rim of the metal body. Once this has been cut off the porcelain insulator and the centre electrode can be removed and discarded. File off the earth electrode, leaving the bare metal body. Using a selection of spacers and washers, arrange a bolt to pass through the body, projecting about $\frac{1}{2}$ to $\frac{3}{4}$ in from the end of the thread. Note that it must still be possible to screw the plug into the head, so check the diameter of any washers used.

3   Remove the right-hand side panel and the fan cowling. Remove the spark plug and fit in its place the piston stop. Check that the crankshaft is stopped short of turning through a complete rotation and make any necessary adjustments to the stop as required. Fit the degree disc to the rotor, then fabricate a wire pointer, attaching it with one of the cowling screws to the crankcase. Set the degree disc so that it reads zero when the piston is against the stop.

4   Turn the crankshaft until the stop is reached again and note the reading. Calculate from this how many degrees of movement exist between the two stop positions, remove the stop, and set the crankshaft exactly at top dead centre (TDC). Reset the disc to zero at this position.

5   It is now necessary to establish at what point the ignition spark occurs. This can be done using a multimeter set on the resistance scale as a continuity tester, or a simple dry battery and bulb arrangement can be employed (see Chapter 6 for details). Trace and disconnect the green contact breaker lead at the junction box, then connect one probe to it and the other to earth. If the crankshaft is now turned slowly it will be noted that the point at which the contacts separate will be indicated by the meter needle moving or the test bulb dimming. Turn the crankshaft slowly clockwise until the points just separate and note the reading on the degree disc. If the timing is correct it should show 21° ± 1° BTDC.

6   If adjustment is necessary, turn the crankshaft slowly until each of the three stator retaining screws is located and slackened. Set the crankshaft at 21° BTDC, then move the stator via the inspection hole until the contacts just separate. Tighten the stator screws and re-check the setting as described above. Once the timing has been set accurately, remove the degree disc and pointer, refit the spark plug and reconnect the contact breaker lead.

7 Checking the ignition wiring: P125 X and P150 X models

1   If the ignition system has ceased to function completely, check that the system has not become earthed out due to a short circuit or damaged lead. Using a multimeter set on the resistance scale, check the various green leads at the terminal in the junction box.

2   Connect one probe to earth and the other to the green lead to the ignition switch, having disconnected this at the junction box. If all is well, the meter should show infinite resistance when the switch is turned to the 'ON' position, and zero resistance when it is turned to the 'OFF' position. If zero resistance is shown in either switch position, the switch or wiring is shorted out, earthing the system.

3   Disconnect the green contact breaker lead and connect one meter probe to it and the other to earth. If the contact breaker points are closed, zero resistance should be shown on the meter. If the crankshaft is now turned, the meter should indicate some resistance (no exact figure is available) as the contacts separate and the circuit is completed via the ignition source coil. If infinite resistance is shown it is likely that the source coil windings have broken, requiring renewal of the coil. If, on the other hand, zero resistance is shown irrespective of the points being open or closed, there is a short in the green lead, the contact breaker assembly or the source coil.

8 Checking and renewing the condenser: P125 X and P150 X models

1   A condenser (or capacitor) is incorporated in the contact breaker circuit to prevent arcing across the contact breaker points as they separate. The condenser, a cylindrical metal-cased component, is connected in parallel with the points and is retained by a single screw to the stator.

2   A failed condenser is characterised by poor starting and misfiring, often getting much worse as the engine warms up. In serious cases the engine may refuse to run at all. Inspection of the contact breaker faces will usually confirm the fault; if the condenser has failed, the

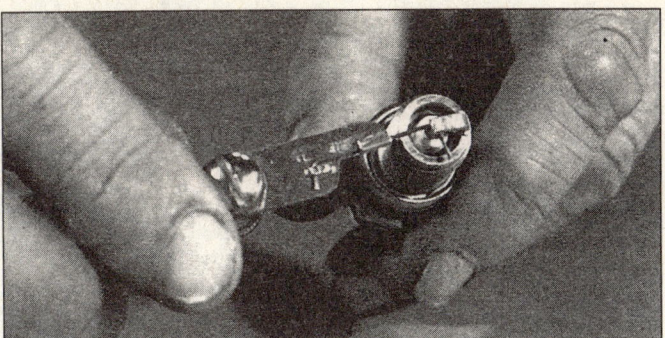

Electrode gap check - use a wire type gauge for best results

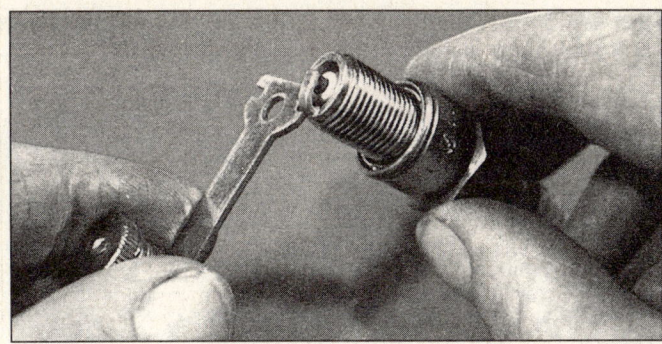

Electrode gap adjustment - bend the side electrode using the correct tool

Normal condition - A brown, tan or grey firing end indicates that the engine is in good condition and that the plug type is correct

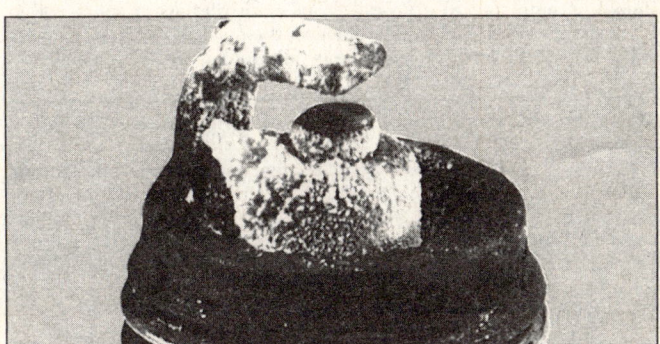

Ash deposits - Light brown deposits encrusted on the electrodes and insulator, leading to misfire and hesitation. Caused by excessive amounts of oil in the combustion chamber or poor quality fuel/oil

Carbon fouling - Dry, black sooty deposits leading to misfire and weak spark. Caused by an over-rich fuel/air mixture, faulty choke operation or blocked air filter

Oil fouling - Wet oily deposits leading to misfire and weak spark. Caused by oil leakage past piston rings or valve guides (4-stroke engine), or excess lubricant (2-stroke engine)

Overheating - A blistered white insulator and glazed electrodes. Caused by ignition system fault, incorrect fuel, or cooling system fault

Worn plug - Worn electrodes will cause poor starting in damp or cold weather and will also waste fuel

contacts will be burnt and eroded due to arcing. If the engine is started and heavy sparking across the contact faces is evident, it is safe to assume that the condenser has failed.

3   To gain access to the condenser it will be necessary to remove the flywheel rotor as described in Section 5 above. In view of the amount of dismantling work required and the low cost of the condenser, it can be considered worthwhile renewing it each time the contact breaker assembly is renewed.

9   Checking and renewing the ignition coil: P125 X and P150 X models

1   In view of the lack of test data on the ignition coil it can only really be checked by substitution of a sound component. If necessary, this should be entrusted to a Vespa dealer who will have a spare coil in stock to facilitate the check. In practice, the coil is a robust unit and is unlikely to fail unless the machine is quite old.

10   Electronic ignition system: general information

1   When performing any work or test procedures on models equipped with electronic ignition, the following points **must** be noted. On no account should the engine be started with any of the ignition leads disconnected or the plug cap removed. Similarly, do not disconnect any leads while the engine is running. If this precaution is not observed it is likely that the ignition unit or the pickup windings will be irreparably damaged.

2   It should also be noted that HT voltages on electronic systems are substantially higher than those of conventional ignition systems. Care should be taken to avoid shocks, which can be very unpleasant and occasionally dangerous.

11   Electronic ignition system: fault diagnosis

1   In the event of an ignition fault, always check the condition of the spark plug, and if in any doubt as to its condition, renew it. Next, physically check the wiring connections, looking for loose terminals and water contamination. These simple checks will often resolve the problem, but if the fault persists, proceed as follows.

2   Check the ignition unit by substituting a new or sound second-hand item. This will require the co-operation of a friend with a similar model or a Vespa dealer. In most cases it is easiest to take the machine to a dealer who will be able to check the unit in a few minutes. If the substitution shows the fault to lie within the ignition unit, there is no alternative to renewal. It is a sealed assembly and cannot be repaired.

3   If the unit proves serviceable and the fault persists, check the stator resistances using a multimeter set on the ohms x 1000 scale. Trace the generator output leads to the junction box on the top of the crankcase and disconnect them. To measure the ignition source coil resistance, connect one meter probe to the white lead and the other to the green lead. If the windings are sound a reading of 500 ± 20 ohms should be shown.

4   To check the ignition pickup windings, connect one meter probe to the white lead and the other to the red lead. A reading of 110 ± 5 ohms should be obtained from a sound pickup. In practice, in either of the above tests a fault is usually indicated by a reading of zero ohms (a short circuit) or infinite resistance (broken windings).

5   If the pickup or the source coil are faulty, it is possible to renew each component separately, no special equipment being required. Note, however, that they are soldered into the stator and some experience is useful when fitting the new units. If in doubt, take the stator to a Vespa dealer to have the job done.

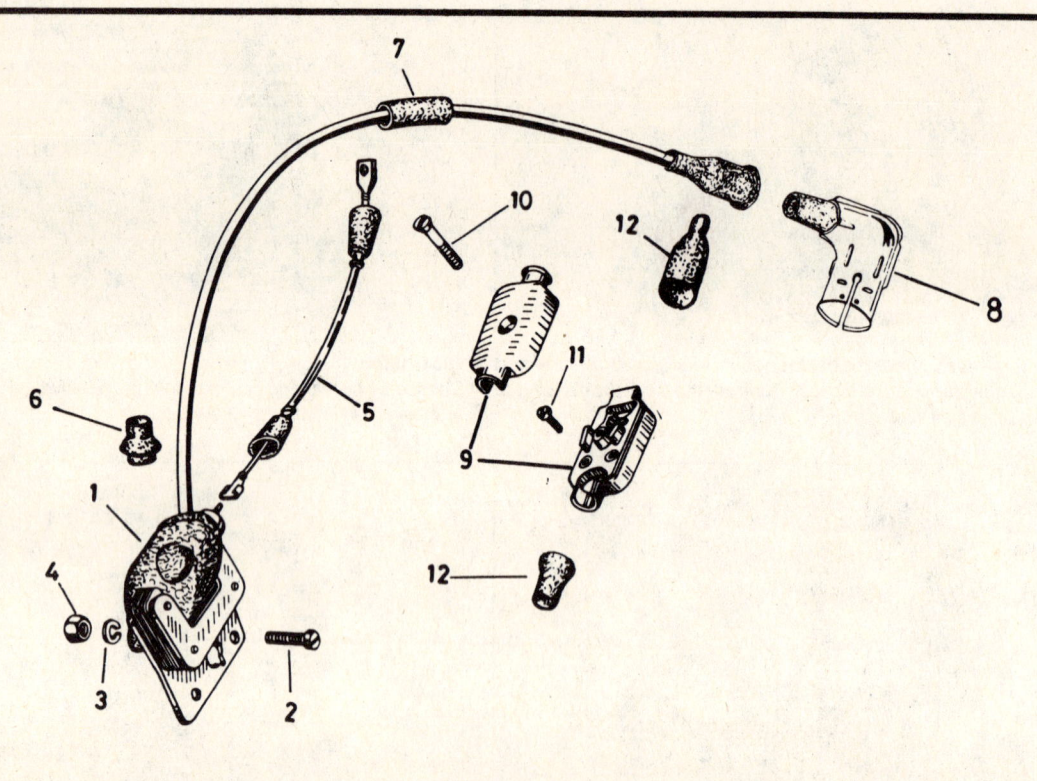

Fig. 3.2 Ignition coil assembly – P125 X and P150 X models

1	Ignition coil	5	Low tension lead	9	Low tension lead terminal
2	Screw	6	Seal	10	Screw
3	Spring washer	7	HT lead	11	Screw
4	Nut	8	Suppressor cap	12	Seal

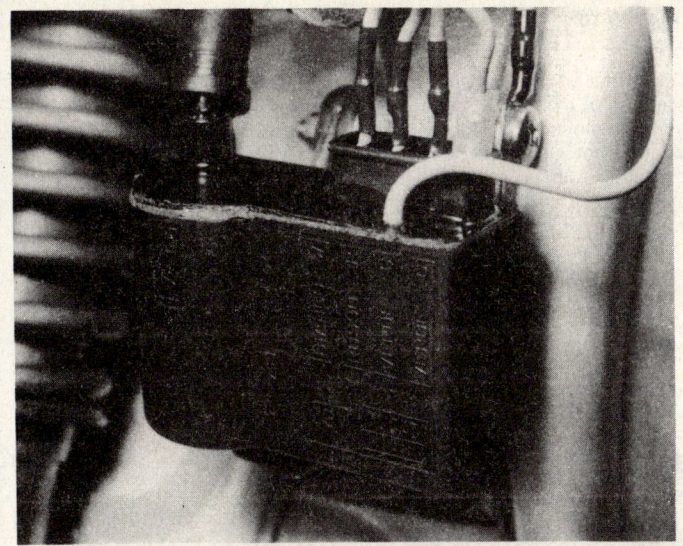

11.2a Check ignition unit connections for corrosion or water contamination

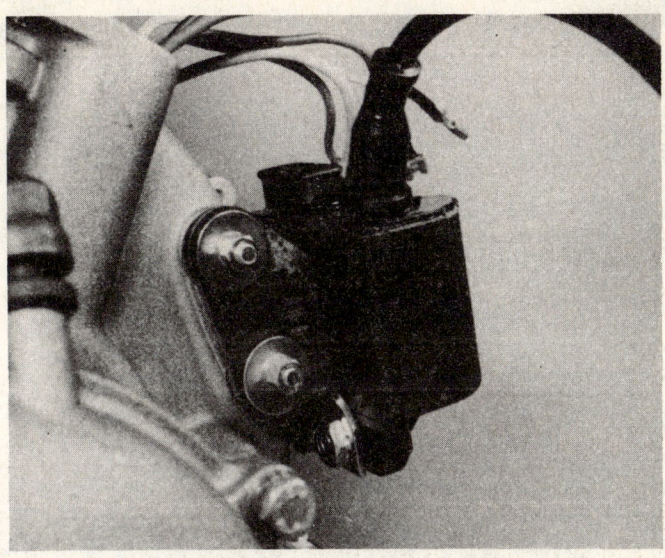

11.2b Ignition unit is bolted to crankcase via rubber mountings

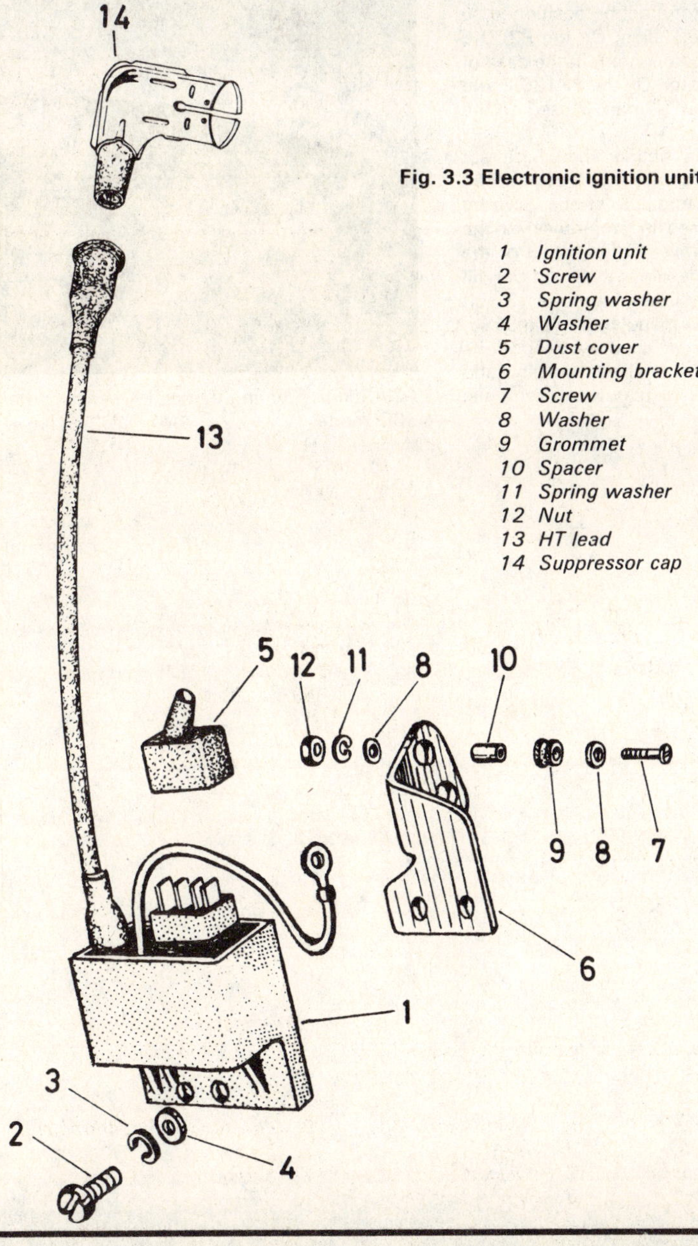

Fig. 3.3 Electronic ignition unit assembly

1 Ignition unit
2 Screw
3 Spring washer
4 Washer
5 Dust cover
6 Mounting bracket
7 Screw
8 Washer
9 Grommet
10 Spacer
11 Spring washer
12 Nut
13 HT lead
14 Suppressor cap

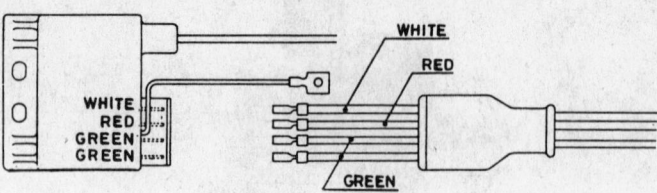

Fig. 3.4 Electronic ignition unit connections – P200 E and all PX models

12 Electronic ignition system: checking the timing

1   It is not usual to have to check the timing other than when the generator stator has been removed in the course of an overhaul. Once set correctly the timing should not require attention, and any apparent change in the ignition timing in normal use is usually due to a fault in the system. The only obvious exception is where the generator stator screws have loosened, allowing the timing to slip.

2   When setting the timing initially, the stator must be positioned so that the timing marks on it and the crankcase align. On the P200 E model, these consist of raised lines on each component. In the case of the PX models there are two marks on the stator. On the PX125 E and the PX 150 E, the 'IT' mark is used, whilst the 'A' mark is used on the PX200 E model.

3   If the marks are aligned correctly, the timing should be set accurately. If there is some doubt as to its accuracy it can be checked dynamically using a stroboscopic timing lamp, or 'strobe'. Where possible, a xenon type strobe should be used in preference to the cheaper neon versions because it will give a clearer indication of the timing mark position. Note, however, that the xenon type strobe will require an independent power supply, usually in the form of a 12 volt car battery. Connect the strobe, following the manufacturer's instructions. If a strobe is not available, or there is some uncertainty about its use, a Vespa dealer can carry out a strobe check quickly and inexpensively and will be able to offer advice about any remedial action that may be required.

4   Start the engine and aim the strobe at the dynamic timing marks. In the case of the P200 E, there is a white line on the pickup coil, and this should appear to align with the two lines on either side of the inspection slot. On the PX series models, the rotor is marked by a small round projection incorporated in one of the cooling fan fins. This should align with the appropriate reference mark stamped into the fan cowling; 'IT' for the 125 and 150, and 'A' for the 200.

5   If the strobe test shows the timing to be inaccurate despite the correct alignment of the static timing marks, it is likely that there is a fault in one of the ignition components, and these should be checked as described above. The most common symptom is likely to be a wavering or unstable image of the timing marks. If the system proves to be operating normally and the inaccuracy persists, slacken the stator screws and make any necessary fine adjustment of the stator position to obtain accurate ignition timing. Note that it is unusual for this step to be required, and that new static marks should be made for subsequent reference.

12.4 Ignition timing marks, PX series. Note 'A' mark which applies to 200 model

Chapter 4 Frame and suspension

For information relating to later models see Chapter 7

Contents

Specifications

Frame
Type .... Welded pressed-steel monocoque body with detachable side panels

Suspension
Front .... Single-sided trailing link, with oil-damped coil spring suspension unit
Rear .... Single-sided, using engine/gearbox unit as suspension member. Single oil-damped coil spring suspension unit

Torque wrench settings

Component	kgf m	lbf ft
Suspension unit mounting plate nuts	2.0 – 2.7	14.5 – 19.5
Suspension unit to mounting plate nut	3.0 – 4.0	21.7 – 28.9
Suspension unit lower mounting nuts	2.0 – 2.7	14.5 – 19.5
Steering head adjuster (preload) – P125/150 X and P200 E	0.6 - 0.7	4.34 - 5.06
Steering head adjuster* PX models	5.0 - 6.0*	36.2 - 43.4*
Steering head locknut – P125/150 X and P200 E	5.0 - 6.0	36.2 - 43.4
Steering head locknut PX models	3.0 - 4.0	21.7 - 28.9
Handlebar pinch bolt	3.0 – 4.4	21.7 – 31.8
Rear suspension unit lower mounting bolt	1.3 – 2.3	9.40 – 16.6
Engine unit pivot bolt	6.1 – 7.5	44.1 – 54.3
Front wheel hub nut	6.0 – 10.0	43.4 – 72.3
Rear wheel hub nut	7.5 – 9.0	54.3 – 65.1
Wheel mounting nuts	2.0 – 2.7	14.5 – 19.5

* After tightening, slacken by approximately $^1/_4$ turn. Steering column should swing freely from lock to lock and all free play should be eliminated.

1 General description

In common with previous Vespa models, the P and PX series employ a pressed steel monocoque body section to which the engine/transmission, suspension and ancillary components are attached. This method of unitary construction is more commonly found in car designs, but has proven successful throughout the Vespa scooter's long production history.

The main body section incorporates a recess on its right-hand side in which the engine unit is accommodated. The latter is attached via a wide pivot point at the front and by the single rear suspension unit at the rear. In this way the engine unit doubles as the rear suspension member, operating in much the same way as a motorcycle swinging arm. The hollow area below the seat is utilised as a housing for the fuel tank, and also the oil tank on models so equipped.

Forward of the main body section lies a flat footboard are , strengthened by a central box section. The latter provides a convenient duct through which the control cables and wiring harness pass. The footboards sweep up to form legshields, and enclose the steering column.

At the top of the steering column is a fully enclosed handlebar arrangement, all of the control cables being concealed within it and passing down into the body next to the steering column. The steering column itself is carried in caged ball steering head races. It emerges inside the deeply valenced front mudguard to form the pivot point for the single-sided trailing link front suspension.

The adoption of single-sided suspension front and rear makes wheel changing considerably easier than on conventional motor-cycle designs, and this combined with the small wheel diameter allows a spare wheel to be carried on the machine. Provision for this is made on the left-hand flank of the body. The spare wheel, where fitted, and the engine/transmission unit, are enclosed by pressed steel side panels retained by quick-release fasteners. On PX series machines the side panel catches are located below the lockable dualseat, providing additional security.

2   Steering column assembly: removal and refitting

1   It is unlikely that it will be necessary to remove the steering column from the machine unless accident damage has been sustained, the front mudguard requires renewal or the steering column bearings are in need of attention. Note, however, the remarks concerning work on the front suspension linkage in Section 5 of this Chapter. If the pins and bushes are to be renewed it is worth removing the steering column and taking this to a Vespa dealer for the work to be carried out. This will minimise the time, and thus the cost, of the renovation work.

2   Place wooden blocks on each side of the rear wheel, then raise the front of the machine about a foot above the ground by placing blocks under the stand feet. Make sure that the machine is stable and in no danger of toppling off the blocks before proceeding further.

3   Disconnect the front brake cable at the hub by unscrewing the knurled adjuster, disengage the cable outer, and refit the trunnion and the adjuster to the end of the cable for safekeeping. Note that it is not necessary to disconnect the speedometer cable. Slacken evenly and progressively the wheel nuts and lift the wheel clear of the brake drum. **Do not** slacken the rim securing nuts.

4   Remove the four cross-head screws which pass up through the underside of the handlebar nacelle to retain the plastic top cover. Lift the cover slightly, taking care not to stretch the cables. If necessary, feed the speedometer and front brake cables up through the steering column from the bottom to gain clearance. Release the speedometer cable by unscrewing the knurled retaining ring, on P125 X, P150 X and P200 E models. In the case of the PX models, squeeze together the tangs on the end of the speedometer cable and pull it clear of the speedometer head. Disconnect the speedometer lamp on the earlier models, or on PX models, unplug the wiring connector from the speedometer head, then lift away the cover.

5   It will now be necessary to release the upper end of the front brake cable. This is accomplished by removing the lever pivot screw locknut followed by the pivot screw itself. Slide the lever blade out of the pivot casting, noting the position of the washers on each side of the pivot and taking care not to lose them. Disengage the cable end from the lever and feed the cable back through the handlebar.

6   It should now be possible to remove the handlebar assembly from the top of the steering column. Slacken and remove the single large pinch bolt which clamps the handlebar casting to the steering column splines. The bolt head is accessible through the hole at the rear of the casting.

7   Grasp the handlebar casting and lift it upwards, rocking it from side to side to assist in freeing it from the splines. The assembly can only be lifted an inch or so before the cables and wiring prevent it from moving further. Take great care not to stretch the cables; if more clearance is necessary, work the cables upwards until the casting clears the splines. Tip the assembly back and away from the steering column, taking care not to damage the speedometer and front brake cables. Support the handlebar assembly so that it lies clear of the steering head and take care to avoid kinking the cables.

8   The steering column can now be removed as an assembly, together with the speedometer and front brake cables and the front mudguard. Using a C-spanner, slacken and remove the steering head locknut, then lift away the tanged washer. Support the column, then

remove the steering head bearing adjuster nut and lift away the upper bearing race. Lower the steering column until it clears the body section and place it to one side. If there is insufficient clearance to permit removal, raise the front further or tip the machine to one side.

9   The assembly is installed by reversing the above procedure. The steering head bearings should be checked prior to assembly and renewed if required, and they should be greased during installation. The bearings must be correctly adjusted, as described below. Fit the adjuster nut, tightening it gradually until all free play is eliminated and no more (torque settings given in Specifications if suitable adaptor can be fabricated); the steering column assembly should swing freely from lock to lock. Note that it is easy to overtighten the head bearings and this must be avoided. Holding the adjuster nut in this position, fit the tanged washer then tighten the locknut securely. If possible use a torque wrench to tighten the locknut to the specified torque setting.

10   When refitting the handlebar casting, check that none of the cables are trapped and align the handlebars with the front wheel before tightening the pinch bolt to 3.0 − 4.4 kgf m (21.7 − 31.8 lbf ft). Refit the front wheel and reconnect and adjust the front brake cable. Check that all controls function correctly before testing the machine.

2.3 Disconnect the front brake cable at the wheel end

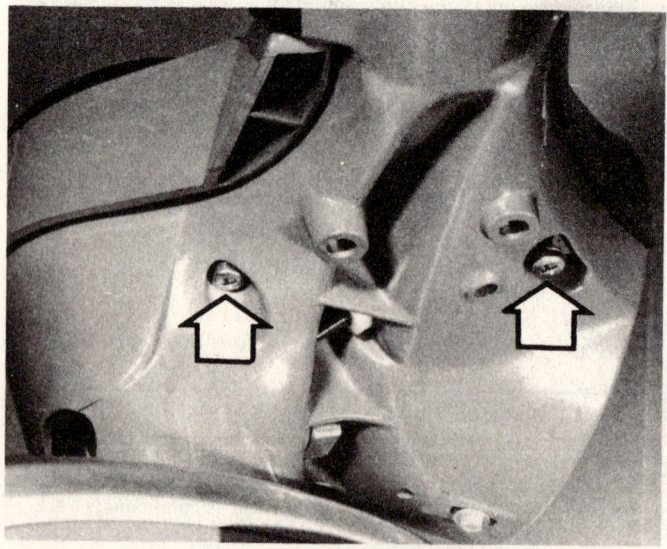

2.4a Remove screws (arrowed) to free handlebar cover

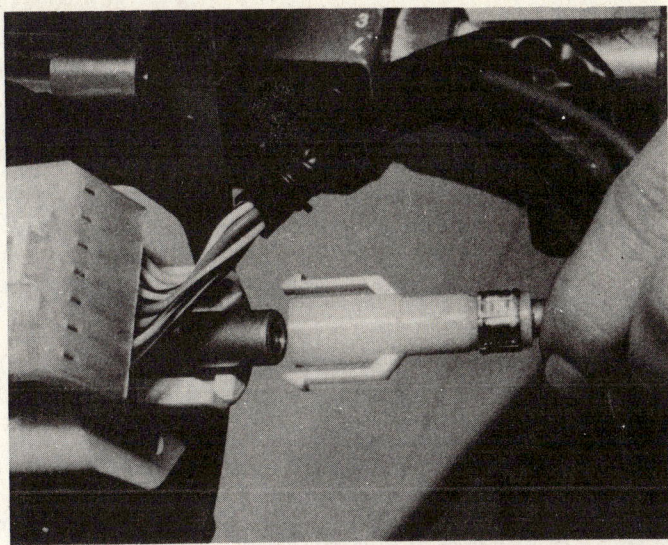

2.4b Disconnect speedometer cable and wiring, then remove cover

2.5a Remove locknut and pivot screw ...

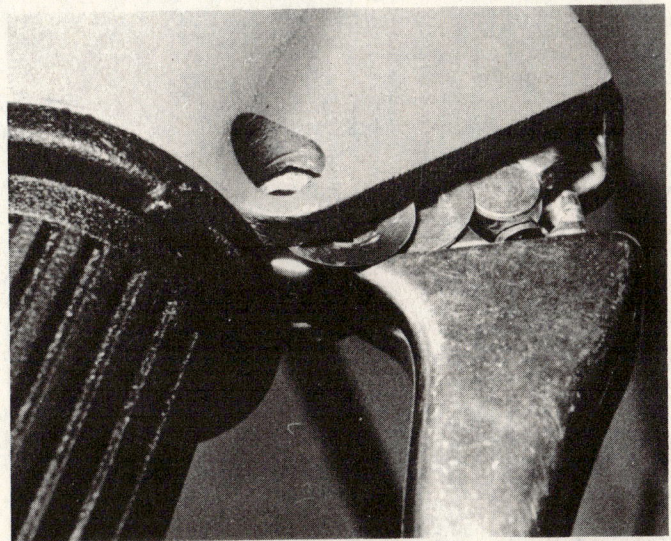

2.5b ... then displace lever, taking care not to lose washers

2.5c Disengage cable from lever and remove trunnion

2.5d Cable can now be pushed through into handlebar unit

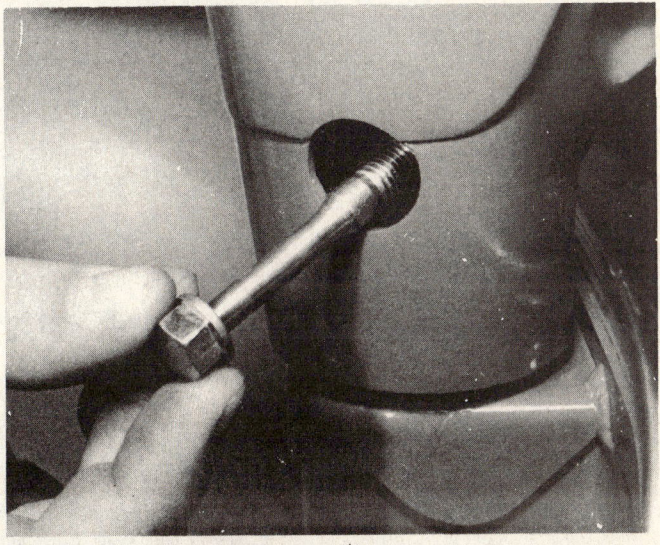

2.6 Remove pinch bolt and lift handlebar off steering column

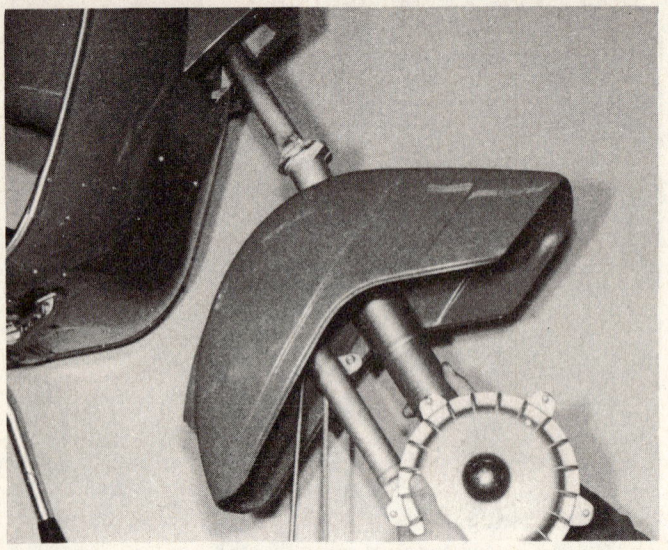

2.8 Slacken steering head nuts and lower column assembly clear of body

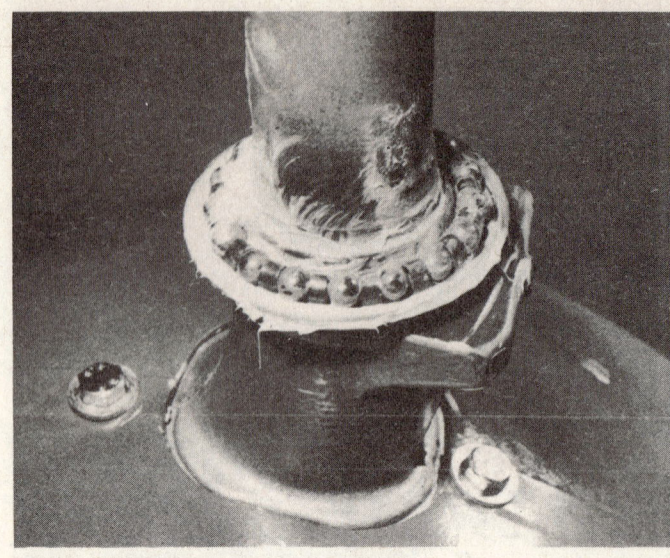

2.9a Grease bearings prior to installation

2.9b Adjust steering head bearings so that play is just taken up

2.9c Fit the tanged washer ...

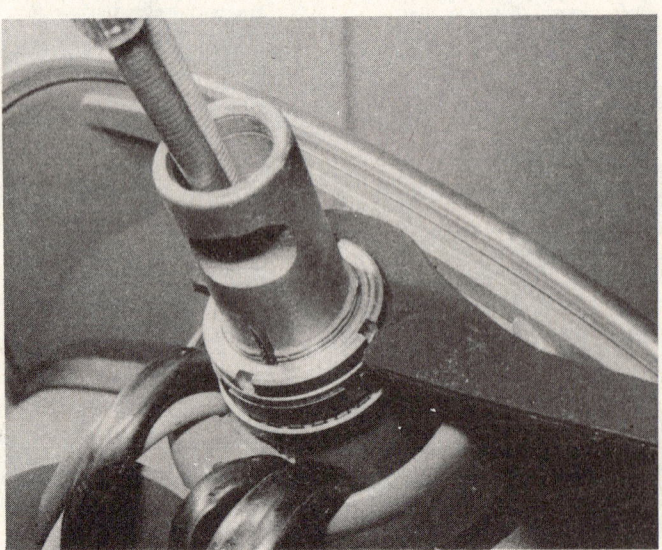

2.9d ... then tighten locknut to secure adjustment

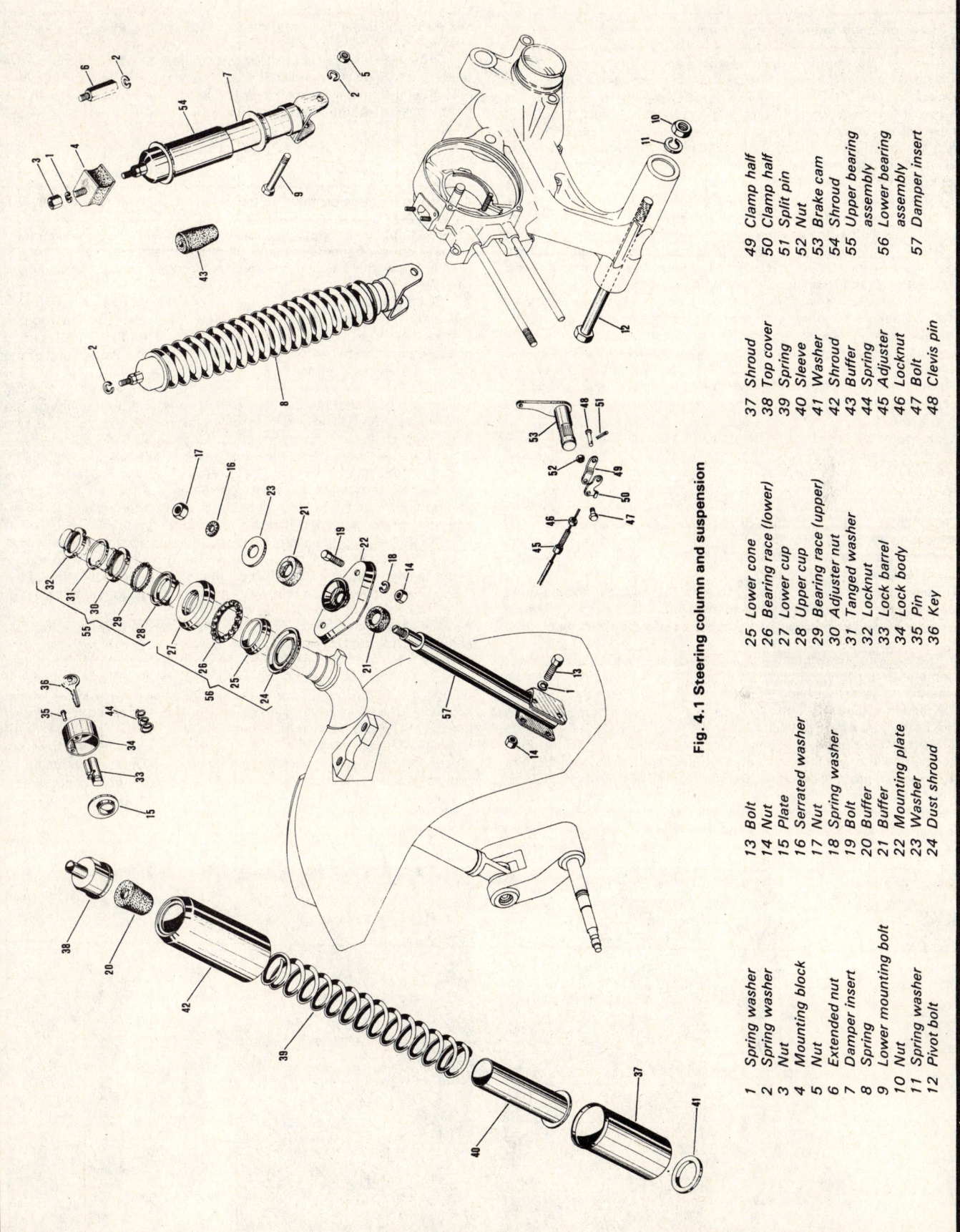

Fig. 4.1 Steering column and suspension

1	Spring washer	25	Lower cone	49	Clamp half
2	Spring washer	26	Bearing race (lower)	50	Clamp half
3	Nut	27	Lower cup	51	Split pin
4	Mounting block	28	Upper cup	52	Nut
5	Nut	29	Bearing race (upper)	53	Brake cam
6	Extended nut	30	Adjuster nut	54	Shroud
7	Damper insert	31	Tanged washer	55	Upper bearing assembly
8	Spring	32	Locknut	56	Lower bearing assembly
9	Lower mounting bolt	33	Lock barrel	57	Damper insert
10	Nut	34	Lock body		
11	Spring washer	35	Pin		
12	Pivot bolt	36	Key		
13	Bolt	37	Shroud		
14	Nut	38	Top cover		
15	Plate	39	Spring		
16	Serrated washer	40	Sleeve		
17	Nut	41	Washer		
18	Spring washer	42	Shroud		
19	Bolt	43	Buffer		
20	Buffer	44	Spring		
21	Buffer	45	Adjuster		
22	Mounting plate	46	Locknut		
23	Washer	47	Bolt		
24	Dust shroud	48	Clevis pin		

3   Steering head bearings: adjustment and renewal

1   The steering column is supported by, and pivots on, two sets of caged ball bearings. In time these will wear and allow free play to develop. Wear of this type should be attended to as soon as it is noticed; if left it will worsen quite quickly and will necessitate bearing renewal if damage or indenting occurs. Check for free play with the machine on its stand. Grasp the handlebar and attempt to push and pull it against the bearings. If any free movement is detected, the bearings are slack or worn and in need of attention.

2   If play has been found, try turning the handlebar from lock to lock. It should move smoothly and easily. If the movement seems notchy or rough it is likely that the bearings are badly worn or damaged. Remove the steering column from the machine as described in Section 2, then check the bearings as follows. If the bearings appear to be in good condition and require adjustment only, move on to paragraph 6.

3   Wash off all old grease with petrol and give the bearings and races a close visual examination. Both the races and the bearing balls should present a highly polished surface; if worn or indented they must be renewed. The lower bearing cup and the upper bearing race are a press-fit in the steering column tube, and can be removed by driving them out with a long drift. The lower bearing cone will remain on the steering column and can be removed by levering it off, using an old screwdriver.

4   Fit the new lower bearing cone, using a length of tubing to drive it squarely home over the steering column. The lower bearing cup and the upper bearing race are best fitted using a drawbolt arrangement to pull them squarely into the steering head tube. A Vespa tool, Part Number T.0021330, is available for this purpose, or it may be possible to improvise using a length of threaded rod obtained from an engineering works or steel stockist. In an emergency, use a large socket as a drift to tap them home, but be very careful to ensure that they seat squarely in the tube.

5   Reassemble the steering column with the new bearings, having greased them and the races prior to installation. The bearings should be adjusted during reassembly, and this is described in Section 2 above.

6   The steering head bearings can be adjusted with the handlebar assembly in position, though to gain access it will normally be necessary to raise the handlebar casting slightly. This is easily done once the large clamp bolt has been removed. The assembly should be lifted up by about half an inch.

7   Slacken the slotted locknut by at least one turn, using a C-spanner. Now tighten the adjuster nut very carefully, until all discernible free play has just been eliminated. **Do not** tighten it any more than is absolutely necessary. It is surprisingly easy to overload the bearings by excessive tightening, and the resulting pressure on the bearings will cause them to wear rapidly or may crack the races. Check that the steering column moves freely from lock to lock. If there is any sign of stiffness, the bearings are too tight; slacken the adjuster and start again.

8   Once adjusted correctly, hold the adjuster in position and secure the locknut. Slide the handlebar casting into position and fit the pinch bolt. Check that the handlebar is aligned correctly in relation to the front wheel, then tighten the pinch bolt to 3.0 – 4.4 kgf m (21.7 – 31.8 lbf ft).

4   Front suspension unit: removal, overhaul and reassembly

1   The front suspension unit can be removed with the remaining front suspension components in place. Note that the accompanying photographs show the steering column and front mudguard removed for clarity.

2   Place the machine on its stand and position wooden blocks below the stand feet to raise the front wheel well clear of the ground. Remove the front wheel, taking care not to disturb the rim securing nuts. Release the two nuts and bolts which retain the lower end of the unit to the suspension link.

3   The upper end of the unit is secured by a single nut to a plate, which is in turn held by two captive bolts and nuts to the lugs on the steering column. Using a socket or a box spanner, remove the two nuts, then lift the unit away together with the mounting plate.

4   If the operation of the suspension unit is suspect, it is recommended that it is taken to a Vespa dealer for overhaul. It is possible to carry out the work at home, but this should not be attempted unless some method of compressing the unit safely can be devised. Where such facilities are available, compress the unit just enough to start compressing the spring, then remove the single nut at the upper end. Release the unit slowly until the spring is no longer under tension and lift away the mounting plate, upper cup and buffers, the spring and the spring shrouds. Lay the various components out in order to avoid confusion during assembly.

5   The operation of the damper insert should be checked by comparing it with a new unit. If the damping effect is weak or non-existent, renew it. No specific data is available on the spring, but as a general rule it will probably be in need of renewal by the time the damper has worn out. The unit is assembled by reversing the above sequence. Note that the retaining nut should be tightened to 3.0 – 4.0 kgf m (21.7 – 28.9 lbf ft).

6   Before installing the unit, displace the two captive bolts from the steering column lugs and clean them thoroughly. Grease the threads to prevent subsequent corrosion, then refit them. Offer up the unit and fit the two mounting plate nuts, tightening them to 2.0 – 2.7 kgf m (14.5 – 19.5 lbf ft). Fit the lower mounting bolts and nuts, tightening these to the same figure.

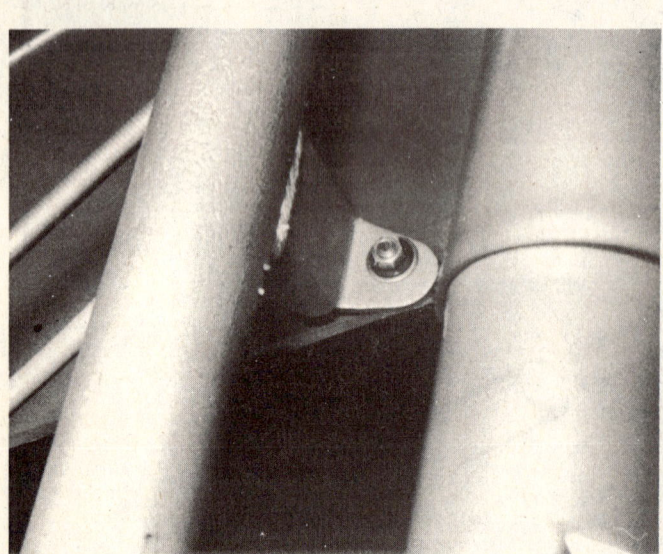

4.1a Front mudguard can be removed with steering column detached. It is held by single bolt at side ...

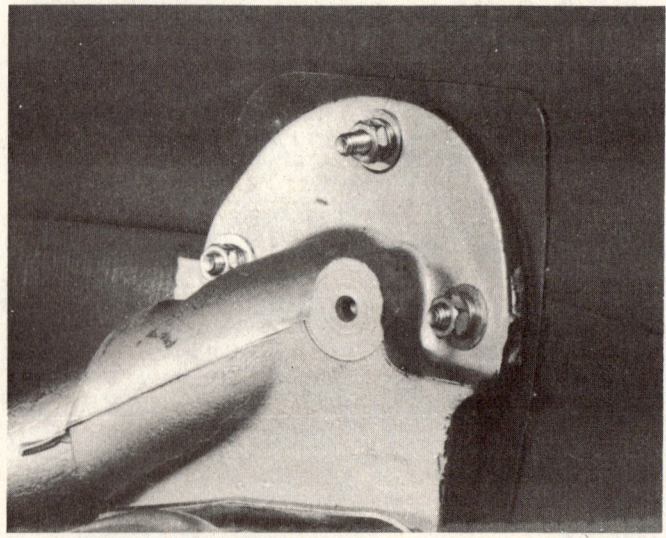

4.1b ... and by three bolts at the top

4.2 Release the two lower mounting bolts

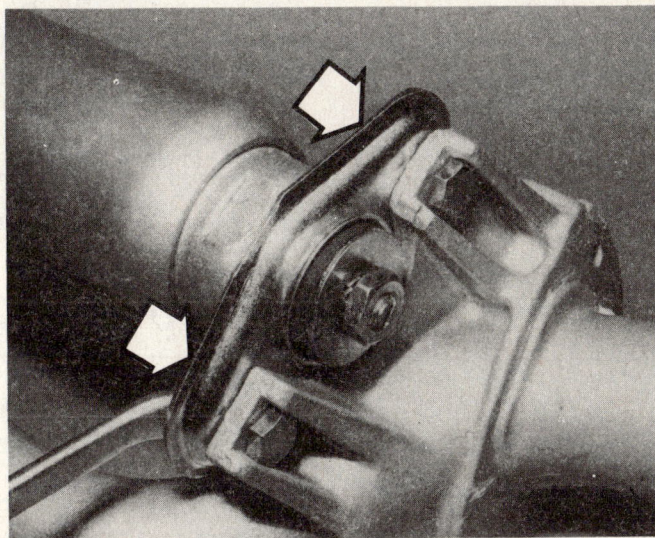

4.3a Remove the two nuts which secure mounting plate to steering column ...

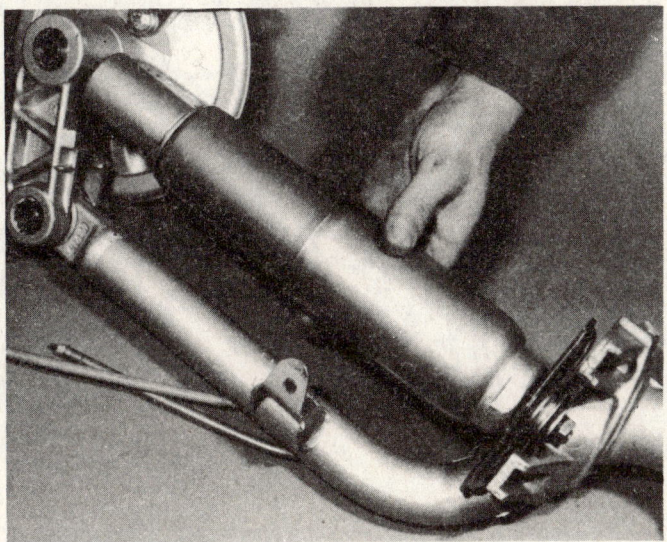

4.3b ... then lift the suspension unit away

Section 2. With the column removed from the machine, release the front suspension unit as described in Section 4, then take the assembly to a Vespa dealer for the overhaul work to be carried out.

6 Rear suspension unit: removal and refitting

1   If it proves necessary to remove the rear suspension unit, the fuel tank must first be removed to gain access to the upper mounting bolt, and reference should be made to Chapter 2 for details. Release the side panels, then raise the rear wheel clear of the ground by placing blocks beneath the rear of the body pressing.
2   Remove the lower mounting nut and displace the bolt to free the lower end of the unit. Working through the tank opening, slacken and remove the upper mounting nut. The unit can now be lifted away. When refitting the unit, tighten the upper mounting nut securely. The lower mounting should be tightened to 1.3 – 2.3 kgf m (9.4 – 16.6 lbf ft).

7 Rear suspension pivot and suspension unit mounting bush: removal and renewal

1   As has been mentioned, the rear suspension arm is formed by the engine/transmission casting which is supported on metal sleeved rubber bushes pressed into the pivot sleeve. The most common problem in this area is where rusting occurs between the inner metal bushes and the pivot bolt. This poses something of a problem because it effectively prevents the removal of the latter by normal methods, and thus the engine unit cannot be removed from the body.
2   The only course of action in these circumstances is to cut or drill away the ends of the pivot bolt to allow the unit to be removed. The remains of the bolt and the sleeves can then be driven through the rubber bushes, which must then be removed and renewed.
3   Renewal of the bushes is, unfortunately, another job which is beyond the resources of most owners. The rubber bushes have to be compressed during fitting and a number of special tools are required to carry out the work. If renewal is required, it is worth removing the engine unit from the body as described in Chapter 1. The unit should then be taken to a Vespa dealer for the new bushes to be fitted.
4   In the case of the rear suspension lower mounting, a similar problem exists, but the work can be carried out with engine installed and with little preliminary dismantling. Once again, special tools are required and the work must be entrusted to a Vespa dealer.

5 Front suspension linkage: overhaul

1   The front stub axle is supported on a forked trailing link, this being carried on a pivot pin and needle roller bearings. Whilst the arrangement is well sealed and will last for a considerable time under normal circumstances, it is likely that the pin and bearings will require renewal during the life of the machine. This is often due to corrosion of the pin or the bearings after failure of one or more of the seals, and little can be done to avoid this other than regular cleaning of the pivot area and application of WD 40 or a similar maintenance fluid.
2   If wear is evident in the pivot, the pin and bearings should be renewed without delay; it will upset the handling at the very least, and is inherently dangerous. In the UK such wear will result in the machine failing its annual MOT test. Unfortunately the necessary repair work is beyond the scope of the owner, requiring specialised service tools. Whilst it will be necessary to have the work carried out by a Vespa dealer, it is well worth removing the steering column assembly to minimise the labour charges incurred. This procedure is described in

Fig. 4.2 Front suspension linkage

1	Steering column	7	Nut	13	Pivot pin
2	Mudguard	8	Cover	14	Screw
3	Trim	9	Suspension link	15	Washer
4	Bolt	10	Bearing	16	Spring washer
5	Washer	11	Seal	17	Nut
6	Spring washer	12	Seal	18	Washer

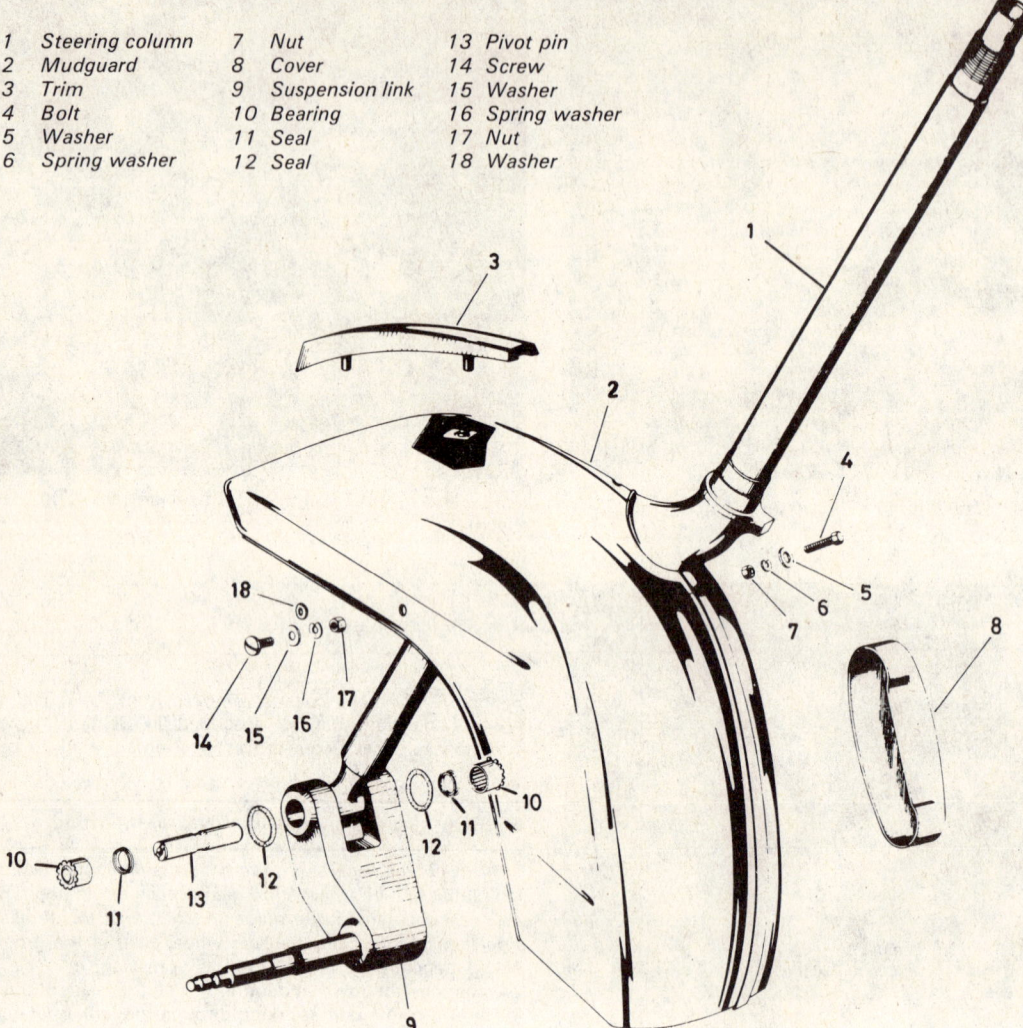

6.2 Lower end of rear suspension unit is retained by bolt passing through rubber-bushed lug

8   Control cable renewal

1   In the event of one of the control cables breaking, it should be noted that, as a rule, the inner cable can be renewed separately. Exceptions to this are the choke and throttle cables which, because of their construction, are best renewed complete. In all cases where the complete cable is to be renewed, note that the damaged cable must be left in position to provide a method of drawing the new cable into place.

2   To gain access to the upper end of all but the rear brake cable, it will first be necessary to detach the handlebar upper cover. This is described in Section 2 of this Chapter. The throttle, clutch, gearchange and rear brake cables pass through the centre section of the body. To ease fitting, it is usually necessary to remove the fuel tank as described in Chapter 2. If any cable becomes stuck in the upper part of the steering column, the horn cover should be removed to gain access to it. This is secured by a single screw which can be reached after the 'Piaggio' badge has been prised away, and by two screws fitted from inside the toolbox. Where cables pass through holes in the bodywork, it is helpful to remove the grommets through which they pass.

Throttle cable

3   Remove the right-hand side panel, then remove the top of the carburettor casing and lift away the air filter element. The lower end of

the cable can now be disengaged and pulled clear of the casing. Unhook the upper end of the cable from the throttle twistgrip pulley. Using strong PVC tape, bind the lower end of the new cable outer to the upper end of the old one, taking care not to leave loose ends which might snag as the cables are pulled through the body. The new cable can now be drawn into position by pulling the old one out.

Clutch cable
4   Release the lower end of the cable by removing the trunnion from the end of the cable inner. To free the upper end, remove the locknut from the lever pivot screw, then remove the screw. Displace the lever, noting the position of the plain and spring washers which will drop free. Release the cable from the lever and push it through into the centre of the handlebar unit.
5   If the inner cable only is to be renewed, pull out the old one and then feed the new one through the outer, having first greased it along its length. If the entire cable is to be renewed, draw the new one into position in the same way as described for the throttle cable.

Gearchange cables
6   Where an inner cable is to be renewed, remove the cover from the selector box and release the lower end of the cable. Pull out the damaged cable from the top, grease the new cable and feed it into position. Clamp the lower end in its trunnion and then set the cable

adjusters so that the gear position marks align correctly and free play in the cables is eliminated.
7   The complete cables are best renewed as a pair because they run through a tightly-fitting sleeve. Disconnect the upper and lower ends of both cables, then tape the new cables to the upper ends of the old ones as described above for the throttle cable. The new cables can then be drawn into place as the old ones are pulled out. Reconnect and adjust the cables as described in paragraph 6.

Rear brake cable
8   Free the rear end of the cable by releasing the nut and retainer plate which secures it to the brake arm and unscrewing the cable adjuster. To gain access to the front of the cable it is necessary to remove the pedal assembly from the body. Start by removing the pedal rubber. Remove the pedal bracket retaining nuts, then manoeuvre the assembly clear of the body, feeding the pedal through the hole in the footboard. Tape the rear end of the new cable to the front end of the old and draw it into position. Once fitted, adjust the cable to give the minimum free play required to prevent the brake from dragging.

Front brake cable
9   Disconnect the lower end of the cable by releasing the nut and retainer plate at the brake arm and then unscrewing the adjuster. The

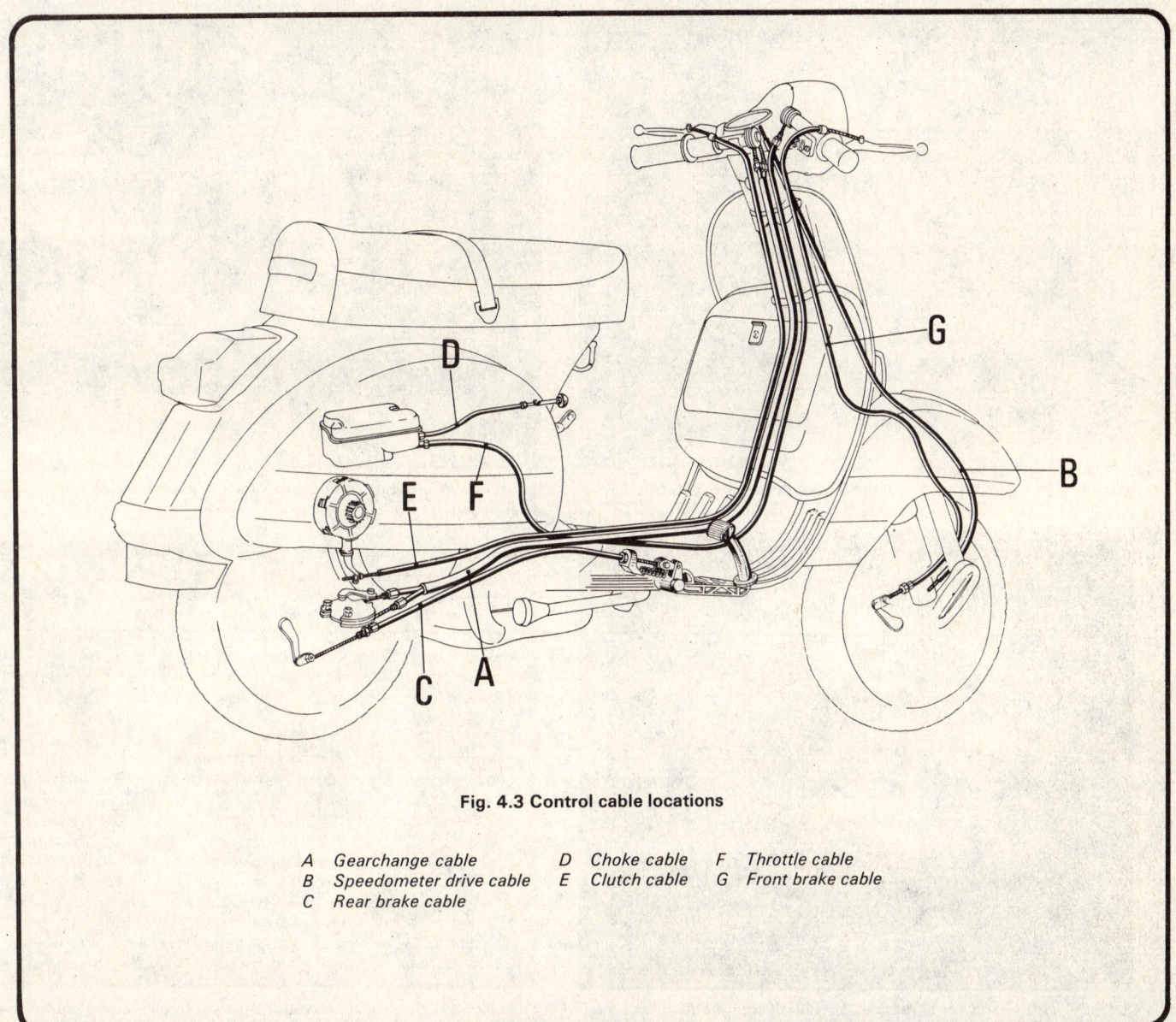

Fig. 4.3 Control cable locations

A Gearchange cable	D Choke cable	F Throttle cable
B Speedometer drive cable	E Clutch cable	G Front brake cable
C Rear brake cable		

upper end is freed as described above for the clutch cable. The cable inner can be renewed by withdrawing the old one, then greasing the new inner and feeding it down from the top. If the entire cable is to be renewed, tape the lower end of the old cable to the upper end of the new one and draw it into place. Note that the cable passes through an S-bend before emerging from the steering column and thus will require careful manoeuvring at this point.

Speedometer cable
10 The inner cable can be renewed by pulling the old one out from the top. Grease all but the top six inches of the cable and feed it into position. If the outer is to be renewed, start by removing the retainer at the lower end. Pull out the inner, then refit it from the **bottom.** Hold the inner in position, then withdraw the outer, leaving the inner in place as a guide. Thread the new outer over the inner cable until it emerges from the steering column. The inner can now be withdrawn and fitted from the top.

Choke cable
11 Remove the right-hand side panel, carburettor cover and the air filter element to gain access to the rear end of the cable, which can then be unhooked and pulled out of the casing. Remove the fuel tank (Chapter 2) to gain access to the front of the cable.

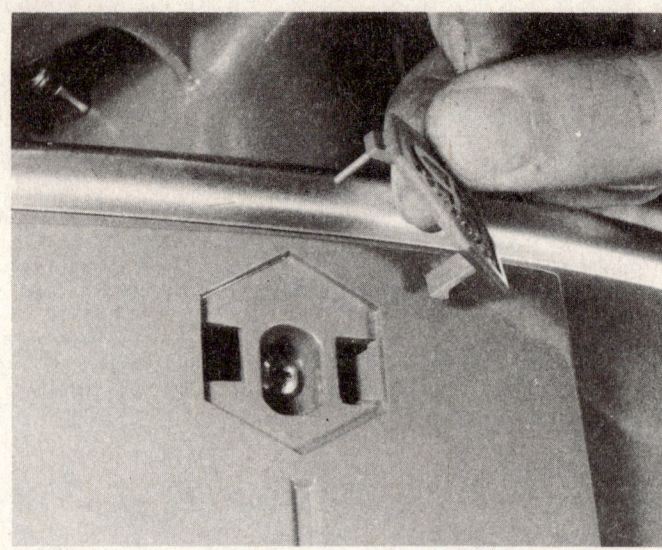

8.2a Prise off the 'Piaggio' badge and remove horn cover upper screw ...

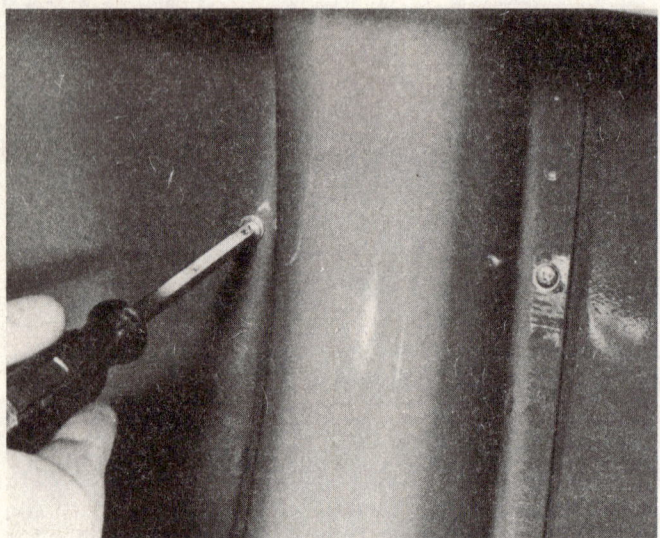

8.2b ... then remove the two screws from inside the toolbox

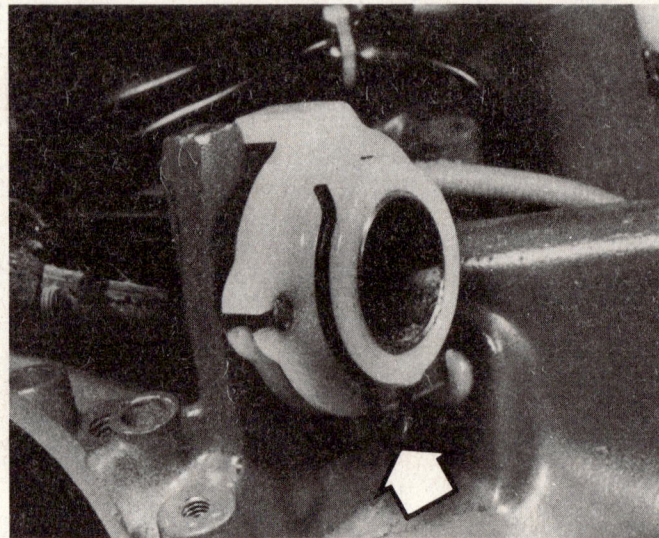

8.3 Remove clip (arrowed) and slide off pulley. Cable can now be disengaged

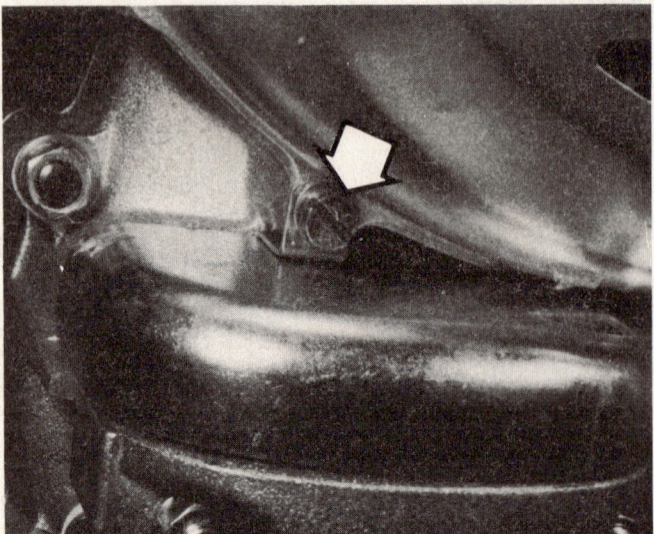

8.6a Selector box cover is retained by one of the fan cowl screws

8.6b As with throttle cable, remove pulley to allow gear cables to be disengaged easily

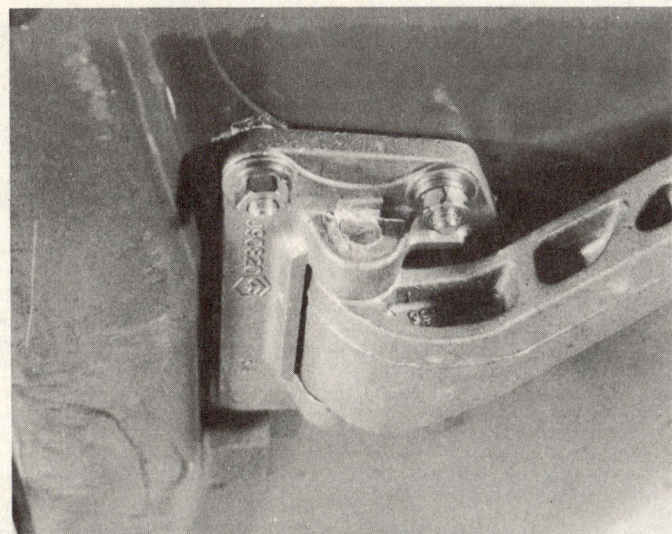

8.8a Remove pedal rubber, then release pedal bracket nuts

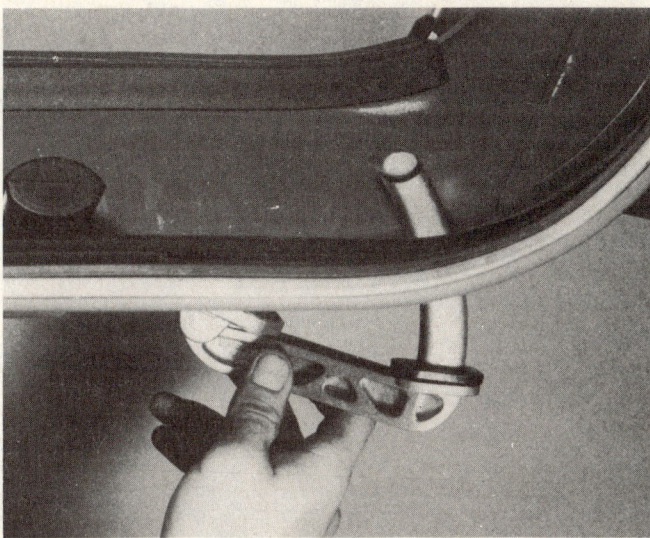

8.8b Lower pedal assembly clear of footboard

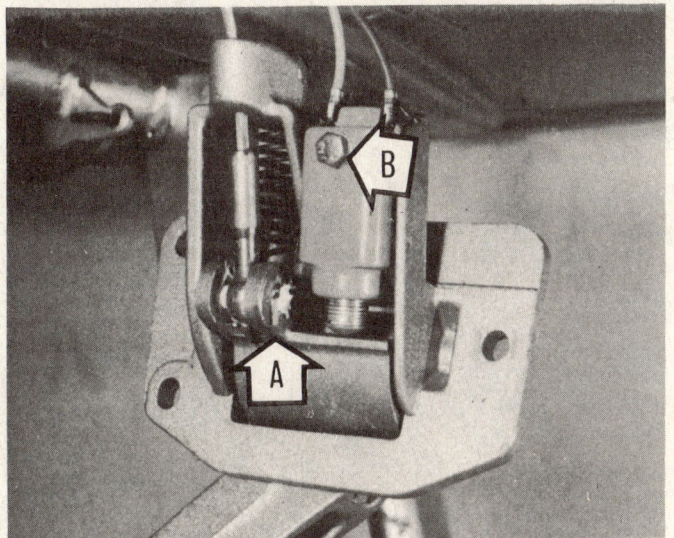

8.8c Cable is retained by clevis pin and split pin (A). Note also the brake switch and retaining bolt (B)

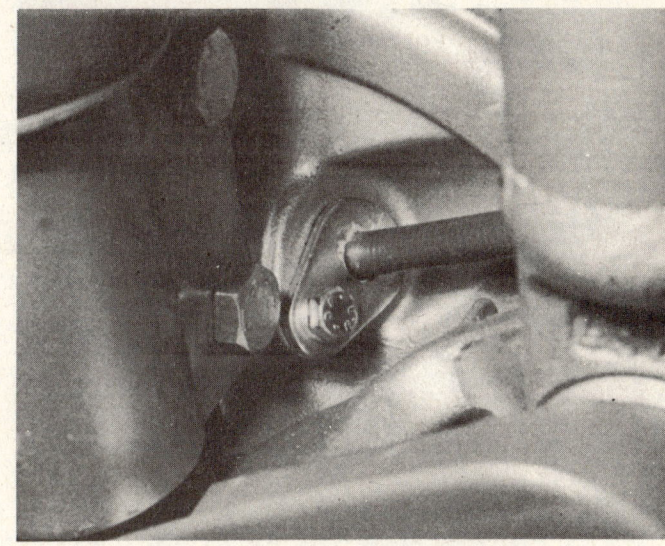

8.10 Speedometer cable is held by retainer plate at lower end

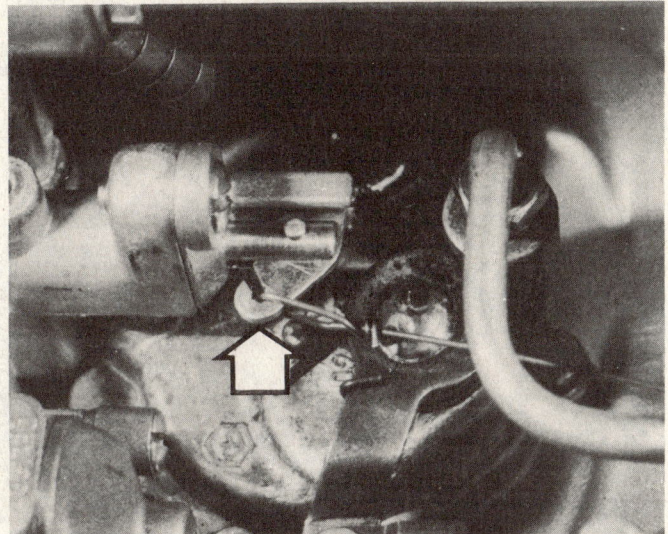

8.11 Lower end of choke cable is hooked over operating link

9 Body: examination and renovation

1   The one-piece main body pressing is unlikely to require attention unless accident damage has been sustained. If this is the case it is strongly advised that the machine is checked by a Vespa dealer, because it is likely that other areas will have been damaged that may not be readily apparent. Repair of the body is likely to prove impracticable unless of a very minor nature. Since such damage is usually subject to insurance claims, it is usual for the machine to be written off in view of the cost of transferring the mechanical and ancillary components to a new body.

2   Some areas of the body are prone to rusting, particularly where paint damage is common. Rusty areas should be refinished promptly to avoid more extensive damage occurring. The affected area should be rubbed down to bare metal, then coated with an aerosol primer. This surface is then keyed using fine abrasive paper before the finishing coats are applied. Aerosol touch-up paints are obtainable from Vespa dealers. For added protection to the area below the footboards it is a good idea to apply an automotive underseal. This forms a tough, resilient film which will resist stone chips.

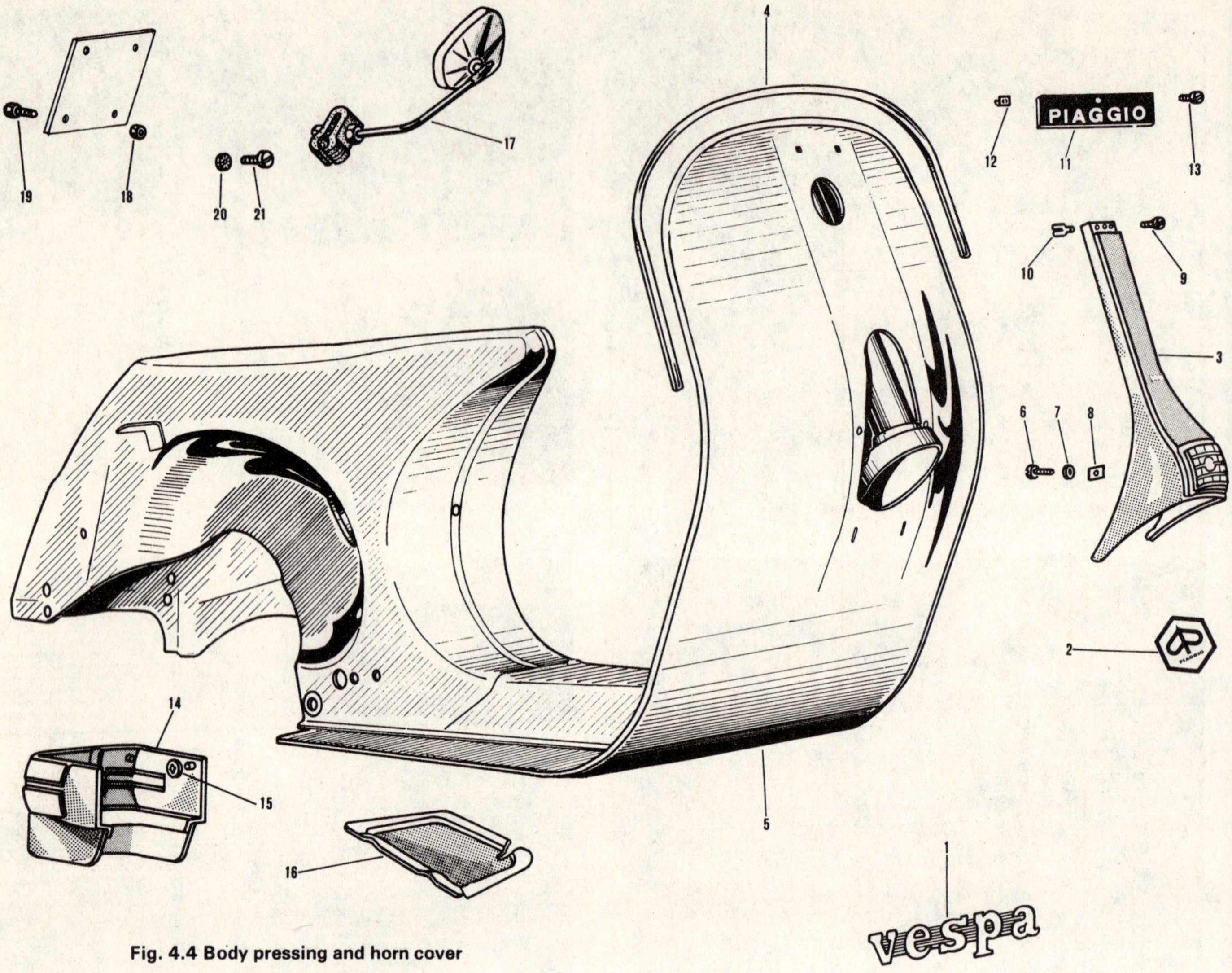

Fig. 4.4 Body pressing and horn cover

1 Badge	12 Fastener
2 Emblem	13 Screw
3 Horn cover	14 Trim
4 Trim	15 Fastener
5 Body pressing	16 Internal body cover
6 Screw	17 Mirror
7 Washer	18 Nut
8 Fastener	19 Bolt
9 Screw	20 Lock washer
10 Plug	21 Screw
11 Badge	

10 Stand: maintenance

1   The machine is fitted with a wide centre stand which is designed to support it with the front wheel raised just clear of the ground. The stand is retained by two brackets, each secured by two bolts and nuts. A coil spring retracts the stand when not in use. Regular cleaning and lubrication of the stand pivots will usually prevent problems occurring, and the condition of the spring can be checked at the same time. Remember that if it breaks, the stand will drop onto the road, and may cause an accident if it catches in a drain cover. For this reason, renew the spring if there is any sign of damage.

2   If it has been abused in the past, the stand stops will eventually bend and the stand will no longer support the machine correctly, necessitating its renewal. This can be avoided by never sitting on the machine when parked and under no circumstances riding the machine off its stand. Note also that the rubber stand feet should be renewed if they have worn through.

10.1 Check stand pivots and condition of return spring

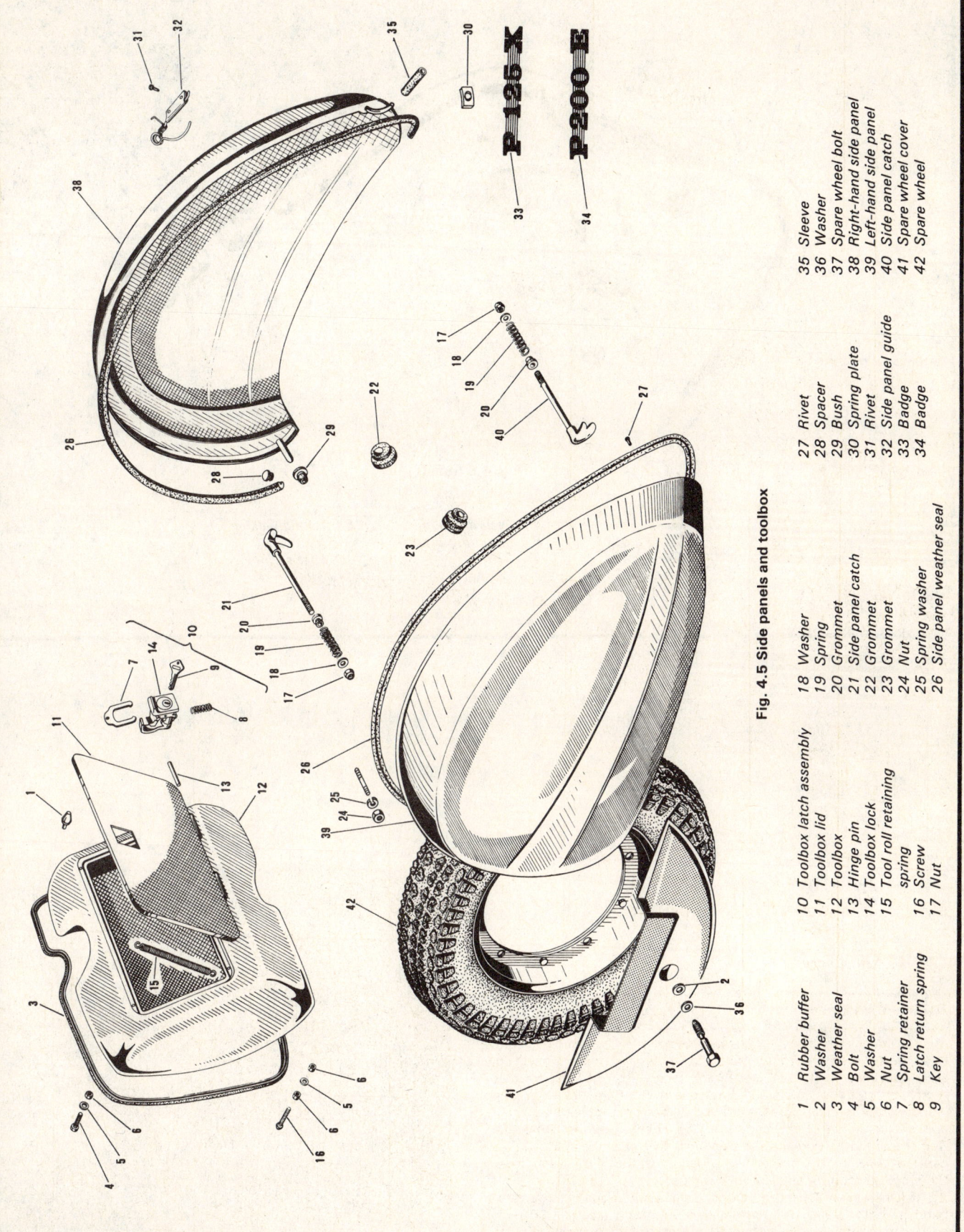

Fig. 4.5 Side panels and toolbox

1	Rubber buffer	10	Toolbox latch assembly	18	Washer	27	Rivet	35	Sleeve
2	Washer	11	Toolbox lid	19	Spring	28	Spacer	36	Washer
3	Weather seal	12	Toolbox	20	Grommet	29	Bush	37	Spare wheel bolt
4	Bolt	13	Hinge pin	21	Side panel catch	30	Spring plate	38	Right-hand side panel
5	Washer	14	Toolbox lock	22	Grommet	31	Rivet	39	Left-hand side panel
6	Nut	15	Tool roll retaining	23	Grommet	32	Side panel guide	40	Side panel catch
7	Spring retainer		spring	24	Nut	33	Badge	41	Spare wheel cover
8	Latch return spring	16	Screw	25	Spring washer	34	Badge	42	Spare wheel
9	Key	17	Nut	26	Side panel weather seal				

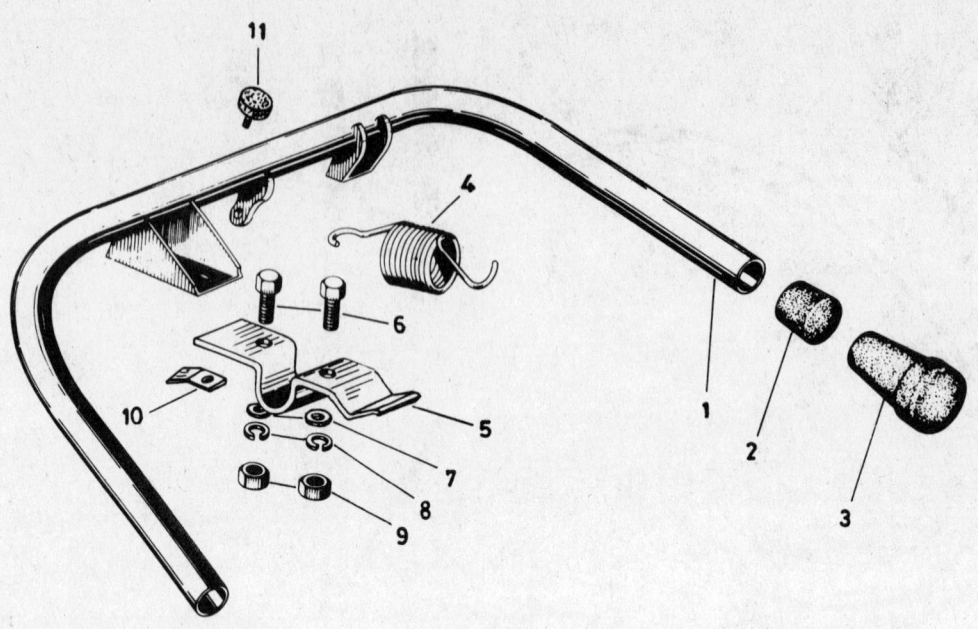

Fig. 4.6 Stand

1	Stand	4	Return spring	8	Spring washer
2	Stand foot	5	Mounting bracket	9	Nut
3	Stand foot – alternative type	6	Bolt	10	Leaf spring
		7	Washer	11	Stop

Chapter 5 Wheels, brakes and tyres

For information relating to later models see Chapter 7

Contents

Specifications

Wheels

Tyre .... Pressed steel split rims, spare wheel available as option. Wheels fully interchangeable

Size .... 2.10 x 10

Brakes

Type .... Internal expanding drum brakes, single leading shoe (sls) type, front and rear

Tyres

Size .... 3.50 x 10, front and rear

Pressures (cold):

Front .... 17.6 psi (1.23 kg/cm^2)

Rear – solo .... 25.8 psi (1.8 kg/cm^2)

Rear – with passenger .... 36.7 psi (2.58 kg/cm^2)

Torque wrench settings

Component	kgf m	lbf ft
Suspension unit mounting plate nuts	2.0 – 2.7	14.5 – 19.5
Suspension unit to mounting plate nut	3.0 – 4.0	21.7 – 28.9
Suspension unit lower mounting nuts	2.0 – 2.7	14.5 – 19.5
Rear suspension unit lower mounting bolt	1.3 – 2.3	9.40 – 16.6
Front wheel hub nut – P125/150 X and P200 E	6.0 - 10.0	43.4 – 72.3
Front wheel hub nut – PX models	7.5 - 9.0	54.3 – 65.1
Rear wheel hub nut – P125/150 X and P200 E	7.5 - 9.0	54.3 – 65.1
Rear wheel hub nut – PX models	9.0 - 11.0	65.1 – 79.5
Wheel mounting nuts	2.0 – 2.7	14.5 – 19.5

1 General description

The wheels on the machines covered in this manual are of pressed steel construction and are fitted with tubed-type tyres. Each wheel consists of two rim halves held together by studs and nuts. This arrangement allows the halves to be separated to simplify tyre changes and puncture repairs. The front and rear wheels are identical and interchangeable, and provision is made for carrying a spare wheel beneath the left-hand side panel.

The front and rear brakes are of the drum type, arranged so that the entire brake, hub and drum remain in place when the wheel is removed. This, allied with the single-sided suspension arrangement, means that the brake need not be disturbed during wheel changes.

1.1 Spare wheel is mounted under left-hand side panel

2 Front and rear wheels: examination and renovation

1   Place the machine on its stand so that the front wheel is raised clear of the ground. Spin the wheel and check the rim alignment. This is made easier if a wire pointer is taped to the steering column and the end positioned near to the rim. There should be little noticeable radial (up-and-down) or axial (side-to-side) runout if the wheel is serviceable. No specific figures are available, but if runout exceeds about 1–2 mm the wheel is probably damaged and vibration may be evident when riding the machine. Do not confuse wheel runout with problems caused by a badly-fitted tyre, which can give similar symptoms.
2   If excessive runout is found, or if the wheel rim is buckled, it is likely that the wheel has suffered quite severe impact damage, perhaps due to the machine having been ridden over a kerb or other obstacle. It is recommended that the condition of the front suspension is also checked since this too may have sustained damage. A damaged rim must be renewed promptly and the tyre checked carefully in case this has been damaged at the same time. If a spare wheel is fitted, use this until the suspect wheel can be checked thoroughly.
3   Check the condition of the wheel bearings by grasping opposite sides of the tyre and attempting to rock the wheel. If there is any noticeable free play, the wheel bearings should be renewed as described in Section 5 of this Chapter. Note that care must be taken not to mistake wear in the front suspension linkage for bearing free play. If suspension wear is noted, refer to Chapter 4.
4   In the case of the rear wheel it will be necessary to prop the rear of the body with blocks to raise the wheel clear of the ground. The rim runout is checked in the same way as has been described for the front wheel, but note that the wheel will spin less freely due to drag in the transmission. If bearing wear is found, it will be necessary to renew the stub axle bearings after the engine/transmission unit has been removed and the crankcase halves separated. See Chapter 1 for details. Wear in the stub axle bearings is usually accompanied by oil leakage from the transmission into the rear hub, rendering the rear brake ineffective, so the repair work must be carried out without delay.

3 Front brake: examination, renovation and reassembly

1   Remove the front wheel by detaching the five retaining nuts and spring washers, noting that the rim securing nuts should **not** be disturbed. Prise off the grease cap at the centre of the hub. Clean off any excess grease, then straighten and remove the split pin which

locks the hub nut. The castellated locking insert can now be lifted away. Slacken and remove the hub nut, then pull the hub off the stub axle. If it proves stubborn, slacken the front brake adjuster and try rocking the hub to loosen it. If absolutely necessary, tap gently on the projecting stud tangs using a hide mallet or a hardwood block and a hammer.
2   Examine the condition of the brake shoes. No specific wear limits are prescribed, but if they have worn thin at the cam end of the lining they should be renewed. As a rough guide, renew the shoes as a pair when worn down to about 1.5 – 2.0 mm at any point. If there appears to be adequate friction material left, but braking performance is poor, the problem is usually due to glazing of the friction surface or grease contamination. In the former case, remove the smooth surface by carefully sanding it down with abrasive paper, but take care not to inhale the toxic asbestos dust which will result. If the linings are contaminated, they should be renewed, after the source of the contamination has been traced and rectified.
3   Clean out the brake drum using a rag moistened in petrol, again taking care to avoid breathing any dust. Check the drum surface for scoring. Light scratching is normal and unavoidable, but if grit has entered the drum at some time it may have become heavily scored and should be renewed together with the brake shoes. It is possible to have the drum skimmed on a lathe to correct scoring or slight warpage, but since this inevitably alters the drum diameter, the standard shoes will not match it correctly. As a general rule, renewal is the best way of resolving the problem.
4   To remove the old brake shoes, release the circlip at the pivot end of each shoe, then work the assembly off the pivots and over the cam, using screwdrivers as levers. When fitting the new shoes, fit the return spring to both shoes and grease the cam faces and pivots before working the assembly into place. It is a good idea to put some masking tape over the lining surfaces to prevent accidental contamination during fitting, but remember to remove it before the drum is fitted.
5   The brake backplate incorporates a needle roller bearing and grease seals. These permit it to move relative to the stub axle, but are prone to corrosion and subsequent failure of the bearing where the grease seals have failed. To remove the brakeplate to permit examination, remove the suspension unit lower mounting bolts. Release the circlip which locates the brake backplate on the stub axle and slide the assembly clear. The precise arrangement of seals, washers and needle roller races varies according to the model, so take care to note the order in which components are removed. The accompanying line drawing illustrates the earlier models, whilst the PX arrangement is shown in the accompanying photographs.
6   The two needle roller races should be cleaned and checked for wear or corrosion. If any of the rollers are less than perfect, renew both races. The old bearings can be driven out using a tubular drift of slightly smaller diameter than the bearings, having first heated the backplate in boiling water. Note that two double-diameter drifts will be required to position the new bearings correctly during assembly, and for this reason it is recommended that they be fitted by a Vespa dealer. If great care is taken, however, and the original positions of the bearings duplicated exactly, careful use of double-diameter drifts will suffice. Once the bearings are in place, press into position the inner and outer grease seals, and grease thoroughly the bearings and the space between them.
7   Before refitting the backplate, examine the condition of the stub axle. If this is worn or indented it must be renewed or the new bearings will be rapidly destroyed. Unfortunately, the stub axle is integral with the suspension link, renewal of which is a job for the dealer. See Chapter 4 for further information.

4 Speedometer drive: maintenance

1   The speedometer drive consists of a skew gear driven by a corresponding gear machined into the hub boss. It requires no regular maintenance, but should be greased whenever the brake is overhauled. In the event of failure, the skew gear, seal and its support block can be displaced as shown in the accompanying photographs. If the gear teeth on the hub become damaged, it will be necessary to renew the hub complete.

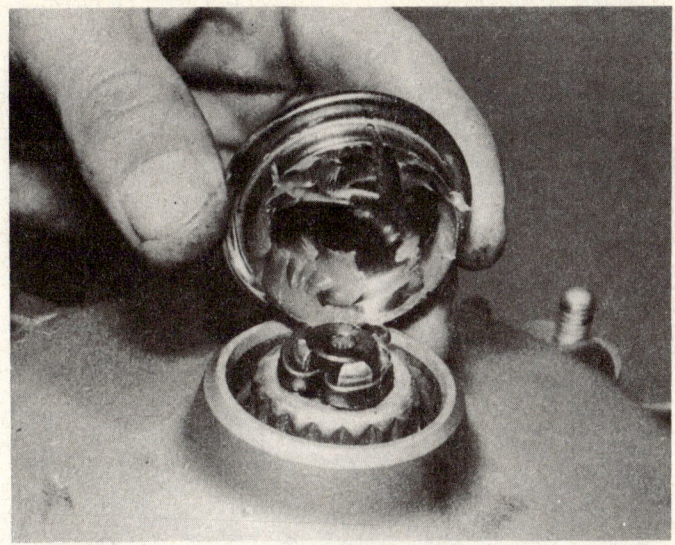

3.1a Prise off the grease cap from hub centre ...

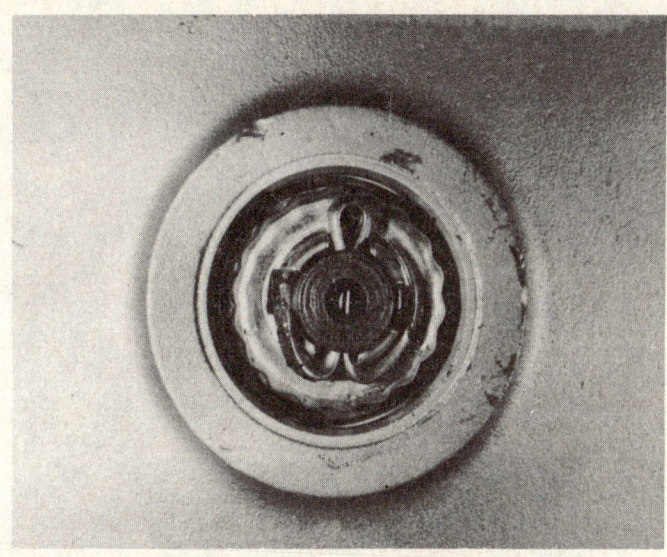

3.1b ... then straighten and remove the split pin

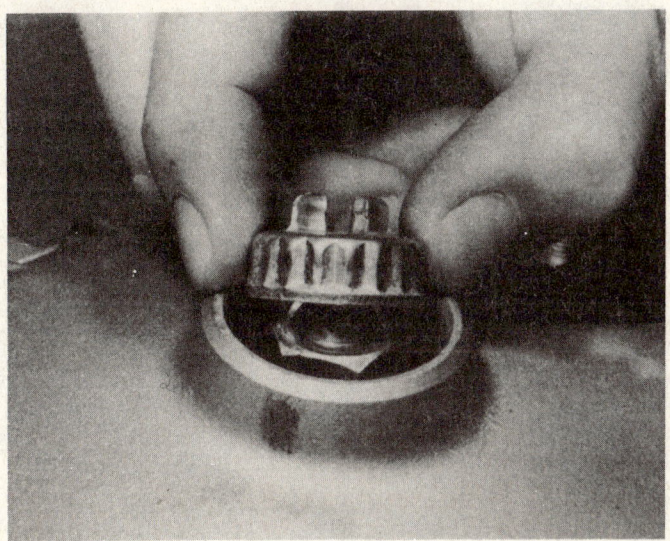

3.1c Lift off the castellated insert and remove nut ...

3.1d ... followed by the plain washer

3.1e Brake drum/hub unit can now be removed to reveal shoes

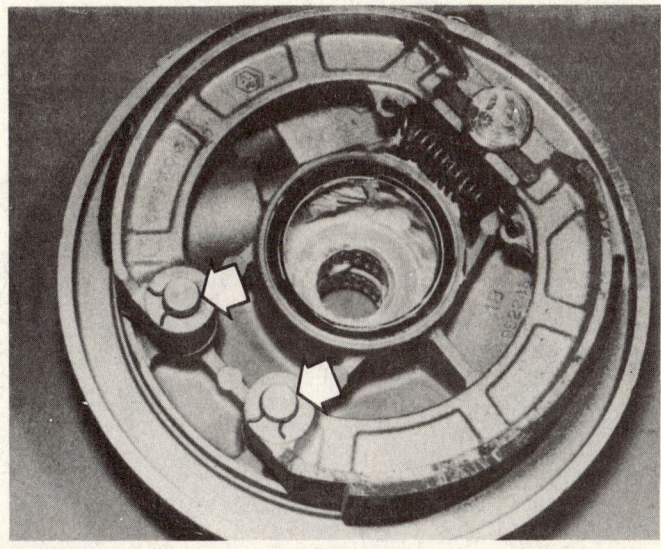

3.4 Brake shoe ends are anchored by circlips (arrowed)

3.5a Free lower end of suspension unit and remove circlip ...

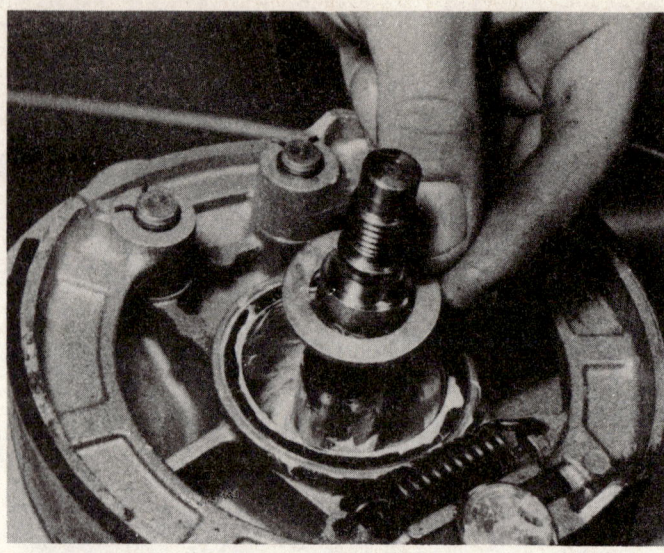

3.5b ... followed by the plain washer

3.5c Brake backplate can now be lifted away ...

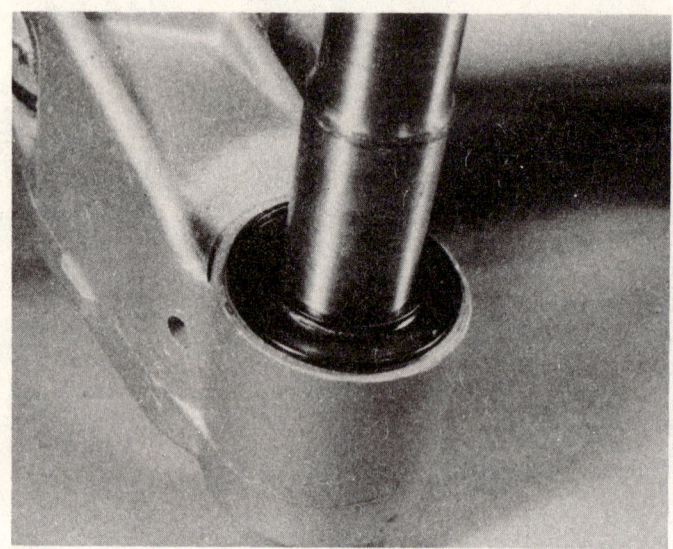

3.5d ... followed by the backplate seal ...

3.5e ... and the shim washer

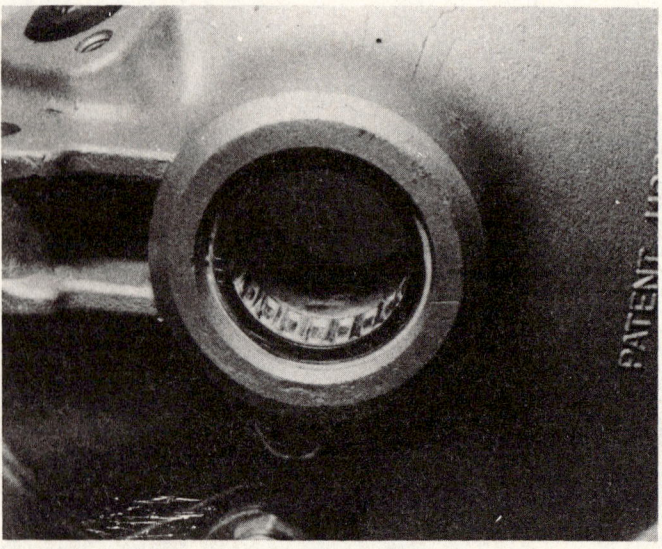

3.6 Check and renew as required the backplate bearings

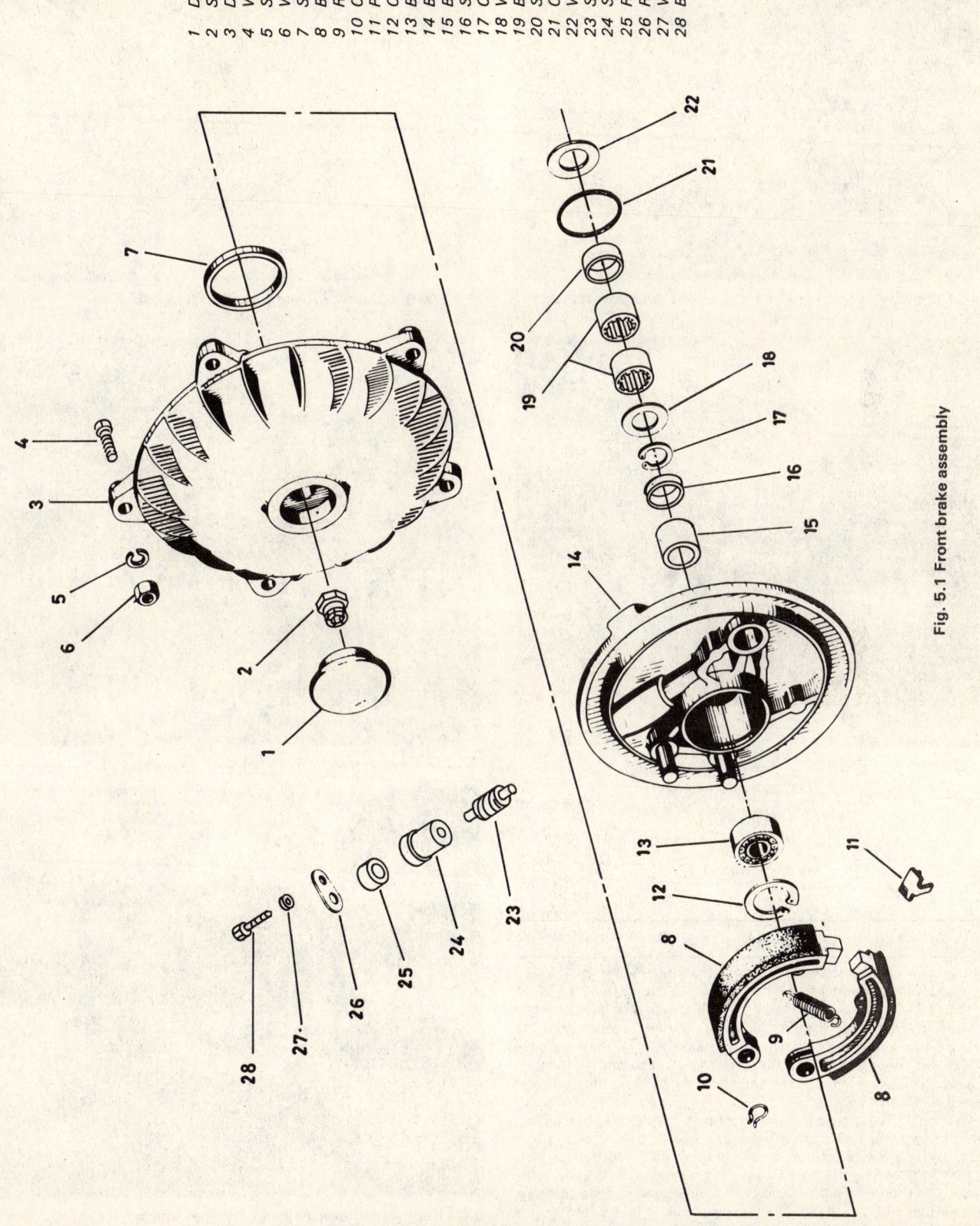

1 Dust cap
2 Stub axle nut
3 Drum/hub assembly
4 Wheel stud
5 Spring washer
6 Wheel nut
7 Seal
8 Brake shoe
9 Return spring
10 Circlip
11 Packing
12 Circlip
13 Bearing
14 Brake backplate
15 Bearing
16 Seal
17 Circlip
18 Washer
19 Bearings
20 Seal
21 O-ring
22 Washer
23 Speedometer drive gear
24 Support block
25 Rubber seal
26 Retainer plate
27 Washer
28 Bolt

Fig. 5.1 Front brake assembly

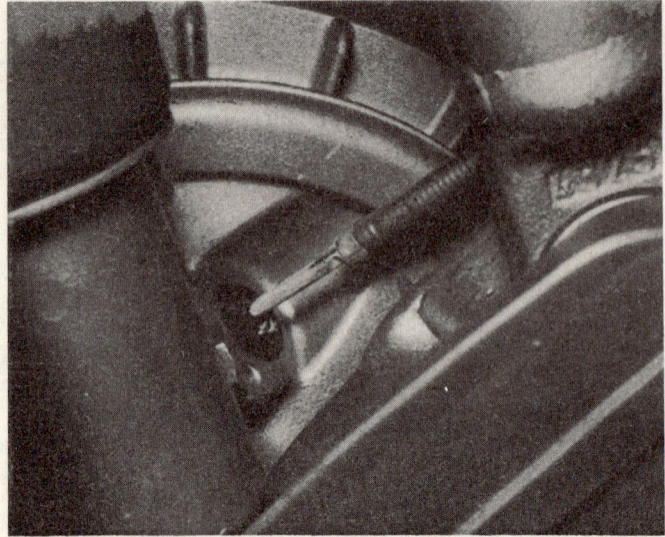

4.1a Speedometer cable is retained and sealed in rubber insert

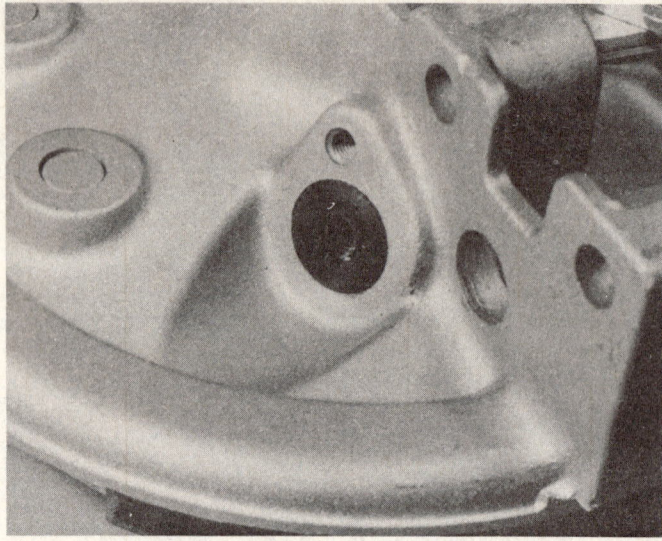

4.1b To remove skew gear, prise out the insert ...

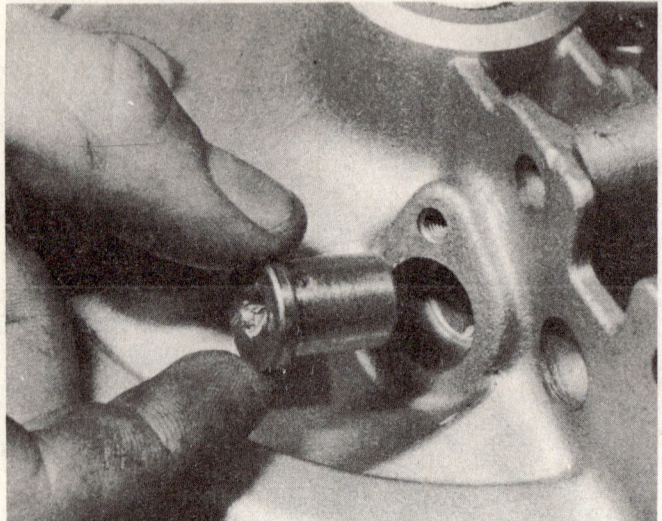

4.1c ... followed by the support block

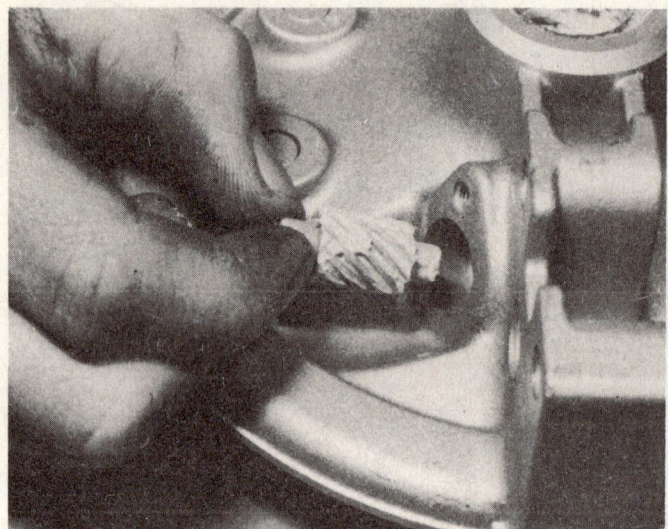

4.1d Skew gear can now be removed for examination

5   Front wheel bearings: renewal

1   If examination has shown the front wheel bearings to be in need of renewal, start by removing the drum as described in Section 3. The outer caged ball bearing is located against a shoulder and retained by a circlip. Remove the circlip, then drive out the old bearing from the inner side using a long drift. Prise out the grease seal on the inner face and note the depth by which the bearing is recessed; it will be necessary to duplicate this when fitting the new one. Drive out and discard the old bearing.

2   Clean out all old grease and heat the hub by immersing it in boiling water. Dry the hub then carefully tap the needle roller bearing into position, using a tubular drift. A small socket is ideal for this purpose. Note that the bearing will be easily distorted if it is not tapped home squarely. Once correctly positioned, fit a new seal. Grease the new outer bearing and tap it squarely home until it is located on its shoulder. Fit the circlip to secure it, then grease both bearings and the area between them.

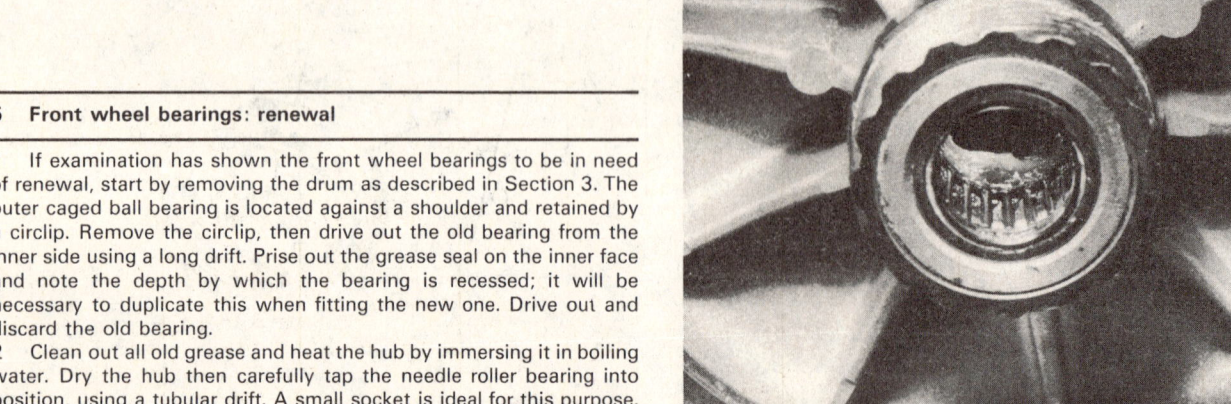

5.2a Tap needle roller bearing home as shown

5.2b Grease outer bearing and hub bore ...

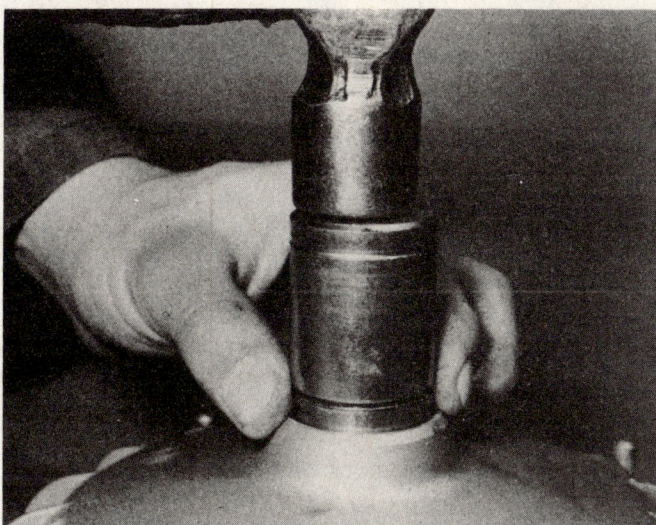

5.2c ... then fit bearing using large socket as drift

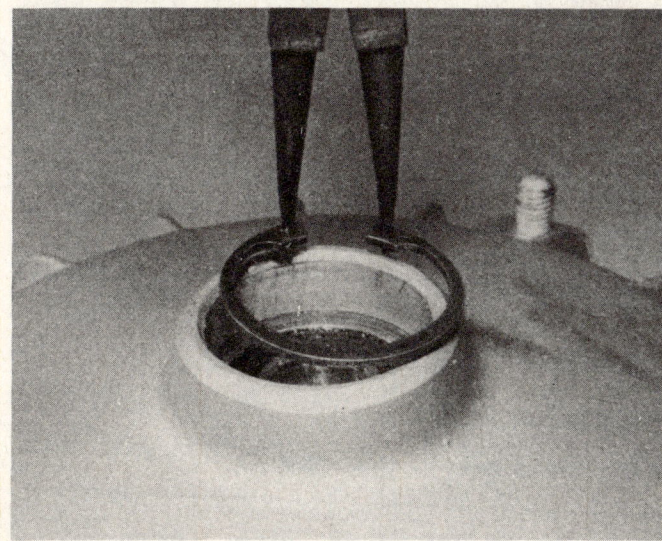

5.2d Secure bearing with circlip

6 Rear brake: examination, renovation and reassembly

1   The rear brake assembly is broadly similar in construction to the front unit, and many of the procedures described in Section 3 can be applied. To gain access to the rear brake components, place the machine on its stand and prop the rear of the body so that the wheel is held clear of the ground. Remove the five wheel nuts and spring washers and remove the wheel, noting that the rim securing nuts should not be disturbed. Prise off the grease cap at the centre of the hub and remove the split pin which locks the hub nut. Slacken and remove the nut, then pull the hub unit off the stub axle splines.

2   Examine the brake shoes for wear, glazing and oil contamination as described for the front brake in Section 3. If it is wished to remove the rear brake backplate it will first be necessary to detach the brake shoes. The backplate is retained by three screws and can be lifted away once these have been unscrewed. Check that the brake cam moves smoothly and easily. If it is stiff, remove the split pin which holds the operating lever to it, then displace the cam. The cam and its bore should be cleaned and re-greased prior to reassembly. When refitting the brake backplate, check that the O-ring seals which fit between it and the casing are undamaged, renewing them if required. Note that if damaged O-rings are used, water and road dirt can enter the brake.

3   If oil contamination is found, check that the stub axle, or output shaft, bearing is unworn. If this is damaged the crankcase halves must be separated to renew it as described in Chapter 1. If the bearing is sound, check the condition of the oil seal. If this is worn out or hardened with age it can be prised out and a new seal fitted.

4   Note that due to modifications to standardise parts across the model range, the seal may be one of two sizes, depending on the type of brake drum fitted. Either seal will fit physically over either drum, but leakage will occur if the wrong size is used. It is a good idea to take the drum when purchasing the seal so that the correct part can be found. The oil seal engages over a projection from the brake drum/hub unit, and it follows that if this is scored or worn the new seal will not last long. Check the surface carefully prior to reassembly, and renew the drum unit if required.

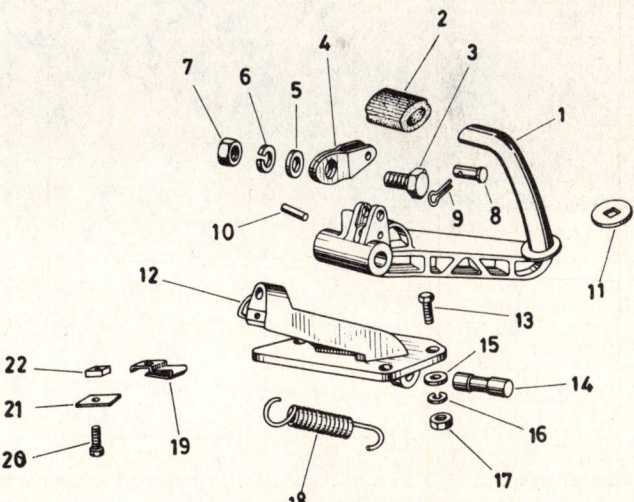

Fig. 5.2 Brake pedal assembly

1	Brake pedal	12	Bracket
2	Pedal rubber	13	Bolt
3	Bolt	14	Pin
4	Cable bracket	15	Washer
5	Washer	16	Spring washer
6	Spring washer	17	Nut
7	Nut	18	Return spring
8	Clevis pin	19	Anchor plate
9	Split pin	20	Bolt
10	Pin	21	Plate
11	Washer	22	Captive nut

6.1 Rear brake is similar to front unit

6.2a Backplate is retained by three screws

6.2b Lift backplate away to gain access to O-ring seals

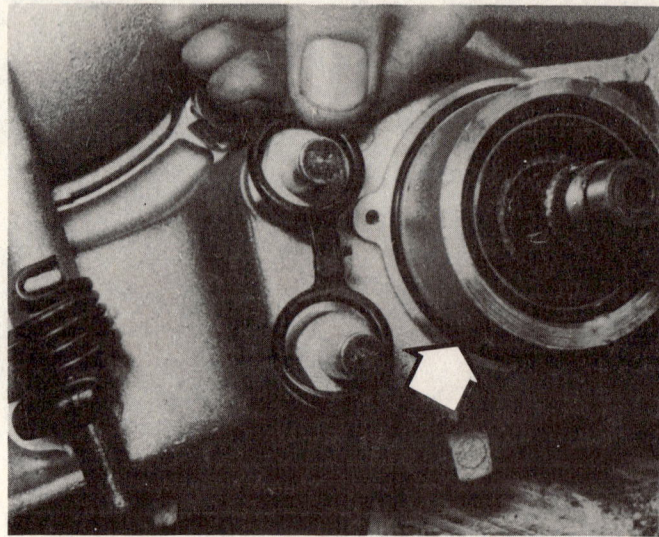

6.2c Note O-rings on pivots and cam boss, and at hub centre (arrowed)

7 Tyres: removal and refitting

1   The split rim construction of the wheels makes tyre changing and puncture repairs a relatively painless process and does not require tyre levers. Start by removing the tyre valve to deflate fully the inner tube. Place the wheel on its side and tread around the tyre close to the rim. This will push the tyre bead towards the centre, making removal easier. Invert the wheel and repeat on the opposite bead.

2   Slacken and remove the five rim retaining nuts and spring washers. The rim halves can now be pulled apart and clear of the tyre. In practice they are often rather stubborn, and it may help if some washing-up liquid is applied between the tyre bead and rim to act as a lubricant. If this fails to free the rims, place wooden blocks between the rim halves and tread the tyre off, taking care not to pinch the tube.

3   The rims are quite likely to have corroded if the machine is more than a few years old, and it is recommended that they are rubbed down and repainted before the tyre is refitted. In extreme cases, rust particles can be trapped between the rim and tube, eventually causing punctures.

4   When joining the rim halves, take great care not to pinch the inner tube between them. To this end it is a good idea to inflate the tube very slightly so that it maintains its shape. To prevent the ingress of water at the rim joint, a thin film of RTV jointing compound can be applied. This will form an effective seal but will not impede subsequent removal. Tighten the rim nuts evenly and progressively, and do not omit the spring washers.

5   When inflating the tyre on a newly assembled wheel, make sure that it sits squarely on the rim. A reference line is moulded on the tyre sidewall for this purpose, and it must be equidistant from the rim at all points. If the tyre is fitted unevenly, wheel vibration will result, so deflate the tyre and re-seat it correctly. The use of washing-up liquid as a lubricant will usually help. Before using the machine, check that the tyres are inflated to the recommended pressures.

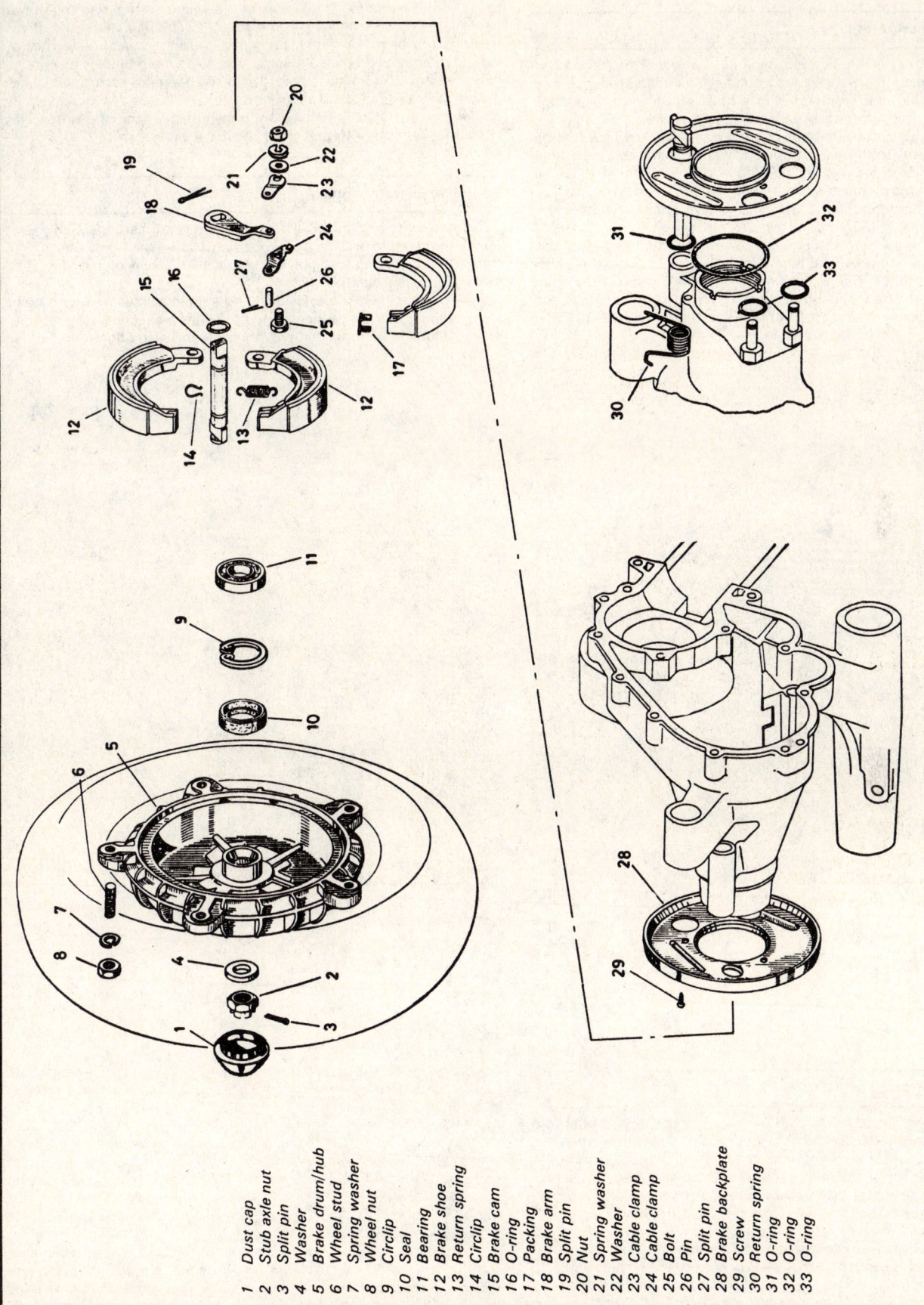

1 Dust cap
2 Stub axle nut
3 Split pin
4 Washer
5 Brake drum/hub
6 Wheel stud
7 Spring washer
8 Wheel nut
9 Circlip
10 Seal
11 Bearing
12 Brake shoe
13 Return spring
14 Circlip
15 Brake cam
16 O-ring
17 Packing
18 Brake arm
19 Split pin
20 Nut
21 Spring washer
22 Washer
23 Cable clamp
24 Cable clamp
25 Bolt
26 Pin
27 Split pin
28 Brake backplate
29 Screw
30 Return spring
31 O-ring
32 O-ring
33 O-ring

Fig. 5.3 Rear brake assembly

8   Tyres: puncture repairs

1   If the tyre has been punctured, separate the wheel rim halves and remove the inner tube as described above. Refit the valve core and reinflate the tube, then immerse it in a bowl of water to locate the source of the leak, marking it with a felt pen or wax crayon. If the puncture is minor and the tube is in good condition, the hole can be patched. If, however, the tube is obviously old or has been patched a number of times before, or if the tube is split or torn, it must be renewed. Remember that a sudden deflation can be very dangerous.

2   Dry the tube thoroughly and clean the area around the puncture with a petrol-soaked rag. Apply a thin, even coating of rubber solution and allow this to dry before applying a self-vulcanising patch. Remove the backing film and press the patch firmly in position. Rub the patch hard to ensure that it bonds onto the tyre, working from the centre outwards. Where fitted, peel off the backing paper from the patch, and apply a little french chalk or talcum powder to any remaining rubber solution on the tube.

3   Before refitting the tyre and tube, try to locate and remove the cause of the puncture. If this was in the vicinity of the tyre tread look for nails or wire embedded in the tread. Check that the fabric of the tyre has not been damaged, particularly after a puncture caused by impact damage. Note that in some cases the internal plies of the tyre may be broken with no outward sign of damage. If in doubt, seek expert advice or play safe and renew the tyre. Punctures in the vicinity of the rim are usually caused by rust particles, and the rim halves should be refinished to prevent a recurrent problem.

9   Valve cores and caps

1   Valve cores seldom give trouble, but do not last indefinitely. Dirt under the seating will cause a puzzling 'slow-puncture'. Check that they are not leaking by applying spittle to the end of the valve and watching for air bubbles.

2   A valve cap is a safety device, and should always be fitted. Apart from keeping dirt out of the valve, it provides a second seal in case of valve failure, and may prevent an accident resulting from sudden deflation.

Chapter 6 Electrical system

For information relating to later models see Chapter 7

Contents

Specifications

Electrical system
Type .... 12 volt alternating current (ac) with electronic ac regulation

Alternator
Type .... 12 volt Ducati "star" type

Regulator
Type .... Electronic ac type

Horn
Type .... Electromagnetic

Bulbs (all 12 volt)
Headlamp 25/25W
Front sidelight 5W
Tail lamp 5W
Stop lamp 10W
Turn signal lamps 21W
Speedometer lamp 3W
Warning lamps 2W

Torque wrench settings

Component	kgf m	lbf ft
Alternator stator screws	0.3 - 0.4	2.17 - 2.89
Alternator rotor nut	6.0 - 6.5	43.4 - 47.0
Pickup mounting screws	0.2 - 0.25	1.45 - 1.81

1 General description

The UK Vespa models covered by this manual are equipped with a 12 volt electrical system. This arrangement is somewhat unorthodox in that it does not employ a battery. In conventional systems the battery not only supplies a reserve of power when the engine is not running, but serves to maintain a constant voltage in the electrical system, even when the engine is idling.

The Vespa system is entirely ac (alternating current), there being no form of rectification to dc (direct current), and in this respect it embodies the simplicity of the rudimentary ac systems normally associated with mopeds. Where it differs, however, is in the high output of the alternator and the fitting of an unusual electronic ac voltage regulator. The combination of the two allows the system to power a full complement of electrical accessories, the regulator maintaining the system voltage over a wide range of engine speeds and loads.

In addition to the usual electrical fittings, turn signals are fitted to the models sold in the UK. These are rather unusual in that the front and rear lamps flash alternately, rather than simultaneously. This adds a further measure of stability to the system, because the operation of the turn signals imposes a constant load, rather than a fluctuating one.

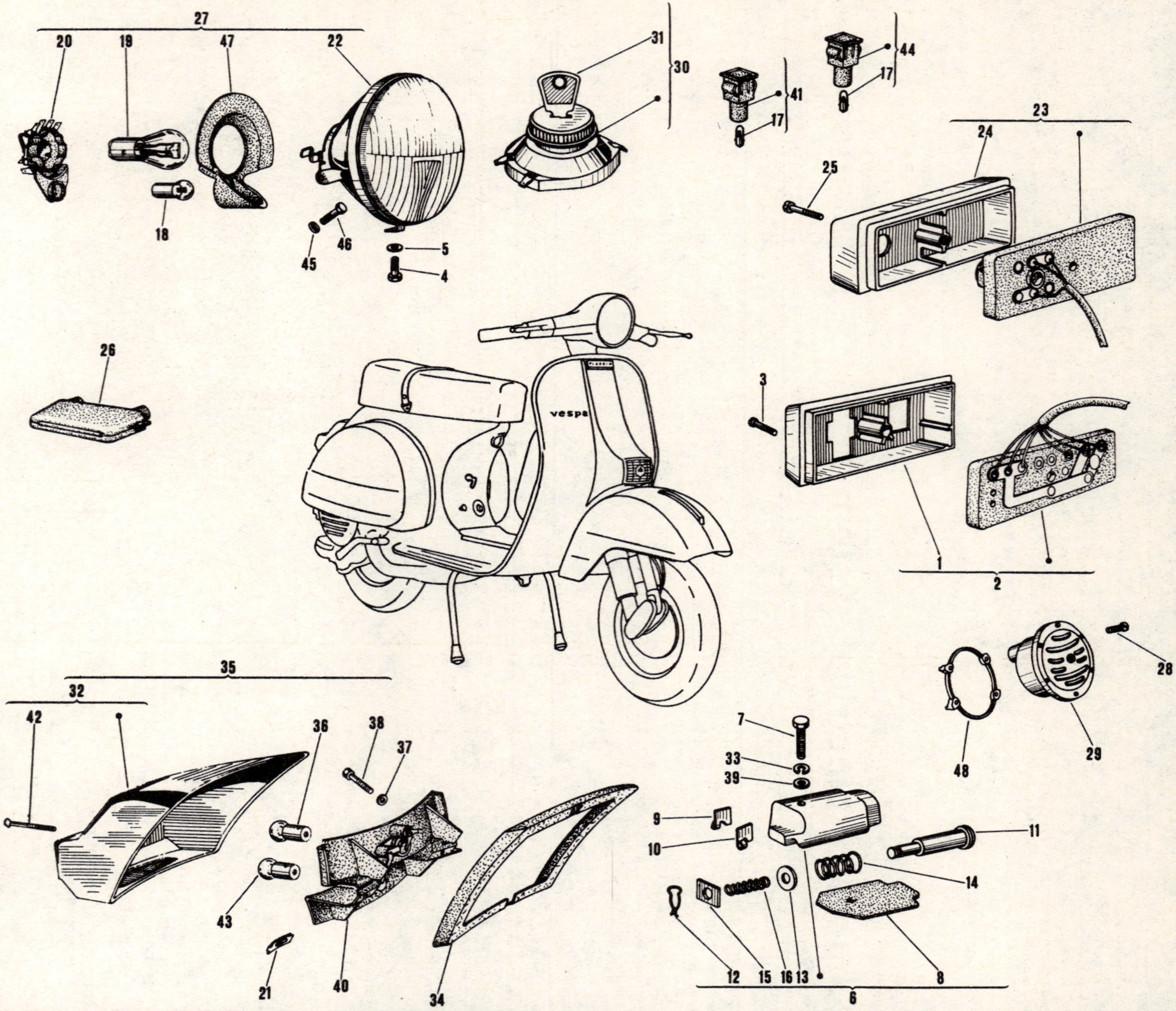

Fig. 6.1 Electrical components

1 Switch cover
2 Handlebar switch assembly
3 Screw
4 Bolt
5 Washer
6 Rear brake switch
7 Bolt
8 Backing
9 Contacts
10 Contacts
11 Plunger
12 Clip
13 Washer
14 Spring
15 Contact bar
16 Spring
17 Warning lamp bulb
18 Parking lamp bulb
19 Headlamp bulb
20 Bulbholder
21 Clip
22 Headlamp
23 Handlebar switch assembly
24 Switch cover
25 Screw
26 Clamp plate
27 Headlamp assembly
28 Screw
29 Horn
30 Ignition switch
31 Ignition key
32 Rear lamp lens
33 Spring washer
34 Gasket
35 Stop/tail lamp assembly
36 Brake lamp bulb
37 Washer
38 Screw
39 Washer
40 Stop/tail lamp unit
41 Warning lamp
42 Screw
43 Tail lamp bulb
44 Warning lamp
45 Washer
46 Screw
47 Seal
48 Spacer

2 Testing the electrical system: general procedures

1   It should be noted at the outset that only a limited amount of testing can be carried out at home. This is due to the need for a special non-inductive resistance and a thermocouple voltmeter for most of the tests, items unlikely to be available to most owners. Where general checks of the system indicate a fault in the alternator or the electronic voltage regulator, the machine must be taken to a Vespa dealer for the fault to be located and remedied. In most instances the dealer will be able to diagnose the fault quickly by the simple expedient of fitting new units until the faulty component is eliminated.

2   Bearing in mind the above, most common faults can be diagnosed and repaired at home without recourse to exotic test equipment. A simple and inexpensive multimeter of the type sold in electronics hobby shops or by many motorcycle dealers is invaluable for checking wiring runs and bulbs, but if unavailable, a simple continuity tester can be made up using a dry battery, a torch bulb and some wire. The accompanying line drawing shows the two arrangements.

3   It is worth keeping in mind that most electrical faults have a mechanical cause, usually a blown bulb, damaged wiring or loose or corroded wiring connections. These can be checked using the multimeter or continuity tester mentioned above, and by visual examination.

3 Wiring and connectors: examination and renovation

1   The leads in the wiring harness are colour-coded to facilitate fault diagnosis, and this is shown in the wiring diagrams at the end of this Chapter. The alternator output leads run from the crankcase via a junction box mounted above and to the rear of the fan. From here they pass through the body to emerge at the main connector block located behind the horn cover. Also connected at this point are the switch harnesses and the leads to the various lamps, so most tests will be made from this connector block to the component concerned. To gain access to the main connector block, prise off the 'Piaggio' badge and remove the single retaining screw, then remove the two retaining screws from inside the toolbox. The horn cover can then be lifted away to expose the main connector block, the horn and on PX models, the ignition switch.

2   To check a lead, disconnect it at each end, using the wiring diagram for guidance, then connect the continuity tester or a multimeter set on the resistance scale. If the lead is intact, the test bulb will light or the meter needle will indicate zero resistance. Check also that the wire covering is intact by checking for conductivity between it and the body pressing. If the test shows a break or short in the wiring, examine it carefully for damage and repair or renew it as required. Most breakages will occur outside the body section and will be easily spotted.

3   Very occasionally a lead may have broken internally or have become damaged within the body. In these cases it will be necessary to feed a new lead through the body to bypass the damaged one. Whilst this is by no means easy, it can usually be accomplished by feeding the wire forwards from the fuel tank recess once this has been removed. A length of curtain wire is a useful tool for this purpose, since this is relatively easy to work through the body section and can then be used to draw the new lead into position.

4   The wiring connectors are well protected from the elements and should not be too vulnerable to saturation in wet weather. Do note, however, that the generally damp climate in the UK can lead to corrosion of the connector terminals. These should be checked visually and any corrosion removed with a wire brush or with abrasive paper. Further corrosion can be prevented by coating the exposed metal terminals with silicone grease or petroleum jelly. Where the system becomes swamped with water, as might happen if the machine is ridden through a flood for example, apply WD 40 or a similar dewatering spray to get the machine running again.

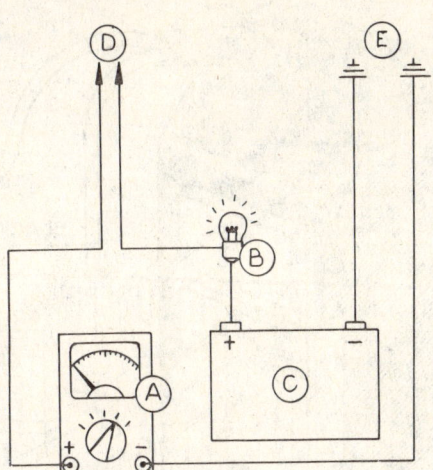

Fig. 6.2 Simple continuity testing arrangements for checking the electrical system

A Multimeter	D Positive probe
B Bulb	E Negative probe
C Battery	

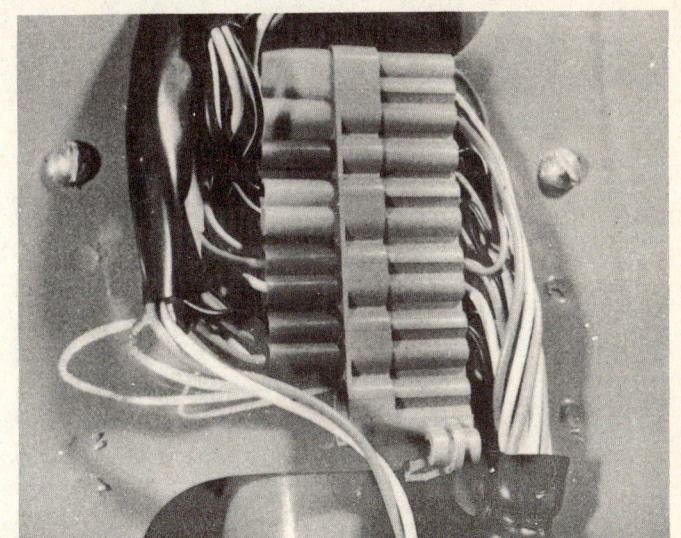

3.1 Main connector block is located behind horn cover

4   Electrical system: fault diagnosis

Total electrical failure

1   This is most commonly associated with the horn circuit, and is due to the fact that the blue output lead from the alternator passes via the main connector block, across the horn button terminals (which are normally closed) to the yellow lead and back to the main connector block. Only after this detour is power fed to the regulator and thence to the rest of the circuit. If there is a break in this circuit, the system will be inoperative.

2   Disconnect the horn leads and check for continuity between the yellow lead and the corresponding yellow lead at the regulator. Then check between the blue horn lead and the blue lead at the alternator output junction box. Trace and repair any break found.

3   A possible associated fault is indicated by continuous horn operation due to jammed contacts. This can often be remedied by releasing the switch retaining screws and spraying WD 40 into the back of the switch. If this fails to cure it, a new switch assembly must be fitted.

4   If the fault still persists, attention must be turned to the alternator source coils. No resistance figures are available for these, but a quick check with a multimeter will give some indication of the state of the coil windings. Disconnect the blue output lead at the junction box, then connect one meter probe to it and the other to earth. The needle should indicate that there is conductivity, but with some resistance. If no reading is shown, there is a break in the blue lead, the coil windings or the coil interconnections. A reading of zero resistance, on the other hand, is indicative of a short circuit.

5   Further investigation requires the removal of the rotor (see Chapter 3) so that the individual coils can be checked. If a faulty coil is found it can be renewed, but note that since it is soldered in place, the job should be left to a Vespa dealer unless the owner has experience of this type of work. Note also that on contact breaker ignition models, the coil **must** be fitted using a special jig and this is therefore impracticable at home.

6   If the alternator seems serviceable, the fault is likely to lie in the electronic regulator unit. In the absence of any passive test data this can only be checked by a dealer or by substitution.

Frequent bulb failure

7   This problem is invariably due to the failure of the regulator unit, and is characterised by persistent bulb blowing and possibly wide variations in headlamp intensity. The blown bulbs will often appear to be silvered inside the glass envelope where the filament metal has been vaporised. The occasional and inevitable bulb failure where the filament has merely broken does not indicate a regulator fault.

8   The recommended test requires an ac voltmeter, a 3.3 ± 0.1 ohm 300 watt non-inductive resistance, a tachometer and another Vespa scooter with an intact electrical system, and so is considered beyond the means of most owners. Have the unit checked by a dealer, or if a friendly Vespa owner can be persuaded, by substituting a regulator known to be in working order. If the unit is faulty it must be renewed, but it may be worth trying a local motorcycle breaker for a good secondhand unit before buying a new one.

5   Lighting system: fault diagnosis

1   The most common fault in the lighting system is failure of the bulbs themselves. This is usually due to old age and road vibration causing a mechanical failure of the filament, but if the bulb(s) fail frequently or have a silvered appearance, the regulator may be at fault (see above).

2   If the affected bulb is undamaged, check first for corrosion in the bulb holder, then check the wiring back to the switch. If the switch itself seems to be at fault, remove the securing screws and try spraying WD 40 or similar into it. This will usually restore normal operation, but if the switch is damaged internally it must be renewed.

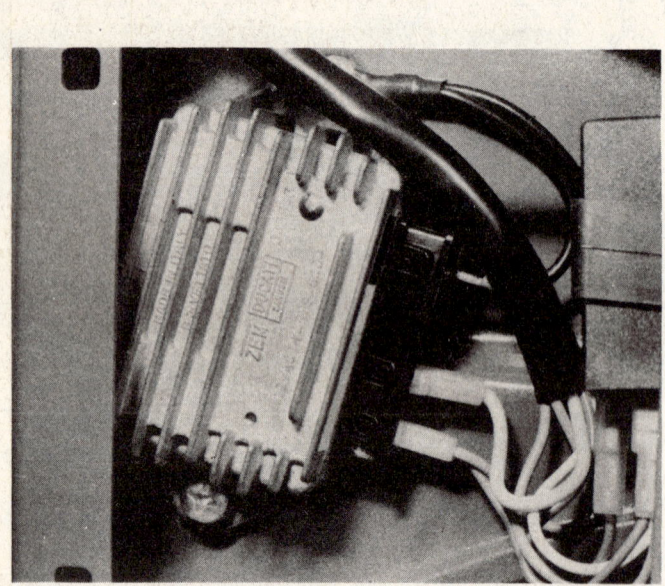

4.7 Electronic regulator unit is mounted behind left-hand side panel

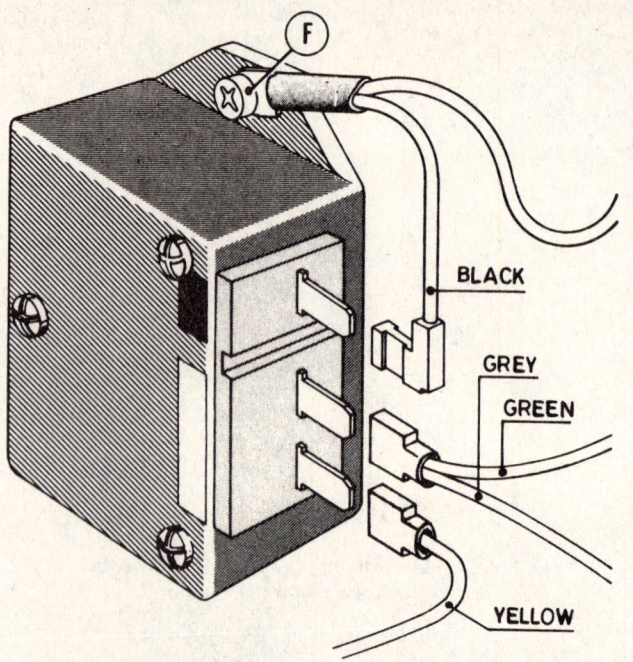

Fig. 6.3 Voltage regulator connections

F   Earth terminal

6 Lighting system: bulb renewal

Headlamp bulb

1   Slacken and remove the four screws which secure the handlebar cover to the main casting. Lift the cover slightly, feeding the speedometer cable up from the bottom where necessary, then disconnect the cable from the underside of the speedometer. The cable is secured by a knurled ring on the P125 X, P150 X and P200 E models, and by a plastic clip arrangement on the PX models. On the earlier models, disconnect the speedometer lamp and warning lamp leads. On PX models, disconnect the wiring connector from the speedometer. The top cover and instrument head can now be lifted away.

2   The headlamp unit is attached to the handlebar casting by screws and need not be removed. The unit incorporates a twin filament headlamp bulb, plus a lower wattage sidelamp bulb, and these can be removed after the bulbholder unit has been unclipped from the headlamp reflector. When fitting the new bulb, check that it is of the correct voltage and wattage.

Speedometer and warning lamp bulbs

3   Access to the speedometer illumination bulb and the warning lamp bulbs is gained after removing the handlebar top cover as described above. On the earlier models the speedometer bulbholder is a push fit in the base of the instrument, whilst the warning lamp bulbs can be removed by pulling the holders out of the separate lamp units. On the PX models, the various bulbholders are a bayonet fit in the base of the speedometer, the capless-type bulbs being integral with the plastic holders. In either case, ensure that the replacement bulbs are of the correct type.

Stop/tail lamp bulbs

4   The stop/tail lamp unit is fitted with separate bulbs, and these can be reached after the plastic lens has been removed. The latter is secured by two screws to the lamp body. When refitting the lens be careful not to overtighten the screws; it is easily damaged.

Turn signal bulbs

5   Access to the front turn signal bulbs is via the toolbox. Unclip the bulbholder from the lamp unit, then remove the bulb by depressing it slightly and turning it anti-clockwise. The rear bulbs can be reached after the lens has been removed. This is secured by two screws, which must not be overtightened during reassembly.

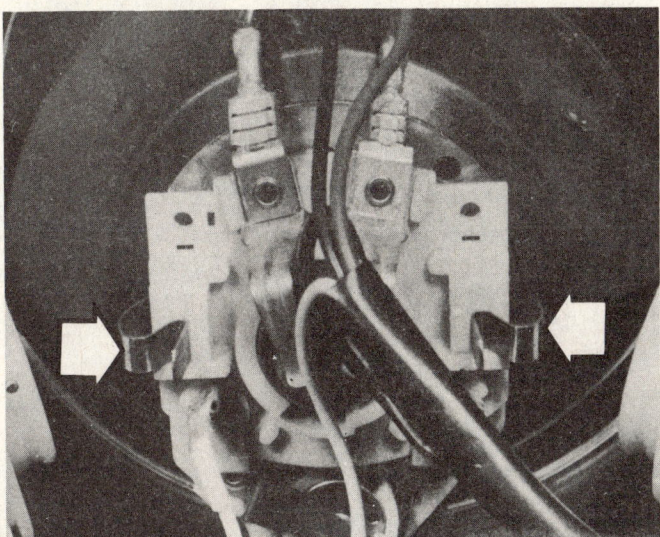
6.1 Instrument wiring connector – PX models

6.2a Headlamp bracket screws need only be removed if unit requires renewal

6.2b To free bulbholder, prise off clips (arrowed) ...

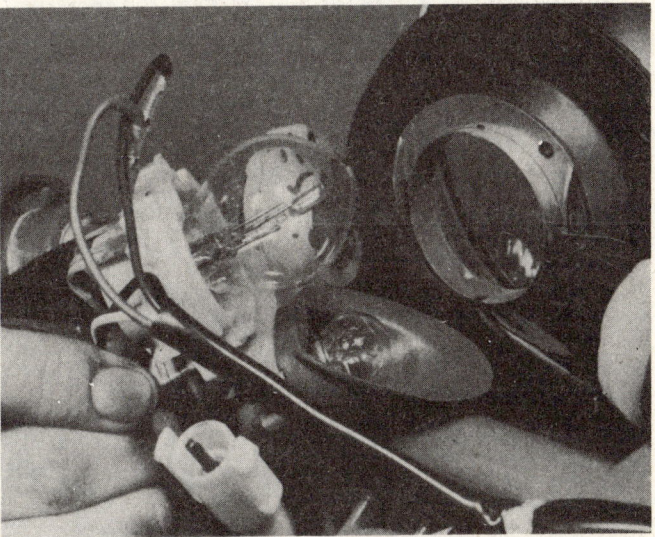
6.2c ... and lift assembly clear of reflector

6.3a On PX models, instrument wiring is of the printed circuit type

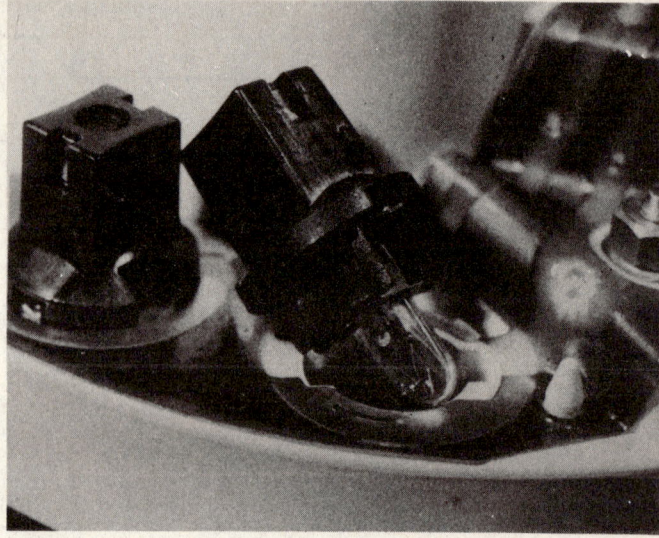

6.3b Bulbs are a bayonet fit in back of speedometer

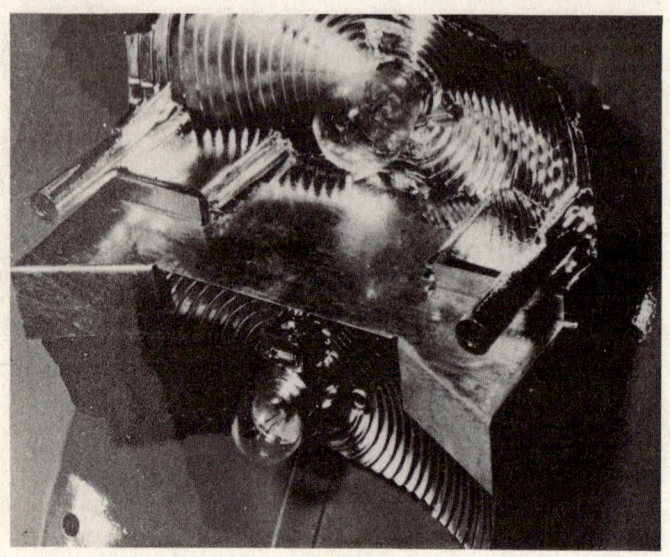

6.4 Remove lens to gain access to separate tail and brake lamp bulbs

6.5a Rear turn signal bulbs can be reached after removing lens

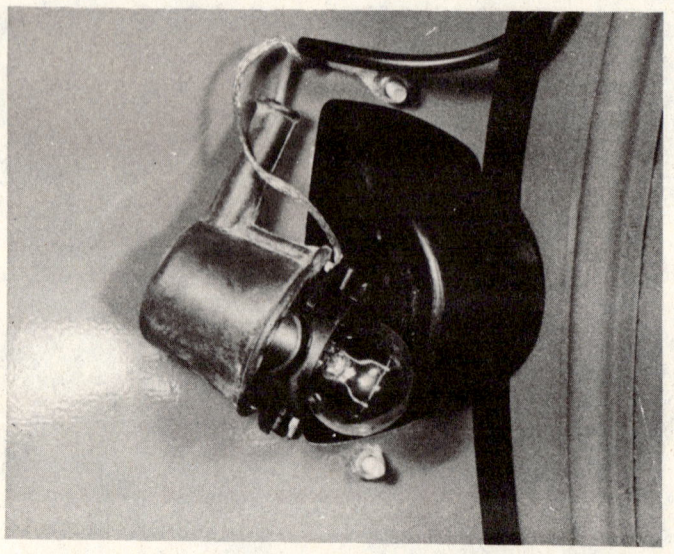

6.5b Front turn signal bulbholders are accessed through the toolbox

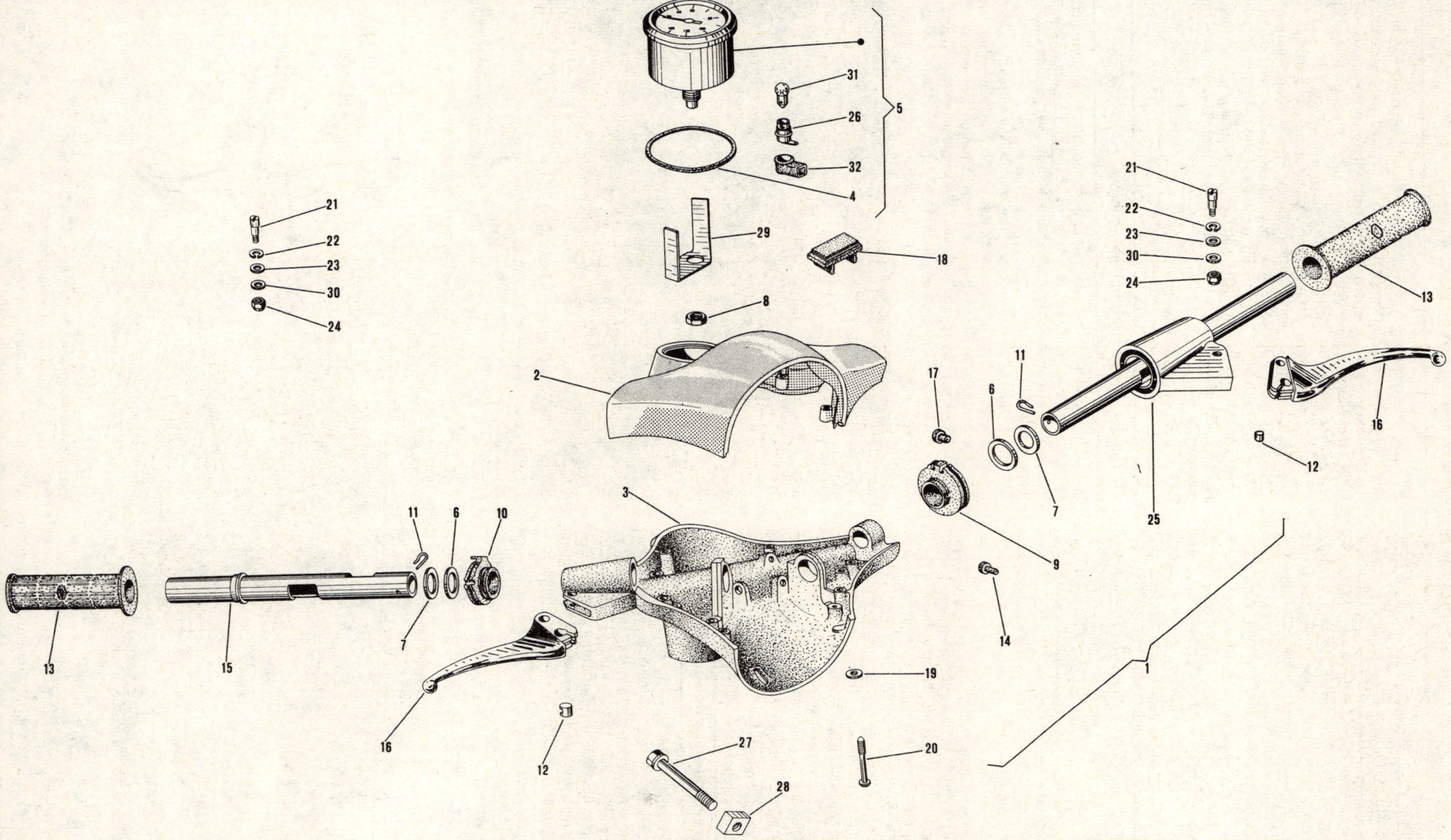

Fig. 6.4 Handlebar assembly

1	Handlebar assembly	14	Ferrule
2	Top cover	15	Right-hand handlebar
3	Handlebar casting	16	Handlebar lever
4	O-ring	17	Ferrule
5	Speedometer assembly –	18	Cover
	early model shown	19	Washer
6	Washer	20	Screw
7	Washer	21	Pivot screw
8	Nut	22	Spring washer
9	Gearchange pulley	23	Washer
10	Throttle pulley	24	Nut
11	Clip	25	Left-hand handlebar
12	Trunnion	26	Bulbholder
13	Grip	27	Pinch bolt
		28	Captive nut
		29	Bracket
		30	Washer
		31	Bulb
		32	Boot

7 Headlamp: adjustment

1 Provision is made for adjusting the vertical alignment of the headlamp beam to obtain adequate illumination without dazzling other road users at night. Adjustment is effected by slackening the single hexagon-headed screw on the underside of the handlebar casting and moving the headlamp to the required position.

2 In the UK, lighting regulations stipulate that the headlamp must be aligned so that it will not dazzle a person standing at a distance greater than 25 feet from the lamp, whose eye level is not less than 3 feet 6 inches above that plain. This can be approximated by placing the machine 25 feet from a wall and on a level surface. Set the dipped beam so that it is concentrated at the same height as the centre of the headlamp. Note that the rider and any regular passenger should be seated normally, with the machine off its stand, when making the adjustment.

8 Turn signal system: fault diagnosis

1 Faults in the turn signal circuit are normally confined to one side of the system, whilst the lamps flash normally on the other side. Where the fault is of this type it is safe to assume that the turn signal relay is serviceable. The first area to check is the bulbs. If these prove sound, check for corrosion in the bulbholders or loose wiring connections. A likely area for intermittent contact is the front side panel catch which acts as the electrical connection for the rear turn signal lamp.

2 Where the system has failed completely, it is possible that the relay is defective, and this should be checked by fitting a new unit. The turn signal relay is held in a rubber mounting next to the regulator unit, under the left-hand side panel. If the fault persists, check the wiring and switch using the wiring diagram for guidance. If the fault lies with the switch and it cannot be resolved by applying WD 40 or similar, it should be renewed.

9 Brake lamp switches: removal and examination

1 If the rear brake switch malfunctions, it will be necessary to remove the brake pedal assembly to gain access to it. Start by removing the brake pedal rubber, then remove the nuts on the underside of the footboard which retain the assembly to the body. Lower the pedal assembly, manoeuvring the pedal end through the hole in the footboard. The switch unit, which is retained by a single bolt to the pedal bracket, can now be removed. (See photograph 4/8.8c)

2 The switch can be dismantled to some extent, allowing the contacts and operating plunger to be cleaned. Before it is reassembled, soak the component parts in WD 40 to inhibit further corrosion. If the switch still fails to function or if it is badly worn, renew it.

3 Later PX models are fitted with a front brake switch incorporated in the brake operating cable. The switch is located in the headlamp housing area, from where it is connected to the main wiring loom. It can be dismantled for inspection or renewal after the front brake cable has been withdrawn.

4 Care must be taken on reassembly of the front brake cable when threading the inner cable lower end through the anchor plate on the brake arm. If the cable strands have separated or are obviously damaged at this point reassembly will be extremely difficult and the inner cable should be renewed. Finally, adjust the brake as described in Routine Maintenance and check brake operation before taking the machine on the road.

10 Ignition switch: location and renewal

1 On the earlier models covered in this manual, the ignition switch is located on the handlebar top cover. It is secured by a knurled ring and can be removed once this has been unscrewed and the switch leads disconnected.

2 In the case of the PX models, the switch is incorporated in the steering lock, and it can be reached after the horn cover has been removed as described in Section 3 above. The switch can be separated from the lock mechanism by removing the single screw which retains it (see photograph). This means that in the event of a faulty switch it is not necessary to renew the lock mechanism.

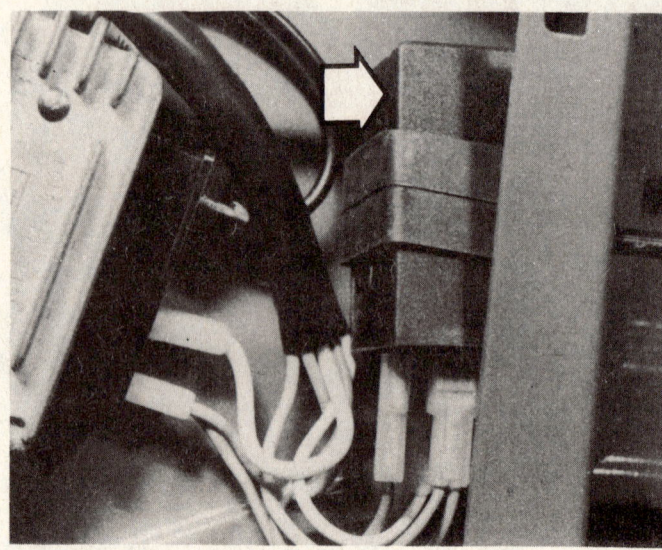

8.2a Turn signal relay is mounted next to regulator unit

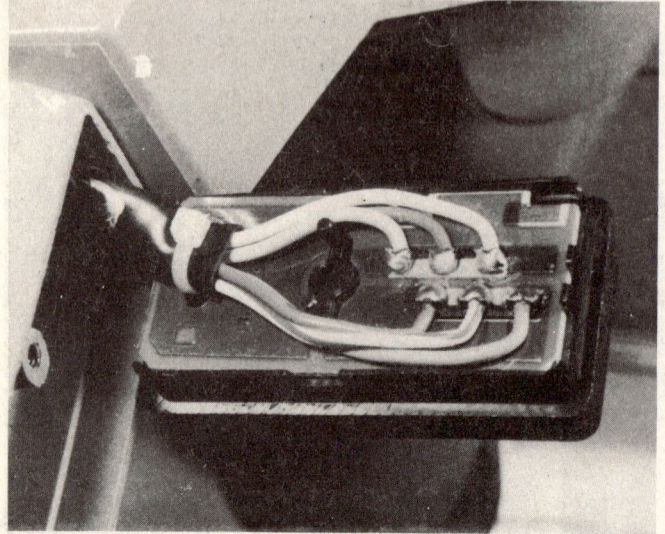

8.2b Handlebar switch can be removed for inspection

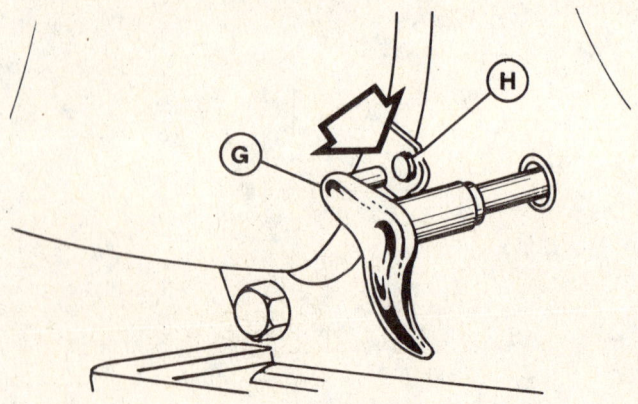

Fig. 6.5 Rear turn signal connection – P125 X, P150 X and P200 E models

G   Side panel catch   H   Terminal

11 Horn: location and renewal

1   The horn unit is retained by four screws on the inside of the horn cover, removal of which is described in Section 3 of this Chapter. Before renewing an inoperative horn, check the wiring and switch contacts, noting the remarks made in paragraphs 1-3 of Section 4. The horn is a sealed unit and therefore cannot be dismantled for repair. Remember that a working horn is a statutory requirement in the UK and most other countries.

12 Fuel gauge circuit: examination

1   On models equipped with a fuel level gauge, this is controlled by a float-operated sender unit housed in the fuel tank. In the event of a fault, check first that the wiring is not shorted or broken. Pay particular attention to the wiring connector near the sender unit. This is pushed inside the body section and can be withdrawn after the grommet has been prised out.

2   To remove the sender unit for inspection, it should be twisted anti-clockwise. In the absence of a suitable tool, the unit can be tapped round until it is freed, using two drifts at diametrically opposite sides of the sender flange. Lift the unit away carefully, manoeuvring it clear of the tank orifice.

3   No resistance figures are available for the sender, but it can be checked visually for corroded or broken resistance windings. If a multimeter is available, connect this to the sender terminals and set it on the resistance scale. If the float is moved up and down the meter needle should move, indicating the changing resistance. If the sender proves faulty, try careful cleaning of the resistance windings. If this fails to effect a cure, renew the unit. If the sender and wiring prove sound, it will be necessary to renew the speedometer head complete.

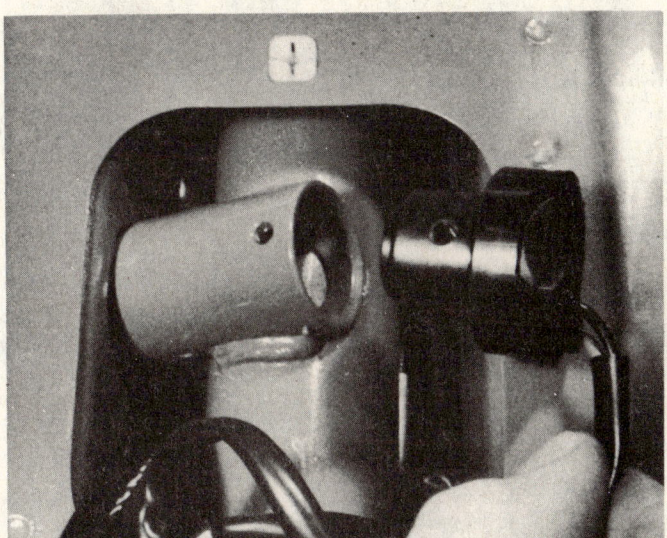

10.2 Ignition switch fits on back of steering/ignition lock on PX models

11.1 Horn unit is mounted inside the horn cover

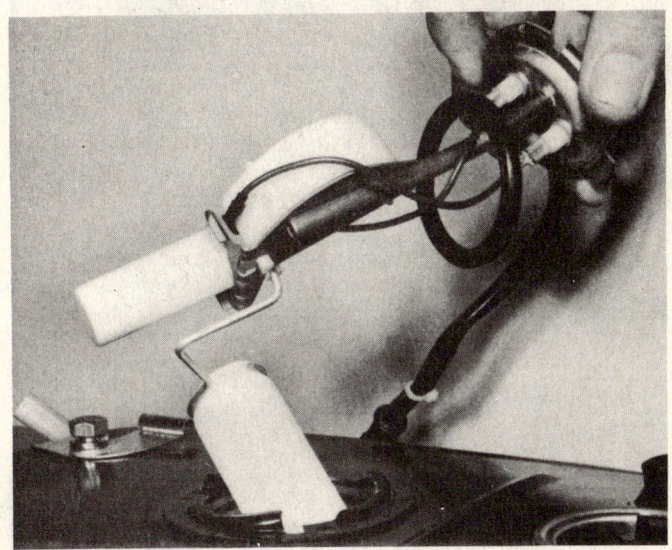

12.2 Fuel gauge sender can be removed by twisting it anti-clockwise. Take care not to damage float or float arm

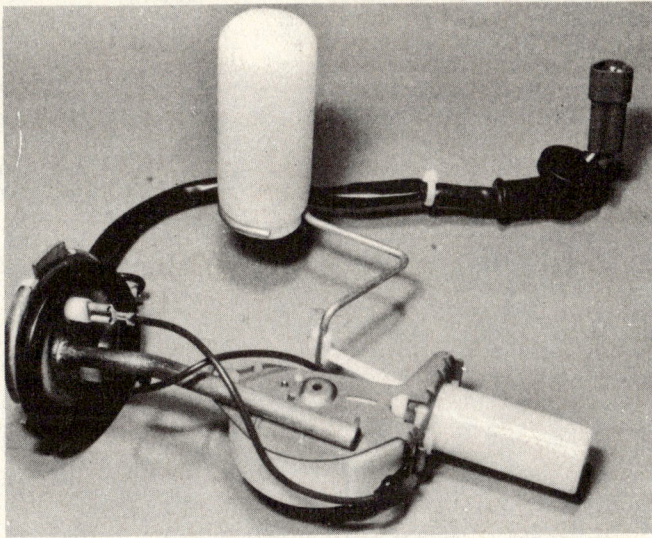

12.3 Check sender wiring and connections. Renew if resistance windings have failed

The PX125 T5 model

Chapter 7 Supplement:
T5 and PX125/150/200 electric start models

Contents

Specifications – PX125 T5 and T5 Classic

The following specifications relate to the models covered in this update Chapter. Where no specifications are shown here, refer to those given for the earlier models at the beginning of Chapters 1 to 6

Model dimensions and weights

Overall length
   T5 model . . . . 1820 mm (71.7 in)
   T5 Classic model. . . . . 1721 mm (67.8 in)
Overall width
   T5 model . . . . 700 mm (27.6 in)
   T5 Classic model. . . . . 686 mm (27.0 in)
Overall height
   T5 model . . . . 1170 mm (46.1 in)
   T5 Classic model. . . . . Not available
Wheelbase
   T5 model . . . . 1250 mm (49.3 in)
   T5 Classic model. . . . . 1219 mm (48.0 in)
Ground clearance . . . . Not available
Dry weight
   T5 model . . . . 112 kg (247 lb)
   T5 Classic model. . . . . 103 kg (227 lb)
Chassis No. prefix. . . . . VNX 5T
Engine No. prefix . . . . VNX 5M

Specifications relating to Chapter 1

Engine

Type	Single cylinder fan-cooled two-stroke
Bore	55 mm (2.17 in)
Stroke	52 mm (2.05 in)
Displacement	123 cc (7.50 cu in)
Compression ratio	11.3:1

Cylinder barrel and piston

Cylinder barrel type	Aluminium alloy, Nikasil coated, 5-port
Nominal bore size	55.0 mm (2.17 in)
Oversizes	Not applicable
Piston/bore clearance	0.0375 – 0.0475 mm (0.0015 – 0.0019 in)
Service limit	0.080 mm (0.0032 in)
Piston measurement point	25 mm (0.985 in) below bottom edge of lower ring groove, at 90° to gudgeon pin bore
Cylinder bore measurement point	25 mm (0.985 in) below gasket face, at 90° to gudgeon pin bore axis
Small-end bearing/gudgeon pin radial clearance	Zero
Service limit	0.02 mm (0.0008 in)

Piston/bore coding and correlation (see Section 4)

	Bore diameter	Piston diameter
Code letter A	54.990 – 54.995 mm (2.1666 – 2.1668 in)	54.950 ± 0.0025 mm (2.1650 ± 0.0001 in)
Code letter B	54.995 – 55.000 mm (2.1668 – 2.1670 in)	54.955 ± 0.0025 mm (2.1652 ± 0.0001 in)
Code letter C	55.000 – 55.005 mm (2.1670 – 2.1672 in)	54.960 ± 0.0025 mm (2.1654 ± 0.0001 in)
Code letter D	55.005 – 55.010 mm (2.1672 – 2.1674 in)	54.965 ± 0.0025 mm (2.1656 ± 0.0001 in)
Code letter E	55.010 – 55.015 mm (2.1674 – 2.1676 in)	54.970 ± 0.0025 mm (2.1658 ± 0.0001 in)
Code letter F	55.015 – 55.020 mm (2.1676 – 2.1678 in)	54.975 ± 0.0025 mm (2.1660 ± 0.0001 in)
Code letter G	55.020 – 55.025 mm (2.1678 – 2.1680 in)	54.980 ± 0.0025 mm (2.1662 ± 0.0001 in)
Code letter H	55.025 – 55.030 mm (2.1680 – 2.1682 in)	54.985 ± 0.0025 mm (2.1664 ± 0.0001 in)
Code letter I	55.030 – 55.035 mm (2.1682 – 2.1684 in)	54.990 ± 0.0025 mm (2.1666 ± 0.0001 in)
Code letter L	55.035 – 55.040 mm (2.1684 – 2.1686 in)	54.995 ± 0.0025 mm (2.1668 ± 0.0001 in)

Piston rings

	Top	2nd
Type	Dykes (L-section)	Plain
End gap (installed)	0.20 – 0.35 mm (0.0079 – 0.0138 in)	0.20 – 0.40 mm (0.0079 – 0.0158 in)
Service limit	2.00 mm (0.079 in)	2.00 mm (0.079 in)

Gearbox

As PX125 E except output shaft thrust washers (see Chapter 1, Section 22)

Initial clearance	0.15 – 0.40 mm (0.006 – 0.016 in)
Standard thickness	1.00 mm (0.0394 in)
1st oversize	1.10 mm (0.0433 in)
2nd oversize	1.20 mm (0.0473 in)
3rd oversize	1.30 mm (0 0512 in)
4th oversize	1.50 mm (0.0591 in)
(All sizes +0.000, – 0.060 mm (+0.000, -0.002 in)	

Torque wrench settings

	kgf m	lbf ft
Crankcase securing nuts	0.6 – 0.8	4.3 – 5.8
Cylinder head nuts	1.6 – 2.6	11.6 – 18.8
Exhaust system to port nut	1.6 – 2.6	11.6 – 18.8
Exhaust system to crankcase bolt	3.3 – 5.3	23.9 – 38.3

Specifications relating to Chapter 2

Carburettor

Make	Dell'Orto
Type	SI 24/24G
Venturi size	24 mm (0.94 in)
Main jet	110/100
Slow running jet:	
Without idle air hole	50/100
With idle air hole	100/100
Main jet air calibrator	120/100
Mixer tube	BE4
Throttle valve	8492.05
Starter jet	60/100

Specifications relating to Chapter 3

Ignition timing
Ignition advance at 2500 – 3000 rpm	16° BTDC

Spark plug
Recommended fitments:

Bosch	W 3 CC
Champion	N-2C

Torque wrench setting
	kgf m	lbf ft
Spark plug	1.8 – 2.4	13.0 – 17.4

Specifications relating to Chapter 4

Torque wrench setting – T5
	kgf m	lbf ft
Slotted handlebar retaining nut	5.5 – 6.5	39.8 – 47.0

Specifications relating to Chapter 5

Tyre pressures (cold)
Front tyre	17.6 psi (1.23 kg/cm^2)
Rear tyre – solo	24.9 psi (1.74 kg/cm^2)
Rear tyre – with pillion	35.5 psi (2.49 kg/cm^2)

Torque wrench settings
	kgf m	lbf ft
Front wheel hub nut	7.5 – 9.0	54.2 – 65.0
Rear wheel hub nut	9.0 – 11.0	65.0 – 79.5

Specifications relating to Chapter 6

Bulbs
Headlamp	12V, 45/40W
Front sidelight	12V, 4W
Tail lamp	12V, 5W
Stop lamp	12V, 10W
Turn signal lamps	12V, 21W
Instrument lamps	12V, 1.2W

Specifications – PX125, PX150 and PX200 electric start models

The following specifications relate to the models covered in this update Chapter. Where no specifications are shown here, refer to those given for the earlier models at the beginning of Chapters 1 to 6

Model dimensions and weights
Overall length	1780 mm (70.1 in)
Overall width	700 mm (27.6 in)
Overall height	1110 mm (43.7 in)
Wheelbase	1245 mm (49.1 in)
Ground clearance	Not available
Kerb weight	104 kg (229 lbs)
Chassis No. prefix	
PX125 with front drum brake	VNX 2T
PX125 with front disc brake	ZAPM09000
PX125 with front disc brake and catalytic converter (Euro 1)	ZAPM09300
PX125 with front disc brake, catalytic converter and SAS (Euro 2 & 3).	ZAPM09302 or VNX 2T
PX150 with front drum brake	VLX 1T
PX150 with front disc brake and catalytic converter (Euro 1)	ZAPM09400
PX150 with front disc brake, catalytic converter and SAS (Euro 2 & 3).	ZAPM09402 or VLX 1T
PX200	VSX 1T
Engine No. prefix	
PX125	VNX 1M
PX150	VLX 1M
PX200	VSE 1M

Specifications relating to Routine maintenance
Engine oil	Fully synthetic 2T scooter oil API TC
Gearbox oil	SAE 80 API GL4

Specifications relating to Chapter 1

Engine
Type	Single cylinder fan-cooled two-stroke
Displacement	
PX125	123.4 cc (7.53 cu in)
PX150	150.6 cc (9.19 cu in)
PX200	197.9 cc (12.07 cu in)
Compression ratio	
PX125, up to Euro 2	8.5:1
PX125 Euro 2 and 3 and PX150	8.0:1
PX200	8.8:1

Cylinder barrel and piston

Cylinder barrel type	Cast iron
Standard bore size	
PX125.	52.5 mm (2.069 in)
PX150.	58 mm (2.283 in)
PX200.	66.5 mm (2.620 in)
Rebore sizes	3, in 0.2 mm (0.008 in) increments
Cylinder bore measurement point	
PX125 and 150	25 mm (1.0 in) below top of the bore, at 90° to gudgeon pin bore axis
PX200.	30 mm (1.2 in) below top of the bore, at 90° to gudgeon pin bore axis
Standard piston size	
PX125.	52.290 – 52.320 mm (2.0586 – 2.0598 in)
PX150.	57.555 – 57.585 mm (2.2659 – 2.2671 in)
PX200.	66.295 mm (2.612 in)
Oversizes	3, in 0.2 mm (0.008 in) increments
Piston measurement point (at 90° to gudgeon pin bore)	
PX125 and 150	5 mm (0.2 in) below bottom edge of lower ring groove
PX200.	7 mm (0.3 in) below bottom edge of lower ring groove
Small-end bearing/gudgeon pin radial clearance	Zero
Service limit	0.02 mm (0.0008 in)

Piston/bore coding and correlation (see Section 5)

PX125 models	Bore diameter	Piston diameter
Code letter B	52.505 mm (2.0671 in)	52.290 mm (2.0587 in)
Code letter C	52.510 mm (2.0673 in)	52.295 mm (2.0589 in)
Code letter D	52.515 mm (2.0675 in)	52.300 mm (2.0591 in)
Code letter E	52.520 mm (2.0677 in)	52.305 mm (2.0592 in)
Code letter F	52.525 mm (2.0679 in)	52.310 mm (2.0594 in)
Code letter G	52.530 mm (2.0681 in)	52.315 mm (2.0596 in)
Code letter H	52.535 mm (2.0683 in)	52.320 mm (2.0598 in)
PX150 models	**Bore diameter**	**Piston diameter**
Code letter B	57.795 mm (2.2754 in)	57.555 mm (2.2659 in)
Code letter C	57.800 mm (2.2756 in)	57.650 mm (2.2697 in)
Code letter D	57.805 mm (2.2758 in)	57.565 mm (2.2663 in)
Code letter E	57.810 mm (2.2760 in)	57.570 mm (2.2665 in)
Code letter F	57.815 mm (2.2762 in)	57.575 mm (2.2667 in)
Code letter G	57.820 mm (2.2764 in)	57.580 mm (2.2669 in)
Code letter H	57.825 mm (2.2766 in)	57.585 mm (2.2671 in)

Piston rings

End gap (installed)	
PX125.	0.20 – 0.35 mm (0.008 – 0.014 in)
PX150.	0.20 – 0.40 mm (0.008 – 0.016 in)
PX200.	0.25 – 0.40 mm (0.010 – 0.016 in)
Service limit	2.00 mm (0.08 in)

Small-end bearings

	Connecting rod marking	Bearing colour
Size 1	I	Copper
Size 2	II	Blue
Size 3	III	White
Size 4	IIII	Green

Clutch

Type	Wet multiplate
No. of friction plates.	4
No. of plain plates	4

Gearbox

Output shaft thrust washers	see Chapter 1, Section 22

Torque wrench settings

	kgf m	lbf ft
Crankcase securing nuts	0.8 – 0.9	5.8 – 6.5
Gear selector box mounting nuts	1.2 – 1.5	8.7 – 10.8
Starter motor bolts.	1.0 – 1.2	7.2 – 8.7
Fan cowling screws	0.8 – 1.0	5.8 – 7.2
Input shaft nut	3.0 – 3.5	21.7 – 25.3

Specifications relating to Chapter 2

Carburettor

	PX125	PX150	PX200
Make	Dell'Orto	Dell'Orto	Dell'Orto
Type	SI 20/20D	SI 20/20D	SI 24/24E
Venturi size	20 mm (0.79 in)	20 mm (0.79 in)	24 mm (0.94 in)
Main jet	96/100	98	118/100
Slow running jet	45/100	45/160	55/100
Air corrector jet.	140/100	150	160/100
Mixer tube.	BE5	BE5	BE3
Throttle valve	6823.09	6823.16.64	8492.04
Starter jet.	60/100	60/100	60/100

Specifications relating to Chapter 3

Ignition timing
Ignition advance at 2500 – 3000 rpm . . . . 18° ± 1° BTDC

Spark plug
Recommended fitments:
PX125/150 up to Euro 2 . . . . Champion L82CN-2C
PX125/150 Euro 2 and 3 . . . . Champion RL82C
PX200 . . . . Champion N4C

Torque wrench setting	kgf m	lbf ft
Spark plug	2.0 – 2.5	14.5 – 18.1

Specifications relating to Chapter 5

Brakes
Brake fluid type . . . . DOT 4
Disc runout service limit . . . . 0.1 mm

Tyre pressures (cold)
Front tyre . . . . 18.8 psi (1.32 kg/cm^2)
Rear tyre – solo . . . . 26.0 psi (1.82 kg/cm^2)
Rear tyre – with pillion . . . . 33.0 psi (2.31 kg/cm^2)

Torque wrench settings	kgf m	lbf ft
Front brake caliper banjo bolt	1.5 – 2.5	10.8 – 18.1
Front brake caliper bleed screw	1.0 – 1.2	7.2 – 8.7
Front brake caliper mounting bolts	2.0 – 2.5	14.5 – 18.1
Front brake master cylinder banjo bolt	0.8 – 1.2	5.8 – 8.7
Front disc mounting bolts	0.5 – 0.6	3.6 – 4.3
Front wheel hub nut	6.1 – 10.1	44.1 – 73.1

Specifications relating to Chapter 6

Battery
Capacity . . . . 12V, 9 Ah
Specific gravity . . . . 1.260 to 1.280

Fuse
PX200 E model . . . . 8 Amp
PX125/200 . . . . 7.5 Amp

Bulbs
Headlamp . . . . 35/35W (later models – 60/55W H4)
Front sidelight 5W
Tail lamp 5W
Stop lamp 10W
Turn signal lamps . . . . 21W (amber bulb and clear lens on later models)
Instrument warning lamps 1.2W

---

1 Introduction

Supplement coverage and usage

This supplement covers the T5 model, introduced in 1986 and superseded by the T5 Classic in 1992, the electric start version of the PX200 E, introduced in the UK in March 1994, and the electric start versions of the PX125 and 150, introduced in 1999.

If working on one of these models, refer first to this Chapter for details of the task required. If no mention is made it can be assumed that the task is unchanged from that described in the earlier Chapters of the manual for the previous model.

Later model changes – T5 model

The 123 cc T5 engine, named after its five transfer ports, is fitted to the PX125 T5 and PX125 T5 Classic. Although the engine retains many features of the unit described in Chapter 1, significant modifications have been made to the top-end.

Most notable is the completely revised cylinder barrel, which features five transfer ports and has a Nikasil finished bore. The bore coating is intended to be long-lasting in use, and thus, periodic reboring to cope with bore wear is eliminated. Where damage does occur with this type of bore, it should be noted that the reboring operation is no longer possible; if it wears out, a complete new barrel and piston will be required.

Additional changes to the engine have seen the strengthening of the flywheel assembly, together with a reduction of the flywheel

weight. This allows the engine to respond faster to the throttle control, making best use of the cylinder design.

The gearbox has seen detail changes, in the form of revised output shaft shimming. Unlike other PX models, the output shaft is now shimmed from both ends in an attempt to resolve the problem of the machine jumping out of gear, which was noted on some of the earlier versions. The heavier-duty clutch of the 200 models is incorporated to cope with the increased power output.

The chassis of the T5 Classic is unchanged from the PX125 E covered in earlier Chapters of this manual. The T5 on the other hand, has more angular styling and redesigned handlebar assembly. The curve at the rear of the body has been replaced by a flat tail section, which aligns with the back of the seat. The handlebar assembly incorporates an instrument panel, housing the speedometer, odometer, fuel gauge and warning lamps, as well as a tachometer. The panel is protected by a small tinted screen, and a rectangular headlamp is fitted. Further detail changes include a re-shaped horn cover and a plastic spoiler at the bottom of the legshield assembly.

Later model changes – PX125, 150 and 200 electric start models

During 1994 electric start became available on PX200 models imported into the UK market, and an electric start PX125 replaced the 125 cc T5 Classic in 1999. The PX125 and 150 were fitted with the same type of three-port engine as the PX200.

The electric starter motor was mounted on top of the right-hand crankcase half with a 90° drive to the engine via a ring gear on the back of the flywheel. With the addition of the electric starter, it was necessary

Vespa PX125, 150 and 200 electric start models component locations – right-hand side

1 Electric starter	4 Front brake stop lamp switch	7 Front disc brake caliper	10 Gearbox drain plug
2 Engine idle speed adjuster	5 Horn	8 Rear brake stop lamp switch	11 Gear change selector box
3 Front brake fluid reservoir	6 Speedometer cable	9 Rear brake cable adjuster	12 Secondary air filter – later models

Vespa PX125, 150 and 200 electric start models component locations – left-hand side

1 Starter safety interlock unit (where fitted)	3 Steering stem	6 Seat lock	9 Fuse
2 Clutch switch	4 Engine oil tank	7 Rear hub	10 Stand pivot and spring
	5 Fuel gauge sender unit	8 Battery	11 Front hub

to uprate the ac-only electrical system, fitted to kickstart models, with a more conventional system using a battery and regulator/rectifier unit.

A redesigned clutch, originally fitted to the Piaggio 'Cosa', was fitted to all electric start PX models.

An hydraulically-operated front disc brake was fitted to the PX200 in 1998 and to the PX125/150 on their introduction the following year.

All models had a retro-style round headlight and the speedometer incorporated a fuel gauge and warning lamps. Clear turn signal lenses were fitted.

Later versions of the PX followed, differing only in their compliance with the increasingly stringent emission requirements imposed by Euro 1, 2 and 3 legislation. Changes have been made to the exhaust system, initially by the fitting of a catalytic converter and then by the addition of a secondary air system. The PX200 did not meet the Euro standards and was discontinued in 2003 following the release of 400 individually numbered Serie Speciale models in black and white paintwork.

A special edition PX125, in white, was produced to mark 30 years of PX production. It had a flyscreen, white-walled tyres on chromed wheel rims, a chromed rear carrier and spare wheel. A plate on the glovebox denoted the model as being a P125X 30 anni Ultima Serie.

A special edition PX150, 150° Anniversario dell'Unità d'Italia, was produced in 2011 to mark 150 years since the unification of Italy. Bodywork was white with green/white/red decals together with an authentication plate.

2 Routine maintenance schedule – PX125, 150 and 200 electric start models

Procedures for all tasks in the schedule are given in Routine maintenance at the beginning of this manual, except where indicated.

Daily (pre-ride) checks
☐ Check the operation of both brakes
☐ Check the level of brake fluid in the front brake master cylinder (Section 3)
☐ Check clutch and throttle operation
☐ Check the oil tank level via the sightglass. Top up via the oil tank under the seat
☐ Check you have enough fuel to complete your journey
☐ Check the tyre pressures and the tread and sidewall condition
☐ Check that the lights and horn are working

After the initial 600 miles (1000 km)
This check will be performed by a Piaggio/Vespa dealer after the first 600 miles (1000 km)
☐ Change the gearbox oil
☐ Adjust the throttle cable
☐ Lubricate the speedometer cable
☐ Check the steering
☐ Grease the brake lever and clutch lever pivots
☐ Check the front brake fluid level
☐ Check tighten all nuts and bolts
☐ Check the battery

Every 3000 miles (5000 km)
Repeat all items under the Daily (pre-ride) heading
☐ Top up the gearbox oil
☐ Replace the spark plug
☐ Adjust the throttle cable
☐ Clean the air filter (Section 3)
☐ Clean the secondary air filters on Euro 2 and 3 models (Section 3)
☐ Carry out general lubrication
☐ Check front brake pad wear and fluid level (Section 3)
☐ Check rear brake cable adjustment
☐ Check the battery (Section 3)

Every 6000 miles (10,000 km)
Repeat all items under the 3000 mile (5000 km) heading
☐ Change the gearbox oil
☐ Replace the spark plug
☐ Check the engine idle speed
☐ Lubricate the speedometer cable
☐ Adjust the throttle cable
☐ Check the steering and suspension
☐ Check tighten all nuts and bolts
☐ Check the headlamp aim

Every 12,000 miles (20,000 km)
☐ Clean off any build-up of dirt from the cylinder head and barrel cooling fins

Every 18,000 miles (30,000 km)
☐ Change the front brake hose

Every two years
☐ Change the brake fluid

3 Routine maintenance procedures – PX125, 150 and 200 electric start models

Brake fluid level check

Note: *Brake hydraulic fluid can harm your eyes and damage painted surfaces, so use extreme caution when handling and pouring it and cover surrounding surfaces with rag. Do not use fluid that has been standing open for some time, as it absorbs moisture from the air which can cause a dangerous loss of braking effectiveness.*

1   Support the machine in an upright position on level ground and turn the handlebars until the hydraulic reservoir is as level as possible. The brake fluid level is visible through the sightglass in the reservoir body – it must be half way up the glass when the reservoir is level.

2   If the brake fluid needs topping-up, wrap a rag around the reservoir to ensure that any spillage does not come into contact with painted or plastic surfaces. Remove the reservoir cover screws and remove the cover, the diaphragm plate and the diaphragm, then top-up with new DOT 4 hydraulic fluid until the level is half way up the sightglass. Do not overfill and take care to avoid spills.

3   Ensure that the diaphragm is correctly seated before installing the plate and cover, then tighten the cover screws securely.

4   The brake fluid should be changed every two years as described in Section 19.

Front brake pad wear check

5   Remove the front wheel, then prise off the brake pad cover to check the condition of the brake pads. The pads are not marked with wear indicators but if the amount of friction material remaining is below 1.5 mm (0.06 in), new pads must be fitted.

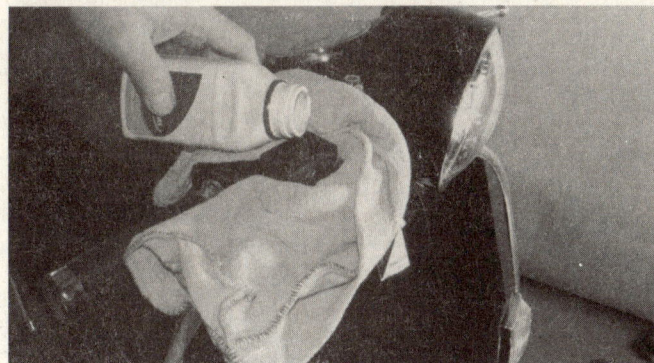

3.2 Topping-up the front brake fluid

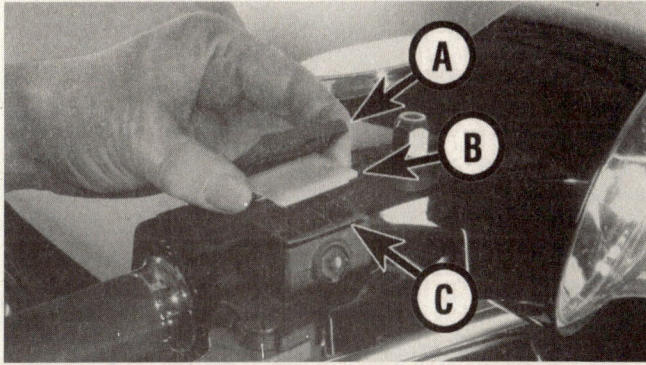

3.3 The hydraulic reservoir cover (A), diaphragm plate (B) and diaphragm (C)

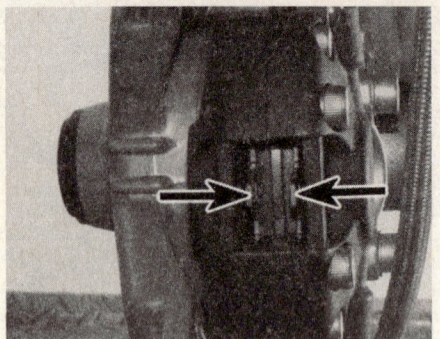

3.6 Location of the front brake pads (arrowed) in the caliper

3.8 Battery electrolyte level must be between UPPER and LOWER marks on casing

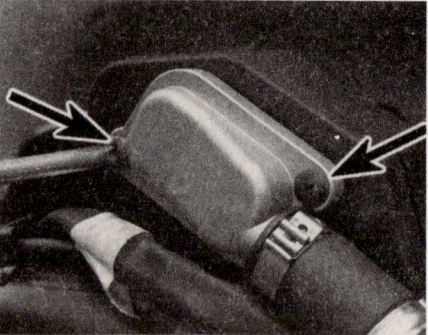

3.13 Secondary air system valve cover screws (arrowed)

6   If the pads are dirty, or if you are in doubt as to the amount of friction material remaining, remove the pads for inspection as described in Section 18.

Battery electrolyte level top up

Note: *Take care when working with the battery that you do not allow the electrolyte to contact your eyes, skin or clothing, as it contains sulphuric acid. Flush any contaminated areas immediately with plenty of water. Any contact with eyes requires prompt medical attention.*

7   Remove the left-hand side panel.
8   The battery electrolyte level is viewed through the battery case. It should lie between the UPPER and LOWER marks on the casing. If not, remove the battery for topping up.

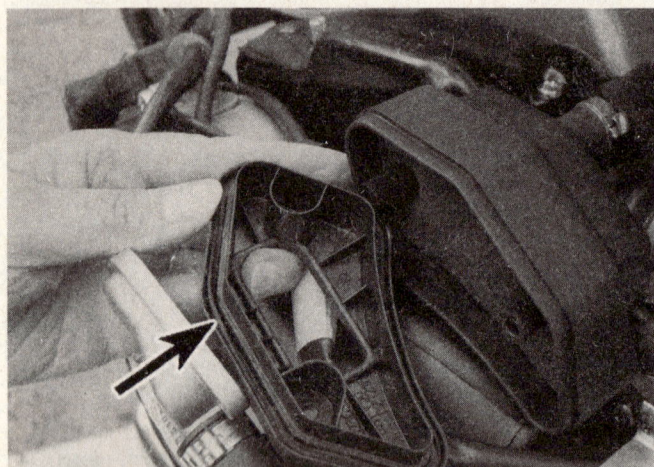

3.14 Remove plastic cover to reveal foam filter, noting the sealing ring (arrowed)

9   If a spare wheel is fitted, this must be removed before the battery can be freed. Disconnect the battery terminals, noting that the negative terminal should be detached first. Release the battery retaining strap and remove the battery from its holder. Remove the cell caps from the battery and top up to the correct level with distilled water only.
10 If the machine is not in regular use, disconnect the battery and give it a refresher charge every month to six weeks, as described in Section 23.

Air filter element clean

11 See Routine maintenance at the beginning of this manual to remove the filter element, then wash the element in a 50% mix of clean engine oil and petrol. Allow the element to air dry before refitting.

Secondary air system clean – Euro 2 and 3 models

12 Remove the right-hand side panel.
13 Undo the screws securing the secondary air filter housing and detach it – the hose can remain attached. Note the location of the reed valve inside the housing.
14 Lift off the plastic cover and pick out the foam filter element. There will be a sealing ring located in the cover groove – check that it is undamaged.
15 Carefully pull the foam intake filter off the pipe which extends from the rear of the housing.
16 Wash the filters in hot soapy water then blow them dry using compressed air. Never wring the filters dry as they may tear. If the filters are excessively dirty and cannot be cleaned properly, or are torn or damaged in any way, fit new ones.
17 Lift the reed valve out of the housing, noting that it is shaped to prevent it being refitted incorrectly. To check the condition of the reed valve, hold it up to the light. The valve should be closed. If light can be seen around the edge of the reed a new valve should be fitted. Clean the reed and stopper plate carefully with a suitable solvent to remove any gum or exhaust gas residue.
18 Install the components in the reverse order of disassembly.

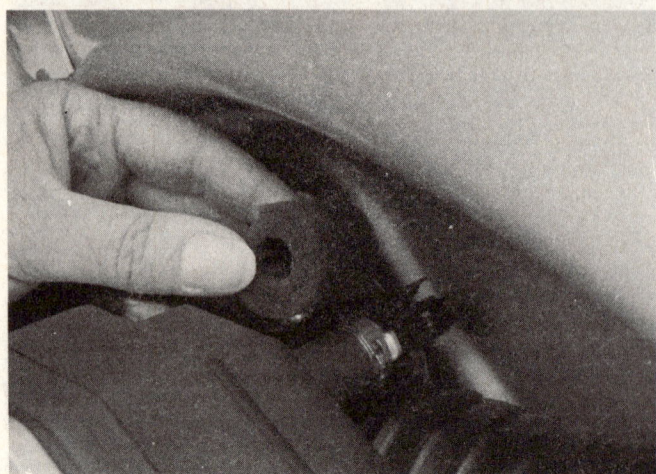

3.15 Handle foam intake filter carefully

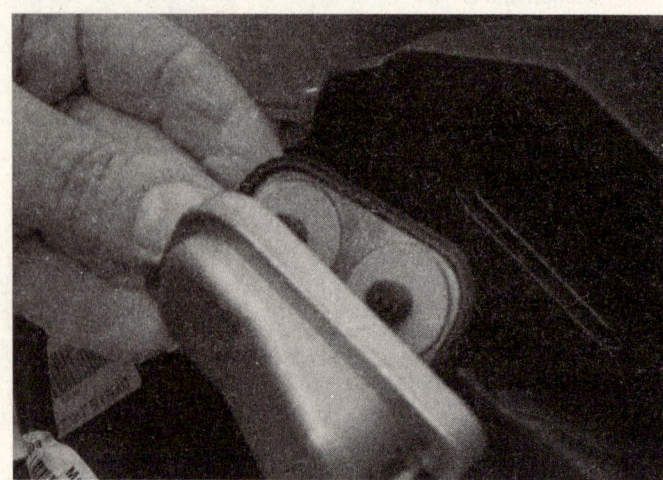

3.17 Reed valve unit locates in housing

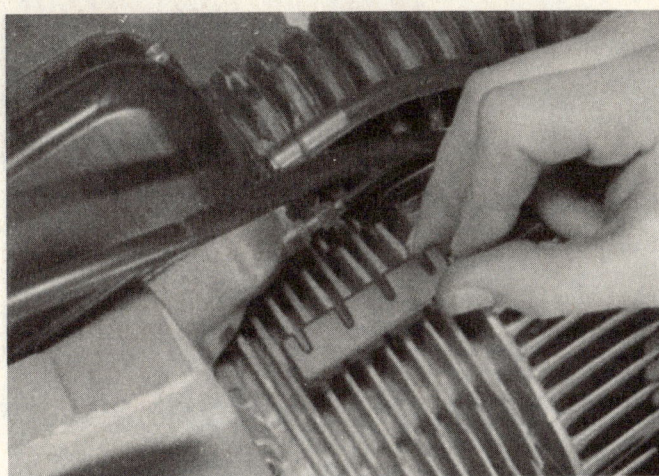

4.2 Rubber damping blocks are fitted between fins of aluminium alloy cylinder barrel

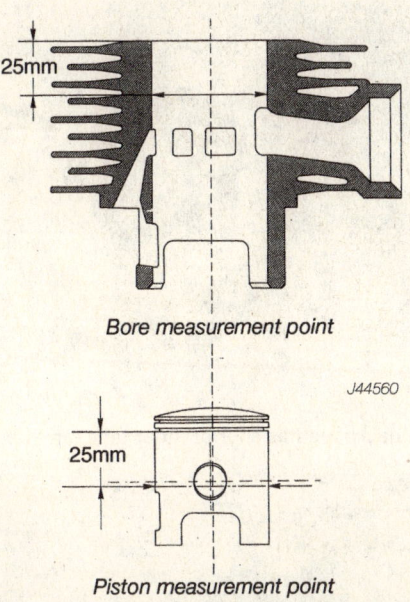

Bore measurement point

J44560

Piston measurement point

Fig. 7.1 Cylinder barrel and piston measurement points (Sec 4)

4   Cylinder barrel and piston: removal, examination and refitting – T5 model

Removal and refitting

1   The T5 engine employs a Nikasil coated light alloy cylinder barrel, and thus a revised approach is required when assessing wear or damage. Preliminary dismantling is similar to that described in Chapter 1, except that a revised exhaust port arrangement is employed. This uses two retaining studs in place of the plain tubular stub previously fitted.

2   Note also that rubber damper blocks are fitted between the cylinder cooling fins. These are designed to prevent the fins from ringing, and should be refitted during reassembly.

Examination

3   Plated alloy cylinder bores provide a very hard-wearing bore surface. The rate of wear of the bore surface is much lower than with conventional types, and high mileages can be expected before attention is required. Where damage or excessive wear does occur, it will be necessary to fit a new cylinder barrel together with a suitably matched piston; reboring is not feasible.

4   The cylinder bore will be marked with a letter to denote its grade, and the code letters and the corresponding bore size are shown in the Specifications section of this Chapter. It is essential that the appropriate grade of piston is selected to maintain the precise piston-to-bore clearance, and to this end the piston is also marked with a grading letter. It follows that if either the piston or the cylinder barrel is to be renewed individually, it is necessary to ensure that one of the correct grade is fitted.

5   Other than obvious damage, such as scoring or flaking of the bore surface, it is not easy to assess wear with sufficient accuracy using normal home workshop tools. If you have access to internal and external micrometers, note that the bore should be checked at a point 25 mm (1.0 in) below the cylinder head gasket face, and at 90° to the gudgeon pin axis. The piston diameter should be checked at a point 25 mm (1.0 in) below the bottom ring groove, again at 90° to the gudgeon pin bore. If either the bore or piston are outside the specified service limits, or if the clearance between the two exceeds the limit of 0.08 mm (0.0032 in), the worn part(s) must be renewed. For most practical purposes, it is probably best to ask your dealer to check these clearances and then to order any necessary replacement parts.

6   During normal use, it is likely that the piston rings will show signs of wear long before the bore surface does, and these should be checked as follows. Remove the rings from the piston (see Chapter 1, Section 19) noting that the lower ring should be marked using a spirit-based felt marker to denote its upper surface. Place each ring in turn into the bottom of the bore, using the base of the piston to position it square to the bore. The ring should be placed at an unworn portion of the bore, about 13 mm (1/2 in) from the bottom.

7   Using feeler gauges, check the ring end gap, comparing the reading obtained with that shown in the specifications at the beginning of this Chapter. If either ring shows an end gap in excess of the wear limit of 2.0 mm (0.079 in), renewal will be required. Note that if bore wear is present, the end gap reading will be increased slightly at the point of maximum wear, though the plated bore surface will mean that bore wear is unlikely to be excessive unless very high mileages have been covered.

5   Piston/barrel and small-end bearing: modifications – PX125, 150 and 200 electric start models

Piston and barrel markings – later models

1   If replacing either the piston or cylinder clean the old component thoroughly to enable it to be checked for a production size code marking. On later models, the piston and cylinder are size-coded during manufacture and it is important that they are of the same size code. Piaggio list 7 size codes (B to H); those for the standard diameter piston are given in the specifications at the beginning of this Chapter. The size codes are stamped into the gasket surface at the top or base of the cylinder, and in the piston crown. When purchasing a new cylinder or piston, always supply the size code letter.

Small-end bearing

2   The small-end bearings for all models are colour-coded for identification and the corresponding connecting rod is either colour coded or marked with a series of lines. See the Specifications at the beginning of this Chapter for bearing fit details.

6   Clutch assembly: modifications – PX125, 150 and 200 electric start models

1   The clutch assembly is broadly similar to that used on earlier models, but there have been modifications to the design of the clutch centre and arrangement of the clutch springs. The clutch centre/primary gear is separate from the inner plain plate, and there are eight small clutch springs located on pins fixed around the centre of the clutch drum. There are four friction plates and four plain plates.

2   To dismantle the clutch, compress the centre into the drum and remove the large circlip as described in Chapter 1, Section 21. The service tool mentioned is no longer listed, but a long bolt with a nut and two large washers is just as effective. Tighten the nut and bolt until pressure is taken off the circlip, then release the circlip from its groove in the outer edge of the drum. Lift out the clutch plates keeping them

6.2a Clutch backplate has shorter inner tabs (arrowed)

6.2b Clutch centre (arrowed) is a separate component

6.3 Spring seat fits over the eight small clutch springs

6.4a Washer must be fitted dished face down

6.4b Coat the friction plates with engine oil before reassembly

in the order they are fitted. The inner plain plate, or backplate, may be a tight fit on the clutch centre so remove the two together if necessary. Note that the inner tabs on the backplate are different to the tabs on the other plain plates. Remove the dished washer, noting how it fits. The clutch centre bush is a tight fit on the shaft of the spring seat and should be left in place unless it is to be renewed.

3   Undo the nut and bolt and remove them, then lift out the spring seat and the clutch springs.

4   There are no service limits available for the clutch components, so inspect them for wear and damage as described in Chapter 1. On reassembly, ensure that the dished washer is fitted with the dished side facing the spring seat. The clutch plates are designed to run in oil so do not wipe them dry before reassembly. If new friction plates are being fitted, soak them in engine oil beforehand.

---

7   Gearbox shaft assembly: modifications – T5 model

Output shaft

1   The output shaft assembly is broadly similar to that used on the earlier PX models, but there has been a modification to the shimming arrangement. A less significant change is the omission of the washer on the selector rod end (item 9 in Fig. 1.9), and this should be taken into account during dismantling and reassembly.

2   On the earlier PX models, output shaft endfloat was controlled by selecting the appropriate size of thrust washer. The thrust washer was fitted to the right-hand end of the assembly, the clearance being measured at the left-hand end of the cluster. This is best shown in the line drawing of the assembly (Fig. 1.10).

3   On the T5 model, thrust washers are fitted at both ends of the gear cluster, the endfloat measurement being taken at the right-hand end of the assembly. This is marked 'A' in the accompanying line drawing. The range of available thrust washer sizes is shown in the Specifications section of this Chapter. Note that the correct clearance remains unchanged at 0.15 – 0.40 mm (0.006 – 0.016 in) and the service limit at 0.50 mm (0.020 in).

Input shaft

4   The input shaft assembly is generally unchanged from the earlier version, the only significant alteration being to the transmission shock absorber assembly. As with the earlier type, dismantling the shock absorber should not normally be undertaken at home due to its riveted construction. If you do tackle this job, note that the inner springs (item 11 in Fig. 1.8) are not fitted to the T5 model.

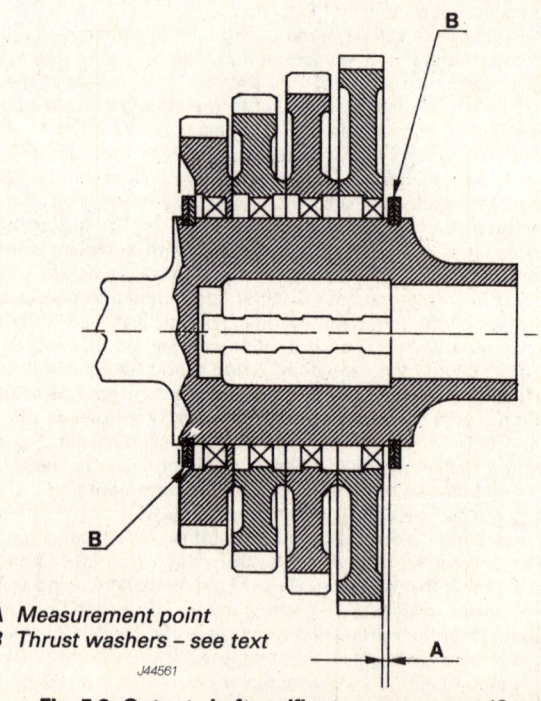

A Measurement point
B Thrust washers – see text

J44561

Fig. 7.2 Output shaft endfloat measurement (Sec 7)

8.2 Lower cowling section contains sound-absorbing material to reduce mechanical noise from the engine/gearbox unit

8   Engine cowling: modifications – T5 model

1   Like previous Vespa models, the engine is cooled by a forced air system, this being powered by the combined external flywheel and fan assembly which forms part of the generator rotor. The cooling air is passed around the cylinder head and barrel fins inside cowling sections, and in the case of the T5 model these are formed from plastic, rather than thin sheet steel.
2   In addition to the cooling system cowling, there is also another addition in the form of an undershield around the gear selector box and gearbox casing. Once again, this is moulded from plastic material, and it also contains a layer of sound insulation material. It follows that access to the gearbox oil filler plug or the gear control cables will require the removal of the undershield.

9   Carburettor: modifications – T5 model

1   The changes to the cylinder porting have resulted in different carburation requirements on the T5 model, and this has led to the fitting of a 24 mm (0.95 in) Dell'Orto instrument in place of the 20 mm (0.79 in) model previously used on other 125 cc engines. The larger carburettor is of similar design, the main alterations being to the various jet sizes. These are given in the specifications section of this Chapter.
2   On some models it is necessary to remove the throttle stop screw in order to remove the air filter for cleaning. Note the position of the screw as described in Chapter 2, Section 6, to aid reassembly, and if necessary adjust the idle speed as described in Routine maintenance.

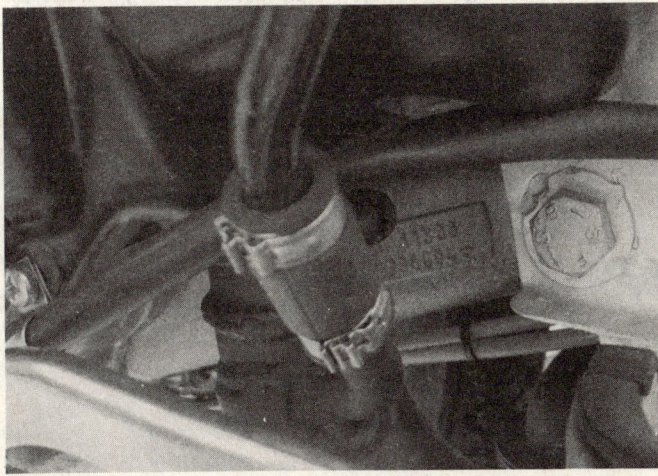

11.3 Disconnect secondary air system hose clip from exhaust pipe stub

10   Carburettor: modifications – PX125, 150 and 200 electric start models

1   The carburettor type and specifications are virtually unchanged from the earlier PX models, although the jetting has been simplified. The revised specifications are shown at the beginning of this Chapter.

11   Exhaust system – PX125 and 150 Euro 1, 2 and 3 models

Catalytic converter – general information

1   The exhaust system contains a simple open-loop catalytic converter. On models which conform to Euro 2 and 3 legislation the catalyst works in conjunction with the secondary air system which promotes the burning of any excess fuel present in the exhaust gases. The exhaust system itself is one-piece on Euro 1 and 2 models; on Euro 3 models a two-piece system is fitted (see Fig. 7.3), the catalyst is housed in the downpipe.
2   The catalytic converter has no link with the fuel and ignition systems, and requires no routine maintenance. However the following points should be noted:
   a) Always use unleaded fuel – the use of leaded fuel or LRP will destroy the converter.
   b) Do not use any fuel or oil additives. Apart from scraping any carbon deposits from the mouth of the downpipe, do not use the exhaust cleaning methods described in Chapter 2.
   c) Keep the fuel and ignition systems in good order – if the fuel/air mixture is suspected of being incorrect, have it checked by a Piaggio/Vespa dealer on an exhaust gas analyser.
   d) When the exhaust system is removed from the scooter handle it with care to avoid damaging the delicate catalytic converter. Note that replacement catalytic converter-equipped systems are expensive.
   e) The catalyst operates at high temperature - be careful at all times to avoid burning your hands or allowing flammable fluids to contact the exhaust system.
   f) Never switch off the ignition whilst the scooter is moving otherwise unburnt fuel will soak the catalytic converter and ruin it.
3   When removing the exhaust system, note that the secondary air system hose should be detached at the flexible link hose.

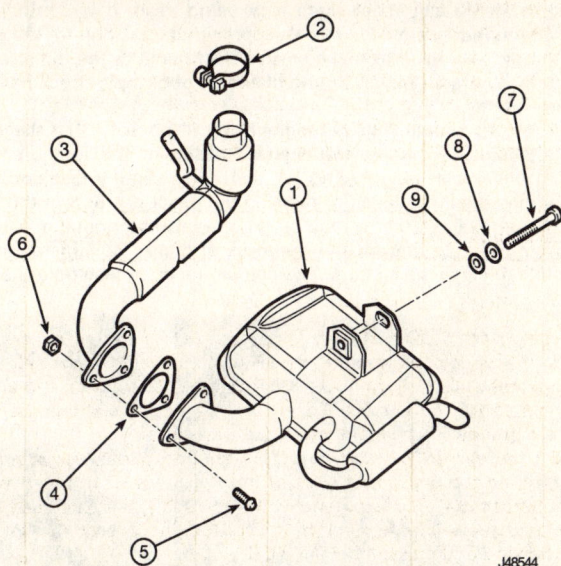

J48544

Fig. 7.3 Exhaust system on Euro 3 models (Sec 11)

1	Silencer	5	Bolt – 3 off
2	Downpipe clamp	6	Nut – 3 off
3	Downpipe (containing catalyst)	7	Bolt
4	Gasket	8	Washer
		9	Washer

12.1 T5 stator assembly is generally similar to previous model

12.2 Revised timing marks on stator

Exhaust CO content check

4   On certain market models, a take-off point is provided on the exhaust system to enable checking of the exhaust gas CO content. If the mixture setting is suspected of being incorrect take the machine to Piaggio/Vespa dealer equipped the specified exhaust gas analyser and gas collecting kit, plus an inductive tachometer to measure engine speed accurately – DIY checks are not possible due to the equipment required.

5   For information, the test requires the secondary air system reed valve to be sealed off temporarily by inserting a plastic sheet between the valve and its housing. It is carried out with the engine warmed up and idling at 1300 ± 100 rpm. The CO value should be $4 \pm 1\%$ with the mixture screw at $2\frac{3}{4}$ turns out.

12 Flywheel generator assembly and ignition timing marks: modification – T5 model

1   A slightly revised ac generator assembly is fitted to the T5 engine, the design being broadly similar to that shown in the photographs which accompany Section 28 of Chapter 1. Note that the stator alignment mark has been simplified from that shown in photograph 28.2b, a single alignment mark now being used. It is worth noting that although these marks give an approximate position for the stator, there may be a need to make small adjustments to the initial setting to attain accurate ignition timing after a stroboscopic check has been made.

2   In the accompanying photograph it will be seen that the marks do not coincide exactly, the precise setting of the ignition timing during initial assembly having left the marks slightly displaced. This underlines the importance of marking the exact position of the stator before removal, so that it may be returned to its original position on reassembly. Note that for the purposes of crankcase separation, it is possible to leave the stator in position on the crankcase outer half.

13 Ignition timing marks: modification – PX125, 150 and 200 electric start models

1   The stator alignment mark for all models is the IT mark, as shown in Chapter 1, Section 28. Always check the alignment of the timing marks and make a note of their position before removing the stator, or make your own alignment marks if necessary.

2   Remember that the marks give an approximate position for the stator and there may be a need to make small adjustments to the initial setting to attain accurate ignition timing after a stroboscopic check has been made as described in Chapter 3, Section 12.

14 Chassis: modifications – T5 model

T5 model

1   Whilst the basic chassis design and layout remain unchanged, there have been a number of cosmetic alterations intended to update the appearance of the model. The front and rear wheels have been fitted with matt silver plastic wheel covers to give them a more contemporary appearance, while items such as the handlebar assembly, horn cover and front mudguard have also been re-styled.

2   The individual rubber footboard strips have been replaced by a one-piece mat, while a front spoiler has been added to the lower edge of the legshield. On the top edge of the glove compartment a moulded plastic tray has been fitted to allow small items to be carried.

3   At the rear of the machine, the slight curvature of the main body pressing which has characterised all Vespas since their inception has been covered by adding a flat sheet steel extension, spot-welded to the normal body pressing below it. Note that it may be worth attempting to inject a rust preventative such as Waxoyl (this product being widely available from car accessory shops) into this cavity to prevent rusting in the future. Similar treatment of the main body pressings will prevent rusting of these areas too, and access is best gained by removing the fuel tank.

14.1a Wheel covers clip over metal tabs on wheels. Note that tabs are secured to the wheel by the rim securing nuts

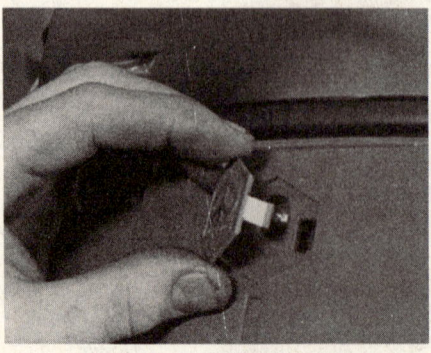

14.1b The clipped-on badge at the top of the horn cover conceals one of the securing screws

14.1c Horn is attached to legshield bracket, not to the inside of the horn cover as on other models

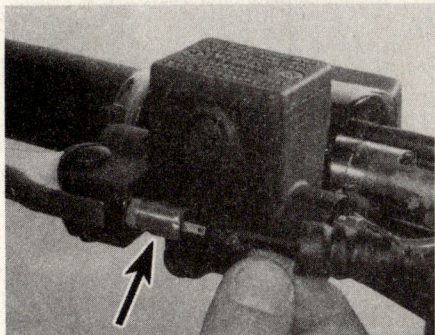

15.2a Front brake light switch (arrowed) has two wiring connectors

15.2b Master cylinder is secured by two bolts (arrowed)

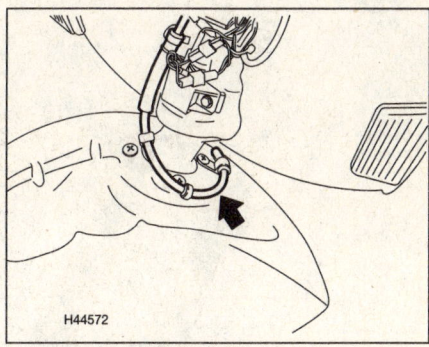

15.3 Note the routing of the front brake hydraulic hose (arrowed)

T5 Classic model

4   Apart from the improvements described in paragraph 2, the T5 Classic chassis components remain unchanged from those fitted to the PX125 E in the main chapters of this manual. Matt silver plastic wheel covers are fitted as standard.

15   Steering column assembly: removal and refitting – PX125, 150 and 200 electric start models

1   The procedure is the same as for earlier models described in Chapter 4, Section 2, with the exception of draining the front brake hydraulic reservoir and disconnecting the brake hose. Take care to avoid spilling brake fluid on painted or plastic surfaces.
2   First disconnect the front brake light switch wiring connectors. Loosen the reservoir cover screws and the hydraulic hose union to the reservoir, then undo the two bolts securing the brake master cylinder assembly to the handlebars. Remove the reservoir cover, diaphragm plate and diaphragm and drain the brake fluid into a suitable container. Wipe any remaining fluid out of the reservoir with a clean rag.
3   Disconnect the hydraulic hose from the reservoir and wrap a clean plastic bag tightly around the end to prevent accidental spillage and dirt entering the system. Remove the horn cover as described in Chapter 4, Section 8, paragraph 2, and feed the hose through the body to the front mudguard. Note how the hose is routed around the back of the steering column and secured to the mudguard with a clip.

4   On reassembly, fill the hydraulic reservoir with new brake fluid and bleed any air out of the system as described in Section 19.

16   Handlebar assembly: removal and refitting – T5 model

Note: This procedure does not apply to the T5 Classic model.
1   The cast alloy handlebar assembly has been abandoned in favour of a pressed steel assembly secured to the steering column, to which is attached upper and lower shrouds and the headlamp unit. Although the steering column assembly and bearings are similar to the previous arrangement, the handlebar assembly is completely different, and its removal and refitting is described below.
2   Start by releasing the four screws which secure the upper and lower handlebar shroud sections. The screws pass up through holes in the underside of the assembly, screwing into the upper section. Remove the single screw which retains the headlamp to the slotted hole in the lower section. Lift the shroud upper section until resistance from the control cables is felt. To ease the upper section away, feed the speedometer and front brake cables up from the lower end of the steering column if required.
3   Release the speedometer drive cable by disconnecting it from the underside of the instrument panel. The cable is retained by two clips on each side of the plastic ferrule. Lift and tilt back the upper shroud until the wiring connectors can be reached. These must be disconnected from the instrument panel carefully to avoid possible damage to the printed circuit. Lift away the shroud upper section and place it safely to one side.
4   It will now be necessary to disconnect the front brake cable at the handlebar lever. Push the speedometer and front brake cable ends down into the steering column until their ends are just above the end of the column. If the complete handlebar is to be removed from the machine, you will also have to disconnect the clutch and gearchange cables. If access to the steering head bearings only is required, it should be possible to leave the cables attached.
5   The handlebar assembly is retained by a slotted nut, for which a special spanner, Part No. 19.1.20055 will be required, this tool also being suitable for the steering head bearing adjuster nut. In the

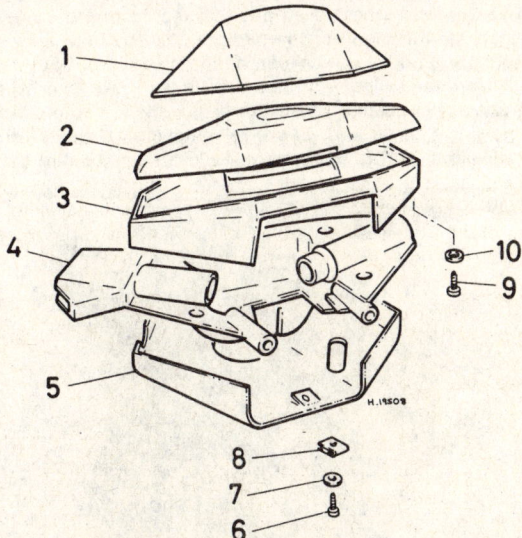

Fig. 7.4 Handlebar shroud assembly (Sec 16)

1 Screen	6 Screw
2 Cover	7 Washer
3 Upper shroud	8 Nut
4 Handlebar	9 Screw – 4 off
5 Lower shroud-	10 Washer – 4 off

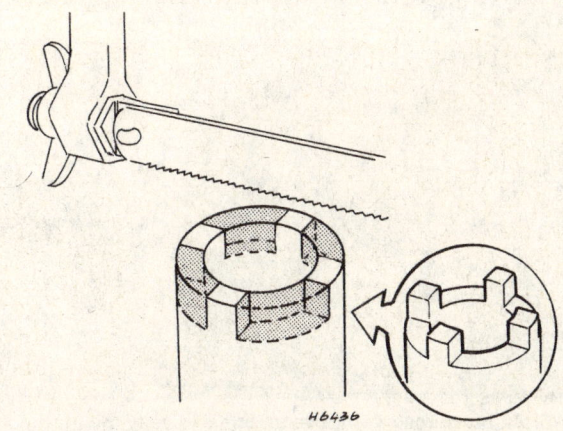

Fig. 7.5 Fabricated handlebar retaining nut removal tool (Sec 16)

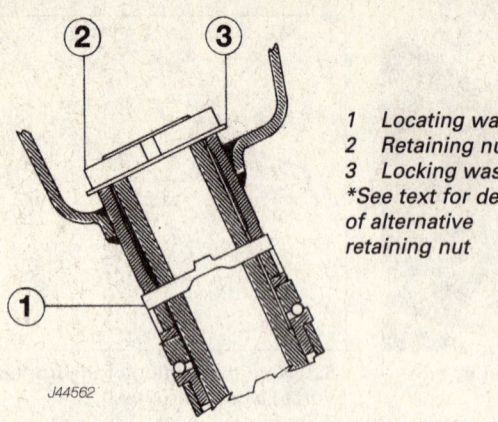

1 Locating washer
2 Retaining nut*
3 Locking washer*
*See text for details
of alternative
retaining nut

Fig. 7.6 Handlebar retaining nut assembly (Sec 16)

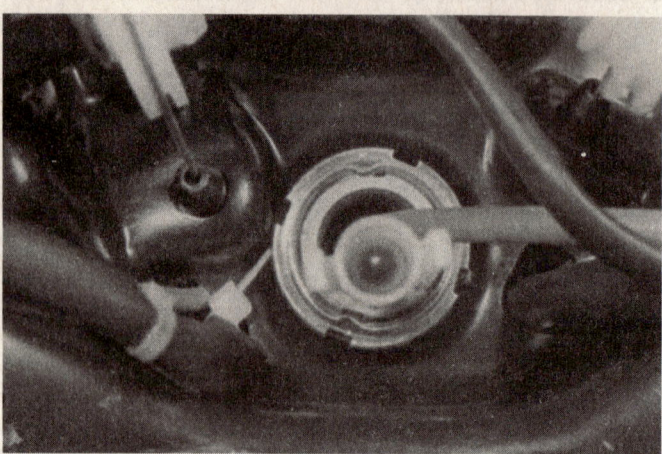

16.7 A single slotted nut (centre of photograph) retains the handlebar assembly. Note also the collar of the nut which is staked into slots in the steering column – see text

absence of the correct tool, a home-made equivalent can be made up from a piece of thick-walled steel tubing of the appropriate diameter. Mark out the position and width of the slots on one end of the tubing and then hacksaw and file the tool as shown in the accompanying line drawing.

6   The handlebar retaining nut will either be locked to the steering column by lockwasher tabs or staked in place. If a lockwasher is fitted, straighten the tab from the nuts slots to allow the nut to be removed, and be sure to fit a new washer during reassembly.

7   Where the handlebar retaining nut has a plain collar section which is staked into the slots in the steering column, the staking will have to be judiciously straightened before the nut can be removed. Note that the staked areas will either split away or will have been weakened during this operation, so use a new nut during installation.

8   Once the retaining nut and any underlying washer has been freed, tip the handlebar assembly back and lift it clear of the steering column. The locating washer fitted below the handlebar assembly can now be lifted away, and the lower section of the shroud removed.

9   Reassembly is a straightforward reversal of the removal procedure, noting that a new locking washer or special nut should be used according to the arrangement applicable to your machine. The slotted nut securing the handlebar assembly should be tightened to 5.5 – 6.5 kgf m (39.8 – 47.0 lbf ft). Note that the headlamp beam aim will have been disturbed during the procedure, and this must be checked and reset when assembly is complete.

---

17   Front brake hose: removal and refitting – 1999-on PX125, 150 and 200 models

1   Remove the handlebar upper cover as described in Chapter 4, Section 2, and the horn cover as described in Chapter 4, Section 8,

paragraph 2. Undo the clip securing the hydraulic hose to the top of the front mudguard.

2   Undo the union securing the hydraulic hose to the reservoir – do not operate the brake lever while the hose is disconnected and wrap some rag around the reservoir to soak up any residual brake fluid. Wrap a clean plastic bag tightly around the end of the hose to prevent accidental spillage. Place a drain tray below the front brake caliper to catch any residual brake fluid and cover the wheel rim and tyre with rag. Note the alignment of the brake hose banjo union with the caliper, then undo the banjo bolt and discard the sealing washers.

3   Carefully feed the hose through the body and the front mudguard, noting its routing. Reverse the procedure to install the new hose, fitting new sealing washers to the banjo union on the caliper, then fill the hydraulic reservoir with new brake fluid and bleed any air out of the system as described in Section 19.

---

18   Front disc brake: examination, renovation and reassembly – 1999-on PX125, 150 and 200 models

Brake pads

1   Remove the front wheel, then prise off the brake pad cover. Prise the circlip off the inner end of the pad pin, then pull out the pin and lift the pad spring out of the caliper, noting how it fits. Withdraw the brake pads from the caliper – do not operate the brake lever while the pads are out of the caliper. Clean the pads with a wire brush which is completely free of oil and grease to remove all traces of dirt and corrosion. If either pad is worn down to less than 1.5 mm (0.06 in),

17.2a Front brake reservoir hose union (arrowed)

17.2b Note the alignment of the brake hose banjo union (arrowed) with the caliper

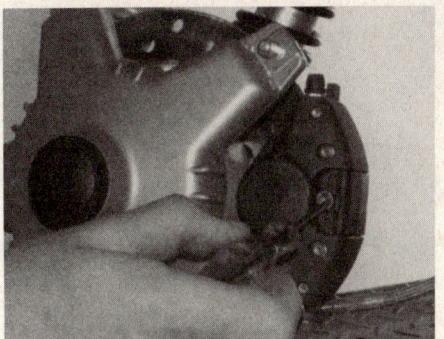

18.1a Remove the circlip . . .

18.1b . . . then pull out the pad pin . . .

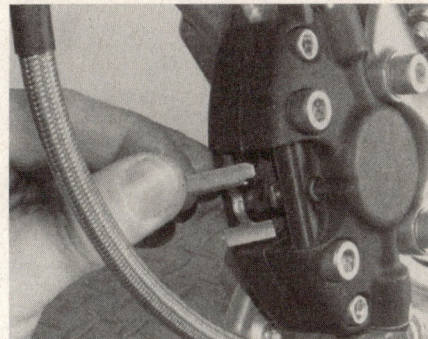

18.1c . . . and remove the pad spring

is fouled with oil or grease, or heavily scored or damaged, both pads must be renewed. Never attempt to degrease the friction material – if the pads are glazed or contaminated in any way they must be renewed. If one pad is worn a lot more than the other, it is likely the corresponding piston is stuck in the caliper. Have the brake checked by a dealer.

2   Spray the inside of the caliper with a dedicated brake cleaner to remove any dust and wipe the caliper and brake disc with a clean cloth. Do not, under any circumstances, use petroleum-based solvents to clean brake parts. Clean any corrosion off the pad pin and pad spring. If new pads are being installed, slowly push the pistons back into the caliper using hand pressure or a piece of wood, but don't lever against the disc as damage may result. Moving the pistons will displace brake fluid back into the hydraulic reservoir, so it may be necessary to remove the reservoir cover, plate and diaphragm and siphon out some fluid. If the pistons are difficult to push back, attach a length of clear hose to the bleed valve and place the open end in a suitable container, then open the valve and try again. Take great care not to draw any air into the system and don't forget to tighten the valve once the pistons have been sufficiently displaced. If in doubt, bleed the brake afterwards (see Section 19).

3   Smear the backs of the pads with copper-based grease, making sure that none gets on the front or sides of the pads, then install them in the caliper. Fit the pad spring, arrow pointing UP, and secure it with the pin. Secure the pin with the circlip – note that it is good practice to use a new circlip whenever the pin is removed. Operate the brake lever several times to bring the pads into contact with the disc and fit the pad cover. Check the level of fluid in the hydraulic reservoir and top-up if necessary.

Brake caliper

4   In order to displace the brake caliper to facilitate work on the front hub, first remove the front wheel, then undo the two bolts securing the caliper to the lower suspension bracket. Pull the caliper off the disc and secure it to the machine with a cable tie to avoid straining the hydraulic hose. The brake pads can be left in place in the caliper.

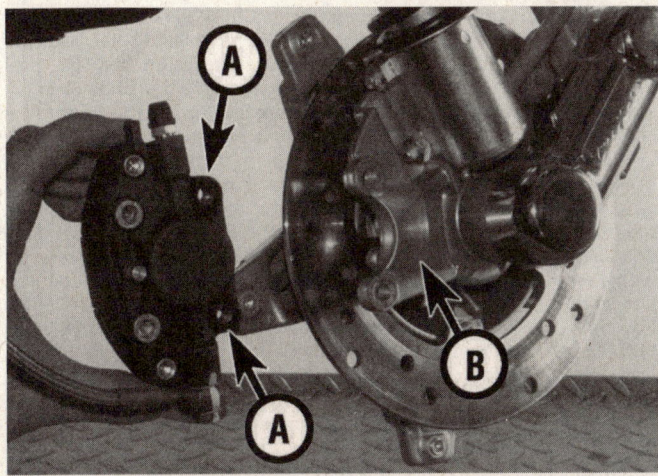

18.4 Brake caliper mounting bolt locations (A) and mounting bracket (B)

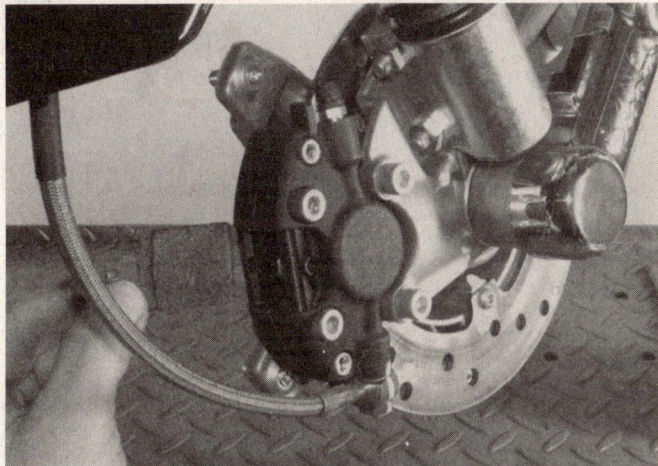

18.1d Pull the brake pads out of the caliper

5   To examine the caliper, remove the brake pads, spray the caliper with a dedicated brake cleaner and wipe it with a clean cloth. If hydraulic fluid is leaking from around the edge of either piston, an internal seal has failed. A caliper rebuild kit is listed but it is recommended that renewing the seals is undertaken by a dealer. Light corrosion can be cleaned off the exposed surface of the pistons carefully with steel wool, but if the pistons are pitted or stuck in the caliper, a new caliper will have to be fitted.

6   To remove the caliper from the machine, disconnect the hydraulic hose at the caliper end only as described in Section 17. When the caliper is refitted, bleed the hydraulic system as described in Section 19.

Brake disc

7   Inspect the surface of the brake disc for score marks and other damage. Light scratches are normal after use and won't affect brake operation, but deep grooves and heavy score marks will reduce braking efficiency and accelerate pad wear. If a disc is badly grooved it must be

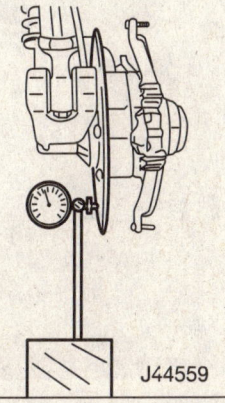

J44559

Fig. 7.7 Set-up for checking brake disc runout (Sec 18)

18.9a Disc is marked with a 'direction of rotation' arrow

18.9b Brake disc is secured by five bolts

machined by a brake specialist or renewed. There is no service limit for the brake disc, but the extent of disc wear will be apparent from the size of the lip around the unworn outer edge.

8   If the brake lever pulses when the brake is applied the disc is probably warped. If available, use a dial gauge as shown in the accompanying line drawing to check the disc runout. If the runout is greater then the service limit, first check the wheel bearings as described in Chapter 5, Section 2. If the bearings are good, fit a new disc.

9   To remove the brake disc, first follow the procedure described in Chapter 5, Section 3, and remove the hub from the stub axle. Note the direction of rotation arrow on the disc and, if the disc is to be refitted, mark the disc and hub so that the disc can be fitted in the same position. The disc is secured by five bolts. On reassembly, apply a suitable non-permanent thread locking compound to the disc bolts and check the position of the direction of rotation arrow before installing the bolts.

19   Bleeding the hydraulic system – 1999-on PX125, 150 and 200 models

1   Bleeding the brake is simply the process of removing air from the hydraulic reservoir, master cylinder, the hose and the brake caliper. Bleeding is necessary whenever a brake system connection is loosened, or when a component is replaced or renewed. To bleed the

19.4 Brake caliper bleed valve (arrowed)

brake, you will need some new DOT 4 brake fluid, a small container partially filled with clean brake fluid, a length of clear vinyl or plastic hose to fit the caliper bleed valve, some rags and a spanner to fit the brake caliper bleed valve.

2   Support the machine in an upright position on level ground and turn the handlebars until the hydraulic reservoir is as level as possible. Cover any painted components with rag to prevent damage in the event that brake fluid is spilled.

3   Remove the reservoir cover, diaphragm plate and diaphragm and slowly pump the brake lever a few times, until no air bubbles can be seen floating up from the holes in the bottom of the reservoir. This bleeds air from the master cylinder end of the line. Temporarily refit the reservoir cover.

4   Pull the dust cap off the caliper bleed valve. To avoid damaging the valve during the procedure, loosen it with a ring spanner and then tighten it temporarily. Attach one end of the clear hose to the valve and submerge the other end in the brake fluid in the container. With the hose attached, the valve can then be opened and closed with an open-ended spanner.

5   Check the fluid level in the reservoir. Do not allow the fluid level to drop below the half-way mark on the inspection window during the procedure. Carefully pump the brake lever three or four times and hold it in while opening the caliper bleed valve. When the valve is opened, brake fluid will flow out of the caliper into the clear hose and the lever will move toward the handlebar. Tighten the bleed valve, then release the brake lever gradually. Repeat the process until no air bubbles are visible in the brake fluid leaving the caliper and the lever is firm when applied. On completion, disconnect the hose, tighten the bleed valve fully and fit the dust cap.

6   Top-up the reservoir, install the diaphragm, diaphragm plate and cover, and wipe up any spilled brake fluid. Check the entire system for fluid leaks. If it's not possible to produce a firm feel to the lever the fluid may be aerated. Let the brake fluid in the system stabilise for a few hours and then repeat the procedure when the tiny bubbles in the system have settled out. To speed this process up, tie the front brake lever to the handlebar so that the system is pressurised.

7   Changing the brake fluid is a similar process to bleeding the brakes and requires the same materials plus a suitable syringe for emptying the hydraulic reservoir. Loosen the bleed valve and attach the hose as before, then remove the reservoir cover, diaphragm plate and diaphragm and siphon out the old fluid. Top-up the reservoir with new fluid. Carefully pump the brake lever three or four times and hold it in while opening the bleed valve to allow brake fluid to flow into the hose. Tighten the bleed valve and release the brake lever gradually, then repeat the process as described in Step 5. Old brake fluid is invariably much darker in colour than new fluid, making it easy to see when all old fluid has been expelled from the system. On completion, ensure there are no air bubbles visible in the brake fluid leaving the caliper and that the lever is firm when applied.

8   Top-up the reservoir and check the operation of the brake before riding the scooter.

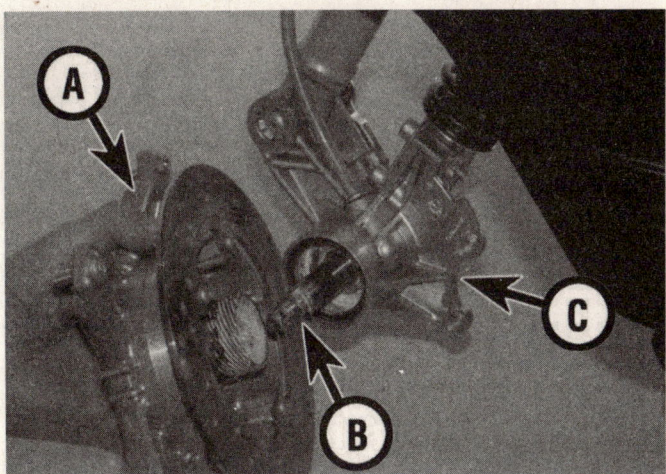

20.1a Front hub (A), stub axle (B) and caliper bracket (C)

20.1b Front suspension unit is secured to the caliper bracket by two bolts (arrowed)

20   Front hub assembly: modifications – 1999-on PX125, 150 and 200 models

1   Despite a move from drum to disc front brake, the front hub arrangement remains much as described in Chapter 5. The hub is still secured by a nut, castellated insert and split pin and the arrangement of the hub bearings and speedometer drive are as before. Likewise, the drum brake backplate has been replaced by the caliper bracket which secures the lower end of the front suspension unit. For details of removal, examination and reassembly see Chapter 5.

21   Lighting system: bulb renewal – PX125, 150 and 200 electric start models

Headlamp bulb

1   The headlamp is fitted with a quartz-halogen bulb – do not touch the bulb glass as skin acids will shorten the bulb's service life. If the bulb is accidentally touched, it should be wiped carefully when cold with a rag soaked in methylated spirit and dried before fitting. Allow the bulb time to cool before removing it if the headlamp has just been on.

2   Remove the handlebar cover as described in Chapter 6, Section 6. Disconnect the bulb wiring connector and remove the dust cover, noting how it fits, then turn the bulbholder anti-clockwise to release it and lift out the bulb. Ensure the tabs on the new bulb fit correctly in the slots in the bulb housing before securing the bulb with the bulbholder.

3   The sidelamp bulbholder is a push fit in the reflector and the bulb is of the capless type.

Turn signal bulbs

4   The turn signal lenses are now clear plastic and the bulbs are orange coloured. Note that the bulb pins are offset and only this type of bulb can be fitted in the bulbholders.

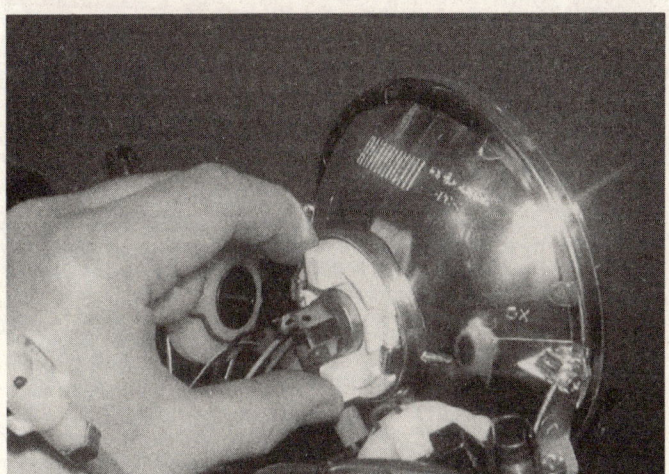

21.2a Turn the bulbholder anti-clockwise to release it

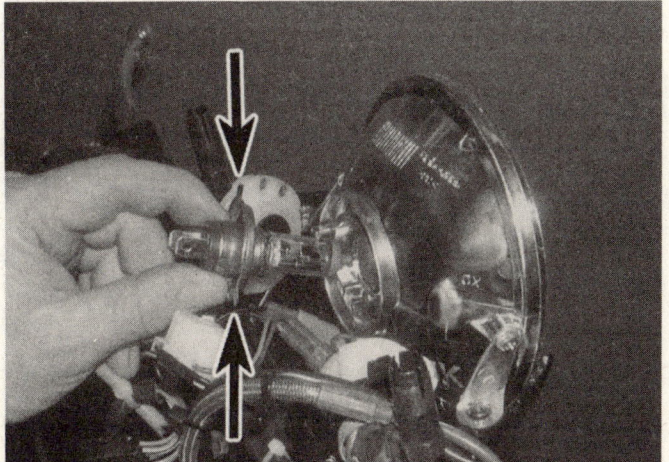

21.2b Align the tabs on the bulb (arrowed) with the slots in the housing

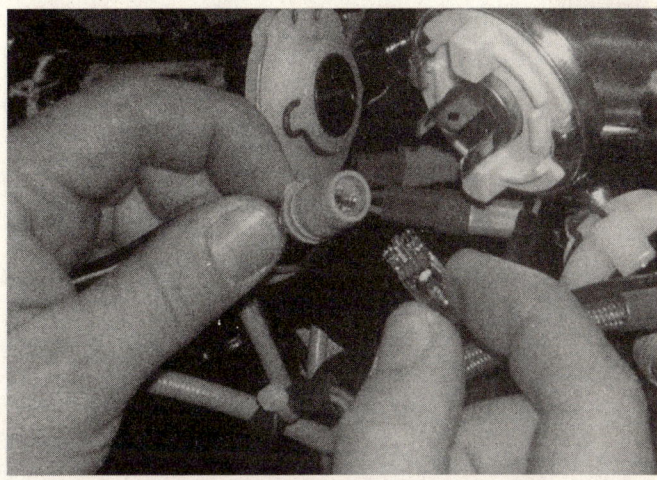

21.3 Sidelamp bulb is a push fit in its holder

22.2a To free the headlamp, release the upper shroud section, lifting it sufficiently to allow the headlamp mounting screws to be removed

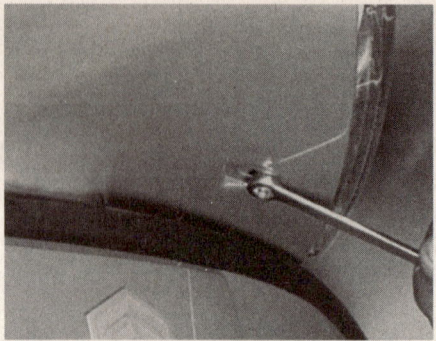

22.2b Release the headlamp adjustment locking screw from the underside of the handlebar . . .

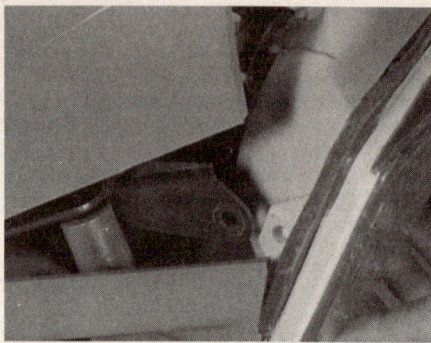

22.2c . . . to allow the headlamp unit to be lifted clear

22.2d Unplug the wiring connector and remove the unit from the machine

22.2e The headlamp bulb is held in place by two spring clips

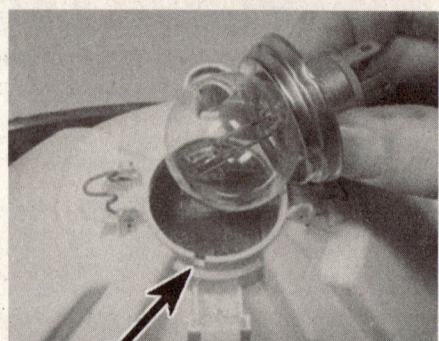

22.2f Note slot in reflector designed to locate pip on bulb flange

22 Headlamp unit: removal and adjustment – T5 model

Note: *This procedure does not apply to the T5 Classic model.*
1   The new rectangular headlamp unit fitted to the T5 model is held in place by two screws to the headlamp subframe. These allow the unit to be tilted to obtain the correct vertical beam setting, the adjustment being secured by means of a single screw immediately below the unit.
2   If it is necessary to remove the unit to permit bulb renewal or for some other reason, note that it is possible to gain access to the two pivot screws after the upper half of the handlebar shroud has been freed. Remove the retaining screws from the underside of the shroud. This will allow the upper half to be eased upwards sufficiently to allow the headlamp screws to be reached. Remove the adjustment screw to free the unit from the shroud lower section, then ease the unit forward and clear of the shroud halves. This approach means that the instrument panel wiring, the control cables and the speedometer cable need not be disturbed.

23 Instrument panel assembly: general information – T5 model

Note: *This procedure does not apply to the T5 Classic model.*
1   The T5 model employs a more sophisticated instrument panel that its predecessor, though the basic layout remains similar. The various instrument functions are incorporated into a single self-contained unit. In addition to the normal speedometer and odometer, the unit houses the fuel gauge, as on the EFL models. In addition, the T5 model features a tachometer.
2   Early T5 models are fitted with a digital tachometer which has a small window through which a two-character LED readout is visible. The system resolves engine speed to the nearest 100 rpm, the display showing 4.5 to indicate 4500 rpm, and so on. Later models are fitted with a conventional analogue tachometer. Note that the method of drive is unchanged.
3   As with most machines, little can be done by way of repair if any aspect of the instrument panel fails; it is effectively a sealed unit for

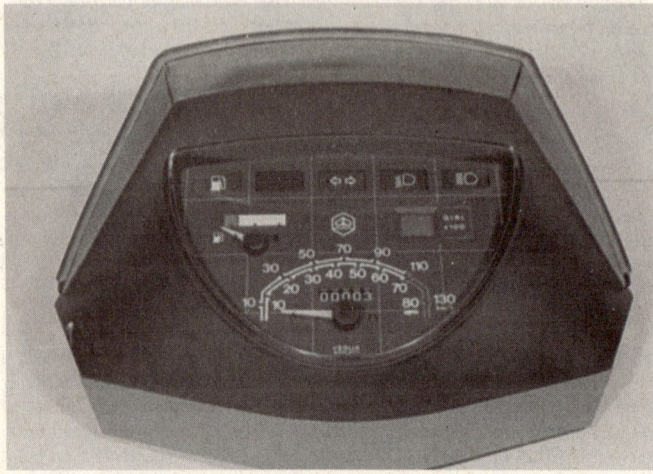

23.1 Top section of handlebar shroud showing the revised instrument panel – early model shown

23.3 Printed circuit layout at rear of panel is retained. Bulbholders are bayonet fitting

which replacement parts are not available, and so it must be renewed if a fault is found. Like the earlier PX models, the instrument panel wiring connects into a printed circuit on the back of the unit. This is fairly fragile, and care should be taken when handling it, or while removing or reconnecting the wiring. Warning bulbs are accessed in the normal way, the bulbholders being twisted anti-clockwise and then pulled out of their mounting holes.

24 Turn signal warning unit: general information

1   Certain models are fitted with an audible warning of turn signal operation, in the form of a small beeper unit housed just inside the glove compartment. Little can be done in the way of testing or repair, other than a check of the wiring and terminal connections. It follows that the unit can only be checked by the substitution of a new item.

25 Battery: inspection and charging – PX125, 150 and 200 electric start models

Inspection

1   Refer to Section 3 for details of battery top up, removal and refitting.
2   Look for sediment in the base of the battery, which is the result of sulphation caused by low electrolyte levels. These deposits will cause internal short circuits, which can quickly discharge the battery. Look for cracks in the case and renew the battery if either of these conditions is found.
3   Check the battery terminals and lead ends for tightness and corrosion. If corrosion is evident, remove the leads (negative lead first) and clean the terminals and lead ends with a wire brush or emery paper. Reconnect the leads (negative lead last). After connection, apply a thin coating of petroleum jelly to the connections to slow further corrosion.
4   The battery case should be kept clean to prevent current leakage, which can discharge the battery over a period of time, especially if the machine sit unused. Wash the outside of the case with a solution of baking soda and water. Do not get any baking soda solution in the battery cells. Rinse the battery thoroughly, then dry it.
5   If acid has been spilled on the bodywork or battery housing, neutralise it with the water and baking soda solution, dry it thoroughly then touch up any damaged paint. Make sure the battery vent tube is not pinched or blocked.

Charging

6   If the machine sits idle for extended periods or if the charging system malfunctions, the battery can be charged from an external source.
7   To properly charge the battery, you will need a charger of the correct rating, an hydrometer, a clean rag, and an syringe for adding distilled water to the battery cells.
8   The maximum charging rate for any battery is 1/10th of the rated

amp/hour capacity. As an example, the maximum charging rate for a 9 Ah battery would be 0.9 amp. If the battery is charged at a higher rate, it could be damaged.
9   Do not allow the battery to be subjected to the so called quick charge (high rate of charge over a short period of time) unless you are prepared to buy a new battery.
10   When charging the battery, always remove it from the machine (see above) and be sure to check the electrolyte level before hooking up the charger (see Section 3). Add distilled water to any cells that are low.
11   Loosen the cell caps, hook up the battery charger leads (red to positive, black to negative), cover the top of the battery with a clean rag then, and only then, plug in the battery charger. *Caution: Remember, the gas escaping from a charging battery is explosive, so keep open flames and sparks well away from the area. Also, the electrolyte is extremely corrosive and will damage anything it comes in contact with.*
12   Allow the battery to charge until the specific gravity is as specified (see below). The charger must be unplugged and disconnected from the battery when making specific gravity checks. If the battery overheats or gases excessively, the charging rate is too high. Either disconnect the charger or lower the charging rate to prevent damage to the battery.
13   If one or more of the cells do not show an increase in specific gravity after a long slow charge, or if the battery as a whole does not seen to want to take a charge, it is time for a new battery.
14   When the battery is fully charged, unplug the charger first, then disconnect its leads from the battery. Install the cell caps and wipe any electrolyte off the outside of the battery case.

Battery specific gravity check

15   A battery condition check to determine the state of charge can be performed with an hydrometer suitable for motorcycle batteries. Remove one of the cell caps and draw some electrolyte into the hydrometer, noting its reading. Compare the reading to the Specifications listed in this Chapter. Note: Add 0.007 points to the reading for every 10°C above 20°C, and subtract 0.007 points from the reading for every 10°C below 20°C. Add 0.004 points to the reading for every 10°F above 68°F, and subtract 0.004 points from the reading for every 10° below 68°F. Return the electrolyte to the cell and repeat the check for the remaining cells. When the check is complete, rinse the hydrometer thoroughly with clean water.
16   If the specific gravity of the electrolyte in each cell is as specified, the battery is in good condition and is apparently being charged by the motorcycle's charging system. If specific gravity is below that specified, the battery needs to be charged (see above). If charging does not cure the problem and it is not due to corroded battery terminals or a charging system fault, the battery is worn out and must be renewed.

26 Electrical system: fault diagnosis – PX125, 150 and 200 electric start models

Warning: To prevent the risk of short circuits, the ignition switch must always be OFF and the battery negative (-ve) terminal should be disconnected before any of the scooter's other electrical components are disturbed. Don't forget to reconnect the terminal securely once work is finished or if battery power is needed for circuit testing.

Tracing faults

1   A typical electrical circuit consists of an electrical component, the switches, relays, etc related to that component and the wiring and connectors that link the component to both the battery and the frame. To aid in locating a problem in any electrical circuit, refer to the wiring diagrams at the end of this Chapter.
2   Before tackling any troublesome electrical circuit, first study the wiring diagram thoroughly to get a complete picture of what makes up that individual circuit. Trouble spots, for instance, can often be narrowed down by noting if other components related to that circuit are operating properly or not. If several components or circuits fail at one time, chances are the fault lies in the fuse or earth connection.
3   Electrical problems often stem from simple causes, such as loose or corroded connections or a blown fuse. Prior to any electrical fault finding, always make a visual check of the fuse, wires and connections in the problem circuit. Intermittent failures can be especially frustrating,

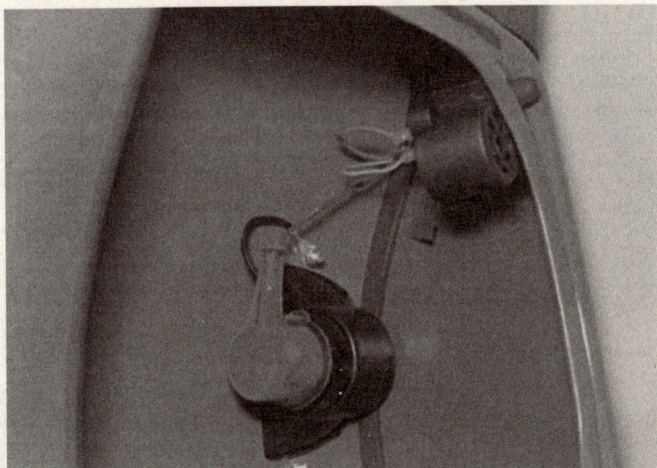
24.1 Inside of glove compartment showing turn signal lamp and the turn signal bleeper unit

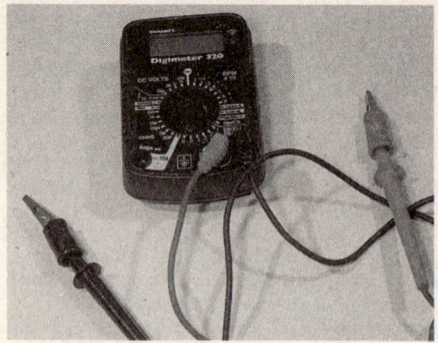

26.5 A multi-meter is capable of reading ohms, amps and volts

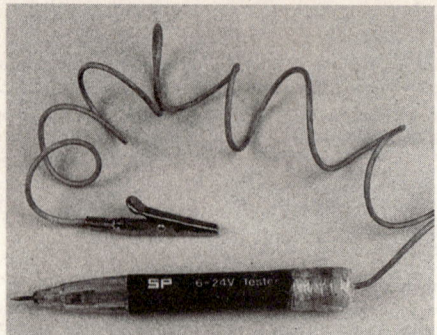

26.6a A simple test light . . .

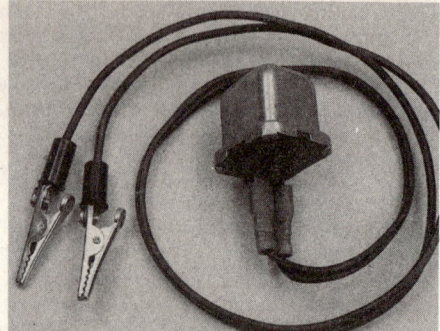

26.6b . . . or a buzzer can be used for simple voltage checks

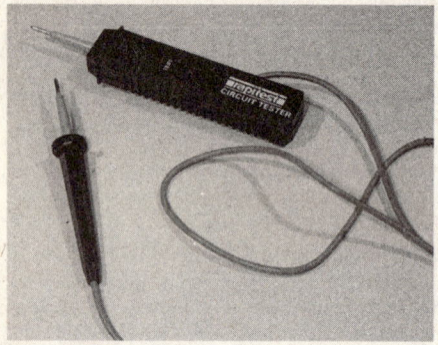

26.8a Continuity can be checked with a battery-powered tester . . .

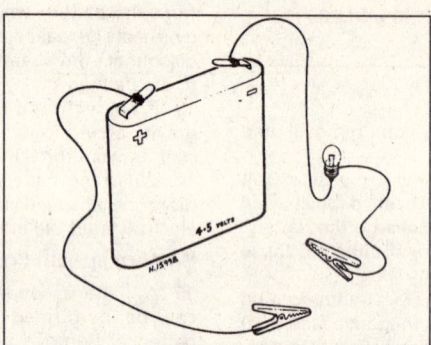

26.8b . . . or a battery and bulb circuit

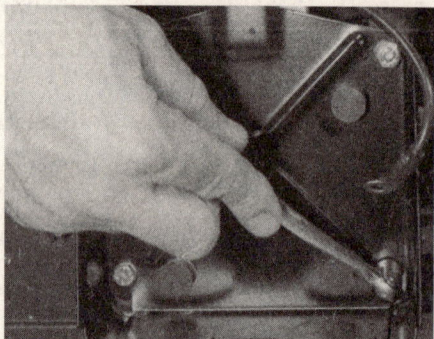

27.2 Battery holder tray is retained by four bolts

since you can't always duplicate the failure when it's convenient to test. In such situations, a good practice is to clean all connections in the affected circuit, whether or not they appear to be good. All of the connections and wires should also be wiggled to check for looseness which can cause intermittent failure.

4   If testing instruments are going to be utilised, use the wiring diagram to plan where you will make the necessary connections in order to accurately pinpoint the trouble spot.

Using test equipment

5   The basic tools needed for electrical fault finding include a battery and bulb test circuit, a continuity tester, a test light, and a jumper wire. A multi-meter capable of reading volts, ohms and amps is also very useful as an alternative to the above, and is necessary for performing more extensive tests and checks.

6   Voltage checks should be performed if a circuit is not functioning properly. Connect one lead of a test light or voltmeter to either the negative battery terminal or a known good earth. Connect the other lead to a connector in the circuit being tested, preferably nearest to the battery or fuse. If the bulb lights, voltage is reaching that point, which means the part of the circuit between that connector and the battery is problem-free. Continue checking the remainder of the circuit in the same manner. When you reach a point where no voltage is present, the problem lies between there and the last good test point. Most of the time the problem is due to a loose connection. Keep in mind that most circuits only receive voltage when the ignition is ON.

7   One method of finding short circuits is to remove the fuse and connect a test light or voltmeter in its place. There should be no load in the circuit (it should be switched off). Move the wiring harness from side-to-side while watching the test light. If the bulb lights, there is a short to earth somewhere in that area, probably where insulation has rubbed off a wire. The same test can be performed on other components in the circuit, including the switch.

8   An earth check should be done to see if a component is earthed properly. Disconnect the battery and connect one lead of a self-powered test light (continuity tester) to a known good earth. Connect the other lead to the wire or earth connection being tested. If the bulb lights, the earth is good. If the bulb does not light, the earth is not good.

9   A continuity check is performed to see if a circuit, section of circuit or individual component is capable of passing electricity through it. Disconnect the battery and connect one lead of a self-powered test light (continuity tester) to one end of the circuit being tested and the other lead to the other end of the circuit. If the bulb lights, there is continuity, which means the circuit is passing electricity through it properly. Switches can be checked in the same way.

27 Regulator/rectifier unit: removal and refitting – PX125, 150 and 200 electric start models

1   The regulator/rectifier unit is a finned aluminium unit located behind the battery. Remove the battery as described in Section 3.

2   Remove the four bolts to release the battery holder tray.

3   Release the two screws, noting that the top screw has the unit's

27.3 Regulator/rectifier top mounting screw also retains earth wire tab

27.4 Colour code label should correspond to regulator/rectifier wire connector colours

28.2a Release thumb screw to free fuse holder cover

28.2b Early models use a ceramic type fuse, held between sprung contacts

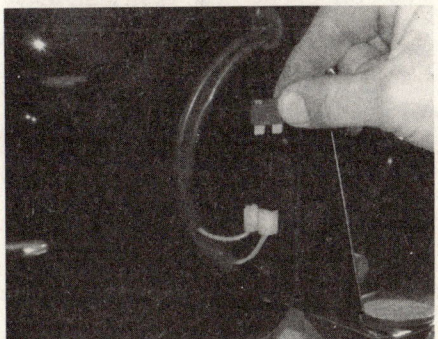

28.2c Later models use a blade type fuse which is a push fit in the holder

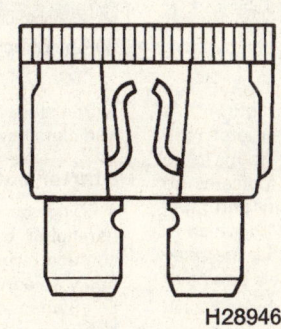

H28946

Fig. 7.8 A blown blade type fuse can be identified by a break in its element (Sec 28)

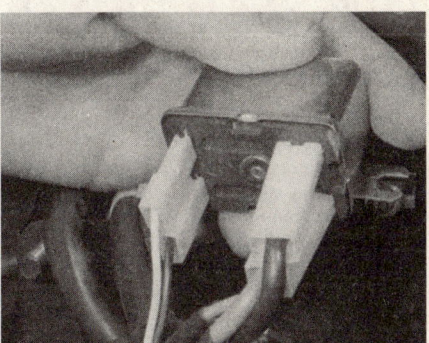

29.2a Release its two nuts and washers to free the starter relay from the bodywork

earth wire attached, to free the regulator/rectifier from the body. Unplug the wire connects to free the unit.
4   When refitting, make sure that the wires are connected to the correct terminals on the unit. Note the colour-coded label which corresponds with the coloured wire connectors. Ensure that the earth tab locates on the regulator/rectifier top mounting.

28   Fuse: location and renewal – PX125, 150 and 200 electric start models

1   The fuse is located in a plastic holder under the left-hand side panel. If a spare wheel is fitted, remove it for access.
2   On early models, release the screw to free the fuse holder cover

and pry the fuse (ceramic type) out of its spring contacts. On later models, lift off the fuse cover and pull the blade-type fuse out of the holder.
3   If the fuse blows, be sure to check the wiring very carefully for evidence of a short-circuit. Look for bare wires and chafed, melted or burned insulation. If a fuse is renewed before the cause is located, the new fuse will blow immediately. Always replace a fuse with one of the same rating. Never put in a fuse of a higher rating or bridge the terminals with any other substitute, however temporary it may be. Serious damage may be done to the circuit, or a fire may start.
4   Occasionally a fuse will blow or cause an open-circuit for no obvious reason. Corrosion of the fuse ends and fuse holder connectors may occur and cause poor fuse contact. If this happens, remove the corrosion with emery paper, then spray the fuse end and terminals with electrical contact cleaner.

29   Starter motor: circuit components – PX125, 150 and 200 electric start models

Note: *Disconnect the battery negative lead before starting work.*

Starter motor and drive unit
1   Refer to Sections 30 and 31.

Starter relay
2   The relay is located behind the battery. Remove the battery as described in Section 3, then remove the four bolts to release the battery holder tray. The starter relay can be identified by the colour of its wiring (see the wiring diagram at the end of this Chapter). On early models, the relay is retained by two nuts and washers. On later models, the relay is retained by a rubber clip.
3   To test the relay, disconnect its wire terminals, then remove the relay from the scooter. Using either a continuity tester or a multimeter set to the ohms x 1 scale, connect to the relay's starter motor and battery lead terminals (terminal nos. 87 and 30). There should be no continuity (infinite resistance). Using a fully-charged 12 volt battery and two insulated jumper wires, connect the battery to the terminals

29.2b Later type relay (arrowed) is retained by a rubber clip

29.4a Starter button is retained to underside of handlebar by two screws

29.4b Check starter button operation and terminal contacts

of the relay wiring connector as shown (terminal nos. 85 and 86). At this point the relay should be heard to click and the multimeter read 0 ohms (continuity). If this is the case the relay is proved good. If the relay does not click when battery voltage is applied and indicates no continuity (infinite resistance) across its terminals, it is faulty and must be replaced with a new one. No test details are available with which to test the unit. If the starter motor does not function, check that the relay wire connectors and starter circuit wiring is sound. On models equipped

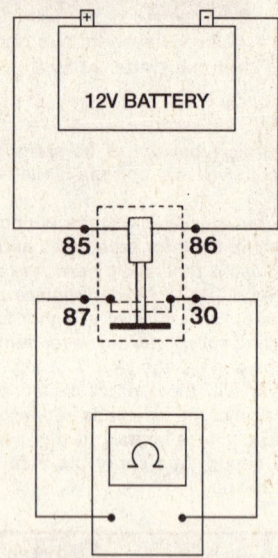

Fig. 7.9 Starter relay test

with a starter safety interlock circuit (see below) check the interlock unit and clutch switch.

Starter button

4   The starter button is retained to the underside of the right-hand handlebar by two screws. If the switch malfunctions, check that its contacts are clean and free from corrosion. Scrape them clean and apply an aerosol contact cleaner to prevent future problems occurring.
5   Switch operation can be checked by making a continuity test between the switch wires. Remove the horn cover (retained by a single screw under the badge) and disconnect the wires from the horn terminals. Identify the starter button wires, using the wiring diagram at the end of this Chapter for identification, and disconnect their connectors.
6   Make sure the ignition switch is OFF, and connect the ohmmeter or continuity tester between the two wires on the starter button side of the connectors. Continuity (0 ohms) should be shown with the starter button depressed, and no continuity (high resistance) with it released. If the switch does not perform as described, remove it from the handlebar for examination.

Starter safety interlock unit – where fitted

7   This unit is located on the steering column under the horn cover. Remove the horn cover (retained by a single screw under the badge) and disconnect the wires from the horn terminals.
8   The purpose of the unit is to prevent the inadvertent operation of the starter button whilst the engine is running and thus preventing damage of the starter drive unit and flywheel ring gear teeth. The clutch lever incorporates a plunger-type switch which must be depressed (by pulling in the clutch lever) to enable the starter motor to operate.
9   Operation of the clutch switch can be checked by removing the handlebar assembly top cover (see Chapter 4, Section 2) and disconnecting the clutch switch wire. Connect an ohmmeter or continuity tester between the switch side of the wire connector and

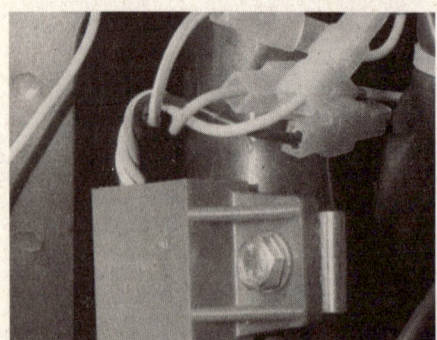

29.7 Starter safety interlock unit is mounted on steering stem

29.8 Clutch switch is located in handlebar casting

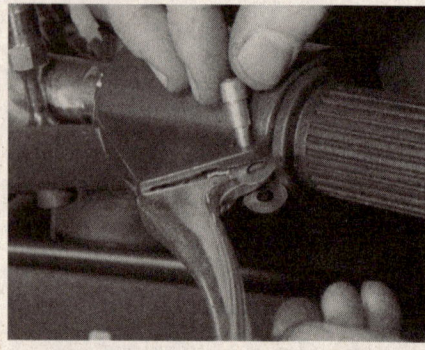

29.10 Remove clutch lever to access clutch switch – note the correct position of the pivot bolt washers

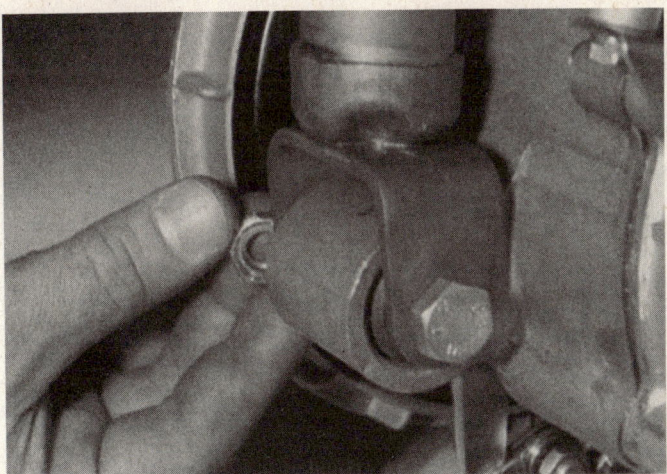

30.2 Remove its through-bolt and nut, then pivot the rear suspension unit away from the starter motor

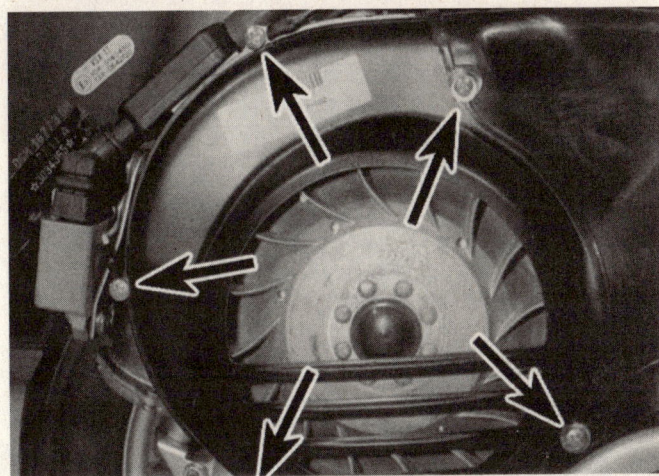

30.3 Fan cowling is retained by five screws (arrowed)

earth on the handlebar casting. Continuity (0 ohms) should be shown with the clutch lever pulled in, and no continuity (high resistance) with it released. If the switch does not perform as described it must be renewed.

10 To remove the clutch switch, disconnect its wire as described in the previous paragraph. Remove the clutch lever pivot bolt nut, washers and bolt and manoeuvre the switch out of the handlebar casting. Use a slim socket to unscrew the switch from the casting.

30 Starter motor and drive: removal and refitting – PX125, 150 and 200 electric start models

Note: *Disconnect the battery negative lead before starting work.*
1 The starter motor and drive mechanism are removed as a single unit. Remove the right-hand side panel for access.
2 Remove the rear wheel (see Chapter 5). Place wood blocks under the engine unit, then remove the rear suspension unit bottom mounting bolt and pivot the end of the unit away from the starter motor. Note that these steps are necessary to gain access to the starter motor mounting nuts.
3 Remove the five screws retaining the fan cowling and manoeuvre it free of the engine front cowling. Note that the gearchange control box cover will also be freed.
4 Also to improve access to the starter motor, it is recommended that the electronic ignition unit be detached from its mounting bracket

and that the mounting bracket be removed from the crankcase. Additionally, the removal of the wire connector case from the casing helps with access.

30.4a Remove ignition control unit from its mounting bracket and unbolt bracket from the engine casing – take note of the bracket's rubber mounting arrangement as a guide to refitting

30.4b Remove wire connector case cover screw, disconnect the wiring . . .

30.4c . . . and unplug the case from the engine casing

30.5 Disconnect the terminal lead from the starter motor

30.6a Starter motor is retained by three nuts with spring and plain washers. Note the pilot mixture screw (arrowed) which may need to be screwed in to allow starter motor removal

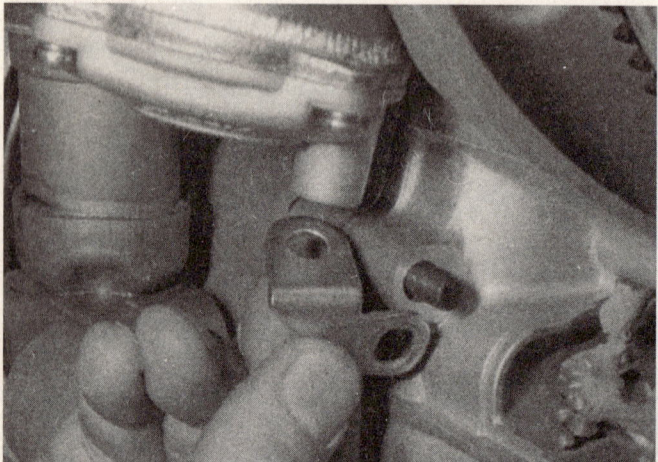

30.6b Starter motor lower support bracket

30.6c Press on the end of the starter drive unit cap to help dislodge the starter motor from the engine casing

5   Peel back the rubber cover, and remove the nut and washers from the starter motor lead terminal. Disconnect the lead from the terminal.
6   Remove the three nuts which hold the starter drive to the casing and the single bolt at the rear which retains the starter motor to the mounting bracket. **Note:** *You may find that the carburettor mixture screw prevents access to one of the starter motor retaining nuts. If*

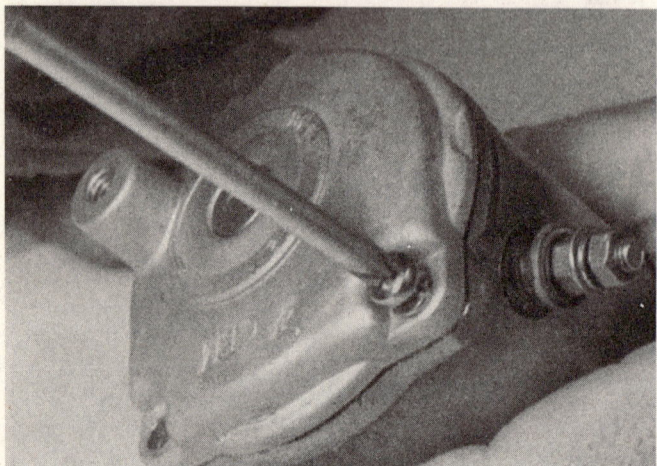

31.2 Remove the three screws to release the starter motor end cover

this is the case, screw the mixture screw inwards until it seats lightly, counting the number of turns (or screw head flats) necessary to seat it – this enables the screw to be returned to its original setting on refitting. Withdraw the starter motor and drive unit from the crankcase, if necessary pressing against the end of the starter drive in the crankcase to free it.
7   Refit the starter motor in a reverse of the removal procedure, noting the following.
   a) *Turn the pilot mixture screw out the number of turns (or flats) recorded on removal.*
   b) *Ensure that the ignition unit HT lead and starter motor lead are secured under the tab of the wire connector case before it is secured to the casing.*
   c) *Ensure that the electronic ignition unit earth lead and main earth lead are secured by the fan cowling screws.*
   d) *Connect the battery negative lead on completion.*

31   Starter motor: overhaul – PX125, 150 and 200 electric start models

Note: *Before overhauling the starter motor, check first whether replacement parts are available.*

Starter motor

1   Remove the starter motor as described in Section 30.
2   If only brush inspection is necessary, remove the three end cover screws and remove the end cover with its gasket.

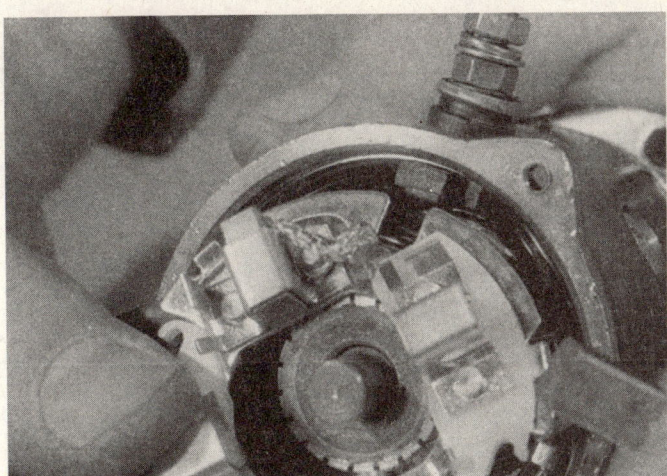

31.6a When fitting brushplate, ensue that its cutout aligns with the body terminal . . .

31.6b . . . and that the field coil brush leads engage the slots in the brushplate

31.6c Place the spring over its post . . .

31.6d . . . hook its shorter end over the tab and stretch the longer end round to tension the brush

31.6e Spring end must locate in brush slot

3   The manufacturer does not specify a figure for brush wear limit. However, if the brushes are worn down so far that their leads contact the base of the holder slots or the springs are no longer capable of applying enough pressure to hold them against the commutator, renew all of them as a set. If the brushes are not worn excessively, cracked, chipped or otherwise damaged, they may be re-used.

4   Release the springs of the two field coil brushes (i.e. the pair which aren't attached to the brushplate) and slip the brushes out of their holders. Prise the brushplate out of the starter motor body. Release the springs to free the remaining two brushes from their holders.

5   If renewing the brushes, check with a dealer if they are supplied separately; if so, they will require soldering in place.

6   When refitting the brushplate, ensure that its cutout engages the lead terminal. Slip the field coil brush leads into their slots, then install the brushes in their holders and install the spring, looping it around the post and tensioning the brush end.

7   Apply a smear of grease to the needle roller bearing inside the brushplate cover, check that the gasket is in place and refit the cover. Secure the cover with the spring washers and screws.

8   If armature removal is necessary, separate the drive unit from the starter motor by removing the two bolts with wave washers. Mark the relationship between the starter motor body and drive unit to ensure correct reassembly. Recover the O-ring and metal distance plate (where fitted).

31.8a Mark the relationship between the drive unit and starter motor as shown, then remove the two bolts (arrowed)

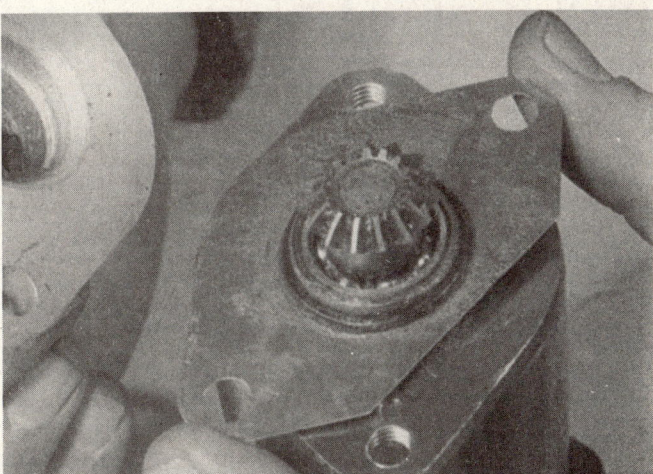

31.8b Lift off the metal distance plate and O-ring

31.9 Remove the roll pin (arrowed) to free the gear from the end of the armature shaft

31.11 Inspect the commutator segments for signs of excessive wear or damage

31.15 Align the shaft hole with the gear pin before drifting the pin back into position

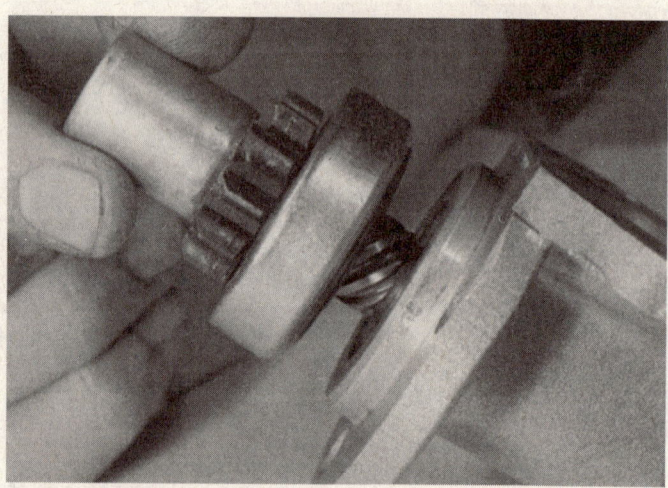

31.19 Check the action of the starter drive unit mechanism

9   Using a 3 mm pin punch, drift the roll pin out of the drive gear body and pull the drive gear off the armature shaft.

10   Remove the brushplate as described in paragraphs 2 to 4 above, then withdraw the armature from the brushplate end of the starter motor body.

11   Inspect the commutator (part on which the brushes bear) for scoring, scratches or discoloration. The commutator may be cleaned and polished with crocus cloth, but do not use sandpaper or emery paper. After cleaning, wipe away any residue with a cloth soaked in electrical contact cleaner. If there is any doubt about the condition of the commutator or armature as a whole, have it inspected and tested by a dealer or auto-electrical expert.

12   Using an ohmmeter or continuity test light, check for continuity between the commutator bars. Continuity should exist between each bar and all of the others. Also check for continuity between the commutator bars and the armature shaft. There should be no continuity (infinite resistance) between the commutator and the shaft. If the checks indicate otherwise, the armature is defective.

13   Check that the ball bearing in the end of the motor body and the needle roller bearing in the brushplate cover turn easily without binding.

14   To reassemble, insert the armature into the motor body so that its shaft passes through the ball bearing. Apply a smear of grease to the bearing.

15   Insert the drive gear, aligning its hole with that in the armature shaft. Drive the roll pin into place to secure it.

16   Install the O-ring and distance plate, align the previously-made matchmarks, and mesh the drive unit and starter motor. Secure with the two bolts and wave washers.

17   Refit the brushplate assembly as described above.

Starter drive unit

18   The starter drive is of the inertia type. As the crown gear of the starter motor rotates it throws the drive unit gear into mesh with the flywheel ring gear, and thus turns the engine. When the starter motor stops, the drive unit gear runs back up its quick thread drive and out of mesh with the flywheel.

19   The drive unit is unlikely to require attention during the life of the machine. Check that the external gear extends away from the body on its quick thread. If it fails to operate as described, and drive is not transmitted to the engine when the starter motor rotates, the drive unit is at fault.

20   Dismantling of the assembly requires the uses of special tools and it is advised that the unit be entrusted to a dealer for overhaul.

21   The machine may be fitted with a starter safety interlock unit to prevent the operation of the starter motor, should the starter button be inadvertently pressed whilst the engine is running (see Section 29).

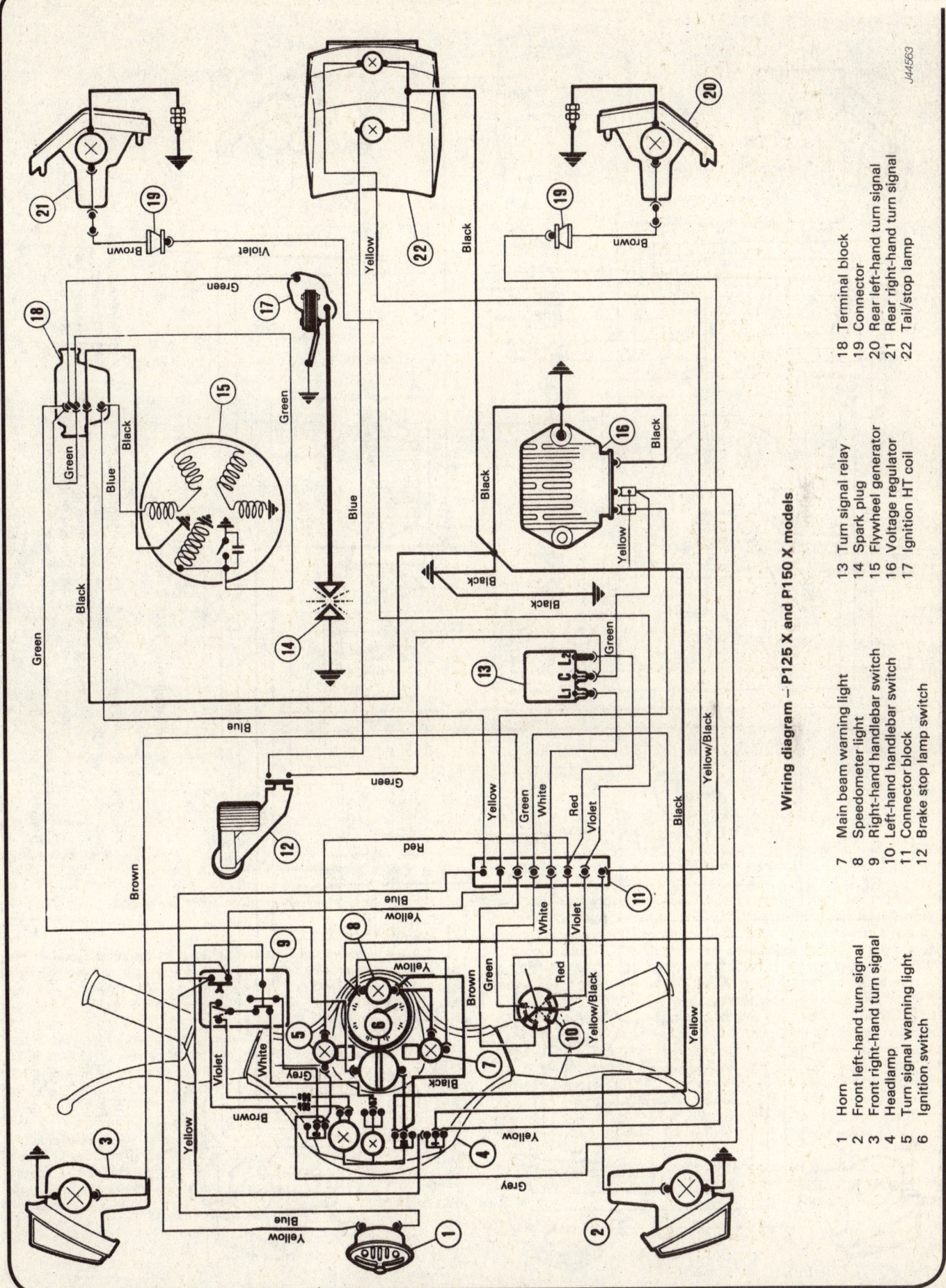

J44563

Wiring diagram – P125 X and P150 X models

1	Horn	13	Turn signal relay
2	Front left-hand turn signal	14	Spark plug
3	Front right-hand turn signal	15	Flywheel generator
4	Headlamp	16	Voltage regulator
5	Turn signal warning light	17	Ignition HT coil
6	Ignition switch	18	Terminal block
7	Main beam warning light	19	Connector
8	Speedometer light	20	Rear left-hand turn signal
9	Right-hand handlebar switch	21	Rear right-hand turn signal
10	Left-hand handlebar switch	22	Tail/stop lamp
11	Connector block		
12	Brake stop lamp switch		

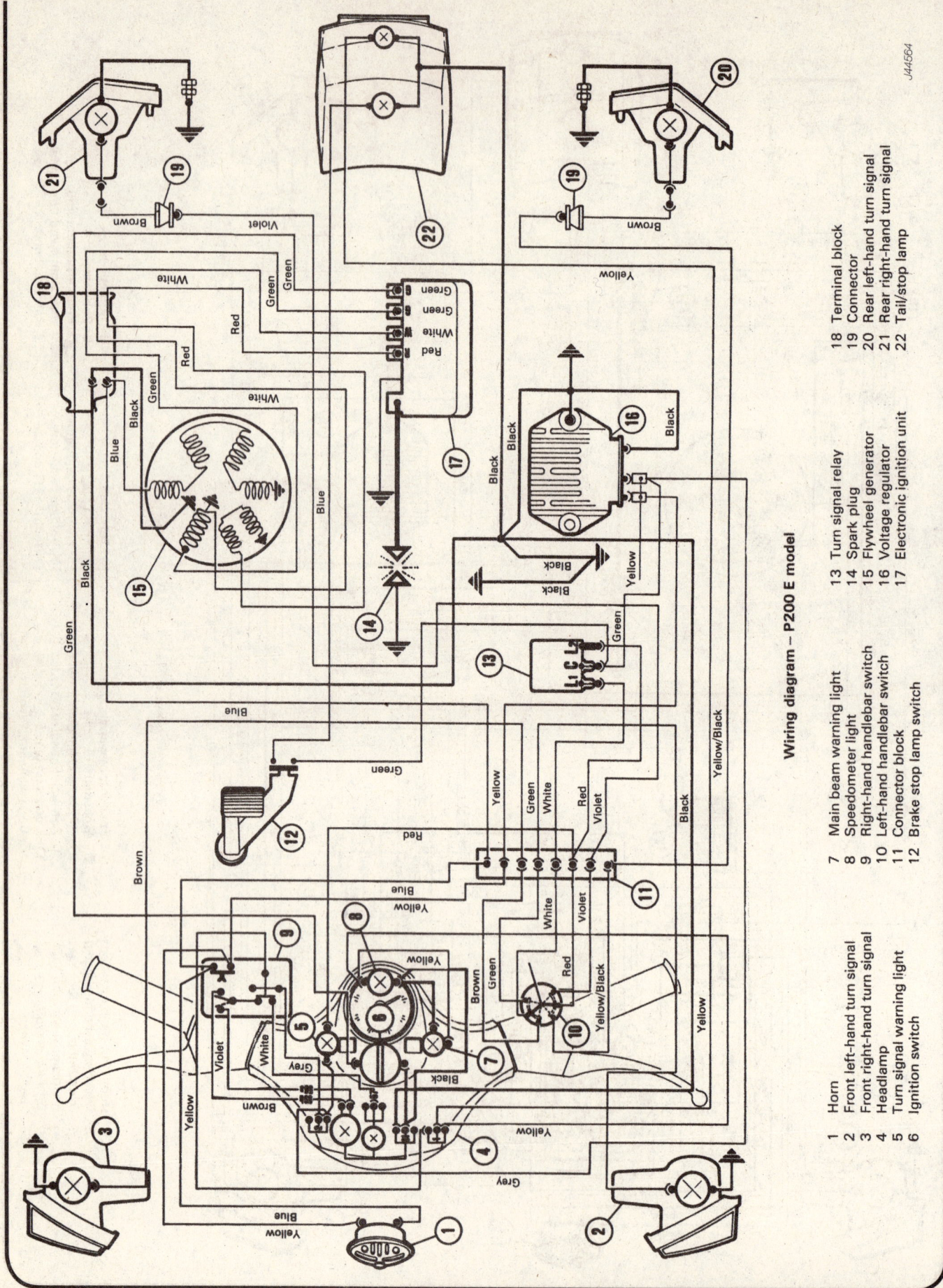

J44564

Wiring diagram – P200 E model

1 Horn
2 Front left-hand turn signal
3 Front right-hand turn signal
4 Headlamp
5 Turn signal warning light
6 Ignition switch

7 Main beam warning light
8 Speedometer light
9 Right-hand handlebar switch
10 Left-hand handlebar switch
11 Connector block
12 Brake stop lamp switch

13 Turn signal relay
14 Spark plug
15 Flywheel generator
16 Voltage regulator
17 Electronic ignition unit

18 Terminal block
19 Connector
20 Rear left-hand turn signal
21 Rear right-hand turn signal
22 Tail/stop lamp

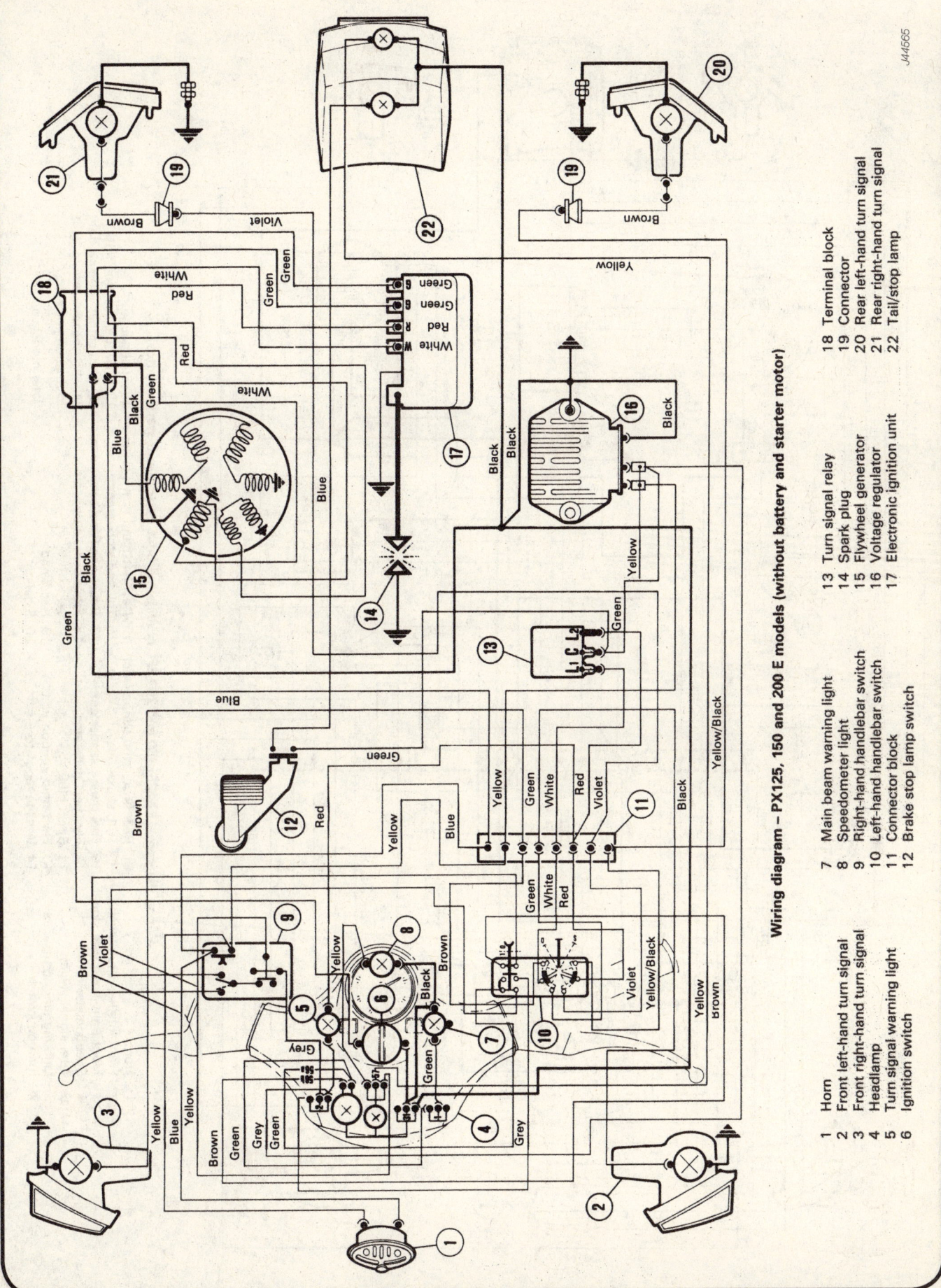

J44565

Wiring diagram – PX125, 150 and 200 E models (without battery and starter motor)

1 Horn	7 Main beam warning light	13 Turn signal relay
2 Front left-hand turn signal	8 Speedometer light	14 Spark plug
3 Front right-hand turn signal	9 Right-hand handlebar switch	15 Flywheel generator
4 Headlamp	10 Left-hand handlebar switch	16 Voltage regulator
5 Turn signal warning light	11 Connector block	17 Electronic ignition unit
6 Ignition switch	12 Brake stop lamp switch	

18 Terminal block	
19 Connector	
20 Rear left-hand turn signal	
21 Rear right-hand turn signal	
22 Tail/stop lamp	

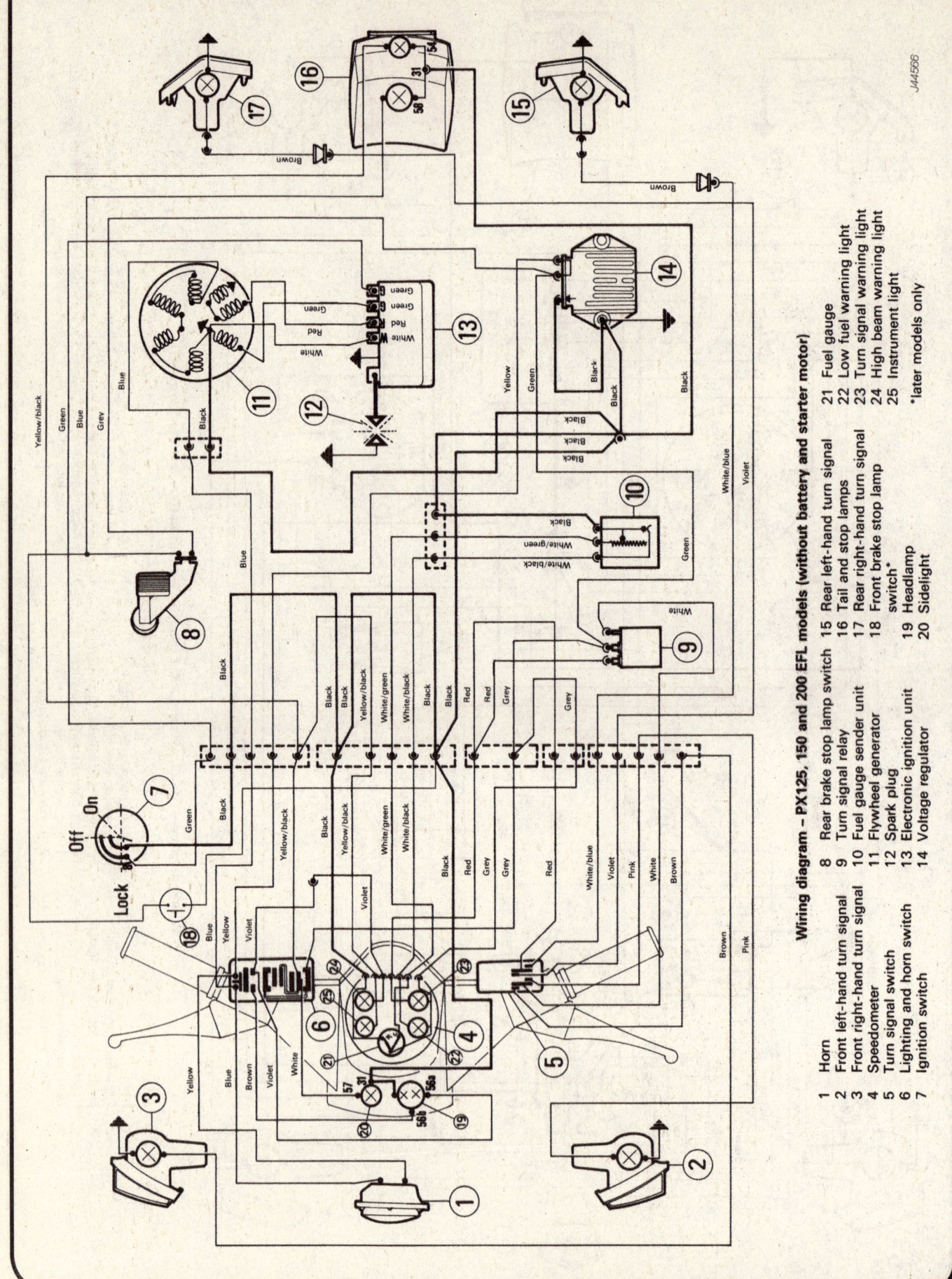

Wiring diagram – PX125, 150 and 200 EFL models (without battery and starter motor)

1 Horn
2 Front left-hand turn signal
3 Front right-hand turn signal
4 Speedometer
5 Lighting and horn switch
6 Turn signal switch
7 Ignition switch

8 Rear brake stop lamp switch
9 Turn signal relay
10 Fuel gauge sender unit
11 Flywheel generator
12 Spark plug
13 Electronic ignition unit
14 Voltage regulator

15 Rear left-hand turn signal
16 Tail and stop lamps
17 Rear right-hand turn signal
18 Front brake stop lamp switch*
19 Headlamp
20 Sidelight

21 Fuel gauge
22 Low fuel warning light
23 Turn signal warning light
24 High beam warning light
25 Instrument light

*later models only

J44566

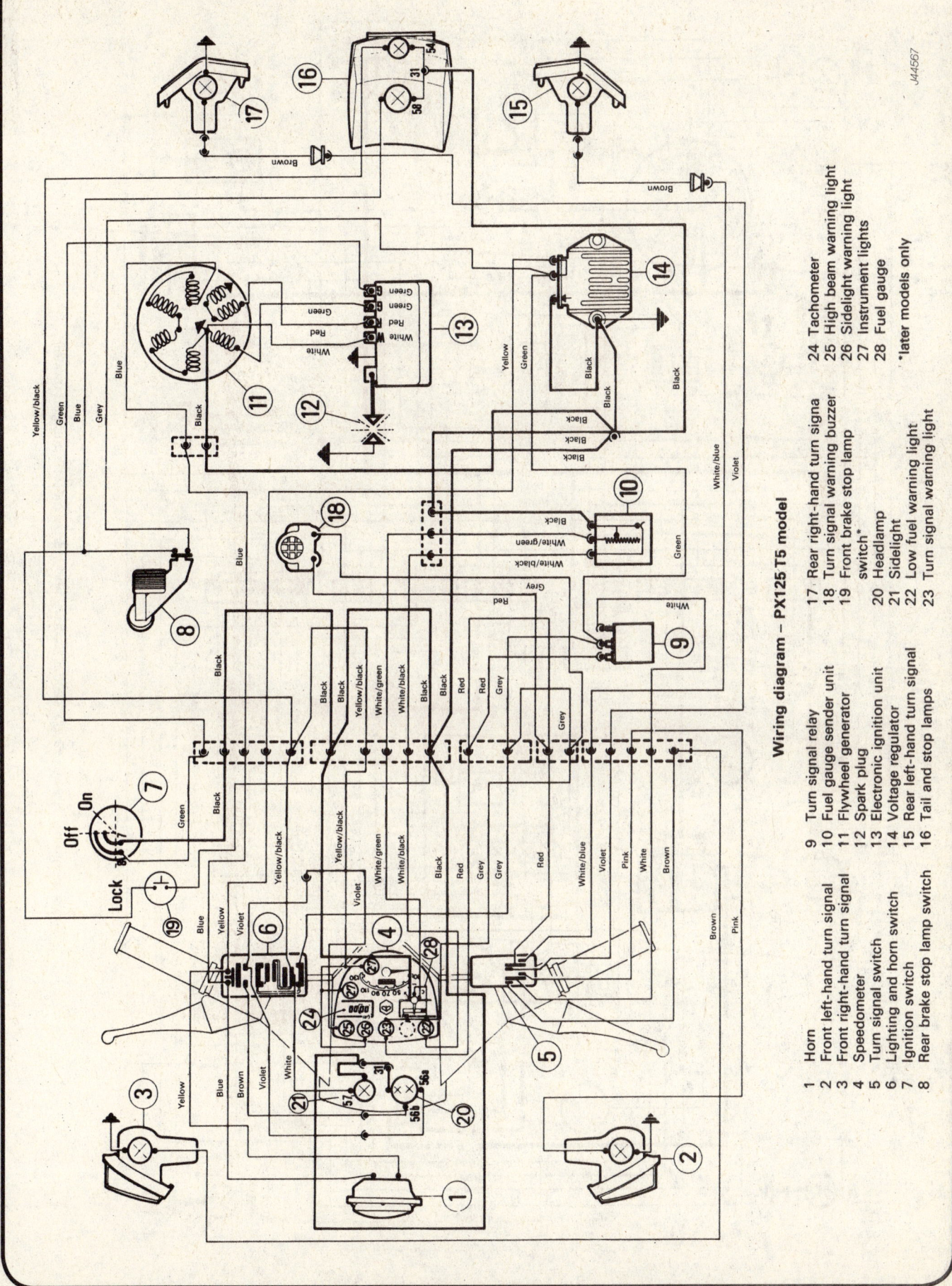

Wiring diagram – PX125 T5 model

1 Horn
2 Front left-hand turn signal
3 Front right-hand turn signal
4 Speedometer
5 Turn signal switch
6 Lighting and horn switch
7 Ignition switch
8 Rear brake stop lamp switch
9 Turn signal relay
10 Fuel gauge sender unit
11 Flywheel generator
12 Spark plug
13 Electronic ignition unit
14 Voltage regulator
15 Rear left-hand turn signal
16 Tail and stop lamps
17 Rear right-hand turn signa
18 Turn signal warning buzzer
19 Front brake stop lamp switch*
20 Headlamp
21 Sidelight
22 Low fuel warning light
23 Turn signal warning light
24 Tachometer
25 High beam warning light
26 Sidelight warning light
27 Instrument lights
28 Fuel gauge
*later models only

J44567

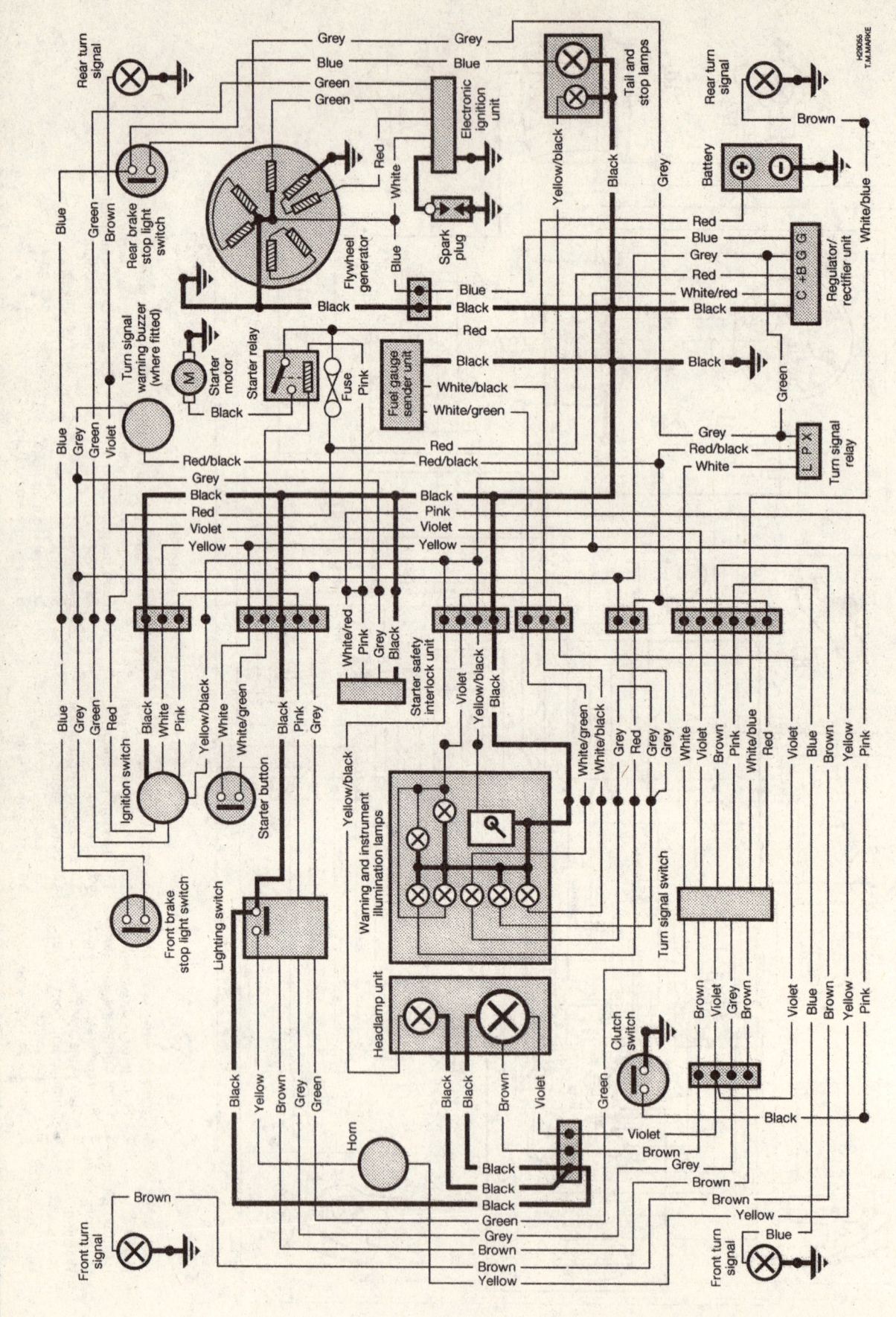

Wiring diagram – 1994 to 1998 PX200 E (battery and starter motor-equipped model)

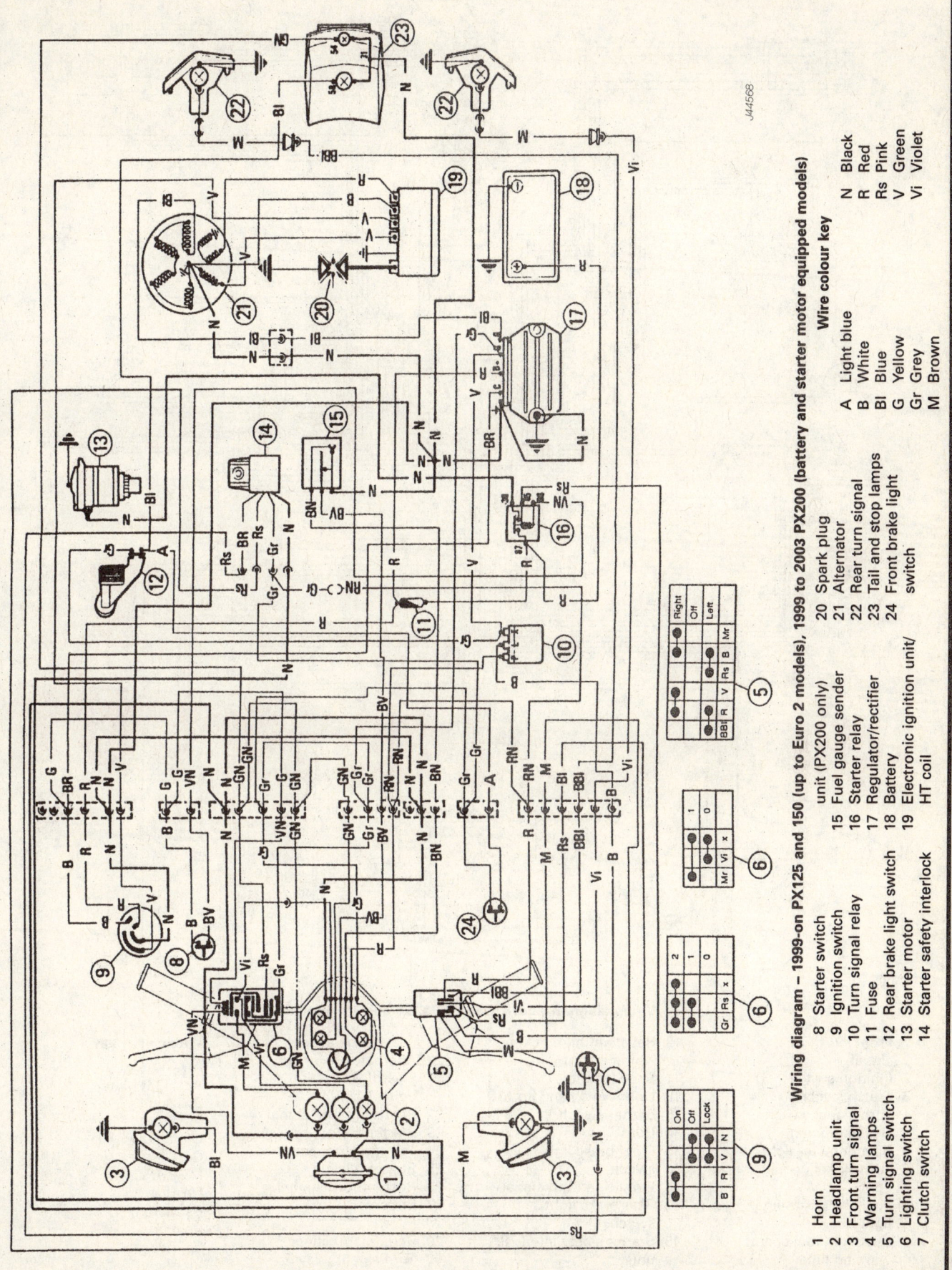

J44568

Wiring diagram – 1999-on PX125 and 150 (up to Euro 2 models), 1999 to 2003 PX200 (battery and starter motor equipped models)

1 Horn
2 Headlamp unit
3 Front turn signal
4 Warning lamps
5 Turn signal switch
6 Lighting switch
7 Clutch switch
8 Starter switch
9 Ignition switch
10 Turn signal relay
11 Fuse
12 Rear brake light switch
13 Starter motor
14 Starter safety interlock

15 Fuel gauge sender
   unit (PX200 only)
16 Starter relay
17 Regulator/rectifier
18 Battery
19 Electronic ignition unit/
   HT coil
20 Spark plug
21 Alternator
22 Rear turn signal
23 Tail and stop lamps
24 Front brake light
   switch

Wire colour key

A	Light blue	N	Black
B	White	R	Red
Bl	Blue	Rs	Pink
G	Yellow	V	Green
Gr	Grey	Vi	Violet
M	Brown		

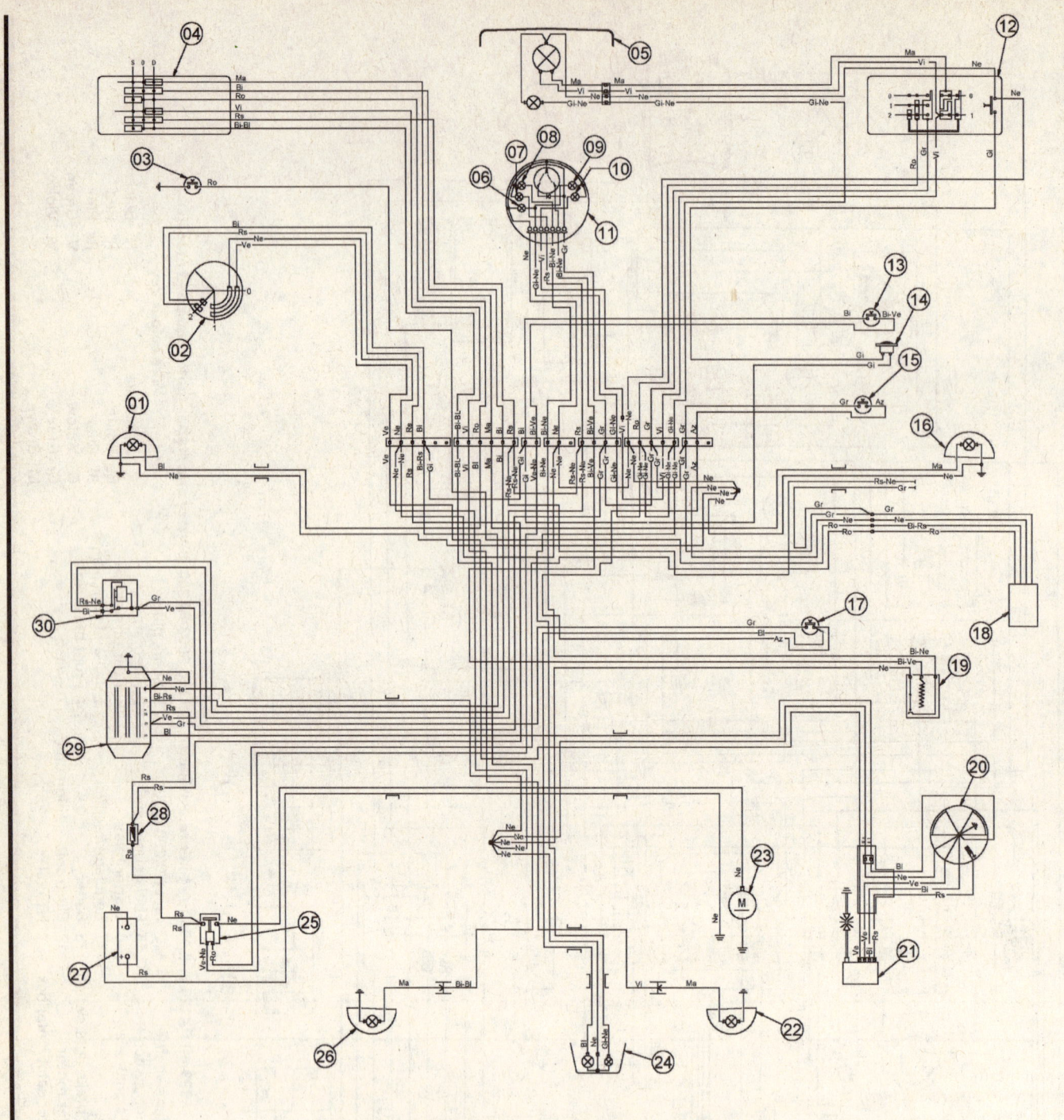

Wiring diagram – Euro 2 and 3 PX125 and 150 models

1 Front left turn signal	10 Headlight high beam warning light	19 Fuel gauge sender	**Wire colour key**
2 Ignition switch	11 Speedometer	20 Alternator	Ar Orange
3 Clutch switch	12 Light switch and horn	21 Electronic ignition unit/HT coil	Az Light blue
4 Turn signal switch	13 Starter switch	22 Rear right turn signal	Bi White
5 Headlamp unit	14 Horn	23 Starter motor	Bl Blue
6 Speedometer light	15 Front brake light switch	24 Tail and stop lamps	Gi Yellow
7 Turn signal warning light	16 Front right turn signal	25 Starter relay	Gr Grey
8 Fuel level warning light	17 Rear brake light switch	26 Rear left turn signal	Ma Brown
9 Headlight low beam warning light	18 Starter safety interlock unit	27 Battery	Ne Black
		28 Fuse	Rs Red
		29 Regulator/rectifier	Ro Pink
		30 Turn signal relay	Ve Green
			Vi Violet

The LML Star 2T

Chapter 8 Supplement:
LML Star 2T model

Contents

Specifications

Model dimensions and weight

Overall length......................................	1760 mm (69.3 in)
Overall width......................................	695 mm (27.4 in)
Wheelbase..	1235 mm (48.7 in)
Seat height	820 mm (32.3 in)
Ground clearance..................................	160 mm (6.3 in)
Wet weight..	109 kg (240 lbs)
Chassis No. prefix	
Europe	MD7M10
US	MD7CG84A
Engine No. prefix	
Europe	EXX
US	E17

Maintenance data

Engine oil	Two-stroke engine oil for injector systems, either fully or semi-synthetic
Gearbox oil	SAE 80 gear oil, SAE 30 engine oil, or 20W/40 engine oil
Gearbox oil quantity	250 cc
Spark plug	
125	NGK BP8HS or Mica R6
150	NGK B6ES, Champion RN9YC, Mico WR8DC
Spark plug gap	0.7 – 0.8 mm (0.0276 – 0.0315 in)
Throttle cable freeplay	2 mm (0.08 in)
Clutch cable freeplay	2 mm (0.08 in)
Rear brake cable freeplay	5 mm (0.2 in)
Tyre pressures – Europe	
Front	17 psi (1.19 kg/cm^2, 1.2 Bars)
Rear – solo	25 psi (1.75 kg/cm^2, 1.7 Bars)
Rear – with passsenger	35 psi (2.45 kg/cm^2, 2.4 Bars)
Tyre pressures – US	
Front	22 psi (1.54 kg/cm^2, 1.5 Bars)
Rear	29 psi (2.03 kg/cm^2, 2.0 Bars)

Engine

Type	Single cylinder, fan-cooled two-stroke
Bore and stroke	
125	52.5 x 57 mm
150	57.8 x 57 mm
Displacement	125 cc or 149.6 cc
Compression ratio	9.0:1
Engine compression pressure	140 ± 20 psi (9.8 kg/cm^2, 9.7 Bars)

Cylinder barrel and piston

Piston-to-cylinder bore clearance	0.225 mm (0.008 in)
Bore size – 125	
Standard	52.5 mm (2.0685 in)
1st oversize	52.7 mm (2.0764 in)
2nd oversize	52.9 mm (2.0843 in)
3rd oversize	53.1 mm (2.0921 in)
Bore size – 150	
Standard	57.8 mm (2.2773 in)
1st oversize	58.0 mm (2.2852 in)
2nd oversize	58.2 mm (2.2931 in)
3rd oversize	58.4 mm (2.3010 in)
Piston size – 125	
Standard	52.305 ± 0.015 mm (2.0608 ± 0.0006 in)
1st oversize	52.505 ± 0.015 mm (2.0687 ± 0.0006 in)
2nd oversize	52.705 ± 0.015 mm (2.0766 ± 0.0006 in)
3rd oversize	52.905 ± 0.015 mm (2.0845 ± 0.0006 in)
Piston size – 150	
Standard	57.585 ± 0.015 mm (2.2688 ± 0.0006 in)
1st oversize	57.785 ± 0.010 mm (2.2767 ± 0.0006 in)
2nd oversize	57.985 ± 0.010 mm (2.2846 ± 0.0006 in)
3rd oversize	58.185 ± 0.010 mm (2.2925 ± 0.0006 in)
Cylinder bore measuring point	25 mm (1.0 in) below top edge of the bore, at 90° to gudgeon pin bore axle
Piston measuring point	5 mm (0.2 in) below bottom edge of lower ring groove
Small-end bearing/gudgeon pin radial clearance	Zero
Service limit	0.02 mm (0.0008 in)

Piston rings

End gap (installed)	0.20 – 0.35 mm (0.0079 – 0.0138 in)
Service limit	1 mm (0.0394 in)

Clutch

Type	Wet, multiplate
No. of friction plates	3
No. of plain plates	2

Gearbox

Oil capacity	250 cc
Oil type	SAE 80 gear oil, SAE 30 engine oil, or 20W/40 engine oil
Type	4-speed, constant mesh
Gear ratios	
1st	15.38:1
2nd	10.46:1
3rd	7.24:1
4th	5.39:1
Output shaft end-float	0.15 – 0.40 mm (0.0059 – 0.0158 in)
Output shaft thrust washer thicknesses	
Standard	1.0 mm (0.0394 in)
1st oversize	1.1 mm (0.0433 in)
2nd oversize	1.2 mm (0.0473 in)
3rd oversize	1.3 mm (0.0512 in)
4th oversize	1.5 mm (0.0591 in)

Torque wrench settings – engine

Alternator rotor nut	6.0 – 6.5 kgf m (43.0 – 47.0 lbf ft)
Alternator stator screws	0.3 – 0.4 kgf m (2.2 – 2.9 lbf ft)
Carburettor sleeve nuts	1.6 – 2.0 kgf m (12.0 – 14.0 lbf ft)
Clutch centre nut	4.0 – 4.5 kgf m (29.0 – 32.5 lbf ft)
Clutch cover bolts	0.6 – 0.8 kgf m (4.3 – 5.8 lbf ft)
Cylinder head nuts	1.3 – 1.8 kgf m (9.4 – 13.0 lbf ft)
Input shaft nut	3.0 – 3.5 kgf m (22.0 – 25.0 lbf ft)
Kickstart lever nut	2.3 – 2.6 kgf m (17.0 – 19.0 lbf ft)
Pickup mounting screw	0.2 – 0.25 kgf m (1.4 – 1.8 lbf ft)
Spark plug	2.0 kgf m (14.0 lbf ft)
Starter motor lower bracket bolt	0.6 – 0.8 kgf m (4.3 – 5.8 lbf ft)
Starter motor nuts	1.0 – 1.5 kgf m (7.2 – 11.0 lbf ft)

Fuel system and lubrication

Fuel tank capacity	8 litres (inc. 1 litre reserve)
Fuel grade	Unleaded
Oil tank capacity	1 litre
Oil type	Two-stroke engine oil for injector systems, either fully or semi-synthetic
Carburettor	Spaco 20/20D
Jet sizes – Europe	not available
Jet sizes – US	
Main jet	92
Slow running jet	40/130
Air corrector jet	140
Mixer tube	E-3
Throttle valve	7.5 x 7.5 SCOOP
Starter jet	60
Pilot screw base setting	½ to 1½ turns out

Ignition system

Ignition timing	
Europe	18° ± 2° BTDC
US	20° ± 2° BTDC
Spark plug	
125	NGK BP8HS or Mica R6
150	NGK B6ES, Champion RN9YC, Mico WR8DC
Spark plug gap	0.7 – 0.8 mm (0.0276 – 0.0315 in)
Ignition source coil resistance	390 ± 20 ohms
Pickup winding resistance	110 ± 15 ohms
HT coil primary winding resistance	0.4 – 0.5 ohm
HT coil secondary winding resistance	3.3 – 3.5 K-ohms
Spark plug cap resistance	5 ± 1.25 K-ohms

Frame and suspension

Frame type	Welded pressed-steel monocoque body with detachable side panels
Suspension type	
Front	Single-sided trailing link, with oil-damped coil spring suspension unit
Rear	Single-sided, using engine/gearbox unit as suspension member. Single oil-damped coil sprung suspension unit

Wheels, brakes and tyres

Type	Pressed steel split rims, with spare under left side panel. All three wheels interchangeable
Front brake	
Type	Hydraulically operated disc brake (two piston, opposed caliper)
Brake fluid	DOT 4
Brake pad thickness – when new	5.9 mm (0.232 in) including pad backing plate
Brake pad thickness – service limit	3.6 mm (0.142 in) including pad backing plate
Brake disc thickness – when new	4 mm (0.158 in)
Rear brake	Cable-operated drum brake (single leading shoe)
Tyre size	3.50 x 10
Tyre pressures – Europe	
Front	17 psi (1.19 kg/cm², 1.2 Bars)
Rear – solo	25 psi (1.75 kg/cm², 1.7 Bars)
Rear – with passsenger	35 psi (2.45 kg/cm², 2.4 Bars)
Tyre pressures – US	
Front	22 psi (1.54 kg/cm², 1.5 Bars)
Rear	29 psi (2.03 kg/cm², 2.0 Bars)

Torque wrench settings – chassis

Front brake caliper and master cylinder	settings not available from LML
Front suspension unit mounting plate nuts	2.0 – 2.7 kgf m (14.5 – 19.5 lbf ft)
Front suspension unit to mounting plate nut	3.0 – 4.0 kgf m (22.0 – 29.0 lbf ft)
Front suspension unit lower mounting nuts	2.0 – 2.7 kgf m (14.5 – 19.5 lbf ft)
Steering head adjuster*	5.0 – 6.0 kgf m (36.0 – 43.0 lbf ft)
Steering head locknut	3.0 – 4.0 kgf m (22.0 – 29.0 lbf ft)
Handlebar pinch bolt	3.0 – 4.4 kgf m (22.0 – 32.0 lbf ft)
Rear suspension unit lower mounting bolt/nut	3.0 – 3.5 kgf m (22.0 – 25.0 lbf ft)
Engine unit pivot bolt	6.0 – 7.5 kgf m (43.0 – 54.0 lbf ft)
Front wheel hub nut	7.5 – 9.0 kgf m (54.0 – 65.0 lbf ft)
Rear wheel hub nut	9.0 – 10.0 kgf m (65.0 – 72.0 lbf ft)

*After tightening, slacken by approximately ¼ turn. Steering column should swing freely from lock to lock and all freeplay should be eliminated.

Electrical system

Type	12 volt alternating current (ac) with electronic ac regulation
Alternator	96 W
Regulated voltage.	14.0 – 14.3 V at 5000 rpm
Battery capacity	9 Ah
Battery specific gravity	1.230
Fuse	8 A
Bulbs (all 12 V)	
Headlamp	35/35 W
Front sidelight.	5 W
Tail lamp	5 W
Stop lamp	10 W
Turn signal lamps.	21 W amber
Speedometer and warning lights	1.4 W capless
Fuel gauge sender unit resistance	110 ± 10 ohms

1 General information

1 From the mid 90s LML (Lohia Machinery Limited) in India have manufactured a version of the Vespa PX125/150 model. Initially models were produced with a drum front brake and kickstart only, but later refinements were made to bring the model in line with the current PX, such as an hydraulic front disc brake, electric start, secondary air system and catalytic converter. Additionally LML made a number of changes to the electrical system, incorporated a pre-air filter (mainly for use in their home market) and fitted reed valve induction. Other differences from the current PX are the provision of a spare wheel under the left-hand side panel as standard, a three-position fuel tap (ON, OFF and RES), and modified instrumentation.

2 The LML two-stroke metal-bodied 4-speed scooters have been sold in the UK under the model names Star 2T, Star DLX/Deluxe and Via Toscana, and in other markets as the NV, Stella, Speedy and Bella Donna.

3 This chapter contains specifications, a maintenance schedule and wiring diagrams. Procedures are given in this chapter where they differ from those for PX models in the preceding chapters; refer first to Chapter 7 and then to the earlier chapters. Note that the revised clutch components described in Section 6 of Chapter 7 are not fitted to LML models.

2 Rountine maintenance schedule

Daily (pre-ride) checks

☐ Check that there is engine oil visible in the sightglass. Top up via the oil tank under the seat if necessary.
☐ Check you have enough fuel to complete your journey
☐ Check the tyre pressures, tread and sidewall condition
☐ Check that the controls, including the brakes, operate correctly
☐ Check the front brake fluid level
☐ Check the operation of all lights and the horn

Every 2500 miles (4000 km)

Repeat all items under the Daily (pre-ride) heading
☐ Clean and adjust the spark plug
☐ Clean the air filter element
☐ Clean the pre air filter
☐ Clean the secondary air filter
☐ Change the gearbox oil

☐ Check the engine idle speed
☐ Check the throttle cable, clutch cable and gearchange cable adjustment
☐ Check the front brake fluid level, pad wear and hose condition
☐ Check the rear brake operation and adjust the cable if necessary
☐ Check battery condition
☐ Lubricate the speedometer cable and drive gear
☐ Lubricate the front wheel bearings
☐ Check the electrical system operation

Every 5000 miles (8000 km)

Repeat all items under the 2500 mile (4000 km) heading
☐ Check tighten all nuts and bolts
☐ Decoke the cylinder head, piston and exhaust port
☐ Renew the spark plug
☐ Check the ignition timing
☐ Lubricate the gearchange control
☐ Lubricate the steering head bearings
☐ Check the steering and suspension

Every two years

☐ Replace the front brake fluid

3 Tool part numbers

The following LML tool part numbers have changed from those stated in the main text for Vespa/Piaggio tools.

Output shaft forked feeler gauge	G-2107025
Generator rotor holding tool	19.1.20095
Fuel tap removal wrench	RS-00231

4 Pre-air filter

1 LML models are manufacturer with a pre-air filter in the main air intake below the seat. The filter is unlikely to become blocked unless the scooter is being operated in a particularly dusty environment. It should be inspected at the same time as the main air filter element is checked.

2 Raise the seat and prise the filter out of the air intake. Use a soft brush to clean away any dust particles and press the filter back into position. There should be a good seal between the rim of the filter and the mouth of the intake to prevent unfiltered air being drawn into the intake system.

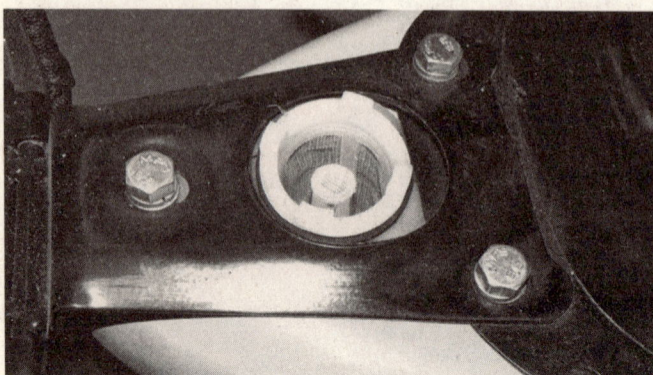

4.1 Raise the seat to access the pre-air filter

4.2 Filter gauze should be clean and free of dust

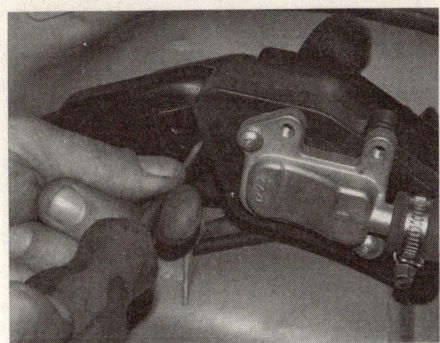

5.2a Single screw secures the secondary air filter

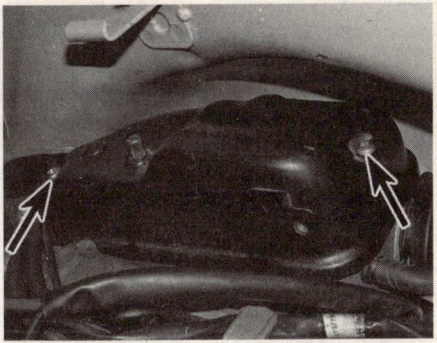

5.2b Remove the air filter lid (two screws arrowed) . . .

5.2c . . . lift off the rubber sleeve . . .

5.2d . . . undo the filter screws and lift off the air filter

5.2e Disconnect the throttle cable (A) and choke cable (B)

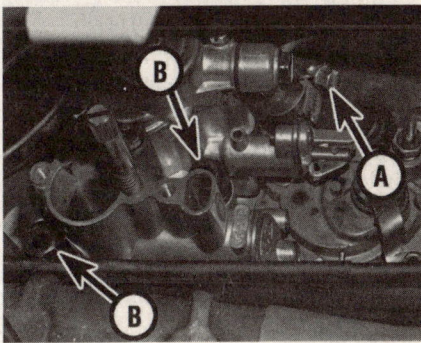

5.2f Slacken the fuel pipe clamp (A) and pull the pipe off its union, then undo the two sleeve nuts (B) . . .

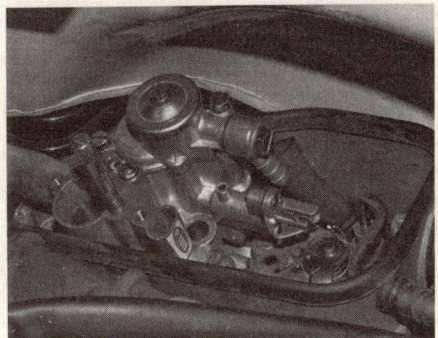

5.2g . . . and lift the carburettor out of the casing

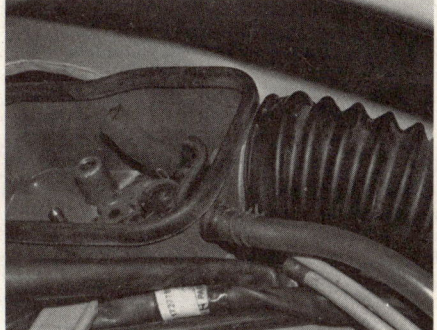

5.2h Pull the air intake trunking off the front of the casing . . .

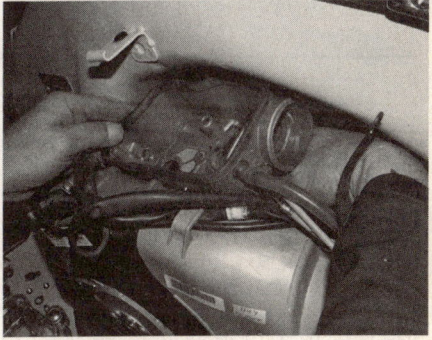

5.2i . . . then ease the casing up off the reed valve block

5 Reed valve

1 The reed valve block is situated between the carburettor and crankcase and mounted in an aluminium block.
2 To access the valve, remove the right-hand side panel and detach the secondary air filter housing from the carburettor cover. Remove the carburettor as shown in the accompanying photo sequence.
3 Remove the two large screws and the smaller Phillips-head screw under the gasket, to free the reed valve block from the crankcase.
4 Handle the reed valve carefully. The reeds should rest fully against their seat, without any dirt preventing them closing. Hold the assembly

5.3a Remove the two slotted-head screws . . .

5.3b . . . and the single Phillips-head screw under the gasket

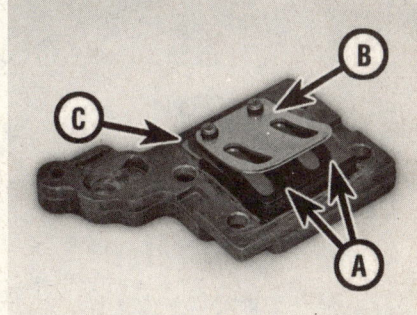

5.4 Reed petals (A) and stopper plate (B). Cut-off on corner (C) indicates correct fitting

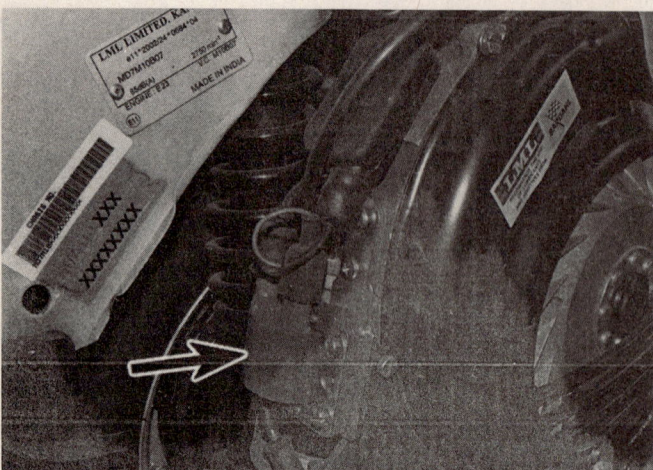
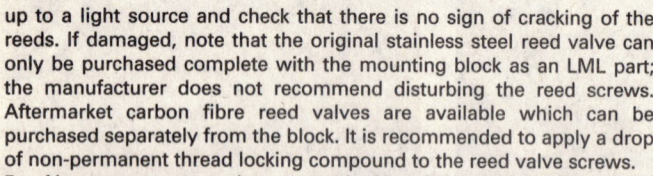

6.2 Ignition HT coil is mounted to the crankcase

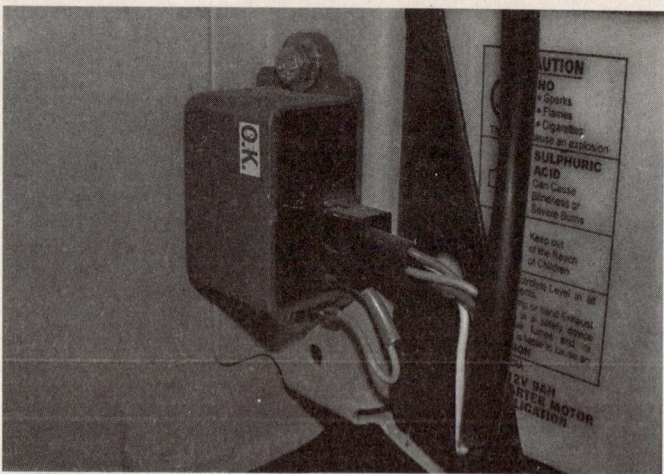

6.3 CDI unit location under left-hand side panel

up to a light source and check that there is no sign of cracking of the reeds. If damaged, note that the original stainless steel reed valve can only be purchased complete with the mounting block as an LML part; the manufacturer does not recommend disturbing the reed screws. Aftermarket carbon fibre reed valves are available which can be purchased separately from the block. It is recommended to apply a drop of non-permanent thread locking compound to the reed valve screws.

5   Always use new gaskets on each side of the reed valve block to ensure full sealing and no air leaks; LML recommended a smear of RTV sealant on both sides of the new gaskets, but take care not to apply an excessive amount as it might ooze out and block the reeds, oilway or enter the crankcase. Fit the gaskets carefully, noting that the top and bottom gaskets differ. Be careful not to block the oilway.

6   Ignition system changes

1   The combined electronic ignition unit and HT coil fitted to PX models is replaced by separate units on the LML.

2   The HT coil is mounted to the crankcase and can be accessed by removing the right-hand side panel. Test values are available for the coil primary and secondary resistances (see Specifications at the beginning of this Chapter). To test the coil, first remove it from the crankcase. Using a multimeter set to the ohms x 1 range, measure the primary winding resistance between the coil's blue wire terminal and the mounting bracket (Fig. 8.1). When measuring the secondary winding resistance, connect the meter between the end of the terminal inside the spark plug cap and the coil's mounting bracket (Fig. 8.2). Compare your test results to the Specifications, noting that the resistance of the spark plug cap must be taken into account when measuring the secondary windings.

3   The CDI unit is bolted to the frame, forward of the battery, under the left-hand side panel. No information is available to test the unit. All that can be done if the CDI unit is suspected of being faulty, and all other ignition system components have been checked, is to test by the substitution of a good CDI unit. When refitting the CDI unit make sure that the earth connection to the frame is good.

4   Values are given for the ignition source coil resistance and pick-up winding resistance at the beginning of this Chapter. Trace the wiring from the alternator and disconnect it at the wire connectors. Make the resistance test on the alternator side of the connectors. To test the source coil, connect the meter between the green and white wire terminals. To test the pick-up coil, connect the meter between the red and white wire terminals.

7   Spare wheel

1   Remove the left-hand side panel to access the spare wheel.

2   Undo the bolt to free the wheel cover, taking care not to lose the spacers. Remove the two nuts and their washers and lift the wheel off its mounting studs.

3   Always ensure the tyre pressure is correct before using the spare wheel.

8   Electrical system changes

1   The turn signal beeper unit described in Chapter 7, Section 24 is located on the steering stem under the horn cover.

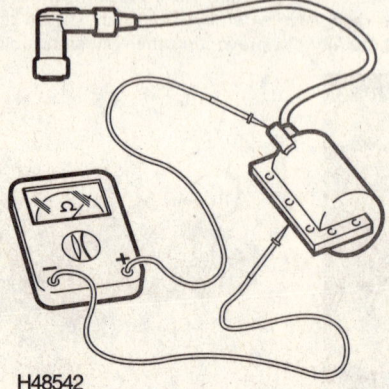

H48542

Fig. 8.1 HT coil primary windings test

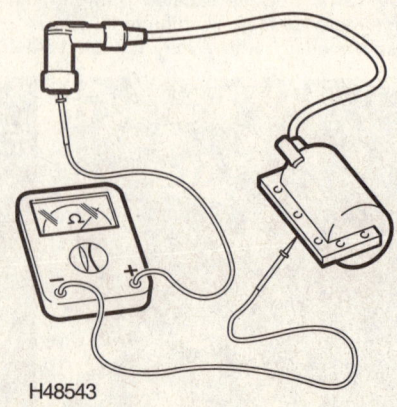

H48543

Fig. 8.2 HT coil secondary windings test

7.2a Remove the wheel cover bolt . . .

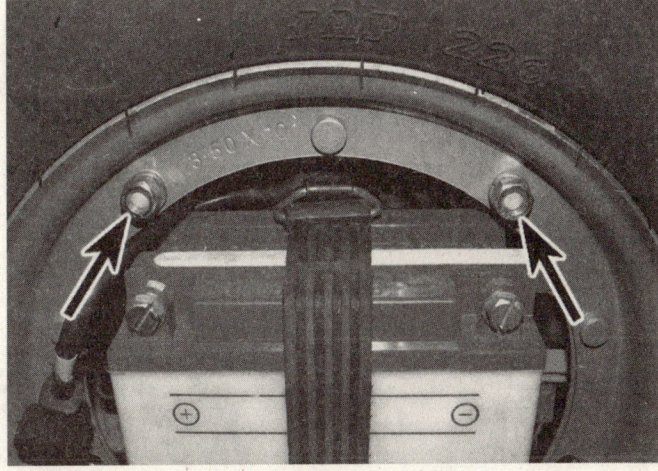

7.2b . . . and the two nuts to free the spare wheel

2   The fuse is located in a separate holder behind the battery carrier under the left-hand side panel. Remove the battery for access, then unscrew the cap and lift out the glass cartridge fuse. The fuse wire can be clearly seen through the glass of the fuse.

3   The starter relay and turn signal relay are located behind the left-hand side panel.

4   LML models use amber turn signal bulbs behind clear lenses. When fitting an amber bulb note that the bulb pins are offset slightly to prevent the use of clear bulbs which have pins spaced 180° apart.

5   Certain US models are equipped with a neutral light switch and indicator light – see the accompanying wiring diagram.

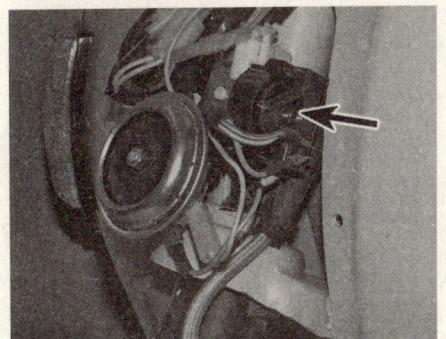

8.1 Turn signal beeper location

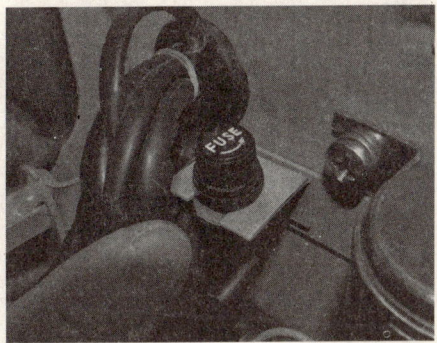

8.2a Fuse holder location under left-hand side panel

8.2b Fuse is an 8A glass cartridge type

8.3a Starter relay . . .

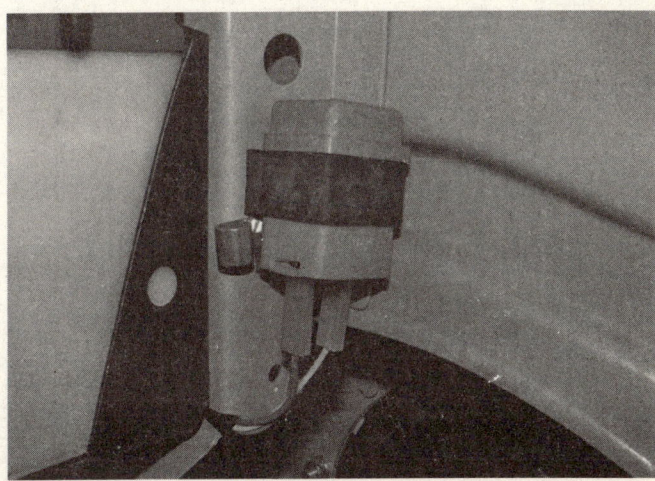

8.3b . . . and turn signal relay

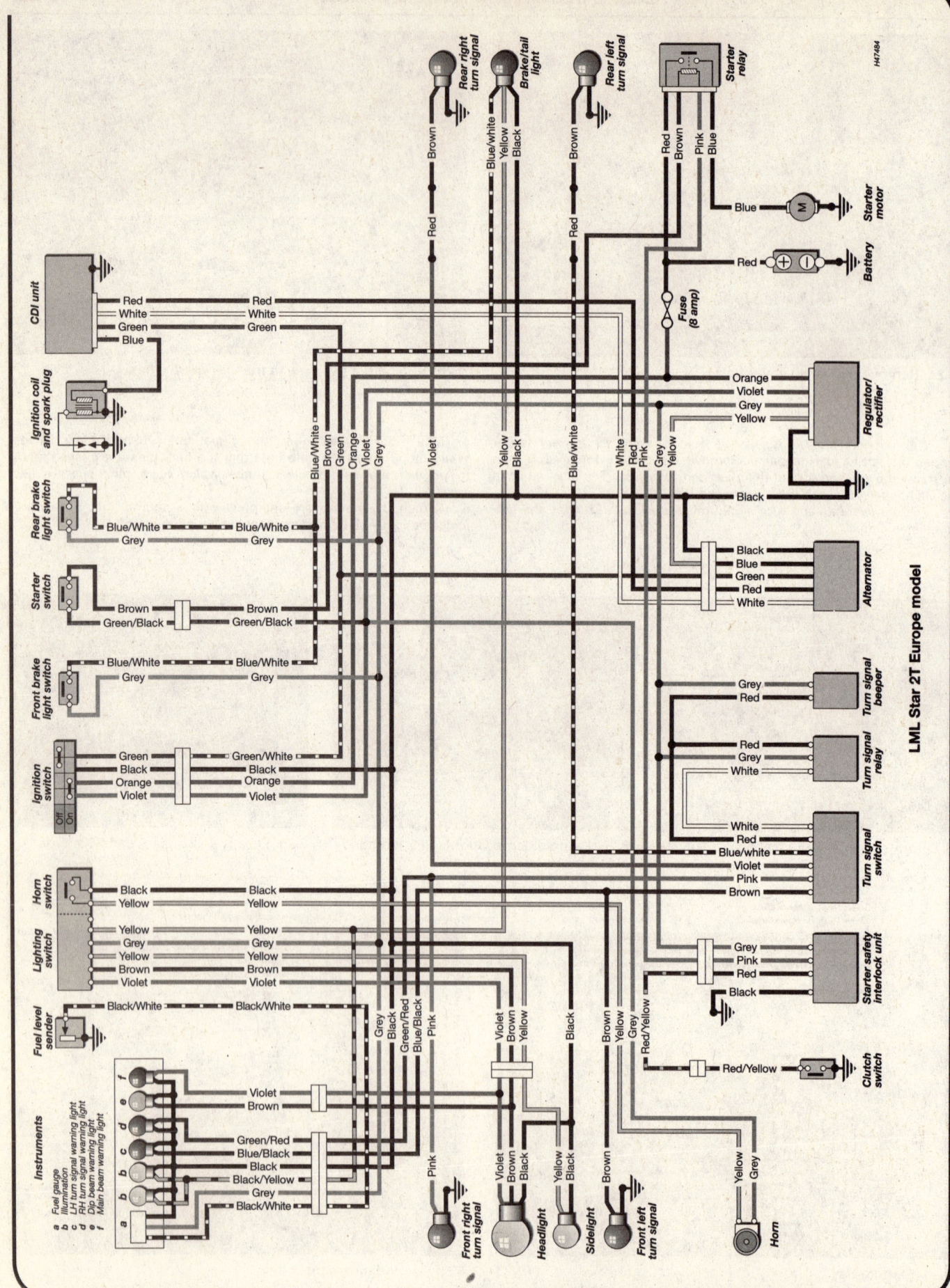

H47484

LML Star 2T Europe model

157

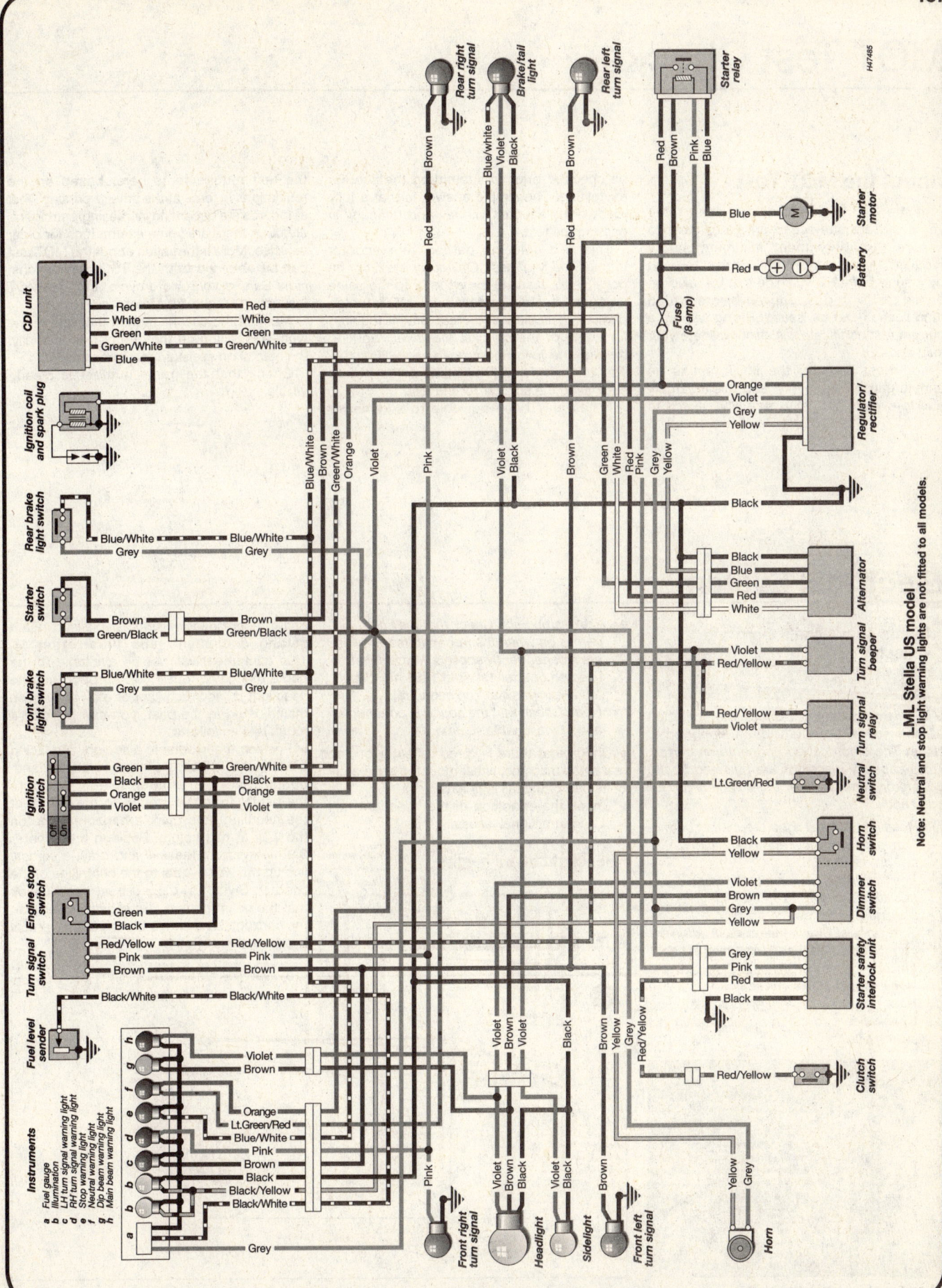

LML Stella US model

Note: Neutral and stop light warning lights are not fitted to all models.

MOT Test Checks

About the MOT Test

In the UK, all vehicles more than three years old are subject to an annual test to ensure that they meet minimum safety requirements. A current test certificate must be issued before a machine can be used on public roads, and is required before a road fund licence can be issued. Riding without a current test certificate will also invalidate your insurance.

For most owners, the MOT test is an annual cause for anxiety, and this is largely due to owners not being sure what needs to be checked prior to submitting the scooter for testing. The simple answer is that a fully roadworthy scooter will have no difficulty in passing the test.

This is a guide to getting your scooter through the MOT test. Obviously it will not be possible to examine the scooter to the same standard as the professional MOT tester, particularly in view of the equipment required for some of the checks. However, working through the following procedures will enable you to identify any problem areas before submitting the scooter for the test.

It has only been possible to summarise the test requirements here, based on the regulations in force at the time of printing. Test standards are becoming increasingly stringent, although there are some exemptions for older vehicles. More information about the MOT test can be obtained from the TSO publications, *How Safe is your Motorcycle* and *The MOT Inspection Manual for Motorcycle Testing*.

Many of the checks require that one of the wheels is raised off the ground. Additionally, the help of an assistant may prove useful.

Check that the frame number is clearly visible.

Electrical System

Lights, turn signals, horn and reflector

✔ With the ignition on, check the operation of the following electrical components. **Note:** *The electrical components on certain small-capacity machines are powered by the generator, requiring that the engine is run for this check.*

a) *Headlight and tail light. Check that both illuminate in the low and high beam switch positions.*
b) *Position lights. Check that the front position (or sidelight) and tail light illuminate in this switch position.*
c) *Turn signals. Check that all flash at the correct rate, and that the warning light(s) function correctly. Check that the turn signal switch works correctly.*
d) *Hazard warning system (where fitted). Check that all four turn signals flash in this switch position.*

e) *Brake stop light. Check that the light comes on when the front and rear brakes are independently applied. Models first used on or after 1st April 1986 must have a brake light switch on each brake.*
f) *Horn. Check that the sound is continuous and of reasonable volume.*

✔ Check that there is a red reflector on the rear of the machine, either mounted separately or as part of the tail light lens.
✔ Check the condition of the headlight, tail light and turn signal lenses.

Headlight beam height

✔ The MOT tester will perform a headlight beam height check using specialised beam setting equipment **(see illustration 1)**. This equipment will not be available to the home mechanic, but if you suspect that the headlight is incorrectly set or may have been maladjusted in the past, you can perform a rough test as follows.
✔ Position the scooter in a straight line facing a brick wall. The scooter must be off its stand, upright and with a rider seated. Measure the height from the ground to the centre of the headlight and mark a horizontal line on the wall at this height. Position the scooter 3.8 metres from the wall and draw a vertical line up the wall central to the centreline of the scooter. Switch to dipped beam and check that the beam pattern falls slightly lower than the horizontal line and to the left of the vertical line **(see illustration 2)**.

Headlight beam height checking equipment

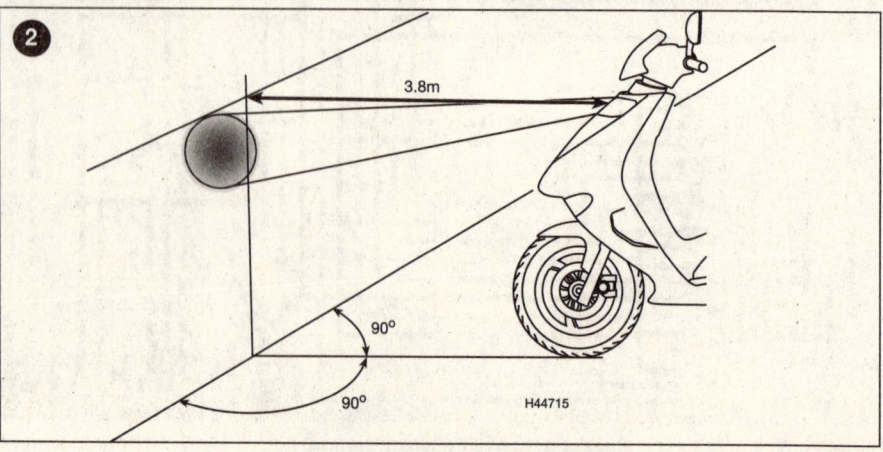
Home workshop beam alignment check

MOT Test Checks

Exhaust System

Exhaust

✔ Check that the exhaust mountings are secure and that the system does not foul any of the rear suspension components.

✔ Start the scooter. When the revs are increased, check that the exhaust is neither holed nor leaking from any of its joints. On a linked system, check that the collector box is not leaking due to corrosion.

✔ Note that the exhaust decibel level ("loudness" of the exhaust) is assessed at the discretion of the tester. If the scooter was first used on or after 1st January 1985 the silencer must carry the BSAU 193 stamp, or a marking relating to its make and model, or be of OE (original equipment) manufacture. If the silencer is marked NOT FOR ROAD USE, RACING USE ONLY or similar, it will fail the MOT.

Steering and Suspension

Steering

✔ With the front wheel raised off the ground, rotate the steering from lock to lock. The handlebar or switches must not contact anything. Problems can be caused by damaged lock stops on the lower yoke and frame, or by the fitting of non-standard handlebars.

✔ When performing the lock to lock check, also ensure that the steering moves freely without drag or notchiness. Steering movement can be impaired by poorly routed cables, or by overtight head bearings or worn bearings. The tester will perform a check of the steering head bearing lower race by mounting the front wheel on a surface plate, then performing a lock to lock check with the weight of the machine on the lower bearing (see illustration 3).

✔ Grasp the fork sliders (lower legs) and attempt to push and pull on the forks (see illustration 4). Any play in the steering head bearings will be felt. Note that in extreme cases, wear of the front fork bushes can be misinterpreted for head bearing play.

✔ Check that the handlebars are securely mounted.

✔ Check that the handlebar grip rubbers are secure. They should by bonded to the bar left end and to the throttle twistgrip on the right end.

Front suspension

✔ With the scooter off the stand, hold the front brake on and pump the front suspension up and down (see illustration 5). Check that the movement is adequately damped.

✔ Inspect the area above and around the front fork oil seals (see illustration 6). There should be no sign of oil on the fork tube (stanchion) nor leaking down the slider (lower leg).

✔ On models with leading or trailing link front suspension, check that there is no freeplay in the linkage when moved from side to side.

Front wheel mounted on a surface plate for steering head bearing lower race check

Checking the steering head bearings for freeplay

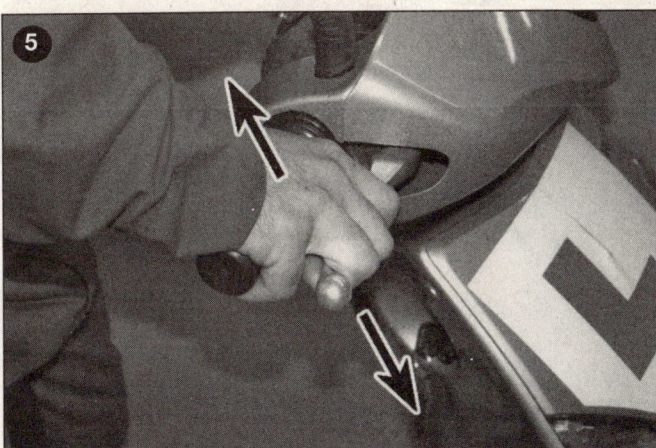

Hold the front brake on and pump the front suspension up and down to check operation

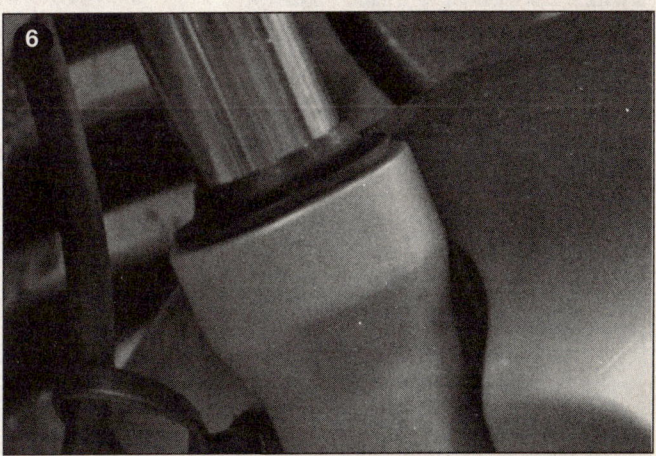

Inspect the area around the fork dust seal for oil leakage

MOT Test Checks

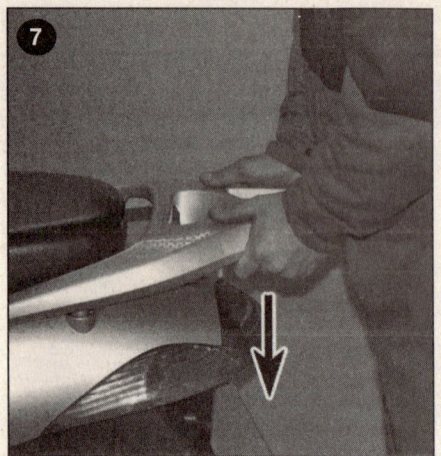

Bounce the rear of the scooter to check rear suspension operation

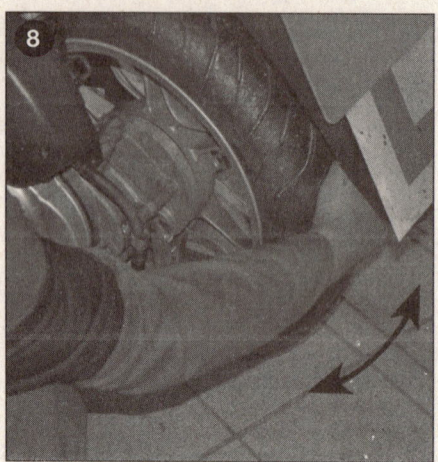

Grasp the rear wheel to check for play in the engine-to-frame mountings

Rear suspension

✔ With the scooter off the stand and an assistant supporting the scooter by its handlebars, bounce the rear suspension **(see illustration 7)**. Check that the suspension components do not foul the bodywork and check that the shock absorber(s) provide adequate damping.

✔ Visually inspect the shock absorber(s) and check that there is no sign of oil leakage from its damper.

✔ With the rear wheel raised off the ground, grasp the wheel as shown and attempt to move it from side to side **(see illustration 8)**. Any play in the engine-to-frame mountings will be felt as movement.

Brakes, Wheels and Tyres

Brakes

✔ With the wheel raised off the ground, apply the brake then free it off, and check that the wheel is about to revolve freely without brake drag.

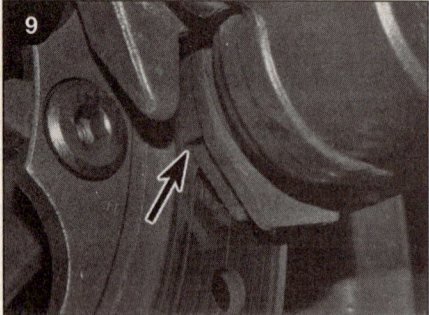

Brake pad wear can usually be viewed without removing the caliper. Some pads have wear indicator grooves (arrow)

Check for wheel bearing play by trying to move the wheel about the axle (spindle)

✔ On disc brakes, examine the disc itself. Check that it is securely mounted and not cracked.

✔ On disc brakes, view the pad material through the caliper mouth and check that the pads are not worn down beyond the limit **(see illustration 9)**.

✔ On drum brakes, check that when the brake is applied the angle between the operating

On drum brakes, check the angle of the operating lever with the brake fully applied. Most drum brakes have a wear indicator pointer and scale

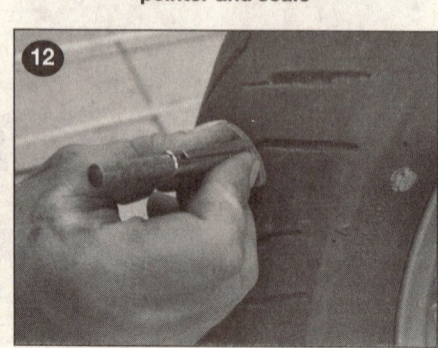

Checking the tyre tread depth

lever and cable or rod is not too great **(see illustration 10)**. Check also that the operating lever doesn't foul any other components.

✔ On disc brakes, examine the flexible hoses from top to bottom. Have an assistant hold the brake on so that the fluid in the hose is under pressure, and check that there is no sign of fluid leakage, bulges or cracking. If there are any metal brake pipes or unions, check that these are free from corrosion and damage.

✔ The MOT tester will perform a test of the scooter's braking efficiency based on a calculation of rider and scooter weight. Although this cannot be carried out at home, you can at least ensure that the braking systems are properly maintained. For hydraulic disc brakes, check the fluid level, lever/pedal feel (bleed of air if its spongy) and pad material. For drum brakes, check adjustment, cable or rod operation and shoe lining thickness.

Wheels and tyres

✔ Check the wheel condition. Cast wheels should be free from cracks and if of the built-up design, all fasteners should be secure.

✔ With the wheel raised off the ground, spin the wheel and visually check that the tyre and wheel run true. Check that the tyre does not foul the suspension or mudguards.

✔ With the wheel raised off the ground, grasp the wheel and attempt to move it about the axle **(see illustration 11)**. Any play felt here indicates wheel bearing failure.

✔ Check the tyre tread depth, tread condition and sidewall condition **(see illustration 12)**.

✔ Check the tyre type. Front and rear tyre types must be compatible and be suitable for

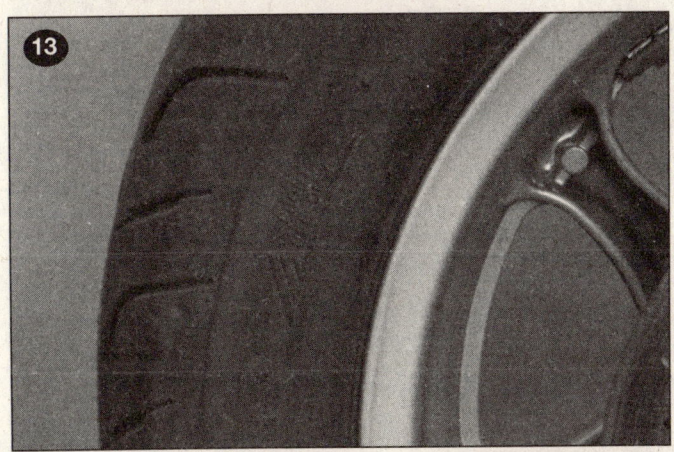

Tyre direction of rotation arrow can be found on tyre sidewall

Two straight-edges are used to check wheel alignment

road use. Tyres marked NOT FOR ROAD USE, COMPETITION USE ONLY or similar, will fail the MOT.

✔ If the tyre sidewall carries a direction of rotation arrow, this must be pointing in the direction of normal wheel rotation **(see illustration 13)**.

✔ Check that the wheel axle nuts (where applicable) are properly secured. A self-locking nut or castellated nut with a split-pin or R-pin can be used.

✔ Wheel alignment is checked with the scooter off the stand and a rider seated. With the front wheel pointing straight ahead, two

perfectly straight lengths of metal or wood and placed against the sidewalls of both tyres **(see illustration 14)**. The gap each side of the front tyre must be equidistant on both sides. Incorrect wheel alignment may be due to a cocked rear wheel or in extreme cases, a bent frame.

General checks and condition

✔ Check the security of all major fasteners, bodypanels, seat and mudguards.

✔ Check that the pillion footrests, handlebar levers and stand are securely mounted.

✔ Check for corrosion on the frame or any load-bearing components. If severe, this may affect the structure, particularly under stress.

Lubricants and fluids

A wide range of lubricants, fluids and cleaning agents is available for motor-cycles. This is a guide as to what is available, its applications and properties.

Four-stroke engine oil

● Engine oil is without doubt the most important component of any four-stroke engine. Modern motorcycle engines place a lot of demands on their oil and choosing the right type is essential. Using an unsuitable oil will lead to an increased rate of engine wear and could result in serious engine damage. Before purchasing oil, always check the recommended oil specification given by the manufacturer. The manufacturer will state a recommended 'type or classification' and also a specific 'viscosity' range for engine oil.

● The oil 'type or classification' is identified by its API (American Petroleum Institute) rating. The API rating will be in the form of two letters, e.g. SG. The S identifies the oil as being suitable for use in a petrol (gasoline) engine (S stands for spark ignition) and the second letter, ranging from A to J, identifies the oil's performance rating. The later this letter, the higher the specification of the oil; for example API SG oil exceeds the requirements of API SF oil. **Note:** *On some oils there may also be a second rating consisting of another two letters, the first letter being C, e.g. API SF/CD. This rating indicates the oil is also suitable for use in a diesel engines (the C stands for compression ignition) and is thus of no relevance for motorcycle use.*

● The 'viscosity' of the oil is identified by its SAE (Society of Automotive Engineers) rating. All modern engines require multigrade oils and the SAE rating will consist of two numbers, the first followed by a W, e.g. 10W/40. The first number indicates the viscosity rating of the oil at low temperatures (W stands for winter – tested at –20°C) and the second number represents the viscosity of the oil at high temperatures (tested at 100°C). The lower the number, the thinner the oil. For example an oil with an SAE 10W/40 rating will give better cold starting and running than an SAE 15W/40 oil.

● As well as ensuring the 'type' and 'viscosity' of the oil match the recommendations, another consideration to make when buying engine oil is whether to purchase a standard mineral-based oil, a semi-synthetic oil (also known as a synthetic blend or synthetic-based oil) or a fully-synthetic oil. Although all oils will have a similar rating and viscosity, their cost will vary considerably; mineral-based oils are the cheapest, the fully-synthetic oils the most expensive with the semi-synthetic oils falling somewhere in-between. This decision is very much up to the owner, but it should be noted that modern synthetic oils have far better lubricating and cleaning qualities than traditional mineral-based oils and tend to retain these properties for far longer. Bearing in mind the operating conditions inside a modern, high-revving motorcycle engine it is highly recommended that a fully synthetic oil is used. The extra expense at each service could save you money in the long term by preventing premature engine wear.

● As a final note always ensure that the oil is specifically designed for use in motorcycle engines. Engine oils designed primarily for use in car engines sometimes contain additives or friction modifiers which could cause clutch slip on a motorcycle fitted with a wet-clutch.

Two-stroke engine oil

● Modern two-stroke engines, with their high power outputs, place high demands on their oil. If engine seizure is to be avoided it is essential that a high-quality oil is used. Two-stroke oils differ hugely from four-stroke oils. The oil lubricates only the crankshaft and piston(s) (the transmission has its own lubricating oil) and is used on a total-loss basis where it is burnt completely during the combustion process.

● The Japanese have recently introduced a classification system for two-strokes oils, the JASO rating. This rating is in the form of two letters, either FA, FB or FC – FA is the lowest classification and FC the highest. Ensure the oil being used meets or exceeds the recommended rating specified by the manufacturer.

● As well as ensuring the oil rating matches the recommendation, another consideration to make when buying engine oil is whether to purchase a standard mineral-based oil, a semi-synthetic oil (also known as a synthetic blend or synthetic-based oil) or a fully-synthetic oil. The cost of each type of oil varies considerably; mineral-based oils are the cheapest, the fully-synthetic oils the most expensive with the semi-synthetic oils falling somewhere in-between. This decision is very much up to the owner, but it should be noted that modern synthetic oils have far better lubricating properties and burn cleaner than traditional mineral-based oils. It is therefore recommended that a fully synthetic oil is used. The extra expense could save you money in the long term by preventing premature engine wear, engine performance will be improved, carbon deposits and exhaust smoke will be reduced.

● Always ensure that the oil is specifically designed for use in an injector system. Many high quality two-stroke oils are designed for competition use and need to be pre-mixed with fuel. These oils are of a much higher viscosity and are not designed to flow through the injector pumps used on road-going two-stroke motorcycles.

Transmission (gear) oil

● On a two-stroke engine, the transmission and clutch are lubricated by their own separate oil bath which must be changed in accordance with the Maintenance Schedule.
● Although the engine and transmission units of most four-strokes use a common lubrication supply, there are some exceptions where the engine and gearbox have separate oil reservoirs and a dry clutch is used.
● Motorcycle manufacturers will either recommend a monograde transmission oil or a four-stroke multigrade engine oil to lubricate the transmission.
● Transmission oils, or gear oils as they are often called, are designed specifically for use in transmission systems. The viscosity of these oils is represented by an SAE number, but the scale of measurement applied is different to that used to grade engine oils. As a rough guide a SAE90 gear oil will be of the same viscosity as an SAE50 engine oil.

Shaft drive oil

● On models equipped with shaft final drive, the shaft drive gears are will have their own oil supply. The manufacturer will state a recommended 'type or classification' and also a specific 'viscosity' range in the same manner as for four-stroke engine oil.
● Gear oil classification is given by the number which follows the API GL (GL standing for gear lubricant) rating, the higher the number, the higher the specification of the oil, e.g. API GL5 oil is a higher specification than API GL4 oil. Ensure the oil meets or

exceeds the classification specified and is of the correct viscosity. The viscosity of gear oils is also represented by an SAE number but the scale of measurement used is different to that used to grade engine oils. As a rough guide an SAE90 gear oil will be of the same viscosity as an SAE50 engine oil.
● If the use of an EP (Extreme Pressure) gear oil is specified, ensure the oil purchased is suitable.

Fork oil and suspension fluid

● Conventional telescopic front forks are hydraulic and require fork oil to work. To ensure the forks function correctly, the fork oil must be changed in accordance with the Maintenance Schedule.
● Fork oil is available in a variety of viscosities, identified by their SAE rating; fork oil ratings vary from light (SAE 5) to heavy (SAE 30). When purchasing fork oil, ensure the viscosity rating matches that specified by the manufacturer.
● Some lubricant manufacturers also produce a range of high-quality suspension fluids which are very similar to fork oil but are designed mainly for competition use. These fluids may have a different viscosity rating system which is not to be confused with the SAE rating of normal fork oil. Refer to the manufacturer's instructions if in any doubt.

Brake and clutch fluid

● All disc brake systems and some clutch systems are hydraulically operated. To ensure correct operation, the hydraulic fluid must be changed in accordance with the Maintenance Schedule.
● Brake and clutch fluid is classified by its DOT rating with most motorcycle manufacturers specifying DOT 3 or 4 fluid. Both fluid types are glycol-based and can be mixed together without adverse effect; DOT 4 fluid exceeds

the requirements of DOT 3 fluid. Although it is safe to use DOT 4 fluid in a system designed for use with DOT 3 fluid, never use DOT 3 fluid in a system which specifies the use of DOT 4 as this will adversely affect the system's performance. The type required for the system will be marked on the fluid reservoir cap.
● Some manufacturers also produce a DOT 5 hydraulic fluid. DOT 5 hydraulic fluid is silicone-based and is not compatible with the glycol-based DOT 3 and 4 fluids. Never mix DOT 5 fluid with DOT 3 or 4 fluid as this will seriously affect the performance of the hydraulic system.

Coolant/antifreeze

● When purchasing coolant/antifreeze, always ensure it is suitable for use in an aluminium engine and contains corrosion inhibitors to prevent possible blockages of the internal coolant passages of the system. As a general rule, most coolants are designed to be used neat and should not be diluted whereas antifreeze can be mixed with distilled water to provide a coolant solution of the required strength. Refer to the manufacturer's instructions on the bottle.
● Ensure the coolant is changed in accordance with the Maintenance Schedule.

Chain lube

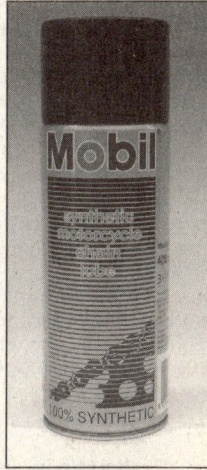

● Chain lube is an aerosol-type spray lubricant specifically designed for use on motorcycle final drive chains. Chain lube has two functions, to minimise friction between the final drive chain and sprockets and to prevent corrosion of the chain. Regular use of a good-quality chain lube will extend the life of the drive chain and sprockets and thus maximise the power being transmitted from the transmission to the rear wheel.
● When using chain lube, always allow some time for the solvents in the lube to evaporate before riding the motorcycle. This will minimise the amount of lube which will 'fling' off from the chain when the motorcycle is used. If the motorcycle is

Lubricants and fluids

equipped with an 'O-ring' chain, ensure the chain lube is labelled as being suitable for use on 'O-ring' chains.

Degreasers and solvents

● There are many different types of solvents and degreasers available to remove the grime

and grease which accumulate around the motorcycle during normal use. Degreasers and solvents are usually available as an aerosol-type spray or as a liquid which you apply with a brush. Always closely follow the manufacturer's instructions and wear eye protection during use. Be aware that many solvents are flammable and may give off noxious fumes; take adequate precautions when using them (see Safety First!).

● For general cleaning, use one of the many solvents or degreasers available from most motorcycle accessory shops. These solvents are usually applied then left for a certain time before being washed off with water.

Brake cleaner is a solvent specifically designed to remove all traces of oil, grease and dust from braking system components. Brake cleaner is designed to evaporate quickly and leaves behind no residue.

Carburettor cleaner is an aerosol-type solvent specifically designed to clear carburettor blockages and break down the hard deposits and gum often found inside carburettors during overhaul.

Contact cleaner is an aerosol-type solvent designed for cleaning electrical components. The cleaner will remove all traces of oil and dirt from components such as switch contacts or fouled spark plugs and then dry, leaving behind no residue.

Gasket remover is an aerosol-type solvent designed for removing stubborn gaskets from engine components during overhaul. Gasket remover will minimise the amount of scraping required to remove the gasket and therefore reduce the risk of damage to the mating surface.

Spray lubricants

● Aerosol-based spray lubricants are widely available and are excellent for lubricating lever pivots and exposed cables and switches. Try to use a lubricant which is of the dry-film type as the fluid evaporates, leaving behind a dry-film of lubricant. Lubricants which leave behind an oily residue will attract dust and dirt which will increase the rate of wear of the cable/lever.

● Most lubricants also act as a moisture dispersant and a penetrating fluid. This means they can also be used to 'dry out' electrical components such as wiring connectors or switches as well as helping to free seized fasteners.

Greases

● Grease is used to lubricate many of the pivot-points. A good-quality multi-purpose grease is suitable for most applications but some manufacturers will specify the use of specialist greases for use on components such as swingarm and suspension linkage bushes. These specialist greases can be purchased from most motorcycle (or car) accessory shops; commonly specified types include molybdenum disulphide grease, lithium-based grease, graphite-based grease, silicone-based grease and high-temperature copper-based grease.

Gasket sealing compounds

● Gasket sealing compounds can be used in conjunction with gaskets, to improve their sealing capabilities, or on their own to seal metal-to-metal joints. Depending on their type, sealing compounds either set hard or stay relatively soft and pliable.

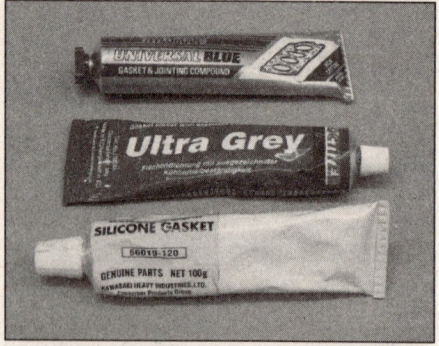

● When purchasing a gasket sealing compound, ensure that it is designed specifically for use on an internal combustion engine. General multi-purpose sealants available from DIY stores may appear visibly similar but they are not designed to withstand the extreme heat or contact with fuel and oil encountered when used on an engine (see 'Tools and Workshop Tips' for further information).

Thread locking compound

● Thread locking compounds are used to secure certain threaded fasteners in position to prevent them from loosening due to vibration. Thread locking compounds can be purchased from most motorcycle (and car) accessory shops. Ensure the threads of the both components are completely clean and dry before sparingly applying the locking compound (see 'Tools and Workshop Tips' for further information).

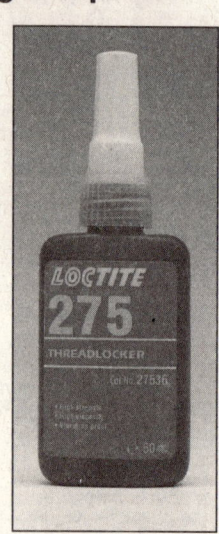

Fuel additives

● Fuel additives which protect and clean the fuel system components are widely available. These additives are designed to remove all traces of deposits that build up on the carburettors/injectors and prevent wear, helping the fuel system to operate more efficiently. If a fuel additive is being used, check that it is suitable for use with your motorcycle, especially if your motorcycle is equipped with a catalytic converter.

● Octane boosters are also available. These additives are designed to improve the performance of highly-tuned engines being run on normal pump-fuel and are of no real use on standard motorcycles.

Index

Haynes Motorcycle Manuals – The Complete List

Title		Book No
APRILIA RS50 (99 – 06) & RS125 (93 – 06)		4298
Aprilia RSV1000 Mille (98 – 03)	♦	4255
Aprilia SR50		4755
BMW 2-valve Twins (70 -96)	♦	0249
BMW F650	♦	4761
BMW K100 & 75 2-valve models (83 - 96)	♦	1373
BMW F800 (F650) Twins (06 – 10)	♦	4872
BMW R850, 1100 & 1150 4-valve Twins (93 – 06)	♦	3466
BMW R1200 (04 – 09)	♦	4598
BMW R1200 dohc Twins (10 – 12)	♦	4925
BSA Bantam (48 – 71)		0117
BSA Unit Singles (58 – 72)		0127
BSA Pre-unit Singles (54 – 61)		0326
BSA A7 & A10 Twins (47 – 62)		0121
BSA A50 & A65 Twins (62 – 73)		0155
CHINESE, Taiwanese & Korean Scooters		4768
Chinese, Taiwanese & Korean 125cc motorcyles		4781
Pulse/Pioneer Adrenaline, Sinnis Apache, Superbyke RMR (07 – 14)	◇♦	5750
DUCATI 600, 620, 750 & 900 2-valve V-twins (91 – 05)	♦	3290
Ducati Mk III & Desmo singles (69 – 76)	◇	0445
Ducati 748, 916 & 996 4-valve V-twins (94 – 01)	♦	3756
GILERA Runner, DNA, Ice & SKP/Stalker (97 – 11)		4163
HARLEY-DAVIDSON Sportsters (70 – 10)	♦	2534
Harley-Davidson Shovelhead & Evolution Big Twins (70 -99)	♦	2536
Harley-Davidson Twin Cam 88, 96 & 103 models (99 – 10)	♦	2478
HONDA NB, ND, NP & NS50 Melody (81 -85)	◇	0622
Honda NE/NB50 Vision & SA50 Vision Met-in (85-95)	◇	1278
Honda MB, MBX, MT & MTX50 (80 – 93)		0731
Honda C50, C70 & C90 (67 – 03)		0324
Honda XR50/70/80/100R & CRF50/70/80/100F (85 – 07)		2218
Honda XL/XR 80, 100, 125, 185 & 200 2-valve models (78 – 87)		0566
Honda H100 & H100S Singles (80 – 92)	◇	0734
Honda 125 Scooters (00 – 09)		4873
Honda ANF125 Innova Scooters (03 -12)	♦	4926
Honda CB/CD125T & CM125C Twins (77 – 88)	◇	0571
Honda CBF125 (09 – 14)	♦	5540
Honda CG125 (76 – 07)	◇	0433
Honda NS125 (86 – 93)	◇	3056
Honda CBR125R (04 – 10)		4620
Honda CBR125R, CBR250R & CRF250L/M (11 – 14)	♦	5919
Honda MBX/MTX125 & MTX200 (83 – 93)	◇	1132
Honda XL125V & VT125C (99 – 11)		4899
Honda CD/CM185 200T & CM250C 2-valve Twins (77 – 85)		0572
Honda CMX250 Rebel & CB250 Nighthawk Twins (85 – 09)	◇	2756
Honda XL/XR 250 & 500 (78 – 84)		0567
Honda XR250L, XR250R & XR400R (86 – 04)		2219
Honda CB250 & CB400N Super Dreams (78 – 84)	◇	0540
Honda CR Motocross Bikes (86 – 07)		2222
Honda CRF250 & CRF450 (02 – 06)		2630
Honda CBR400RR Fours (88 – 99)	◇♦	3552
Honda VFR400 (NC30) & RVF400 (NC35) V-Fours (89 – 98)	◇♦	3496
Honda CB500 (93 – 02) & CBF500 (03 – 08)	◇	3753
Honda CB400 & CB550 Fours (73 – 77)		0262
Honda CX/GL500 & 650 V-Twins (78 – 86)		0442
Honda CBX550 Four (82 – 86)	◇	0940
Honda XL600R & XR600R (83 – 08)	♦	2183
Honda XL600/650V Transalp & XRV750 Africa Twin (87 – 07)	♦	3919
Honda CB600 Hornet, CBF600 & CBR600F (07 – 12)	♦	5572
Honda CBR600F1 & 1000F Fours (87 – 96)	♦	1730
Honda CBR600F2 & F3 Fours (91 – 98)	♦	2070
Honda CBR600F4 (99 – 06)	♦	3911
Honda CB600F Hornet & CBF600 (98 – 06)	◇♦	3915
Honda CBR600RR (03 – 06)	♦	4590
Honda CBR600RR (07 -12)	♦	4795
Honda CB650 sohc Fours (78 – 84)		0665
Honda NTV600 Revere, NTV650 & NT650V Deauville (88 – 05)	◇♦	3243
Honda Shadow VT600 & 750 (USA) (88 – 09)		2312
Honda NT700V Deauville & XL700V Transalp (06 -13)	♦	5541
Honda CB750 sohc Four (69 – 79)		0131
Honda V45/65 Sabre & Magna (82 – 88)		0820
Honda VFR750 & 700 V-Fours (86 – 97)	♦	2101
Honda VFR800 V-Fours (97 – 01)	♦	3703
Honda VFR800 V-Tec V-Fours (02 – 09)	♦	4196
Honda CB750 & CB900 dohc Fours (78 – 84)		0535
Honda CBF1000 (06 -10) & CB1000R (08 – 11)	♦	4927
Honda VTR1000 Firestorm, Super Hawk & XL1000V Varadero (97 – 08)	♦	3744
Honda CBR900RR Fireblade (92 – 99)	♦	2161
Honda CBR900RR Fireblade (00 – 03)	♦	4060
Honda CBR1000RR Fireblade (04 – 07)	♦	4604
Honda CBR1000RR Fireblade (08 – 13)	♦	5688
Honda CBR1100XX Super Blackbird (97 – 07)	♦	3901
Honda ST1100 Pan European V-Fours (90 – 02)	♦	3384
Honda ST1300 Pan European (02 -11)	♦	4908
Honda Shadow VT1100 (USA) (85 – 07)		2313

Title		Book No
Honda GL1000 Gold Wing (75 – 79)		0309
Honda GL1100 Gold Wing (79 – 81)		0669
Honda Gold Wing 1200 (USA) (84 - 87)		2199
Honda Gold Wing 1500 (USA) (88 – 00)		2225
Honda Goldwing GL1800	♦	2787
KAWASAKI AE/AR 50 & 80 (81 – 95)		1007
Kawasaki KC, KE & KH100 (75 – 99)		1371
Kawasaki KMX125 & 200 (86 – 02)	◇	3046
Kawasaki 250, 350 & 400 Triples (72 – 79)		0134
Kawasaki 400 & 440 Twins (74 – 81)		0281
Kawasaki 400, 500 & 550 Fours (79 – 91)		0910
Kawasaki EN450 & 500 Twins (Ltd/Vulcan) (85 – 07)		2053
Kawasaki ER-6F & ER-6N (06 -10)	♦	4874
Kawasaki EX500 (GPZ500S) & ER500 (ER-5) (87 – 08)	♦	2052
Kawasaki ZX600 (ZZ-R600 & Ninja ZX-6) (90 – 06)	♦	2146
Kawasaki ZX-6R Ninja Fours (95 – 02)	♦	3451
Kawasaki ZX-6R (03 – 06)	♦	4742
Kawasaki ZX600 (GPZ600R, GPX600R, Ninja 600R & RX) & ZX750 (GPX750R, Ninja 750R) (85 – 97)	♦	1780
Kawasaki 650 Four (76 – 78)		0373
Kawasaki Vulcan 700/750 & 800 (85 – 04)	♦	2457
Kawasaki Vulcan 1500 & 1600 (87 – 08)	♦	4913
Kawasaki 750 Air-cooled Fours		0574
Kawasaki ZR550 & 750 Zephyr Fours (90 – 97)	♦	3382
Kawasaki Z750 & Z1000 (03 – 08)	♦	4762
Kawasaki ZX750 (Ninja ZX-7 & ZXR750) Fours (89 – 96)	♦	2054
Kawasaki Ninja ZX-7R & ZX-9R (94 – 04)	♦	3721
Kawasaki 900 & 1000 Fours (73 – 77)		0222
Kawasaki ZX900, 1000 & 1100 Liquid-cooled Fours (83 – 97)	♦	1681
Kawasaki ZX-10R (04 – 10)	♦	5542
KTM EXC Enduro & SX Motocross (00 – 07)	♦	4629
LAMBRETTA Scooters (58 – 00)	♦	5573
MOTO GUZZI 750, 850 & 1000 V-Twins (74 – 78)		0339
MZ ETZ models (81 – 95)	◇	1680
NORTON 500, 600, 650 & 750 Twins (57 – 70)		0187
Norton Commando (68 – 77)		0125
PEUGEOT Speedfight, Trekker & Vivacity Scooters (96 – 08)	◇	3920
Peugeot V-Clic, Speedfight 3, Vivacity 3, Kisbee & Tweet (08 – 14)	◇♦	5751
PIAGGIO (Vespa) Scooters (91 – 09)	◇	3492
SUZUKI GT, ZR & TS50 (77 – 90)	◇	0799
Suzuki TS50X (84 – 00)	◇	1599
Suzuki 100, 125, 185 & 250 Air-cooled Trail bikes (79 – 89)		0797
Suzuki GP100 & 125 Singles (78 – 93)	◇	0576
Suzuki GS, GN, GZ & DR125 Singles (82 – 05)	◇	0888
Suzuki Burgman 250 & 400 (98 – 11)	♦	4909
Suzuki GSX-R600/750 (06 – 09)	♦	4790
Suzuki 250 & 350 Twins (68 – 78)		0120
Suzuki GT250X7, GT200X5 & SB200 Twins (78 – 83)	◇	0469
Suzuki DR-Z400 (00 – 10)	♦	2933
Suzuki GS/GSX250, 400 & 450 Twins (79 – 85)		0736
Suzuki GS500 Twin (89 – 08)	♦	3238
Suzuki GS550 (77 – 82) & GS750 Fours (76 – 79)		0363
Suzuki GS/GSX550 4-valve Fours (83 – 88)		1133
Suzuki SV650 & SV650S (99 – 08)	♦	3912
Suzuki DL650 V-Strom & SFV650 Gladius (04 – 13)	♦	5643
Suzuki GSX-R600 & 750 (96 – 00)	♦	3553
Suzuki GSX-R600 (01 – 03), GSX-R750 (00 – 03) & GSX-R1000 (01 – 02)	♦	3986
Suzuki GSX-R600/750 (04 – 05) & GSX-R1000 (03 – 06)	♦	4382
Suzuki GSF600, 650 & 1200 Bandit Fours (95 – 06)	♦	3367
Suzuki Intruder, Marauder, Volusia & Boulevard (85 – 09)	♦	2618
Suzuki GS850 Fours (78 – 88)		0536
Suzuki GS1000 Four (77 – 79)		0484
Suzuki GSX-R750, GSX-R1100 (85 – 92) GSX600F, GSX750F, GSX1100F (Katana) Fours (88 – 96)	♦	2055
Suzuki GSX600/750F & GSX750 (98 – 02)	♦	3987
Suzuki GS/GSX1000, 1100 & 1150 4-valve Fours (79 – 88)		0737
Suzuki TL1000S/R & DL V-Strom (97 – 04)	♦	4083
Suzuki GSF650/1250 Bandit & GSX650/1250F (07 – 14)	♦	4798
Suzuki GSX1300R Hayabusa (99 – 14)	♦	4184
Suzuki GSX1400 (02 – 08)	♦	4758
TRIUMPH Tiger Cub & Terrier (52 – 68)		0414
Triumph 350 & 500 Unit Twins (58 – 73)		0137
Triumph Pre-Unit Twins (47 – 62)		0251
Triumph 650 & 750 2-valve Unit Twins (63 – 83)		0122
Triumph 675 (06 – 10)	♦	4876
Triumph Tiger 800 (10 – 14)	♦	5752
Triumph 1050 Sprint, Speed Triple & Tiger (05 -13)	♦	4796
Triumph Trident & BSA Rocket 3 (69 – 75)		0136
Triumph Bonneville (01 – 12)	♦	4364
Triumph Daytona, Speed Triple, Sprint & Tiger (97 – 05)	♦	3755
Triumph Triples & Fours (carburetor engines) (91 – 04)	♦	2162
VESPA P/PX125, 150 & 200 Scooters (78 – 12)		0707
Vespa GTS125, 250 & 300 (05 – 10)		4898
Vespa Scooters (59 – 78)		0126

Title		Book No
YAMAHA DT50 & 80 Trail Bikes (78 – 95)	◇	0800
Yamaha T50 & 80 Townmate (83 – 95)	◇	1247
Yamaha YB100 Singles (73 – 91)	◇	0474
Yamaha RS/RXS 100 & 125 Singles (74 – 95)		0331
Yamaha RD & DT125LC (82 – 87)	◇	0887
Yamaha TZR125 (87 – 93) & DT125R (88 – 07)	◇	1655
Yamaha TY50, 80, 125 & 175 (74 – 84)	◇	0464
Yamaha XT & SR125 (82 – 03)	◇	1021
Yamaha YBR125 & XT125R/X (05 – 13)		4797
Yamaha YZF-R125 (08 – 11)	♦	5543
Yamaha Trail Bikes (81 – 03)		2350
Yamaha 2-stroke Motocross Bikes (86 – 06)		2662
Yamaha YZ & WR 4-stroke Motorcross Bikes (98 – 08)		2689
Yamaha 250 & 350 Twins (70 – 79)		0040
Yamaha XS250, 360 & 400 sohc Twins (75 – 84)		0378
Yamaha RD250 & 350LC Twins (80 – 82)		0803
Yamaha RD350 YPVS Twins (83 – 95)		1158
Yamaha RD400 Twin (75 – 79)		0333
Yamaha XT, TT & SR500 Singles (75 – 83)		0342
Yamaha XZ550 Vision V-Twins (82 – 85)		0821
Yamaha FJ, FX, XY & YX600 Radian (84 – 92)		2100
Yamaha XT660 & MT-03 (04 – 11)	♦	4910
Yamaha XJ600S (Diversion, Seca II) & XJ600N Fours (92 – 03)	♦	2145
Yamaha XJ6 & FZ6R (09 – 15)	♦	5889
Yamaha YZF600R Thundercat & FZS600 Fazer (96 – 03)	♦	3702
Yamaha FZ-6 Fazer (04 – 08)	♦	4751
Yamaha YZF-R6 (99 – 02)	♦	3900
Yamaha YZF-R6 (03 – 05)	♦	4601
Yamaha YZF-R6 (06 – 13)	♦	5544
Yamaha 650 Twins (70 – 83)		0341
Yamaha XJ650 & 750 Fours (80 – 84)		0738
Yamaha XS750 & 850 Triples (76 – 85)		0340
Yamaha TDM850, TRX850 & XTZ750 (89 – 99)	◇♦	3450
Yamaha YZF750R & YZF1000R Thunderace (93 – 00)	♦	3720
Yamaha FZR600, 750 & 1000 Fours (87 – 96)	♦	2056
Yamaha XV (Virago) V-Twins (81 – 03)	♦	0802
Yamaha XVS650 & 1100 Drag Star/V-Star (97 – 05)	♦	4195
Yamaha XJ900F Fours (83 – 94)	♦	3239
Yamaha XJ900S Diversion (94 – 01)	♦	3739
Yamaha YZF-R1 (98 – 03)	♦	3754
Yamaha YZF-R1 (04 – 06)	♦	4605
Yamaha FZS1000 Fazer (01 – 05)	♦	4287
Yamaha FJ1100 & 1200 Fours (84 – 96)	♦	2057
Yamaha FJR1300 (01 – 13)	♦	5607
Yamaha XJR1200 & 1300 (95 – 06)	♦	3981
Yamaha V-Max (85 – 03)	♦	4072
ATVs		
Honda ATC 70, 90, 110, 185 & 200 (71 – on)		0565
Honda Rancher, Recon & TRX250EX ATVs		2553
Honda TRX300 Shaft Drive ATVs (88 – 00)		2125
Honda Foreman (95 – 11)		2465
Honda TRX300EX, TRX400EX & TRX450R/ER ATVs (93 – 06)		2318
Kawasaki Bayou 220/250/300 & Prairie 300 ATVs (86 – 03)		2351
Polaris ATVs (85 – 97)		2302
Polaris ATVs (98 – 07)		2508
Suzuki/Kawasaki/Artic Cat ATVs (03 – 09)		2910
Yamaha YFS200 Blaster ATV (88 – 06)		2317
Yamaha YFM350 & YFM400 (ER & Big Bear) ATVs (87 – 09)		2126
Yamaha YFZ450 & YFZ450R (04 – 10)		2899
Yamaha Banshee and Warrior ATVs (87 – 10)		2314
Yamaha Kodiak and Grizzly ATVs (93 – 05)		2567
ATV Basics		10450
SCOOTERS		
Twist and Go (automatic transmission) Scooters Service and Repair Manual	◇	4082
TECHBOOK SERIES		
Motorcycle Basics Techbook (2nd edition)		3515
Motorcycle Electrical Techbook (3rd edition)		3471
Motorcycle Fuel Systems Techbook		3514
Motorcycle Maintenance Techbook		4071
Motorcycle Modifying		4272
Motorcycle Workshop Practice Techbook (2nd edition)		3470

◇ = not available in the USA ♦ = Superbike

The manuals on this page are available through good motorcycle dealers and accessory shops.
In case of difficulty, contact: **Haynes Publishing**
(UK) **+44 1963 442030** (USA) **+1 805 498 6703**
(SV) **+46 18 124016**
(Australia/New Zealand) **+61 2 8713 1400**

MCL 07.05.15